Words in th

Words in the Mind
— An Introduction to the Mental Lexicon —

THIRD EDITION

JEAN AITCHISON

Blackwell
Publishing

BLACKWELL PUBLISHING
350 Main Street, Malden, MA 02148-5020, USA
9600 Garsington Road, Oxford OX4 2DQ, UK
550 Swanston Street, Carlton, Victoria 3053, Australia

First published 1987
Second edition published 1994
Third edition published 2003 by Blackwell Publishing Ltd
5   2005

Library of Congress Cataloging-in-Publication Data

Aitchison, Jean, 1938–
    Words in the mind : an introduction to the mental lexicon / Jean Aitchison. — 3rd ed.
        p. cm.
    Includes bibliographical references and index.
    ISBN 0-631-23243-5 (alk. paper) — ISBN 0-631-23244-3 (pbk. : alk. paper)
    1. Lexicology—Psychological aspects. 2. Psycholinguistics. I. Title.
    P326.5.P75 A38 2002
    401'.9—dc21

                                                                2002066637

ISBN-13: 978-0-631-23243-8 (alk. paper) — ISBN-13: 978-0-631-23244-5 (pbk. : alk. paper)

A catalogue record for this title is available from the British Library.

Set in 10/12 pt Ehrhardt
by Graphicraft Ltd, Hong Kong
Printed and bound in the United Kingdom
by TJ International, Padstow, Cornwall

The publisher's policy is to use permanent paper from mills that operate a sustainable forestry policy, and which has been manufactured from pulp processed using acid-free and elementary chlorine-free practices. Furthermore, the publisher ensures that the text paper and cover board used have met acceptable environmental accreditation standards.

For further information on
Blackwell Publishing, visit our website:
www.blackwellpublishing.com

We thought a day and night of steady rain
was plenty, but it's falling again, downright tireless . . .
. . . Much like words
But words don't fall exactly; they hang in there
In the heaven of language, immune to gravity
If not to time, entering your mind
From no direction, travelling no distance at all,
And with rainy persistence tease from the spread earth
So many wonderful scents . . .

Robert Mezey, 'Words'

Contents

Preface

This book deals with words. It sets out to answer the questions: how do humans manage to store so many words, and how do they find the ones they want? In brief, it discusses the nature of the human word-store, or 'mental lexicon'.

This is a topic which has recently attracted the attention of a large number of researchers. Unfortunately, much of the work is tucked away in scholarly journals and conference proceedings. It is also excessively fragmented, since many of those working on the subject have concerned themselves with only a small section of it. This book is an attempt to make recent findings on the mental lexicon available to a wide range of people, and to provide a coherent overall picture of the way it might work. Hopefully, it will prove of interest to anyone concerned with words: students of linguistics and psychology, speech therapists, language teachers, educationists, lexicographers, and the general reader who would just like to know how humans remember words and how children learn them. It could also be regarded as a general introduction to linguistics from a novel angle.

The book does not presuppose any previous knowledge of linguistics or psychology. It contains a minimum of jargon, and all technical terms are fully explained. For those interested in pursuing any topic further, there are copious references and suggestions for further reading in the notes at the end of the book.

Work on the lexicon has exploded since the earlier editions of this book were published (the first in 1987, the second in 1994). From being a minor interest of a few, the lexicon has become a major interest of many. This is reflected in this new edition, which contains substantial additional material. One new chapter has been added, on change of meaning. And chunks have been added to a variety of other chapters, on linguistic corpora, on idioms, on verbs, on metaphor and metonymy, on word formation. In addition, new paragraphs and new references have been added throughout.

In the second edition, I thanked by name those people who particularly helped in the preparation of the edition, by sending me offprints, making helpful suggestions and so on. Such a list has now got so long that I would undoubtedly (and accidentally) leave off valuable names. So I will thank everybody together, and say please continue to send me e-mails and letters about my book, especially if any errors have inadvertently crept it, and please continue sending offprints. I really do read them, even if there was (this time) insufficient space to include everything.

However, two people must be thanked by name: first, my research assistant Diana Lewis, who as usual was brilliant at bashing the references into shape, and at tracking down obscure ones. Second, my husband, the lexicographer John Ayto, whose books, loving kindness, and brilliant cooking made my task an easier one.

Of course, the views expressed in this book are my own, and I alone am responsible for any errors which remain.

Jean Aitchison
Oxford, 2002

Acknowledgements

The author and publisher gratefully acknowledge the permission granted to reproduce the copyright material in this book:

page v Robert Mezey, lines from 'Words', in Leonard Michaels and Christopher Ricks (eds), *The State of the Language*. Berkeley: University of California Press, 1980. © 1980 The Regents of the University of California.

pages 3 and 102 Norton Juster, extracts from *The Phantom Tollbooth*. London: Collins, 1962. © 1961 by Norton Juster. Reprinted by permission of HarperCollins Publishers, London, and Mildred Marmur Associates, Larchmont, New York.

page 3 Stevie Smith, lines from 'In the Park' in *The Collected Poems of Stevie Smith*. London: Allen Lane, 1975. Reprinted by permission of James MacGibbon.

pages 9, 12 and 174 Douglas Adams, extracts from *Life, the Universe, and Everything*. London: Pan, 1982. Reprinted by permission of Macmillan, London, UK.

page 29 Ira Levin, extract from *The Stepford Wives*. London: Michael Joseph Ltd, 1972.

page 41 Roald Dahl, extract from *My Uncle Oswald*. London: Michael Joseph Ltd and Penguin Books Ltd, 1979. © 1979, 1980 by Roald Dahl. Reprinted by permission of Alfred A. Knopf, Inc.

pages 42 and 215–16 T. S. Eliot, lines from 'Burnt Norton' and 'Little Gidding' (two of the 'Four Quartets') in *The Collected Poems, 1909–1962*. London: Faber, 1969. © 1943 by T. S. Eliot, renewed 1971 by Esme Valerie Eliot. Reprinted by permission of Faber and Faber Ltd and Harcourt Brace Jovanovich Inc.

page 44 T. S. Eliot, lines from 'Macavity the Mystery Cat', in *Old Possum's Book of Practical Cats*. London: Faber, 1939. © 1939 by T. S. Eliot, renewed 1967 by Esme Valerie Eliot. Reprinted by permission of Faber and Faber Ltd and Harcourt Brace Jovanovich Inc.

page 54 Clive (no 848) by Angus McGill, 1970. Reproduced by kind permission of the *Evening Standard* (London).

pages 70, 126, 127, 133, 184–5 and 200 Ogden Nash, lines from 'Who Called that Pied-billed Grebe a *Podilymbus podiceps podiceps?*' (first printed in the *New Yorker*), © 1968 by Ogden Nash; 'Any Millenniums Today, Lady?' (first printed in the *New Yorker*), © 1948 by Ogden Nash; 'The Joyous Malingerer' in *There's Always Another Windmill* (London: André Deutsch, 1969), © 1967 by Ogden Nash; 'Are You a Snodgrass?' (first printed in the *Saturday Evening Post*), © 1934 by Ogden Nash; 'Away from it All' in *I Wouldn't Have Missed It* (London: André Deutsch, 1983), © 1975 by Frances Nash, Isobel Eberstadt Nash and Linnell Nash Smith; 'Thunder over the Nursery', © 1936 by Ogden Nash. All extracts reproduced courtesy of the Curtis Brown Group and the author's estate.

page 88 Couples by Calman. © The Estates of Mel Calman. Reprinted by permission of Methuen Publishing Limited.

page 162 Laurence Lerner, lines from 'Meanings' in *Rembrandt's Mirror*. London: Secker and Warburg, 1987. © 1987 by Laurence Lerner and reproduced by kind permission.

page 188 Spike Milligan, lines from 'The Bongaloo' in *Silly Verse for Kids*. London: Puffin Books, 1959.

page 206 Youens cartoon. Reproduced by kind permission of *The Observer*.

page 215 Samuel Beckett, extract from *All That Fall* in *The Complete Dramatic Works* by Samuel Beckett. London: Faber, 1986. Reproduced by permission of Faber and Faber Ltd and Grove Press Inc.

page 227 Douglas Adams, extract from *So Long and Thanks for All the Fish*. London: Pan, 1982. Reprinted by permission of Macmillan, London, UK.

page 240 Stephen Jay Gould, extract from *The Panda's Thumb: More Reflections in Natural History*. New York: W. W. Norton, 1980.

page 249 Pete Seeger, lines from 'Words, Words, Words. © 1967 Harmony Music Ltd, 19/20 Poland Street, London W1V 3DD, international copyright secured, all rights reserved, used by permission; © 1967, 1968 by Sanga Music Inc., all rights reserved, used by permission.

Every effort has been made to trace copyright holders and to obtain their permission for the use of copyright material. The publisher apologizes for any errors or omissions in the above list and would be grateful if notified of any corrections that should be incorporated in future reprints or editions of this book.

Abbreviations and Symbols

The following abbreviations are used for standard dictionaries after their first mention in the text, where they are referred to by their full title:

CCED	*Collins Concise English Dictionary*
CED	*Collins English Dictionary*
COD	*Concise Oxford Dictionary*
EWED	*The Encarta World English Dictionary*
NODE	*The New Oxford Dictionary of English*
NSOD	*New Shorter Oxford Dictionary*
OED	*Oxford English Dictionary*
LCED	*Longman Concise English Dictionary*
LDEL	*Longman Dictionary of the English Language*
LLA	*Longman Language Activator*

In order to make the text easier to read, spoken words have been mostly represented by their conventional written form. Where the use of phonetic symbols is unavoidable, these are put in square brackets [ ], regardless of their linguistic status (phones or phonemes, on which see Aitchison, 1999). Most of the phonetic symbols are obvious, as [d] in *did*. The following non-obvious IPA (International Phonetic Alphabet) symbols occur in the text:

[θ] as at the beginning of *thin*
[ʃ] as at the beginning of *shin*
[ŋ] as at the end of *sing*

An asterisk *indicates an impossible word, phrase, or sentence, such as *kbad*, which is not a possible English word.

An exclamation mark (!) indicates an unacceptable or odd sentence.

Part I
Aims and Evidence

1

Welcome to Dictionopolis!

— The human word-store —

Before long they saw in the distance the towers and flags of Dictionopolis sparkling in the sunshine, and in a few moments they reached the great wall and stood at the gateway to the city.

'A-H-H-H-R-R-E-M-M-', roared the sentry, clearing his throat and snapping smartly to attention. 'This is Dictionopolis, a happy kingdom, advantageously located in the Foothills of Confusion and caressed by gentle breezes from the Sea of Knowledge . . . Dictionopolis is the place where all the words in the world come from. They're grown right here in our orchards.'

Norton Juster, *The Phantom Tollbooth*

'Words glisten. Words irradiate exquisite splendour. Words carry magic and keep us spell-bound . . . Words are like glamorous bricks that constitute the fabric of any language . . . Words are like roses that make the environment fragrant,' asserts the writer of a textbook urging people to improve their vocabulary.[1]

Few people regard words with the awe and reverence of this author. Most of us use them all the time without thinking. Yet words are supremely important. Everyone needs them, and a normal person probably comes into contact with thousands in the course of a normal day. We would be quite lost without them: 'I wanted to utter a word, but that word I cannot remember; and the bodiless thought will now return to the palace of shadows,' said the Russian poet Mandelstam.[2]

The frustration of being without words is vividly expressed in Stevie Smith's poem 'In the park':

'Pray for the Mute who have no word to say.'
Cried the one old gentleman, 'Not because they are dumb,
But they are weak. And the weak thoughts beating in the brain
Generate a sort of heat, yet cannot speak.
Thoughts that are bound without sound
In the tomb of the brain's room, wound. Pray for the Mute.'

On a less poetic level, someone who has had a stroke can illustrate clearly the handicap suffered by those who just cannot think of the words they want. For example, K.C., a highly intelligent solicitor, was quite unable to remember the name of a box of matches: 'Waitresses. Waitrixies. A backland and another bank. For bandicks er bandiks I think they are, I believe they're zandicks, I'm sorry, but they're called flitters landocks.' He had equal difficulty when shown a telephone: 'Ooh that, that sir. I can show you then what is a zapricks for the elencom, the elencom, with the pidland thing to the . . . and then each of the pidlands has an eye in, one, two, three, and so on'.[3]

Most people are convinced that they need to know a lot of words, and become worried if they cannot recall a word they want. Yet most of the time they will have relatively little difficulty in remembering the thousands of words needed for everyday conversation. This is a considerable feat.

However, speakers of a language are unlikely to have given much thought to this remarkable skill. Even those who deal with language professionally, such as speech therapists and teachers, know relatively little about how humans cope with all these words. Their lack of knowledge is not surprising since there is little information readily available about key issues, such as 'How are words stored in the mind?', 'How do people find the words they want when they speak?', 'Do children remember words in the same way as adults?', and so on.

This is the topic of this book. It will primarily consider how we store words in our mind, and how we retrieve them from this store when we need them. The overall aim is to produce outline specifications, as it were, for a working model of the word-store in the human mind. This turns out to be a huge subject. In order to narrow it down somewhat, the book will focus on the spoken words of people whose native language is English. English has been selected because, up till now, more work has been done on it than on any other language. And spoken speech has been chosen because native speakers of English talk it before they learn to read or write it. Reading, writing and other languages will therefore be mentioned only intermittently, when work on them illuminates the topic under discussion. The decision to concentrate on spoken English means that bilingualism and multilingualism are not directly discussed – though hopefully the findings will shed light on how people cope with the vocabulary of more than one language.

Mazes Intricate

Mazes intricate,
Eccentric, intervolved, yet regular
Then most, when most irregular they seem.

Milton's description of the planets in *Paradise Lost*[4] could apply equally well to the human word-store. Planets might appear to the untrained observer to wander randomly round the night sky, yet in fact their movements are under the control of natural laws which are not obvious to the naked eye. Similarly, words are not just stacked higgledy-piggledy in our minds, like leaves on an autumn bonfire. Instead, they are organized into an intricate, interlocking system whose underlying principles can be discovered.

Words cannot be heaped up randomly in the mind for two reasons. First, there are so many of them. Second, they can be found so fast. Psychologists have shown that human memory is both flexible and extendable, provided that the information is structured.[5] Random facts and figures are extremely difficult to remember, but enormous quantities of data can be remembered and utilized, as long as they are well organized.

However, to say that humans know 'so many' words and find them 'so fast' is somewhat vague. What number are we talking about? And what speed are we referring to? Let us briefly consider these two points.

Native speakers of a language almost certainly know more words than they imagine. Educated adults generally estimate their own vocabulary at only 1 to 10 per cent of the real level, it has been claimed.[6] Most people behave somewhat like the rustics in Oliver Goldsmith's poem 'The Deserted Village'. The villagers gather round to listen in awe to the schoolmaster, whose verbal knowledge amazes them:

> Words of learned length and thund'ring sound
> Amazed the gazing rustics rang'd around,
> And still they gaz'd, and still the wonder grew,
> That one small head could carry all he knew.

While admiring the word power of their local schoolteacher, the rustics did not realize that the word-store within each one of their heads was probably almost as great as that of the teacher. Even highly educated people can make ludicrously low guesses. In the middle of the last century Dean Farrar, a respected intellectual, pronounced on the vocabulary of some peasants after eavesdropping on them as they chatted: 'I once listened for a long time together to the conversation of three peasants who were gathering apples among the boughs of an orchard, and as far as I could conjecture, the whole number of words they used did not exceed a hundred.'[7] They managed with this small number, he surmised, because 'the same word was made to serve a multitude of purposes, and the same coarse expletives recurred with a horrible frequency in the place of every single part of speech'.

More recently, the French writer Georges Simenon was reported as saying that he tried to make his style as simple as possible because he had read somewhere that over half the people in France used no more than a total of 600 words.[8] Simenon's figure is perhaps as much the product of wishful thinking as his claim to have slept with 10,000 women in his life. At the very least one should probably exchange the numbers of words and women, though 10,000 words is still likely to be an underestimate.

An educated adult might well know more than 150,000 words, and be able to actively use 90 per cent of these, according to one calculation.[9] This figure is controversial, because of the problems of defining 'word' and the difficulty of finding a reliable procedure for assessing vocabulary knowledge. However, Seashore and Eckerson were pioneers of a method now widely used for measuring vocabulary size. It might be useful, therefore, to consider how they reached their conclusions, even though they are now thought to have overestimated the total, and their techniques have been subsequently modified.

Seashore and Eckerson defined a 'word' as an item listed in the 1937 edition of Funk and Wagnall's *New Standard Dictionary of the English Language*, which contains approximately 450,000 entries. They reduced this to 370,000 by omitting alternative meanings. Of these, they reckoned that just under half, about 166,000, were 'basic words' such as *loyal*, and the remaining 204,000 or so were derivatives and compounds, such as *loyalism*, *loyalize*, *loyally* and *Loyal Legion*. Obviously it is impractical to test anyone on all the words in the dictionary, so a representative sample of the total needs to be obtained. The researchers did this by taking the third word down in the first column of every left-hand page. This gave a list of 1,320 words, which they divided into four. Several hundred college students were tested on their ability to define the words on each list and to use them in illustrative sentences.

Seashore and Eckerson found that their subjects were surprisingly knowledgeable. On average, the students knew 35 per cent of the common 'basic words' on the list, 1 per cent of the rare 'basic words' and 47 per cent of the derivatives and compounds. When these proportions were applied to the overall number of words in the whole dictionary, the average college student turned out to know approximately 58,000 common 'basic words', 1,700 rare 'basic words' and 96,000 derivatives and compounds. The overall total comes to over 150,000. The highest student score was almost 200,000, while even the lowest was over 100,000.

Later researchers have pointed out a number of flaws in Seashore and Eckerson's methodology. The students might have been able to guess the meaning and use of derivatives from a knowledge of the 'basic words' to which they are related. Also, bright students tend to overestimate their knowledge. Take the word *kneehole*. This is the space under a desk for a person's knees. Yet someone who was 'quite sure' he knew the word, suggested it was a hole worn by a person's knee through thin fabric trousers. In contrast, less good pupils think they know words which are similar to others. When asked to use the word *burrow* in a sentence, one child wrote: 'May I *burrow* your pencil?', confusing it with *borrow*, and another: 'You take away rubbish in a *wheelburrow*', instead of *wheelbarrow*.

The 'big dictionary effect' is another problem: the bigger the dictionary used, the more words people are found to know, partly because bigger dictionaries include more homonyms (different words with the same form). The word *must* probably elicits the meaning 'should, is obligated to' ('You *must* wash your hands') in the mind of someone asked about it. Yet a dictionary sample might have picked on *must* 'the newly pressed juice of grapes', or even *must* 'a state of frenzied sexual excitement in the males of large mammals, especially elephants'.

It's also difficult to know what level of knowledge is being tapped. One person claiming to know *aardvark* might think of it only as a strange wild animal, but another might be able to describe it as a nocturnal mammal with long ears and a snout which feeds on termites and inhabits the grasslands of Africa.[10]

In spite of these problems, self-assessment of a dictionary sample has turned out to be the best way of estimating vocabulary size, mainly because it allows a large number of words to be reviewed. The method has been refined somewhat since Seashore and Eckerson's pioneering work: non-words are normally included in the sample, in order to detect unreliable respondents. Different levels of list are tested, each controlled for the frequency of occurrence of the words selected. Students are no longer always asked to give a straight 'yes–no' answer to whether they know it, but can also reply 'maybe' if the word sounds vaguely familiar.[11]

On the basis of this method, some conclusions are possible. An educated adult speaker of English can understand, and potentially use, at least 50,000 words, with a word provisionally defined as a 'dictionary entry'. Modern dictionaries usually include different forms of a word under the same entry, so *sing, sings, sang, sung* would all come under the headword *sing*. However, they normally provide separate entries for derivatives whose meaning cannot be reliably guessed, so *singer* would have an entry to itself, because it does not just mean 'someone who sings', but more usually 'someone who sings for a living'.

This guestimate of 50,000 is based on informal tests with British English university students. But the total may be on the low side. The reading vocabulary of the average American high school graduate has been assessed at about 40,000 words,[12] with the total rising to 60,000 or perhaps even 80,000 if all the proper names of people and places and all the idiomatic expressions are also included.[13] Only a few thousand of these words will be routinely used, but many more, such as *anteater, barometer, crustacean, derogatory*, can be understood or actively produced if required.

Compare these totals with the vocabulary of any of the 'talking apes', animals who have been taught a language-like system in which signs stand for words. The chimps Washoe and Nim actively used around 200 signs after several years of training, while Koko the gorilla supposedly used around 400. None of these animals approached the thousand mark, something which is normally achieved by children soon after the age of 2. And animals trained more recently, such as Lana (a female chimp) and Kanzi (a male bonobo) have an even more limited vocabulary, since they have been taught to manipulate pre-set symbols on a keyboard whose number does not exceed 200.[14]

In conclusion, the number of words which an educated adult native speaker of English knows, and can potentially use, is unlikely to be less than 50,000, and may be much higher. These high figures suggest that the mental lexicon is arranged on a systematic basis.

The second reason why words are likely to be well organized in the mind is that they can be located so fast, literally in a split second. This is apparent above all from the speed of normal speech, in which six syllables a second, making three or more words, is fairly standard.[15] And experiments have confirmed this figure, showing that native speakers can recognize a word of their language in 200 ms (milliseconds) or less from its onset, that is, approximately one-fifth of a second from its beginning.[16] In many cases this is well before all the word has been heard. Indeed, the average duration of words used in the experiments was around 375 ms – almost twice as long as the recognition time. One way in which the researchers demonstrated this was by pointing to the behaviour of subjects in a 'speech shadowing' task. Shadowing is a fairly common technique in psycholinguistic experiments, and is reminiscent of simultaneous interpretation. The experimenter asks the subjects to wear headphones into which a stream of speech is played. Subjects are then asked to repeat what they hear as they hear it. People who are good at shadowing can repeat back speech with a delay of little more than 250–275 ms – around one-quarter of a second. If we assume that 50–75 ms is taken up with the actual response, and deduct this from the overall time taken, then we get the figure of 200 ms (one-fifth of a second) quoted above. These good shadowers are not just parroting back what they hear. They are genuinely 'processing' the words, since they correct mistakes, such as changing *tomorrance* to 'tomorrow'.

The detection of non-words provides further evidence of fast and efficient word-searching ability. Subjects are able to reject a sound sequence which is a non-word in around half a second. This has been shown by means of a lexical decision task, an experiment in which subjects are asked to decide whether a sequence of sounds is a word of the language or not.[17] Some of the sequences presented were real words, others non-words, such as *vleesidence*, *grankiment*, *swollite*. Subjects were asked to press a button as soon as they heard a non-word. They did this surprisingly fast, in just under half a second (450 ms) from the point at which the sound sequence diverged from being a possible real word. Once again, this suggests that speakers are able to conduct an orderly search through their mental word-store in a surprisingly short length of time.

Of course, the fact that speakers are usually able to distinguish fast between real words and non-words is something which we can also sometimes see happening for ourselves, as in the following extract from a short story, 'De Bilbow' by Brigid Brophy. Barney is questioned by his foreign girlfriend about the meaning of a word:

> 'There is an English word I am not knowing. I am not finding it in the dictionary . . . "Bilbow".'
>   'Bilbow?'
>   'Yes.'
>   'There's no such word. It's a surname, not an ordinary word.'
>   'Please? You are not knowing this English word?'
>   'I AM knowing,' Barney said. 'I'm knowing damn well the word doesn't exist.'

Note that Barney responded without hesitation. This is quite a feat. Suppose he knew 60,000 words. If he had checked through these one by one at the rate of

100 per second, it would have taken him ten minutes to discover that *bilbow* didn't exist. The problem sequence *bilbow*, incidentally, came from Shakespeare's *Henry V*,[18] in a passage in which the French-speaking Katherine mispronounces the English word *elbow*.

Native speakers, then, seem able to carry out a thorough search of their word-store in well under a second, when they need to recognize a real word or reject a non-word. These figures relate to words that are clearly words and non-words that are unlike actual words, since most of us have a grey area of sequences such as *concision* which sound as if they might be 'real' words, but we are not quite sure.

Most humans are also impressively fast at finding the words they need when they produce speech. Unfortunately, we cannot time the production process as easily as we can measure recognition speed. Some researchers have made attempts in this direction by arguing that pauses in speech, which are measurable, often occur before major lexical items. They may therefore have been caused by word searching.[19] However, the pauses vary in length, and their interpretation is controversial: we cannot easily tell whether a speaker is pausing to choose the words themselves or the order in which they will occur. So we cannot produce convincing figures for selection times, especially as some words seem to be easier to find than others.

Indeed, some words seem to be particularly hard to seek out. Almost everybody has had the annoying experience of not being able to think of the particular word they want, even though they are sure they know it. Yet such problems probably seem more frequent than they really are. Even when struggling to find a particular word, normal speakers have plenty of others at their disposal in order to carry on a reasonable conversation. This can be illustrated by a fictional but not unrealistic dialogue from Douglas Adams's science-fiction satire *Life, the Universe and Everything*.

> Arthur shook his head in a sudden access of emotion and bewilderment.
> 'I haven't seen anyone for years,' he said, 'not anyone. I can hardly even remember how to speak. I keep forgetting words. I practise you see. I practise by talking to . . . talking to . . . what are those things people think you're mad if you talk to? Like George the Third.'
> 'Kings?' suggested Ford.
> 'No, no,' said Arthur. 'The things he used to talk to. We're surrounded by them for heaven's sake. I've planted hundreds myself. They all died. Trees! I practise by talking to trees.'

Arthur cannot remember the word *trees*. Yet while he struggles to retrieve it he uses approximately 50 other different words seemingly effortlessly, with no conscious searching. Such fast and efficient retrieval must be based on a structured system, not on random rummages around the mind.

Our conclusions so far, then, are as follows: the large number of words known by humans and the speed with which they can be located point to the existence of a highly organized mental lexicon.

However, the requirements of massive storage capacity and fast retrieval are not necessarily the same. This can be illustrated by an analogy. Suppose the words in the mental lexicon were like books. If we wanted to store thousands of books, how would we do this? The simplest method would be to find a large room and to stack them up in heaps which go from floor to ceiling. We would start at the side of the room opposite the door and carry on heaping them up until the room was quite full. Then we would shut the door. In this way we could store the maximum possible number of books. But suppose we then needed to consult one of them. How would we find it? We might never locate the book we wanted, unless it happened to be one of the few stored near the door.

In brief, the system which allowed the greatest storage capacity might not be compatible with efficient retrieval. And there might be further discrepancies between storage requirements and speedy retrieval. To continue with the book analogy, libraries often keep all really big and heavy books near the floor. But this means that they cannot be kept in strict sequence. Similarly, in the human mind, extra long words might need a specialized storage system which could separate them from shorter words, and which might cause some delay when it came to retrieving them.

In dealing with words in the mind, therefore, we must treat storage and retrieval as interlinked problems but not identical ones. Although common sense suggests that the human word-store is primarily organized to ensure fast and accurate retrieval, we cannot assume that this is inevitable. Humans might have adopted a compromise solution which is ideal neither for storage nor for retrieval.

Words in the Mind and Words in Books

The human word-store is often referred to as the 'mental dictionary' or, perhaps more commonly, as the *mental lexicon*, to use the Greek word for 'dictionary'. There is, however, relatively little similarity between the words in our minds and words in book dictionaries, even though the information will sometimes overlap. Let us therefore look at some of the differences between a human's mental dictionary and a book dictionary. The dissimilarities involve both organization and content.

With regard to organization, book dictionaries standardly list words in alphabetical order. As a first guess, one might suggest that the mental lexicon of someone who can read and write could also be organized in this way. After all, many of us spend a considerable amount of time looking things up alphabetically in telephone directories and indexes. So, one might assume that educated English speakers had set up their mental lexicons to fit in with their alphabetical expectations.

This is an easy hypothesis to test. People occasionally make mistakes when they speak, selecting one word in error for another. If the mental lexicon was organized in alphabetical order, one might expect speakers to accidentally pick an adjacent entry when making errors of this type. So, in place of the musical instrument 'zither' one would predict, perhaps, the wrong selection of *zit* 'a spot on the skin', or *ziti* 'pasta in the form of tubes resembling large macaroni' which precede and follow *zither* in *The New Oxford Dictionary of English* (*NODE*). Similarly, in error for the word 'guitar' one might expect someone to accidentally pick *guinea* or *guipure* or *guise*, or perhaps *guiver*, *Gujerati*, *gulch*, *gulden*, *gules*, *gulf*, all words which are near neighbours in *NODE*.

But mistakes of this type are quite unlikely, as becomes clear when we look at a few 'slips of the tongue', such as 'He told a funny antidote', with *antidote* instead of 'anecdote', or 'The doctor listened to her chest with his periscope', with *periscope* replacing 'stethoscope'. These errors suggest that even if the mental lexicon turns out to be partially organized in terms of initial sounds, the order will certainly not be straightforwardly alphabetical. Other aspects of the word's sound structure, such as its ending, its stress pattern and the stressed vowel, are all likely to play a role in the arrangement of words in the mind.

Furthermore, consider a speech error such as 'The inhabitants of the car were unhurt', where the speaker presumably meant to say *occupants* rather than 'inhabitants'. Such mistakes show that, unlike book dictionaries, human mental dictionaries cannot be organized solely on the basis of sounds or spelling. Meaning must be taken into consideration as well, since humans fairly often confuse words with similar meanings, as in 'Please hand me the tin-opener' when the speaker wanted to crack a nut, so must have meant 'nut-crackers'.

Arrangement in terms of meaning is found in some collections of synonyms, such as *Roget's Thesaurus*, but not generally in book dictionaries, where a desire to be neat and tidy in an alphabetical fashion may outweigh other considerations. For example, the word *horsehair* occurs soon after *horse* in the *Encarta World English Dictionary* (*EWED*), but there is no mention of it near the entry *hair*. Similarly, *workhorse* occurs soon after the entry for *work*, but does not appear with *horse*. In brief, the organization of the mental lexicon is likely to be considerably more complex than that of book dictionaries, for whom orderliness is a prime requirement.

As for content, a book dictionary contains a fixed number of words which can be counted. Book dictionaries are therefore inescapably outdated, because language is constantly changing, and vocabulary fastest of all. As the eighteenth-century lexicographer Samuel Johnson pointed out in the preface to his famous *Dictionary of the English Language* (1755): 'No dictionary of a living tongue can ever be perfect, since while it is hastening to publication, some words are budding, and some fading away.' Everyone must at times have been frustrated to find occasions when a book dictionary concentrates on an archaic meaning of a word or omits a moderately common item. *COD* (7th edn, 1982), for example, defined *buzz* only in terms of sound. It did not mention its more recent and perhaps equally frequent meaning in the 1980s of 'a thrill, a euphoric sensation' until almost a decade later (8th edn, 1990). Or take the word *wimp*, meaning 'a weak ineffectual person'. This was a vogue word in the early 1980s, as in the 'lonely hearts' ad 'Wimp needs bossy lady' (*Time Out*, July 1984), or the comment by a singing group that 'the trying-hard wimps' were an easy target for humour (*Guardian*, July 1984), or the magazine column which noted that 'your cad, pale-faced wimp, Byron with malnutrition, Little Boy Lost . . . have a great appeal for women since they are vulnerable' (*Cosmopolitan*, July 1984). Its adjectives were also widespread: a Sunday newspaper referred to 'the wimpish young schoolmaster' (*Mail on Sunday*, May 1982), and a women's magazine called attention to a calendar featuring 'six most decidedly wimpy males in varying states of undress' (*Over 21*, August 1984). Yet *wimp*-words were slow to find their way into British book dictionaries. The *Oxford English Dictionary* Supplement (1987) finally included them, and showed that they had been around for decades: *wimp* (first occurrence 1920), *wimpish* (1925), *wimpy* (1967), and *wimpishness* (1978). Meanwhile, the teenage vogue greeting *whassup*, from 'what's up?', is still absent from many dictionaries.

The way in which written dictionaries dodder along behind language is amusingly satirized in Douglas Adams's *Life, the Universe and Everything*:

> The mattress globbered. This is the noise made by a live, swamp-dwelling mattress that is deeply moved by a story of human tragedy. The word can also, according to 'The Ultra-Complete Maximegalon Dictionary of Every Language Ever', mean the noise that is made by the Lord High Sanvalvwag of Hollop on discovering that he has forgotten his wife's birthday for the second year running. Since there was only ever one Lord High Sanvalvwag of Hollop, and he never married, the word is only ever used in a negative or speculative sense, and there is an ever-increasing body of opinion which holds that 'The Ultra-Complete Maximegalon Dictionary' is not worth the fleet of lorries it takes to cart its microstored edition around in. Strangely enough, the dictionary omits the word 'floopily', which simply means 'in the manner of something which is floopy'.

– though this judgment on dictionaries is now somewhat unfair. In the last decade dictionaries have narrowed the gap between the first occurrence of a word and its appearance in print, due to the development of computerized databases, which themselves are based on the electronic scanning of recent material. A new word can now make it into a dictionary within months.

Turning to the mental lexicon, its content is by no means fixed. People add new words all the time, as well as altering the pronunciation and meaning of existing ones. Humans, however, do not just add on words from time to time, in between utterances. They often create new words and new meanings for words from moment to moment, while speech is in progress. A caller asking an American telephone operator about long-distance charges was told: 'You'll have to ask a zero.' The caller had no difficulty in interpreting this as 'a person you can reach on the telephone by dialling zero'. Similarly, it was not difficult for native speakers to guess that 'The newsboy porched the newspaper yesterday' meant 'The newsboy left the newspaper in the porch', or that the instruction 'Please do a Napoleon for the camera' meant posing with one hand tucked inside the jacket, as in most pictures of Napoleon, even though they had probably never come across these usages before.[20]

In the examples above, the speakers and hearers were already familiar with other uses of the word *zero* and *porch* and with the characteristics of a famous character such as Napoleon. They simply reapplied this knowledge in a new way. But human creativity goes beyond this. Quite often, totally new lexical items can be created and interpreted on the spur of the moment. This skill has been tested experimentally.[21] The researchers gave a short description of a somewhat eccentric imaginary character to a number of students: 'Imagine that a friend of yours has told you about his neighbour, Elvis Edmunds. Elvis loves to entertain his children in the evenings with several magic tricks that he knows. He often surprises them by pulling dollar bills out of his ear. During the day, Elvis is employed as a professional skywriter. He likes to work best on days when there is not a cloud in the sky. To supplement his income, Elvis carves fruit into exotic shapes for the delicatessen down the road.' The students were then quizzed about the meaning of the phrase 'doing an Elvis' in various contexts, a task they found easy. They were confident, for example, that a sentence they could not possibly have heard before, such as 'I have often thought about doing an Elvis Edmunds to some apples I bought', meant 'carving apples into exotic shapes'. The fluidity and flexibility of the mental lexicon, then, contrasts strongly with the fixed vocabulary of any book, or even an electronic dictionary.

But the biggest difference between a book dictionary and the mental lexicon is that the latter contains far, far more information about each entry. All book dictionaries are inevitably limited in the amount they contain, just because it would be quite impracticable to include all possible data about each word. In any case it is unlikely that anyone has ever assembled the total range of knowledge which could be brought together about any one dictionary entry. As one linguist notes: 'There is no known limit to the amount of detailed information . . . which may be associated with a lexical item. Existing dictionaries, even large ones, specify lexical items only incompletely.'[22]

For example, one popular dictionary suggests that the verb *paint* means 'cover surface of (object) with paint'. But 'If you knock over the paint bucket, thereby covering the surface of the floor with paint, you have not thereby painted the floor'.[23] Nor can one patch up the dictionary definition by suggesting that one must intentionally cover something with paint: 'For consider that when Michelangelo dipped his brush into Cerulian Blue, he thereby covered the surface of his brush with paint and did so with the primary intention that his brush should be covered with paint in consequence of his having so dipped it. But MICHELANGELO WAS NOT, FOR ALL THAT, PAINTING HIS PAINTBRUSH.'[24] All this suggests that people have a much more detailed knowledge of the meaning of words than any book dictionary would have the space to specify.

Furthermore, why don't people wear rancid socks? Or find fetid milk? Nothing suggests that this is abnormal in *EWED*. It defines the word *rancid* as 'having the strong disagreeable smell or taste of decomposing fats or oils' and *fetid* as 'with a rotten or offensive smell'. This suggests that one ought to be able to attach both words to bad eggs or cow dung or even dirty socks. Yet it would sound very odd to say 'Alphonse was ashamed of his rancid socks' or 'Mary's egg was fetid.' Written dictionaries list only a small selection of the range of words with which a lexical item can occur. As one lexicographer comments: 'The world's largest data bank of examples in context is dwarfed by the collection we all carry around subconsciously in our heads.'[25]

Moreover, in book dictionaries, words are mostly dealt with in isolation. A *child* is defined by *NODE* as 'a young human being below the age of full physical development'. But this fails to inform us how the word *child* relates to all the other words for young human beings, such as *baby, infant, toddler, youngster*. Similarly, *NODE* tells us that *warm* means 'of or at a fairly or comfortably high temperature'. Yet in order to fully understand *warm*, one needs to know how it slots into the range of temperature words such as *cold, tepid, hot*. This type of information seems to be an intrinsic part of one's mental lexicon.

To continue this list of differences between words in the mind and words in books, a book dictionary tends to give information that is spuriously cut and dried. It is likely to tell you that *pelicans, sparrows, parrots* and *flamingos* are all birds, but will not rank them in any way. Humans seems able to judge that a sparrow is a more 'birdy' bird than a pelican or a flamingo. Or more likely, a human would say that a pelican is a 'funny' kind of bird. In addition, book dictionaries do not often spare the space to comment on frequency of usage. There is no indication in *NODE* that *abode* is less usual than *house*, or that *coney* is uncommon beside *rabbit*. People, on the other hand, seem well aware of which words are rare and which not. Recently, however, a number of dictionaries have started to include this kind of information.[26]

Or, to take another facet of words, book dictionaries contain only a very small amount of data about the syntactic patterns into which each word can slot. *Wide* and *main* are both classified as adjectives in *NODE*. But it does not tell us that you can say 'The road is wide' but not 'The road is main.' Both *eat* and *resemble* are classified as verbs which take an object, but it does not tell us that whereas 'A cow was eaten by my aunt' is possible, 'A cow was resembled by my aunt' is not.

If we move on to consider how book dictionaries cope with sounds, we note that they normally specify only one pronunciation for each word. Yet native speakers of a language are likely to be able to understand quite different pronunciations by different speakers. In addition, they are likely to have more than one pronunciation in their own repertoire, depending on the formality of the occasion and how fast they are speaking. Sometimes, for example, one might pronounce a word such as *handbag* with all the sounds found in the conventional spelling, and at other times it might sound like 'hambag'.

The examples listed above could be multiplied. They show that the mental lexicon is indeed a mammoth structure.[27] The relationship between a book dictionary and the human mental lexicon may be somewhat like the link between a tourist pamphlet advertising a seaside resort and the resort itself. A tourist pamphlet gives us a small, partial glimpse of a place as it was at some point in the past, with no real idea of how the different parts of the resort fit together to form a whole, living town. Similarly, a book dictionary gives us a spuriously neat, static and incomplete view of the mental lexicon.[28]

The differences between words in the mind and words in books are therefore profound. The point of this section, however, was not to point out the shortcomings of book dictionaries, which serve a useful, though limited, purpose, enabling us to check on the conventional spelling of a word and to find out its approximate meaning. Indeed, if we did expect a book dictionary to include the same information as the mental lexicon, then we would undoubtedly require a fleet of lorries to cart its microstored edition around in, like the 'Ultra-Complete Maximegalon Dictionary' mentioned earlier. The comparison between mental dictionaries and book dictionaries was made in order to show that we cannot deduce much about our mental lexicons from studying the way words are dealt with in books. In the next two chapters, therefore, we shall consider how we can build up a more adequate picture of the human word-store.

Summary

In this chapter we have noted that humans know tens of thousands of words, most of which they can locate in a fraction of a second. Such huge numbers, and such efficiency in finding those required, suggest that these words are carefully organized, not just stacked in random heaps. This book will discuss the storage and retrieval of words by both adults and children, bearing in mind that a system which is ideal for storage might not necessarily be the best for fast retrieval. Its overall aim is to provide outline specifications for a working model of the human word-store.

We further noted that most ordinary dictionaries are limited in scope in comparison with the mental lexicon. Their organization is oversimple, their content is fixed and outdated, and they contain only a relatively small amount of information about each item – even though the situation is improving, as new sophisticated electronic databases are increasingly being used as the basis for recent dictionaries.

The mental lexicon, then, is both large and complex. In the next two chapters we shall consider how we should set about studying this mammoth structure.

2

Links in the Chain
— Assessing the evidence —

I picked up a magazine from the table . . . One of the articles attempted to show how much an observant man might learn by an accurate and systematic examination of all that came in his way . . .

'From a drop of water', said the writer, 'a logician could infer the possibility of an Atlantic or a Niagara without having seen or heard of one or the other. So all life is a great chain, the nature of which is known whenever we are shown a single link of it.'

Arthur Conan Doyle, *A Study in Scarlet*

The writer who made the grandiose claims in the article quoted above was the fictional detective Sherlock Holmes. And psycholinguists investigating the human word-store have been likened to Sherlock Holmes in pursuit of the master-criminal Professor Moriarty, the elusive director of a vast criminal organization.[1] The detective had to work out what the master-mind was like with the aid of limited resources: his knowledge of the world, his deductive powers, his imagination, and a simple magnifying glass, with which he examined the isolated clues left by Moriarty's crimes. Psycholinguists similarly have few powerful tools with which to build up a model of the mental lexicon – mainly their own intelligence and a heterogeneous collection of different types of clue.

These clues are the topic of this chapter. They are of various types (figure 2.1): word searches and 'slips of the tongue' of normal speakers; the word-finding efforts of people with speech disorders; psycholinguistic experiments; the findings of linguistics. In this chapter we shall consider what these sources of evidence have to offer, and discuss some of the problems associated with them. We shall also outline some newish, recently developed tools: brain scans and electronic databases.

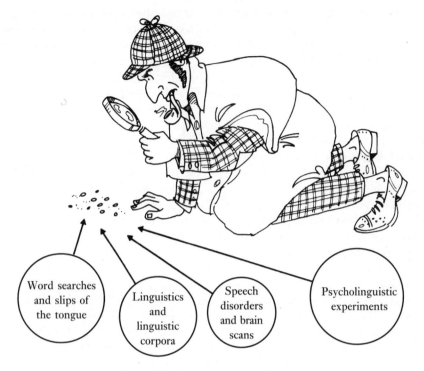

Figure 2.1   Clues to the mental lexicon

Word Searches: Black Holes and Oysters

'The name of those fabulous animals (pagan, I regret to say) who used to sing on the water, has quite escaped me.'

Mr George Chuzzlewit suggested 'Swans'.

'No,' said Mr Pecksniff, 'Not swans. Very like swans, too. Thankyou.'

The nephew . . . propounded 'Oysters'.

'No,' said Mr Pecksniff . . . 'nor oysters. But by no means unlike oysters; a very excellent idea, thankyou my dear sir, very much. Wait! Sirens, of course.'

In the passage above, Mr Pecksniff, a character in Charles Dickens's novel *Martin Chuzzlewit*, has difficulty in retrieving a word which ordinarily he knows quite well. When such word searches occur in real life, they may provide valuable information about the mental lexicon if we assume, as did the psychologist William James at the end of the last century, that 'We make search in our memory for a forgotten idea, just as we rummage our house for a lost object. In both cases we visit what seems to be the probable neighbourhood of that which we miss.'[2] The intermediate stages through which a person passes in the struggle to locate a missing item may give us clues to the general organization of a whole area – though the notion of 'neighbourhood' should not be taken too literally: words which seem to be closely related may be stored close together, or they may be more distant but have strong links binding them.

Of course, sometimes the searcher feels completely blocked, unable to remember anything about the word required, like George, a character in Iris Murdoch's novel *The Philosopher's Pupil*, who likens his inability to remember his wife's whereabouts to the 'black hole' left by an elusive word: 'He thought, I know, but I've forgotten . . . she's there in the form of a black hole, like not being able to find a word. I can't remember anything about her. . . .'

Quite often, however, the hole left by the missing word is far from empty. As William James noted: 'There is a gap . . . but no mere gap. It is a gap that is intensely active. A sort of wraith of the name is in it, beckoning us in a given direction, making us at moments tingle with the sense of our closeness. . . .'[3] This wraith can sometimes lead us to the required word, as shown by Sigmund Freud's insightful account of a successful word search:

> One day I found it impossible to recall the name of the small country of which Monte Carlo is the chief town. The substitute names for it ran: Piedmont, Albania, Montevideo, Colico. Albania was soon replaced in my mind by Montenegro; and it then occurred to me that the syllable 'Mont' (pronounced 'Mon') was found in all the substitute names except the last. Thus it was easy for me, starting from the name of Prince Albert [the ruling prince], to find the forgotten name Monaco. Colico gives a pretty close imitation of the sequence of syllables and the rhythm of the forgotten name.[4]

The same type of rooting around can be observed quite often today. For example: 'He took a . . . er . . . something interest in it. What's the word I want? It's something like *salient*, but I may be confusing it with *prurient*. I know it begins with an *s*. Ah, yes, SALACIOUS.' These intermediate guesses may indicate groups of words which the mental lexicon treats as closely related.

Word searches, then, can provide useful evidence. But they also have certain drawbacks. First, the words mislaid tend to be relatively uncommon ones, so the method of finding them may not be the same as that for frequently used ones. Second, perhaps the speakers were taking a roundabout and unnatural route to the target, because the straightforward way was blocked.[5] Therefore evidence from word searches needs to be supplemented by other types of information.

Looking in on the Cogs

Minor malfunctions can often reveal more about underlying mechanisms than a perfectly working system. If we turn on a tap (faucet), and pure water runs out, we may have no idea where this water was stored before it splashed down into the sink. If, however, some pigeon feathers arrive with the water (as reputedly happened in an old hospital), then we might surmise that the water supply came from a tank on the roof to which pigeons had access. Similarly, 'slips of the tongue' – errors which occur involuntarily in spontaneous speech – can give us clues about speech mechanisms which are normally hidden. In the words of two researchers at the end of the last century, 'the cover is lifted from the clockwork and we can look in on the cogs.'[6]

Speech error evidence is valuable for several reasons. First, when speakers pick a wrong word in error, they often think, perhaps only momentarily, that they have grabbed the right one. Therefore they are unlikely to have approached the target by a roundabout route, so we are witnessing the results of a normal retrieval process. Second, everybody makes slips of the tongue, no matter how well educated they may be: so they reflect the working of normal brains, not diseased or senile ones. But the major reason why tongue-slips are useful is that they are 'rule-governed' in the sense that they follow predictable patterns, a fact expressed in the title of a well-known paper on the topic: 'The non-anomalous nature of anomalous utterances'.[7] This means that we can build up a data bank of recurring types of error from which we can investigate the nature of the normal processes involved.[8]

Tongue-slips fall into two major categories: *assemblage errors* and *selection errors*. In the first, we find errors such as *patter-killer* for 'caterpillar', or *par cark* for 'car park', in which the right items have been chosen but assembled in the wrong order. Such errors probably have relatively little to do with the mental lexicon. In this book, therefore, we shall concentrate mainly on the second type of error.

In this second type, a wrong item appears to have been selected from the mental word-store. For example, in a television interview about his old school, Prince Edward of England noted: 'Corporal punishment is a last resort. It is difficult to use capital punishment in any institution. A beating is very valuable: it shows people you have come to the end of your tether.' In the second sentence, he appears to have mistakenly substituted the word *capital* for 'corporal'. Such selection errors can shed light on the mental lexicon if we assume that anyone who accidentally produces a wrong word is likely to have picked one closely related to the intended word or 'target'.

It is popularly assumed that selection errors are 'Freudian slips', based on Freud's claim that slips of the tongue often reveal suppressed thoughts which have involuntarily pushed their way to the surface. This does happen occasionally. However, if one looks objectively at the examples Freud quotes, they give us more information about the mental lexicon and less about secret thoughts than he would have us believe.[9] For example, one of his patients made a fairly common slip, saying *week* when she meant 'day'. Freud recounts the incident as follows: 'A woman patient who was acting entirely against my wishes in planning a short trip to Budapest, but who was determined to have her own way, justified herself by telling me that she was going only for three days, but she made a slip of the tongue and actually said "only three WEEKS". She was betraying the fact that, to spite me, she would rather spend three weeks than three days there in the company which I considered unsuitable for her.'[10] An alternative interpretation is that Freud's obvious disapproval distracted the patient from what she was saying, and led her to pick the wrong word out of several closely related words. But it is unnecessary to assume that the word *week* had any special significance in the conversation.

Selection errors may be based on meaning similarity, sound similarity, or both. For example:

> MEANING:
> I wonder who invented *crosswords* (jigsaws)?
> He came *tomorrow* (yesterday).
> SOUND:
> The emperor had several *porcupines* (concubines).
> There were lots of little *orgasms* (organisms) floating in the water.
> MEANING AND SOUND:
> You can hear the *clarinets* (castanets) clicking.
> I don't have much sympathy with rich-looking *burglars* (beggars).

The examples above are all single words which replaced the target, the word intended. However, each of the types of error mentioned above can also occur as 'blends', cases in which two words have been combined into one. For example:

> MEANING BLEND:
> I don't *expose* (expect/suppose) anyone will eat that.
> SOUND BLEND:
> Akbar Khan was a *lustrious* (lustful/illustrious) and passionate man.
> SOUND AND MEANING BLEND:
> My *tummach* (tummy/stomach) feels funny.

These types are summarized in figure 2.2.

Such tongue-slips can provide valuable clues to the way the human word-store works. But the evidence must be used with care, for several reasons. There can be slip-ups both in the collection of data and in its interpretation. Let us consider these problems.

	SINGLE ERRORS	BLENDS
MEANING	*crosswords* (jigsaws)	*expose* (expect/suppose)
SOUND	*orgasms* (organisms)	*lustrious* (lustful/illustrious)
MEANING/SOUND	*burglars* (beggars)	*tummach* (tummy/stomach)

Figure 2.2   Types of selection errors

In order to gather data, many tongue-slip collectors carry round a small notebook in which they write down errors whenever they hear them – on a bus, at parties or at mealtimes. This can produce a lot of interesting data – but even trained researchers sometimes hear inaccurately or fail to note the surrounding context properly. The obvious alternative is to use only tape-recorded data. But since one cannot keep a tape-recorder running all the time, many errors would be missed. Moreover, the number of errors produced in any one hour of spoken speech is fairly small, and we would need hundreds of hours of tape-recordings in order to write a single paper. In brief, the notebook type of data may be unreliable, and tape-recorded data produces too few errors to be regarded as a representative sample.

The interpretation of the evidence can also be tricky. Not all slips fit neatly into one or other of the categories suggested earlier. For example, is *conversation* for 'conservation' a selection error, in which one similar-sounding word has been picked instead of another? Or an assemblage error, in which the [s] and [v] were reversed? Or what about the student who, describing her new boyfriend, said: 'He's such a lovely *huskuline* man.' Was this a genuine blend, in which the similar-meaning words *husky* and *masculine* had been bundled together, when she meant to say only one? Or was it simply a 'telescopic' blend, in which two adjacent words had been telescoped together in a hurry, so that what she had really meant to say was 'husky AND masculine'? Or what went wrong in the slip *peach seduction* for 'speech production'?[11] This one is especially hard to categorize.

A further problem is that it is often difficult to know whether we are dealing with a momentary selection error or an error of ignorance, in which the speaker was simply unaware of the correct word, like the fictional Mrs Malaprop in Sheridan's play *The Rivals*, who repeatedly confused similar-sounding words such as *alligator* and *allegory*: 'She was as headstrong as an allegory on the banks of the Nile.' Sometimes the strangeness of the mistake indicates that the hearer had no idea of the appropriate word, as with *blue bonnet plague* instead of 'bubonic plague',[12] but at other times the distinction is quite unclear.

We also need to be careful about the conclusions we draw. Suppose we find many more tongue-slips involving nouns than verbs. This does not automatically mean that humans find nouns harder to cope with than verbs: our evidence may just reflect the fact that the English language contains more nouns than any other part of speech.[13]

In brief, the spontaneous word selection errors of normal speakers provide useful evidence. But they are not without problems, and one needs to be aware of the possible ways in which they could be misleading. Let us now move on to the somewhat more bizarre errors produced by people with speech disorders.

Lost for Words

'I often had the impression that I had the . . . word within my power but through a tempestuous cleavage another element would come and take its place and this would give to my speech a quality often incomprehensible and fantastic. . . .'[14] This is a description by a recovered patient of what it was like to suffer from aphasia – severe speech difficulties, which are most commonly caused by a stroke or head injury.

Word-finding difficulties are the commonest aphasic symptom, and are present in almost all types of aphasia. A typical example is the case of Mr Philip Gorgan, a 72-year-old retired butcher.[15] When asked to name objects, his responses were hardly ever wholly wrong: he said *chair* for 'table', *knee* for 'elbow' and *hair* for 'comb'. 'Clip' came out as *plick*, 'butter' was renamed *tubber* and 'ceiling' became *leasing*. For 'ankle' he said 'ankely, no mankel, no kankle'; 'paper' was named 'piece of handkerchief, pauper, hand pepper, piece of hand paper'; 'fork' was called *tonsil, teller, tongue, fung*. As these examples show, 'Sometimes . . . he would manage to hit, or at least circle in upon, the sought-for target; sometimes not . . . Like a soldier in a strange country, who knows there is an enemy somewhere but is unfamiliar with the terrain and type of warfare, he searches about, periodically lunging in various directions, sometimes coming close to, or even to grips with, the enemy; but he is just as likely to shoot completely wide of the mark or get caught in a booby trap.'[16]

Mr Gorgan is not mad. He does not try to sit on the table or spear food with his tongue, though obviously it is important to distinguish people like Mr Gorgan from someone who is truly confused, such as the 53-year-old painter who insisted that a bedpan was a paint pot.[17] When asked what a paint pot was doing in his hospital bed, he replied that his job was to paint automobiles, so he always worked with a paint pot. At this stage of his illness the patient genuinely believed that he had a paint pot beside him.

Researchers study aphasics because they assume that 'certain symptom patterns would not be possible if the normal intact cognitive system were not organized in a particular way'.[18] Those who carry out this type of work hope above all to find patients whose mental lexicon is selectively impaired, in that some parts are damaged, others not. This might indicate possible subsystems within the mental lexicon. Suppose, for example, we found a patient who could remember nouns but not verbs. This would suggest that these were organized differently from one another in the mind.

Another justification for studying speech disorders is that, in a number of cases, the problems of aphasic patients are simply an exaggeration of the difficulties which normal speakers may experience. Freud observed in 1891 that the errors of aphasics do 'not differ from the incorrect use and the distortion of words which the healthy person can observe in himself in states of fatigue or divided attention or under the influence of disturbing affects'.[19] And similarities between the the errors of aphasics and the slips of the tongue of normal speakers have been found in more recent work.[20]

The lexicon of aphasics can be studied either by analysing their spontaneous speech or by attempting to elicit words through showing pictures or pointing. A really thorough investigation tests the ability to name not only objects the patient can see but also things he or she can touch or smell or hear, such as identifying handclapping or the smell of lavender. It also tests different categories of objects, such as body parts, countries of the world, colours, as well as the ability to list members of these categories: 'How many types of fruit can you think of?' It would also see if the patient could name an item from a description of its use, such as 'What type of a machine would you use to clean carpets?', and would see if cues, such as hearing the initial sound, could jog their memory.[21]

There are, however, two major problems in dealing with aphasics. The first and most obvious is that damaged brains may not always be representative of normal ones. Strange effects may occur not only as a result of the original injury, as when patients use bizarre nonsense words such as *rugabize* for 'TV set', *lungfab* for 'window' and *dop* for 'nose',[22] but also because patients may develop strange and idiosyncratic strategies to deal with their speech problems. One helpless patient whom I met objected to being treated as a baby by the hospital staff. In her speech she sometimes gave the impression that long, strange words were easier to access than short common ones. For example, when shown a picture of someone knitting, she said: 'My dear, she's reticulating.' This may have been a genuine symptom of her illness. On the other hand, it may have been a conscious attempt to sound 'grown-up'.

A second problem is that the same output might be due to a variety of underlying causes, and only careful probing can reveal the difference. At the very least, one needs to distinguish between patients who have totally lost the word and those who just cannot locate it temporarily. One patient failed utterly to name a comb. When told it was a comb, he commented: 'You may call it a comb, but that's not the word I would use.'[23] The word seemed to have been obliterated from his mental lexicon. Another also failed to remember the name *comb*, but when reminded said: 'Yes, of course, a comb.' In the latter case, to quote a nineteenth-century researcher: 'The words representing his ideas were preserved in the treasury of his memory, but the mere origination of the idea was not sufficient to effect the verbal expression of them.'[24] And there are a few patients who may be perfectly aware of the word *comb* in their mind, but may be quite unable to 'spit it out'.

A third problem is variability. On one day, a patient said *didjog* for 'hedgehog', then on another suggested *ig, os, hidjog, egog*, and proposed HE as the first two letters.[25]

These examples suggest that, as in the case of normal slips of the tongue, the errors and word-finding attempts of aphasics can provide valuable evidence, provided they are treated with caution and compared with information from other sources. Let us now go on to consider another of these sources, the results of psycholinguistic experiments.

Controlling the Situation

One day towards the end of the nineteenth century the pioneering British psychologist Francis Galton wrote down 75 words on slips of paper, then put them aside until he had forgotten the particular words selected. After a few days he glanced at a word at a time, and, taking a pen in one hand, quickly wrote down the first two ideas which came into his head. In his other hand he held a watch, so that he could time his reactions. He notes: 'The records lay bare the foundations of a man's thoughts with curious distinctness and exhibit his mental anatomy with more vividness and truth than he himself would probably care to publish to the world.'[26] This is the first recorded experiment on the organization of words in the mind.

Galton's idea was immediately seized on by a number of other psychologists. This basic word association experiment, slightly modified, is still in use today. The experimenter presents the subject with a series of words, and for each item asks her to name the first word which comes to mind: 'Give me the first word you think of when I say *day*.' The subject will say, perhaps, 'night' or 'light' or anything else which pops into her mind in response to *day*. The advantage of this type of experiment is that it is extremely simple. Furthermore, it is likely to be useful, since different people tend to give rather similar responses, so much so that one can talk about 'norms of word association' – the title of a well-known book on the topic.[27] An analysis of these responses may therefore give useful information about how words might be linked together in a person's mind.

Another famous though more recent experiment involves the 'tip of the tongue' (TOT) phenomenon. In the mid-1960s two American psychologists tried to artificially induce the state in which people feel that a word is 'on the tip of their tongue' but cannot quite remember it.[28] Subjects in a 'TOT state' are left with 'a disembodied presence, like the grin without the Cheshire cat'.[29] The experimenters evoked this state by reading out definitions of relatively uncommon words, such as 'navigational instrument used in measuring angular distances, esp. the altitude of sun, moon and stars at sea'. Some people didn't know the word *sextant* at all, but a few went into a 'TOT state'. The experimenters then quizzed them about the word they could almost remember. Could they name words with similar meaning? Or suggest similar-sounding words? Could they guess the initial consonant or the number of syllables? Some of them managed to do all these things. These findings, and those of others who have replicated this experiment, provide a useful supplement to the information gleaned from spontaneous word searches.

These days, experimental psychology has become highly sophisticated, utilizing expensive and accurate equipment. However, in any one area of enquiry a few basic techniques tend to recur. Lexical decision tasks, 'priming', 'phoneme monitoring' and 'gating' are particularly common in investigations of the mental lexicon. Let us briefly outline what these involve.

A lexical decision task has already been mentioned in chapter 1. In its simplest form, the experimenters present subjects with a number of sound or letter sequences, asking them to say whether each is a word or not. Their reaction times are measured in milliseconds (thousandths of a second). This is likely to provide information as to which words are the most readily available in a person's mental lexicon – though care must be taken to distinguish between word-finding time and various processes which might be happening in the mind after the word has been found and before the response has been given.[30]

The basic lexical decision task can be varied in several ways, most obviously by altering the type of word being tested. Reaction time to common words might be compared with responses to uncommon ones. Or the rejection speed for nonsense words which are similar to real ones might be checked against that for non-words which are quite different from actual words.

Another way of varying this task is to see whether a subject's response to a word is altered by the words presented before it. For example, suppose you had measured the recognition time for a word such as *game* when the previous word was another common word, such as *level*. You might then check whether this recognition time was significantly altered if you put a less common word in front of it, such as *tithe*.[31]

Preactivating a listener's attention, as in the example above, is known as 'priming', the assumption being that if a word 'primes' another (facilitates the processing of another), the two are likely to be closely connected. A variety of possibilities can be tested in this way. Suppose one found that subjects responded faster to the words *spider* or *bug* after hearing the word *insect*. One might then check whether the word *insect* still primed *bug* even when the bug in question was clearly an electronic bug.[32]

Numerous ingenious variants of priming exist. In 'cross-modal priming', for example, subjects hear first a spoken word, then see a written version. In this way, some researchers hope to gain information about a possible abstract, underlying version of the word[33] – though as the techniques become more varied, so controversy about the results increases.[34]

If a person is having trouble in dealing with a word, then she will have less attention for handling other tasks. This is the rationale behind another technique known as 'phoneme monitoring', which means listening for the presence of a particular sound: 'Press the button when you hear a [b].' If the required sound comes immediately after a complicated word, then the listener's response is likely to be slower. For example, one might want to check whether a word such as *yellow* was harder or easier or the same as *empty*, and ask subjects to listen for a [b] in a sentence such as:

The dog sniffing round the yard stuck its nose into the empty bucket.

The time taken to find [b] would be measured. Then, some time later, the sentence would be presented again, but with *yellow* in place of 'empty'.[35]

'Gating' is a more recent technique.[36] It relies on highly sophisticated equipment which can cut an utterance up into minute slices, as small as 1/40th of a second (25ms). Its name reveals how it works: it allows a certain amount of a word through, then cuts off the rest with a 'gate'. Suppose you have two words which start the same and finish differently, such as *scoop* and *scoot*. You can let through a progressively larger portion of each word, and ask people to predict what the ending will be. This allows a researcher to find out just how much information is needed before word recognition takes place.[37]

In addition to lexical decision tasks, priming, phoneme monitoring, and gating, there are a number of other psycholinguistic experiments which can be used to find out about the mental lexicon. For example, word-learning experiments seem to be particularly useful with children.[38] The experimenters teach children new words, and then, some time later, check how well they have been remembered. Misremembered words, such as *puss-puss* for 'cuscus', *gandigoose* for 'bandicoot', can show which parts of the word children find easiest to recall.[39]

The advantage of experiments is that the experimenter can simplify the situation and manipulate one variable at a time, instead of being faced with the tens or even hundreds of uncontrollable factors found in ordinary speech. But this creates a problem. In order to be fully in control, it is necessary to create a quite artificial situation. This sometimes leads people to devise abnormal strategies for coping, which they would never use in a normal situation. Another problem is that a psychologist may not always be aware of all the variables which exist, and so may unwittingly have falsified the experiment.[40] So it is important to be aware of this possibility and not place too much reliance on any one experiment.

Experiments, then, can give interesting insights into the mental lexicon, but cannot be trusted blindly, since quite misleading conclusions may be drawn from unnatural or badly designed experiments.

The Messiness of Minds

'Linguists like any other speakers of a language cannot help focusing their attention on the word, which is the most central element in the social system of communication.'[41] As the above quotation suggests, those involved in the study of linguistics have treated words as important for a long time, and there are countless discussions of their sounds, their meaning and their syntax. Anyone working on the mental lexicon needs to become acquainted with the enormous and often valuable literature on the topic of words.

There are, however, some problems with the conclusions reached. Linguists are primarily trying to describe the facts of language in as simple a way as possible. But there is no guarantee that human minds work in this neat and economical fashion. It has been claimed that 'A linguist who could not devise a better system than is present in any speaker's brain ought to try another trade'.[42]

A second problem with the writings of linguists is that until recently they have regarded syntax, which involves combinations of words, as more important than the words themselves: 'The principal task of linguistics is to investigate and describe the ways in which words can be combined and manipulated to convey meanings.'[43] This has led many of them to underestimate the complexities of the lexicon and to characterize it as a finite list which concentrates on irregularities and idiosyncrasies: 'A list of lexical items as provided in the lexicon . . . is unquestionably finite. That is to say, the lexical items of a language can indeed be presented as a mere list.'[44] 'The lexicon is really an appendix of the grammar, a list of basic irregularities.'[45] 'Regular variations are not matters for the lexicon, which should contain only idiosyncratic items.'[46] Only recently has this viewpoint been challenged, and much that was ignored or placed elsewhere in a grammar is now being shifted back into the lexicon.[47]

The findings of linguists, then, like the other types of evidence discussed in this chapter, provide useful clues to the mental lexicon, but need to be treated with caution.

Brain Scans

New tools for the study of the mental lexicon are speeding up and even revolutionizing methods of research.

Brain scans are the most spectacular of these new developments.[48] So-called PET (positron emission tomography) scans became established in the 1970s. Blood surges in the brain when someone uses language, just as extra blood is pumped into the legs when someone runs. This blood flow can be recorded. Radioactive water is injected into a vein in the arm. In just over a minute, the water accumulates in the brain. The subject is asked to perform a series of progressively more difficult linguistic tasks, such as speaking a word they see or hear, or, later, providing a verb to fit with a noun, such as *hit* with *hammer*. The more complex the task, the more brain areas are involved – though with practice, the activity grows less.

But injecting anything into the body involves a minor risk, and non-invasive techniques have since been developed. So-called fMRI (functional magnetic resonance imaging) relies on manipulating particles (protons) which are numerous in the body, and which have magnetic properties. They emit detectable radio signals, which can be measured. As with PET scans, MRI studies can show which areas of the brain are active at any time, though with no risk to the patient.

The electrical activity produced by different areas of the brain can be revealed by ERP (event-related potential) studies. Electrodes are attached to the skull, and these measure the amount of activity in the area beneath them.[49]

A drawback of all these neurological techniques is that they pick up a huge amount of cortical hustle and bustle. It is not at all clear how much of this seething activity relates to language. But the use of these new techniques has confirmed some points which have long been suspected by linguists, such as basic differences between the treatment of nouns and verbs, and between different types of verb. And future work will undoubtedly provide more insights.

From Drudge to Whiz-kid

'LEXICOGRAPHER. A writer of dictionaries; a harmless drudge . . .' according to Samuel Johnson in his famous dictionary published in the mid-eighteenth century.[50] Even in the early part of the twentieth century, dictionary writers had to behave like drudges. They painstakingly copied words onto cards, which they then sorted. But now, lexicographers have to be computer whiz-kids.

By the end of the twentieth century, books and newspapers could be electronically scanned onto computers. Electronic databases contain massive amounts of language material and are accessible at the touch of a few keystrokes. On-line dictionaries which are continuously updated are perhaps the most obvious bonus to those working on the lexicon.

Meanwhile, a new branch of linguistics, **corpus linguistics**, has emerged, which explores the ways in which these huge databases can be exploited. The pioneers of corpus linguistics restricted themselves to simple tasks: for example, they counted how many words were two-letter, three-letter or four-letter. Or how many words were nouns, and how many verbs or adjectives. Or they looked at the different endings which could be added to words, and so on.

But as computers grew more powerful, data could be stored and manipulated in more sophisticated ways. A word's immediate neighbours and near neighbours can be revealed with a few computer keystrokes. The British National Corpus, for example, is a large database which contains both written and spoken language from multiple registers (styles). It enables researchers to choose how many words they want to consider either side of their selected word.[51] They can then identify often subtle co-occurrence patterns: 'For example, *big* commonly co-occurs with *toe*, while *large* commonly co-occurs with *number*.'[52]

Summary

In this chapter we have outlined various ways in which we can gather clues about the mental lexicon: word searches and slips of the tongue of normal people, the word-finding problems of aphasics, psycholinguistic experiments, the work of linguists, brain-scans, and electronic databases. We have shown that each of these can provide valuable information, though each has its own inbuilt problems. We therefore need to combine all these sources, but with some degree of caution.

In the next chapter we shall consider how these clues can be used in relation to our long-term aim, that of providing outline specifications for a working model of the mental lexicon.

3

Programming Dumbella
— Modelling the mental lexicon —

'I've got this project I've been working on in my spare time', he said. . . . 'Maybe you've heard about it. I've been getting people to tape-record lists of words and syllables for me.'. . .

He gave her eight yellow-boxed cartridges and a black looseleaf binder.

'My gosh, there's a lot', she said, leafing through curled and mended pages typed in triple columns.

'It goes quickly', Claude said. 'You must say each word clearly in your regular voice and take a little stop before the next one.'. . .

She went to the desk . . . and switched the recorder on. With a finger to the page, she leaned towards the microphone . . . 'Taker. Takes. Taking', she said. 'Talcum. Talent. Talented. Talk. Talkative. Talked. Talker. Talking. Talks.'

Ira Levin, *The Stepford Wives*

The best way of finding out about something is to try to make it oneself. If we were trying to discover the principles underlying, say, a sewing machine, a working replica would be proof that we had understood the basic mechanisms involved.

Often, however, it is too expensive or impractical to build a complete replica. If one was trying to find out how a spacecraft was likely to respond to different temperatures, it might be better to start by building a scale model of the original, and to check its performance in different freezer and furnace heats. In this case, and in many others, models are likely to be more practical than replicas, so 'model building' is the name given to this type of activity.

In this book, the overall aim is to provide the outline specifications for a 'model' of the mental lexicon. This covers both the way it is organized and how it works. We shall behave as if we were trying to program a robot to behave like a human being as far as its word-storage and word-finding abilities are concerned, a situation proposed by Ira Levin in his novel *The Stepford Wives*. In this work of science fiction, the women of a small town in America are killed by their menfolk and replaced by smiling robots who do everything the men want. These dummies are programmed to speak just like normal humans. The basis of this ability is a long list of words, since, prior to her death, every woman has been persuaded to read out the contents of a dictionary on to a tape, which has been incorporated into the workings of the robot. Let us call the archetype of these dummies 'Dumbella'. In this book we shall try to find out how the words should be organized inside her, so that she may be regarded as a 'model' of a human being as far as the mental lexicon is concerned.

First, however, we need to say more about the nature and limitations of 'models'. After that, we shall make suggestions as to how to deal with this task.

Models and Maps

The term 'model building' has a fairly modern ring to it, but the activity of building working models in order to understand something is quite old, and is mentioned by the seventeenth-century poet John Milton. In *Paradise Lost* the angel Raphael tells Adam that God has allowed men to argue about the stars and planets, perhaps so that he can laugh at their attempts to model the mechanisms underlying them:

> He his Fabric of the Heav'ns
> Hath left to their disputes, perhaps to move
> His laughter at their quaint Opinions wide
> Hereafter, when they come to model Heav'n
> And calculate the Starrs . . .[1]

However, the word 'model' may be misleading, because it gives the impression that we are always dealing with scaled-down copies of originals. In many cases this is false, for two reasons: first, models are often highly simplified, and second, they often represent guesswork rather than copying. Let us discuss these two matters.

Perfect scale models, in which every single detail of the original has been replicated, are time-consuming and expensive to build. It therefore makes sense to leave out insignificant trivia and concentrate on the important characteristics of the 'real thing' that is being simulated: 'Models embody only the essential features of whatever it is they are intended to represent. If a model of an automobile is intended for wind tunnel tests, then the outside shape of the model car is important, but no seats nor any other interior furnishings of the real automobile need be present in the model.'[2] Sometimes, concentration on only the bare essentials can lead to a model being very far away from the original indeed. When men come to 'model Heav'n', the most important feature may be the 24-hour cycle caused by the rotation of the planet Earth. Therefore, one can claim that 'Clocks are fundamentally models of the planetary system,'[3] – and so are digital watches.

The fact that models can be very different from the original, yet still embody some of its essential features, has meant that model building can be used by a wide range of researchers, even people who do not deal with strictly physical things at all, such as economists, psychologists, and linguists.[4] When economists build a 'model' of the economy, they attempt to encapsulate the crucial features of the present-day economic situation and to show the principles which underlie it. This enterprise helps them to lay plans for the future, since ideally their model will predict what is likely to happen next.

Models, then, are not necessarily scaled-down replicas, but more usually simplified versions of what they represent. But they may be different from the thing they are modelling in another way also: they are likely to be guesses rather than copies. Although it is perfectly possible to unscrew a sewing machine and copy it piece by piece, this approach is just not feasible in a number of situations. For example, scientists studying the hidden thermonuclear reactions in the sun's interior cannot, in the current state of science, place a laboratory inside the sun. All they can do is study the light emitted at the outermost layers of the sun and then rely on elaborate guesswork in trying to construct models which might explain why the sun's light converts into heat.[5] If they succeed in building a model which produces the same effect as the sun, then they may have guessed right about the underlying principles involved.

However, the fact that some models have to rely on guesses raises a problem. Even if we are successful in simulating some general effect with a model, such as the light and heat emitted by the sun, how do we know that we have got its inner workings right? It is sometimes possible to produce the same output by very different mechanisms. For instance, the chemical insulin is produced by the human body, but scientists have also discovered how to manufacture it artificially. But there is no reason to believe that the two processes are the same. Similarly, when dealing with the mental lexicon, two or more models might produce the same output even though their internal mechanisms could be quite different.

Scientists, then, are faced with two similar but related problems. First, they have to build a model which produces the right end result. Second, they have to decide whether the inner mechanism of their model is a 'real' replica, or simply one which does the same task in a different way. It may happen that two teams of researchers each build a different model which has the same effect. In that case, they will need to decide which is the better one. A number of different models of the mental lexicon have been proposed. In the course of this book we will be discussing why we might want to choose one type of model in preference to another.

Mental Maps

Models of the mind built by psycholinguists are somewhere in between the concrete models of spacecraft and the abstract models of economists. Perhaps the best analogy is that of a map, which in some ways fits a 'real life' state of affairs and in other ways is quite different. It is obvious that 'the most useful map is often not an exact representation of the terrain. The well-known map of the London underground . . . provides an elegant way of summarizing essential information . . . It sacrifices realism but given its purpose is a better map for doing so.'[6] The London Underground map tells one clearly which train-lines connect which stations. There is a line on the map linking Holborn and Covent Garden, and correspondingly there are sets of metal rails linking these two stations. In this way, it presents a true picture of 'reality'. On the other hand, the various lines are represented by different colours on the map. We do not expect either the trains or the railway lines to be painted this colour. Nor do we expect the distances between stations to be accurately represented.

We are trying, then, to produce a diagram of the connections in the mental lexicon which is in some respects comparable to a plan of the London Underground. However, there is one way in which this mental map is quite different. We can go down into the Underground and map the connections between stations. But we cannot yet view the connections in the mind directly though brain scans might enable us to do so at some time in the future. We are instead in the situation of observers who could watch passengers entering and leaving train stations but could neither enter the system nor communicate directly with the travellers. In this situation, we would probably conclude that it was possible to get from any single station to any other, but would argue about whether one spaghetti-like line linked all the stations or whether there were a number of different lines, so that passengers had to change trains. If a journey took a long time, some observers might propose that the length of time was due to a single train taking a roundabout route. Others might argue that a passenger must have changed trains, and had to wait between them. Similarly, a fast journey between stations might be because they were located near one another or because there was a speedy non-stop train linking them. This is the kind of argument which takes place between psycholinguists when they cannot decide how to interpret evidence on the mental lexicon.

Another way in which a mental map is likely to differ from the London Underground map is that we may be dealing with a system or set of systems which are quite disparate in nature, as if one line involved a train, another a bus, another a camel. Or, to take another analogy, we could be in the same sort of situation as a person trying to reconstruct the processes going on inside the mouth, assuming one could not see inside.[7] One might well come to the conclusion that, in order to cope with food, there was some kind of grinder to pulverize it and some kind of wetting mechanism to moisturize it. But what would ever lead us to suggest that in addition there is a tongue that has a strong muscle in it for the manipulation of food? We could equally well have concluded that there was simply a suction mechanism which held the food in place for the grinder and moisturizer, and never discovered the tongue.

The mouth image is useful partly because it reminds us that logical thinking is not necessarily going to lead us to the right conclusions, since the mind may work in a way that is quite counter-intuitive. But the mouth image is useful for another reason also. It suggests that human behaviour is often the end result of the interaction of a number of quite different components, subsystems or 'modules', a term borrowed from computer terminology. The same is likely to be true of the mental lexicon.

Birdcages and Libraries

If researchers have to make guesses about the structure of something unknown, where do they get their inspiration from? How does one pull a guess out of thin air, as it were? The mouth and London Underground analogies indicate one fruitful way in which humans are able to contemplate something which is not well understood. They hypothesize that it is like something we already know about, and then test this hypothesis. As one writer notes: 'Since finding out what something is is largely a matter of discovering what it is like, the most impressive contribution to the growth of intelligibility has been made by the application of suggestive metaphors.'[8]

Birdcages, treasure-houses, attics, libraries. These are all suggestions which have been put forward for describing human memory.[9] They reflect a recurrent notion that memory is a place of some kind, a metaphor which has persisted for centuries. The ancient Greek philosopher Plato attributes the birdcage analogy to Socrates: 'Let us suppose that every mind contains a kind of large birdcage stocked with all kinds of birds, some in flocks, some in small groups, and some flying around alone . . . When we are babies, we must assume that this container is empty, and suppose that the birds stand for pieces of knowledge. Whenever a person acquires some piece of knowledge, he puts it into the enclosure.'[10] The Roman orator Cicero referred to memory as the 'treasure-house of all things'.[11] A similar metaphor is put into the mouth of Sherlock Holmes by his inventor Conan Doyle: 'I consider that a man's brain originally is like a little empty attic and you have to stock it with such furniture as you choose.'[12]

The trouble with birdcages, treasure-houses and attics is that their contents are somewhat varied and difficult to put into order. So the most popular of these place metaphors has involved the notion of a place whose contents could be easily organized – above all, a library. The German philosopher Kant, writing at the end of the eighteenth century, suggested that the material in one's memory was divided into general headings 'as when we arrange the books in a library on shelves with different labels'.[13] The library is a recurring metaphor not only for memory in general, but in particular for the mental lexicon, where words are likened to books on shelves. As a medical writer suggested at the beginning of the century: 'After some brain shock, a person may be able to speak, but the wrong word often vexatiously comes to his lips, just as if . . . shelves had become badly jumbled.'[14]

Metaphors, then, can suggest hypotheses for testing, and identify questions to ask. To return to libraries, they normally have a central catalogue which gives outline information about each book and specifies a detailed location for each. This observation might lead one to hypothesize a similar central catalogue for the mental lexicon, where one could check the location of a word. Or, to take another example, libraries often have to decide what to do with popular books. Should they be stored on a shelf just inside the library, so that readers can find them easily? And should there be several copies of each? In dealing with the mental lexicon a similar question arises. Are all words to be regarded as equal? Or are frequent words and rare words treated differently? Each analogy, therefore, can provide researchers with a whole range of ideas for testing.

But libraries are not at the moment the main source of cerebral metaphors. There is a tendency for the dominant technology of the era to take over, so that almost all modern systems which involve storing information or sending messages have had their turn at providing suggestive metaphors.[15] Earlier in this century the mind was compared to a telephone exchange. More recently, memory traces have been likened to laser holograms. These days, however, computers provide the most powerful suggestive analogies. Computers can sort phenomenally quickly and store huge amounts of data. It is perhaps not surprising that they have taken over as the main metaphor for the mind, including the mental lexicon.

Computers, however, are not timeless objects. Like bathrooms or aeroplanes, they develop over the years. Modern computers are very different from the early ones. So what inspires the computers? This will potentially affect any models based on them.

Early computers were partially inspired by typewriters.[16] Just as a typewriter could be in a state in which it could type either capital or lower-case letters, so computers were envisaged as machines which had a finite number of possible internal states. Then there were strict limits on what could be done in each state, just as typewriters were limited by the number of keys.

Over the years, these old-style computers have become invaluable for sorting bank accounts and for similar number-crunching. But they cannot simulate human behaviour. So a new style of computer is in the process of explosive development. This has been inspired by the human brain, with its billions of interlocking connections. We are therefore faced with a potentially rewarding situation: modern computers are inspired by the brain, and models of the mind are simulated on these computers. 'We wish to replace the "computer metaphor" as a model of the mind with the "brain metaphor" as a model of the mind,' as one group of researchers expressed it.[17] Some of these new-style models, known under the general name of 'connectionism', will be discussed later in the book.

Testing Ideas

'I was just thinking that detection must be like science. The detective formulates a theory, then tests it. If the facts he discovers fit, then the theory holds. If they don't, then he has to find another theory, another suspect.'

Dr Howarth said drily: 'It's a reasonable analogy. But the temptation to select the right facts is probably greater.'

These lines, from P. D. James's novel *Death of an Expert Witness*, illustrate a problem faced both by detectives and by psycholinguists. Logically, the idea comes first, then the evidence is examined. Indeed, until one has an outline theory, it's difficult to know what kind of evidence to collect. But this means that researchers might subconsciously select speech samples or devise experiments which fit in with their ideas. This is a danger which researchers have to be aware of as they check to see how well facts and theories fit. A theory is likely to be on the right track if it can account for a whole range of facts, in particular extra ones which the theorist did not at first take into consideration. For example, treating the heart as a pump explains not only why blood flows round the body but also why it makes a thumping sound.

In practice, evidence and theory are somewhat more intertwined than the above 'logical order' suggests. Quite often, a chance piece of evidence suggests an idea, which is then checked against further evidence. Aunt Agatha might repeatedly confuse the words *cup* and *saucer*. This could give her nephew the idea that words for crockery were stored near one another in the mind. He could then check this out by devising an experiment which required her to name cups, saucers, plates and jugs. Overall, the situation is somewhat like trying to crack a code. The best way to do this is described by an elderly monk in Umberto Eco's novel *The Name of the Rose*: 'The first rule in deciphering a message is to guess what it means . . . Some hypotheses can be formed on the possible first words of the message, and then you see whether the rule you infer from them can apply to the rest of the text.' Similarly, psycholinguists find a piece of evidence, form a hypothesis about it, then check it out on new evidence. In the course of this book we shall be adopting this procedure in relation to the mental lexicon. Of course, we cannot deal with the whole of it straight away, so we shall concentrate at first on finding out about smallish sections of it.[18] Later we can make hypotheses about how these sections fit together.

What is a Word?

We have been calling the mental lexicon 'the human word-store'. Yet so far we have said little about one crucial question. What exactly is a word? We need to consider this before we proceed with our investigation.

Everybody thinks that they know what a word is. But the matter, which seems so simple, is in fact enormously problematical.[19] Consider the rhyme below:

> There once was a fisher named Fisher
> Who fished for a fish in a fissure.
> But the fish with a grin
> Pulled the fisherman in
> Now they all fish the fissure for Fisher.

How many words does this contain? This is easy to answer if one is dealing with a written version of the rhyme, since English conventionally leaves gaps between written words. Therefore one can simply count the overall total, which is 33. But the overall number of words in a passage (word-tokens) does not necessarily correlate with the number of different words (word-types).

How many different words are there in the limerick from the point of view of the mental lexicon? Presumably *fish* (noun) needs to be distinguished from *fish* (verb), since they have different roles in the sentence, even though they sound the same. However, what about *fished* and *fisher*? Do these have entries to themselves? Or is *fished* listed under the verb *fish*? And what about *fisher*?

Surely, some people might say, we could simply consult a dictionary. But, as we saw in chapter 1, book dictionaries are quite unlike the mental lexicon. Moreover, book dictionaries disagree over which words should have entries to themselves and which should not. *Fisher* is given an entry to itself in one well-known dictionary (*CCED*), but is listed under the verb *fish* in another (*LCED*). Yet both dictionaries give a similar word *runner* a separate entry. In short, 'Dictionaries not only differ from one another as to which words they have the space or inclination to recognize but also tend to be inconsistent within their own covers.'[20] And theoretical linguists show similar disagreements among themselves over what to count as 'words'.

'The wordishness of words'[21] presents a further problem. Not all words, especially spoken words, are as word-like as others. At one end *er*, *um* and *ah!* are typically left out of dictionaries, but *aargh*, *splat*, *weeow*, *whoop* and similar 'cartoon sounds' are mostly left in.

This type of inconsistency shows that, in our discussion of the mental lexicon, we cannot rely on any prior definition of either 'word' or 'lexical entry'. This will have to be determined in the course of the book. Furthermore, how do we know that the mental lexicon is composed of whole words? Perhaps words such as *fisher* are in pieces, with *fish* stored separately from *-er*. This is a question which we need to discuss.

Because of these complications, we shall restrict our discussion in the early stages to items such as *cow*, *tiger*, *square*, *bachelor*, which seem relatively straightforward, at least when compared with *fisher*. Let us assume that these and similar items are 'words' which have their own entries in the mental lexicon. Then, at a later stage, we can move on to the more complicated cases.

Dividing up the Work

At the very least, humans must know three things about a word in order to be able to use it: its meaning, its role in a sentence (whether it is a verb or a noun, for example) and what it sounds like. These three facets of words will be discussed in the next few chapters (Part II: Basic Ingredients, chapters 4–12). We will also consider whether words are stored as wholes or in pieces. After that, we will consider how humans deal with new situations, when they need to extend an old word or create a new one. We shall also explore how children learn words. (Part III: Newcomers, chapters 13–17). Finally, we shall discuss how all these various facets combine together (Part IV: The Overall Picture, chapters 18–21).

Summary

The overall aim of this book is to build a 'model' of the mental lexicon. In this chapter, therefore, the notion of models was discussed. We noted that models of the mind are somewhat like plans of the London Underground system: they are simplified diagrams which encapsulate crucial features of something that is in reality considerably more complex.

However, mental maps are unlike real-life maps in that they have to depend on inspired guesswork, since we cannot easily look into the head and see the connections we hypothesize. Our models are therefore often based on metaphors, as when we test out the notion that the mind may be like something else we know about, such as a library or a computer.

We then pointed out that we cannot, in advance, decide what we mean by a word: this will have to be determined in the course of the book. So will the question of whether words are stored as wholes or in pieces.

Furthermore, we noted that it was impossible to deal with the whole of the mental lexicon at once. We need to subdivide our enquiry. In the next chapter we will turn to the first of these subdivisions: word meaning.

Part II
Basic Ingredients

4

Slippery Customers
— Attempts to pin down the meaning of words —

'And now we need as it were a tompion to protect the contents of this flask from invading bacteria. I presume you know what a tompion is, Cornelius?'

'I can't say I do, sir', I said.

'Can anyone give me a definition of that common English noun?' A. R. Woresley said.

Nobody could . . .

'Oh, come on, sir', someone said. 'Tell us what it means.'

'A tompion', A. R. Woresley said, 'is a small pellet made out of mud and saliva which a bear inserts into his anus before hibernating for the winter, to stop the ants getting in.'

Roald Dahl, *My Uncle Oswald*

'Words have basic inalienable meanings, departure from which is either conscious metaphor or inexcusable vulgarity,' claimed the novelist Evelyn Waugh.[1] Words, according to this viewpoint, are precision instruments which should be used with care and accuracy. 'Words matter,' asserted the writer A. P. Herbert, 'for words are the tools of thought, and you will often find that you are thinking badly because you are using the wrong tools, trying to bore a hole with a screw-driver, or draw a cork with a coal-hammer.'[2] Supposedly, educated people will know exactly which word to use when, because in the course of their education they will have learnt precisely what each word means. If this point of view is correct, then the semantic entries in one's mental lexicon will be fairly cut and dried, and failure to achieve this ideal state will be due either to lack of education or to mental laziness. The overall assumption is that there exists, somewhere, a basic meaning for each word, which individuals should strive to attain. We can label this the 'fixed meaning' assumption.

There is, however, an alternative viewpoint, which argues that words cannot be assigned a firm meaning, and that 'Natural language concepts have vague boundaries and fuzzy edges.'[3] Word meanings cannot be pinned down, as if they were dead insects. Instead, they flutter around elusively like live butterflies. Or perhaps they should be likened to fish which slither out of one's grasp: 'Words have often been called slippery customers, and many scholars have been distressed by their tendency to shift their meanings and slide out from under any simple definition.'[4] Or perhaps word meanings should be likened to birds wheeling in mid-air: 'The proper meaning of a word . . . is never something upon which the word sits perched like a gull on a stone; it is something over which the word hovers like a gull over a ship's stern.'[5] This alternative viewpoint can be called the 'fuzzy meaning' assumption. If it is correct, then it may be extremely difficult to characterize the entries in a person's mental lexicon.

Why should intelligent people hold such divergent opinions? One possibility is that these are both uninformed, popular viewpoints, which have been put forward solely on the basis of the personality of the proposer. Perhaps the notion of a fixed meaning is promoted mainly by lexicographers and schoolmasters, since their jobs would clearly be simpler if words did have precise definitions. The fictional A. R. Woresley, quoted at the start of the chapter, obviously enjoyed handing over his dogmatic definition of a tompion, which, incidentally, is somewhat narrower than most dictionary definitions of the word. These mostly agree that a tompion or tampion is a plug for stopping an aperture, but the aperture does not have to belong to a bear – it could belong to a wide range of things, such as a cask, a gun or an organ pipe.

In contrast, we might find that the 'fuzzy meaning' adherents were poets and mystics, such as T. S. Eliot, who complained in 'Burnt Norton' that

> Words strain
> Crack and sometimes break, under the burden,
> Under the tension, slip, slide, perish,
> Decay with imprecision, will not stay in place,
> Will not stay still.

Unfortunately, this simple solution will not work. It turns out that there is no simple correlation between the type of person and the viewpoint held. Well-known and respected philosophers, psychologists and linguists are found on each side of the debate – though, on balance, philosophers have tended to favour the fixed meaning viewpoint, while psychologists often opt for fuzziness.[6] As far as the mental lexicon is concerned, we need to know whether it is possible to assign a firm definition to any word or whether words inevitably have fuzzy meanings. The answer will obviously affect our view of how people represent them in their minds. In this chapter, therefore, we will consider the fixed–fuzzy issue. In the next two, we will discuss the mental representation of word meaning in more depth (chapters 5–6). After that, we will move on to the organization of words in the mind in relation to one another (chapters 7–8).

In what follows we shall concentrate on the information which might be in a person's mind, rather than on trying to come to grips with the abstract philosophical problems involved in 'the baffling word "meaning"'.[7] The opinions of philosophers

Figure 4.1   The word and thing problem

will be mentioned only when these seem likely to illuminate the issues under discussion.[8]

Similarly, we shall not be particularly concerned with what has been called 'the inscrutability of reference',[9] the complex relationship between a word and the real-world thing it labels. Most people assume that words are linked to things via 'concepts', though exactly how is unclear (see figure 4.1).

The intermeshing of words and concepts is an area of study which is 'a morass of complexity and ignorance . . . The intricate connection between the labels people use and their conceptions of the things labeled is poorly understood.'[10] People argue as to whether there is an abstract layer of concepts which is separate from word meaning or whether the word meanings and the concepts are identical.[11] In this book we will assume, first, that people translate the real world into 'concepts', which in cases such as *tiger, moon* reflect the external world fairly well, in that there is likely to be considerable agreement over what they are, even between people speaking different languages. Second, we will treat the 'meaning' of a word as overlapping with the concept to a large extent, though not necessarily totally: the overall concept may extend beyond the sections labelled with a word (figure 4.2). This viewpoint will hopefully become clearer as the book progresses – and so will some of the problems involved.

Let us now consider the fixed–fuzzy issue. We will begin by outlining some ideas put forward by proponents of the fixed meaning viewpoint.

Snapshots and Checklists

Yes. I remember Adlestrop –
The name, because one afternoon
Of heat the express-train drew up there
Unwontedly. It was late June.

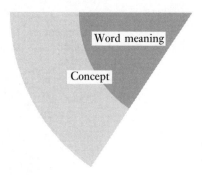

Figure 4.2   The relationship between concepts and word meanings

These lines from Edward Thomas's poem 'Adlestrop' exemplify the simplest possible viewpoint that one could have of fixed word meaning. They suggest that we have words filed as a series of snapshots. The word Adlestrop conjures up a particular photo from the file, in this case a view through a train window.

It seems likely that we all have our Adlestrops: psychologists sometimes talk about 'episodic memory', cases in which a particular episode is remembered with great clarity, sometimes with a word label attached.[12] However, there are a number of difficulties with the snapshot viewpoint as a general theory of word meaning. One major problem is that we have usually seen any object we are talking about from a number of angles. Take the word *cat*. Are we talking about a cat which is awake and walking about? Or one which is curled up asleep? Or one which is licking milk from a saucer? At the very least we need a number of different snapshots, representing a cat in each of these positions. Furthermore, cats can be different colours and sizes, often with quite personal characteristics, as with T. S. Eliot's mystery cat, Macavity:

> Macavity's a ginger cat, he's very tall and thin;
> You would know him if you saw him, for his eyes are sunken in.
> His brow is deeply lined with thought, his head is highly domed;
> His coat is dusty from neglect, his whiskers are uncombed.

So do people need a whole dossier of photographs for every single cat they have ever seen in every single position? And if so, how could they possibly label a new cat as *cat* if it wasn't in the dossier?

Moreover, the more general a term is, the more difficult it is to specify an associated image. Consider the term *animal*: 'If the generic image is four-footed, how is it that we can identify man as an animal; if it is short-necked how can we identify the giraffe?'[13]

These problems explain why the notion that meaning involves a mental image has generally proved unsatisfactory. It had some popularity at the beginning of the century, when the influential psychologist Edward Bradford Titchener claimed to have a fixed mental image for every word. For him, *cow* was 'a longish rectangle with a certain facial expression, a sort of exaggerated pout', and the word *meaning* called to mind 'the blue-grey tip of a kind of scoop which has a bit of yellow about it'.[14] But since then, the vast majority of psychologists have abandoned the idea that word meaning involves any straightforward imagery, apart from the occasional Adlestrop-type snapshot.

These observations suggest that a word such as *cat* refers not to the image of a cat but to a somewhat more abstract amalgam. Anyone who understands the word *cat* must have performed some type of analysis which has isolated the essential 'cattiness' involved in being a cat. Perhaps it is these essential characteristics which constitute its basic meaning.

This is the viewpoint of a number of philosophers. They argue that in order to capture the meaning of a word, one should establish a set of 'necessary and sufficient conditions', in other words, a list of conditions which are absolutely necessary to the meaning of the word, and which, taken together, are sufficient or adequate to encapsulate the meaning. Take the word square. This has four necessary conditions:[15]

1   a closed, flat figure
2   having four sides
3   all sides are equal in length
4   all interior angles are equal.

Each of these conditions is, by itself, necessary in order for something to be a square, and when combined, they are sufficient to define and identify a square, and only a square. Presumably anyone who understands the concept of a square must be aware of these conditions, even if they could not express them in quite this way. These conditions are also called 'conditions of criteriality' or 'criterial attributes' since they are the criteria which one uses to judge whether something is a square or not.

We may refer to this as a 'checklist' theory.[16] This theory suggests that for each word we have an internal list of essential characteristics, and we label something as *cat,* or *square,* or *cow* only if it possesses the 'criterial attributes', which we subconsciously check off one by one. This 'checklist' theory is intuitively satisfying to some people, perhaps because it is fairly familiar, as many dictionaries implicitly work on a checklist principle. However, the checklist theory also involves a number of problems. Let us consider some of these.

A major problem with the checklist theory is deciding which attributes go on to the list. Only a very few words have a straightforward set of necessary conditions, though occasionally officials can decree that words have fixed meanings within a particular context, as in the following bureaucratic definition of a cow: 'A cow is a female bovine animal which has borne a calf, or has, in the opinion of the Minister, been brought into a herd to replace one which has borne a calf.'[17]

However, most people's notion of a cow would perhaps be more like that of the following 10-year-old: 'A cow is a mammal. It has six sides – right, left, an upper and below. At the back it has a tail on which hangs a brush. With this it sends the flies away so that they do not fall into the milk. The head is for the purpose of growing horns and so that the mouth can be somewhere. The horns are to butt with and the mouth is to moo with. Under the cow hangs the milk. It is arranged for milking. When people milk, the milk comes and there is never an end to the supply.'[18] This child seems to have the word *cow* in its active mental lexicon. But how much of this description involves the actual 'meaning' of *cow* and how much is additional, non-essential information? Is it possible to isolate from people's overall knowledge a basic hard core of fixed meaning?

A number of linguists and philosophers have claimed that such a distinction is a useful one. Like the Greek philosopher Aristotle, they assume that words have a hard core of essential meaning which it is, in principle, possible to extract and specify. Surrounding this core are a number of fairly accidental facts which can be added or omitted without altering the basic meaning in any important way. The core meaning is assumed to be entered in some kind of linguistic dictionary, whereas the surrounding non-essential facts are stated in an encyclopaedia of general knowledge. Two influential researchers who promoted this viewpoint claimed that they were trying to characterize speakers' internal knowledge of their language, and so seem to be suggesting that there may be a division between a lexicon and an encyclopaedia in the human mind.[19]

If this is likely to be so, how might one identify the semantic core? Some people propose using the 'That's impossible' test. Suppose you were analysing the meaning of the word *bachelor*. If you say to someone, 'Harry is a bachelor who has been married ten years,' you would be likely to get the response: 'That's impossible. Bachelors can't be married, unless you're talking about Harry's first degree or using the word metaphorically.' This suggests that UNMARRIED is a core condition of *bachelor*. You would probably get a similar response of incredulity if you said, 'My aunt Fenella is a bachelor,' on the grounds that a *bachelor* has to be male. Similarly, if you stated, 'My baby brother is a bachelor' or 'My tadpole is a bachelor,' you would probably be told that bachelors have to be adult and human. So HUMAN, MALE, ADULT, UNMARRIED might be regarded as components of the 'real meaning' of *bachelor*, in that each of these characteristics seems to be absolutely necessary in order for a person to be labelled *bachelor*. Of course, people might well have additional knowledge or beliefs about bachelors. For example, they might expect bachelors to be childless or to drive fast cars. But this type of information would be a non-necessary extra, which might help in a conversation with a bachelor, but would not have anything to do with the meaning of the word.

The idea of sorting out a core meaning which can be distinguished from encyclopaedic knowledge is an enticing one. Unfortunately, however, there are relatively few words which can be sorted out in this apparently useful way. Most words cause considerably more difficulty. Take the word *tiger*. Everybody claims to know what a tiger is, but no one is at all clear about exactly what makes a tiger a tiger.

A tiger is a 'large Asian yellow-brown black-striped carnivorous maneless feline' according to one dictionary[20] and 'a very large Asiatic cat having a tawny coat transversely striped with black' according to another.[21] Which of these characteristics are essential? Here the 'That's impossible' test is likely to yield inconclusive results. Most people would accept that ANIMAL is a necessary condition of tigerhood, since if you said 'Harry's tiger's not an animal,' you would probably get the reply: 'Then it can't be a tiger.' People might also agree that tigers needn't be carnivorous. If you said 'Harry's tiger's a vegetarian,' it would be quite plausible to receive the reply: 'I'm not surprised, he probably can't afford to feed it on meat.' What about stripiness? 'Of course tigers have to be striped. Whoever heard of an unstriped tiger?' say a few people. But many people are more permissive, and make comments such as: 'I read in the paper that you can have white tigers, so stripiness can't be essential' – though white tigers, incidentally, are quite a disappointment: they are in fact honey-coloured, with faint stripes.

The general permissiveness over core characteristics is a problem. 'It's not at all hard to convince the man on the street that there are three-legged, lame, toothless, albino tigers, that are tigers all the same . . . What keeps them tigers?'[22] How does one cope with these apparently 'coreless concepts'?

The checklist viewpoint, therefore, is faced with two critical problems. First, it seems to be extremely difficult to decide what goes on to the checklist, since there appears to be no obvious way to draw a dividing line between essential and non-essential characteristics. Second, for some things the checklist seems to be virtually non-existent, since there appear to be hardly any necessary conditions.

Does this mean that the fixed meaning assumption has to be abandoned if, in practice, it is impossible to fix the meaning for most words? A well-known philosophical viewpoint is that words do indeed have a fixed, correct meaning, but that only a few experts know it.[23] Ordinary people must consult these experts if they need to know about the essential nature of something. Only a specialist, for example, might be able to specify the true nature of gold or arsenic. The problem here is that specialists sometimes disagree, and sometimes change their minds. This leaves us with a quite extraordinary state of affairs: that there might be a 'real meaning' of something which at present nobody can actually specify. But this type of meaning, even if it exists, is not very interesting to someone working on the mental lexicon: 'Either it is in an expert's mind (though no one can know for sure that the right meaning is there), or it is in no one's mind and accordingly an idle wheel in the intellectual traffic of the world.'[24]

In brief, even if the 'true meaning' of, say, *gold, measles* or *arsenic* exists in the abstract or in the minds of experts, it is clear that we non-experts bumble along quite happily with a working approximation of our own for most words, as indeed the philosophers admit. Moreover, even if we are told of an expert's viewpoint, we sometimes choose to ignore it. For example, botanists tell us that an onion is a member of the lily family,[25] information which seems to be unnecessary for a working knowledge of onions and lilies, and even if known is likely to be disregarded. We conclude, therefore, that even if there is somewhere a 'true' meaning for each particular word, this meaning is fairly irrelevant in relation to the mental lexicon. A possible compromise is to distinguish 'broad content' meaning in the world from 'narrow content' or mental representations[26] – which is what we shall be concerned with in this book.

In this section, then, we have found that, for some words, it seems to be impossible to identify a firm semantic core. Does this mean that the notion of fixed meanings must be abandoned? Yes it does, according to the fuzzy meaning supporters. Let us now consider their viewpoint.

Fuzzy Edges and Family Resemblances

Fuzzy meaning supporters argue that word meanings are inevitably fluid, for two reasons: the 'fuzzy edge phenomenon' and the 'family resemblance syndrome'. Let us illustrate these. Words have fuzzy edges in the sense that there is no clear point at which one word ends and another begins. This was demonstrated by the socio-linguist William Labov when he showed students pictures of containers and asked them to label each as either a *cup*, a *vase* or a *bowl*.[27] The students all agreed on certain shapes. For example, they all considered tall thin containers without handles to be vases and low flat ones to be bowls. But they were quite confused when faced with something that was in between the two. Was it a vase or a cup? And suppose vase and bowl shapes were given handles (figure 4.3), what then? They had difficulty in deciding, and they came to different conclusions from one another. As Labov pointed out: 'In any kitchen, there are many containers that are obviously bowls, cups, mugs, and dishes. But there are others that might be called cups or might not; or might be a kind of cup, according to some, but a kind of dish according to others.'[28]

Figure 4.3   Vase, cup or bowl?

If it was just that they disagreed with one another, one could simply have said that people's mental lexicons differ. But it turned out that individuals were inconsistent in their own responses. For example, after confirming that a particular container was likely to be called a *bowl* when it was seen empty, Labov then asked the students what they would call it when it was filled with various things. A bowl remained a *bowl* if it was full of mashed potatoes, but tended to be relabelled a *vase* if it contained flowers and a *cup* if there was coffee in it. Labov notes: 'A goal of some clear thinkers has been to use words in more precise ways. But though this is an excellent and necessary step for technical jargon, it is a self-defeating programme when applied to ordinary words.'[29] Fuzzy edges, then, seem to be an intrinsic property of word meaning.

Let us now turn to the family resemblance syndrome. This can be illustrated by a mythical family called the Mugwumps. The Mugwumps, let us say, have certain family characteristics which tend to surface in generation after generation of Mugwumps: ears which stick out, squinting eyes, eyebrows which meet in the middle and a ferocious temper. However, it might well happen that although two or three of these features occurred in lots of Mugwumps, there was no single Mugwump who actually had all of them. The same thing happens in relation to words.

The family resemblance syndrome has been described vividly by the philosopher Wittgenstein:

> Consider . . . the proceedings that we call: 'games'. I mean board-games, card-games, ball-games, Olympic games, and so on. What is common to them all? – Don't say: 'There must be something common, or they would not be called "games"' – but look and see whether there is anything common to all. – For if you look at them you will not see something that is common to all, but similarities, relationships, and a whole series of them at that. To repeat: don't think, but look! – Look for example at board-games, with their multifarious relationships. Now pass to card-games; here you find many correspondences with the first group, but many features drop out, and others appear. When we pass next to ball-games, much that is common is retained, but much is lost. – Are they all 'amusing'? Compare chess with noughts and crosses. Or is there always winning and losing, or competition between players? Think of patience. In ball-games there is winning and losing; but when a child throws his ball at the wall and catches it again, this feature has disappeared. Look at the parts played by skill and luck; and at the difference between skill in chess and skill in tennis. Think now of games like ring-a-ring-a-roses; here is the element of amusement, but how many other characteristic features have disappeared! And we can go through the many, many other groups of games in the same way; can see how similarities crop up and disappear.[30]

Wittgenstein concludes that although every game has some similarity with other games, there is no one factor which links them all. We are faced with 'a complicated network of similarities overlapping and criss-crossing'.[31] He continues: 'I can think of no better expression to characterize these similarities than "family

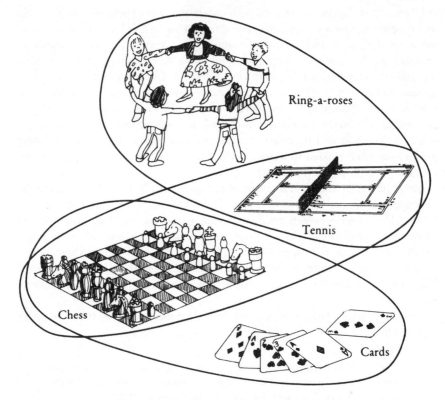

Figure 4.4   Family resemblances among games

resemblances"; for the various resemblances between members of a family: build, features, colour of eyes, gait, temperament, etc. etc. overlap and criss-cross in the same way. – And I shall say: "games" form a family'[32] (figure 4.4).

The word *game*, then, illustrates the family resemblance syndrome clearly. But this word is not an isolated, special instance, and there are numerous other equally common ones which exhibit the same problem, such as *furniture, employment* or *vegetable*.

The Fixed–Fuzziness Issue

Let us now summarize the fixed–fuzziness issue. There are a small number of words such as *square* or *bachelor* which appear to have a fixed meaning; that is, they are words for which we can specify a set of necessary and sufficient conditions. The majority of words, however, do not behave in this way. They suffer from one or more of the following problems: first, it may be difficult to specify a hard core of meaning at all. Second, it may be impossible to tell where 'true meaning' ends and encyclopaedic knowledge begins. Third, the words may have 'fuzzy boundaries', in that there may be no clear point at which the meaning of one word ends and another begins. Fourth, a single word may apply to a 'family' of items which all overlap in meaning but do not share any one common characteristic.

These are insuperable obstacles to the fixed meaning viewpoint. We conclude that, for the majority of words, meanings in the mind are fuzzy, not fixed. Language, it seems, has an inbuilt 'property of "limited sloppiness"', and 'only some areas are marked by a degree of "terminologization"' – the setting of firm boundaries.[33] In the next chapter we shall consider how humans cope with this hazy mush of meanings. However, before we tackle this topic, we need to consider one further point. Can we assume that everyone operates with the same meanings? Or is there a huge discrepancy from person to person? Let us discuss this problem.

Plank, Slab, Block, Brick, Cube

'Plank, slab, block, brick, cube' are the first five words spoken in Tom Stoppard's play *Dogg's Our Pet*. A man called Charlie is planning to build a platform, and he shouts instructions about the pieces he wants thrown to him. A plank, a slab, a block, a brick and a cube duly arrive, in that order. But then strange things start to happen. When Charlie shouts 'Plank' again, a block arrives. When he calls for a block, he gets a brick, and when he yells 'Cube', there is no response. What has gone wrong?

It transpires that Charlie and the thrower are speaking a different language. In Charlie's language, words such as plank, block and cube have their conventional meaning. But to the thrower they mean something different, perhaps 'Here!', 'Next!' and 'Thankyou!' If Charlie had needed only the first five pieces named, the discrepancy might never have been discovered, since the thrower's language fitted in sufficiently well with the context of platform-building for the work to proceed.

This is an extreme and literary situation. But the play makes a serious point. If I ask someone to fetch me a glass of water and a glass of water arrives, it is possible that the person fetching it simply thinks that the word *water* means 'colourless liquid' and so chose randomly between water, gin and vodka. Only if there is a misunderstanding and a tumblerful of vodka arrives, would I suspect a problem. And such misunderstandings might continue for some time, being discovered only by chance, as when I overheard a schoolchild who was viewing lemurs at the London Zoo enquire of her teacher: 'Please, miss, are they extinct?', or when a horrified mother heard her teenage daughter say to an elderly lady: 'Can I relieve you of your nether garments?' as she helped the visitor out of her coat.

Furthermore, we are not in general on the look-out for problems of this kind. If someone uses a word strangely, we rarely assume that their use of it is defective by our standards. If someone said, 'Look out! There's a rhinoceros sitting in the tree just above your head,' we would assume that they were either joking or mad. We would be unlikely to consider the possibility that the speaker thought *rhinoceros* meant 'pigeon'. In brief, in real life we operate by assuming that, for the most part, people have beliefs similar to our own about what words mean.[34] We as psycho-linguists work in the same way. We assume that there will be sufficient overlap between the meaning of words in the minds of different speakers for us to come to some useful conclusions – though we shall be on the look-out for discrepancies which might reveal idiosyncratic ideas.

Summary

In this chapter we examined the controversy between those who claim that words have fixed meanings and those who argue that word meanings are essentially fluid.

Our conclusion was that, for many words, it is impossible to specify hard-core semantic information, and equally impossible to distinguish essential meaning from encyclopaedic knowledge. There is no firm boundary between the meaning of one word and another, and the same word often applies to a whole family of things which have no overall common characteristic. We concluded therefore that words are indeed slippery customers, with vague boundaries and fuzzy edges.

But if words are so fuzzy, how do speakers cope with this hazy mush of meanings? This is the topic of the next chapter.

5

Bad Birds and Better Birds
— Prototype theories —

> The Hatter . . . had taken his watch out of his pocket, and was looking at it
> uneasily, shaking it every now and then, and holding it to his ear . . .
> 'Two days wrong!' sighed the Hatter, 'I told you butter wouldn't suit the works!' . . .
> Alice had been looking over his shoulder with some curiosity. 'What a funny
> watch!' she remarked. 'It tells the day of the month, and doesn't tell what o'clock it
> is!'
>
> Lewis Carroll, *Alice's Adventures in Wonderland*

If words have a hazy area of application, as we decided in the last chapter, we are
faced with a serious problem in relation to the mental lexicon. How do we manage
to cope with words at all? The quotation above from *Alice in Wonderland* gives us
a clue. Alice appears to have some notion of what constitutes a 'proper watch'.
This enables her to identify the butter-smeared object owned by the Hatter as a
watch, and to comment that it is a 'funny' one.

A feeling that some examples of words may be more central than others appears
to be widespread, as shown by a dialogue between two small girls in a popular
cartoon strip (p. 54):

Augusta:	What colour did you say the Martians are?
Friend:	Green.
Augusta:	What sort of green? I mean are they an emerald green or a pea green or an apple green or a sage green or a sea green or what?
Friend:	Well I think they're a sort of greeny green.

Humans, then, appear to find some instances of words more basic than others.
Such an observation may shed light on how people understand their meaning.
Take birds. Perhaps people have an amalgam of ideal bird characteristics in their
minds. Then, if they saw a pterodactyl, they would decide whether it was likely to
be a bird by matching it against the features of a bird-like bird, or, in psycholinguistic
terminology, a 'prototypical' bird. It need not have all the characteristics of the

prototype, but if the match was reasonably good, it could be labelled *bird*, though it might not necessarily be a very good example of a bird. This viewpoint is not unlike the checklist viewpoint, but it differs in that in order to be a bird, the creature in question does not have to have a fixed number of bird characteristics. It simply has to be a reasonable match.

This is an intriguing idea. But, like any intriguing idea, it needs to be tested. How could we find out if people really behave in this way? In fact, psychologists showed quite a long time ago that people treat colours like this.[1] However, this type of study has also been extended to other types of vocabulary items. Let us consider one of the pioneering papers on the topic.

Birdy Birds and Vegetabley Vegetables

About 30 years ago Eleanor Rosch, a psychologist at the University of California at Berkeley, carried out a set of experiments in order to test the idea that people regard some types of birds as 'birdier' than other birds, or some vegetables as more vegetable-like or some tools more tooly.

She devised an experiment which she carried out with more than 200 psychology students: 'This study has to do with what we have in mind when we use words which refer to categories' ran the instructions.

> Let's take the word red as an example. Close your eyes and imagine a true red. Now imagine an orangish red . . . imagine a purple red. Although you might still name the orange red or the purple red with the term red, they are not as good examples of red . . . as the clear 'true' red. In short, some reds are redder than others. The same is true for other kinds of categories. Think of dogs. You all have some notion of what a 'real dog', a 'doggy dog' is. To me a retriever or a German shepherd is a very doggy dog while a Pekinese is a less doggy dog. Notice that this kind of judgment has nothing to do with how well you like the thing; you can like a purple red better than a true red but still recognize that the color you like is not a true red. You may prefer to own a Pekinese without thinking that it is the breed that best represents what people mean by dogginess.[2]

The questionnaire which followed was ten pages long. On each page was a category name, such as 'Furniture', 'Fruit', 'Vegetable', 'Bird', 'Carpenter's Tool', 'Clothing', and so on. Under each category was a list of 50 or so examples. *Orange, lemon, apple, peach, pear, melon* appeared on the fruit list, and so did most of the other fruits you would be likely to think up easily. The order of the list was varied for different students to ensure that the order of presentation did not bias the results. The students were asked to rate how good an example of the category each member was on a seven-point scale: rating something as '1' meant that it was considered an excellent example; '4' indicated a moderate fit; whereas '7' suggested that it was a very poor example, and probably should not be in the category at all.

The results were surprisingly consistent. Agreement was particularly high for the items rated as very good examples of the category. Almost everybody thought that a *robin* was the best example of a bird, that *pea* was the best example of a vegetable and *chair* the best example of furniture. On the bird list, *sparrow, canary, blackbird, dove* and *lark* all came out high (figure 5.1). *Parrot, pheasant, albatross, toucan* and *owl* came somewhat lower. *Flamingo, duck* and *peacock* were lower still. *Ostrich, emu* and *penguin* came more than halfway down the seven-point rating, while last of all came *bat*, which probably shouldn't be regarded as a bird at all. Similar results were found for the other categories, that is, *shirts, dresses* and *skirts* were considered better examples of clothing than *shoes* and *stockings*, which were in turn higher than *aprons* and *earmuffs*. *Guns* and *daggers* were better examples of weapons than *whips* and *axes*, which were better than *pitchforks* and *bricks*. *Saws, hammers* and *screwdrivers* were better examples of carpenters' tools than *crowbars* and *plumb-lines*.

Psychologists on the other side of America obtained very similar results when they repeated the experiment,[3] so the results are not just a peculiar reaction of Californian psychology students. And Rosch carried out other experiments which

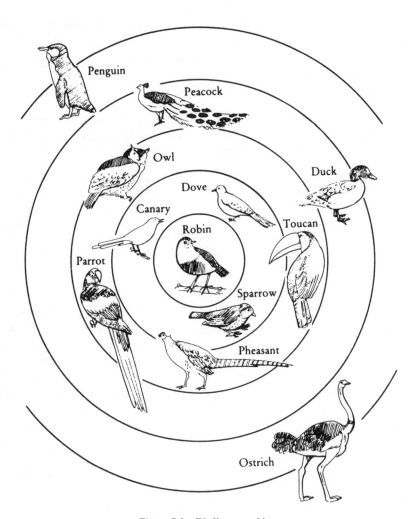

Figure 5.1   Birdiness rankings

supported her original results. For example, she checked how long it took students to verify category membership. That is, she said, 'Tell me whether the following is true,' and then gave the students sentences such as 'A penguin is a bird' or 'A sparrow is a bird.' She found that good exemplars (her name for examples) of a category were verified faster than less good exemplars, so that it took longer to say 'Yes' to 'A penguin is a bird' than it did to 'A sparrow is a bird.'[4]

The results of these experiments are fairly impressive. But there is one obvious criticism: were the students just responding faster to more common words? After all, people come across sparrows far more frequently than penguins, and hammers more often than crowbars. Obviously, frequency of usage is likely to have some effect: in California nectarines and boysenberries are commoner than mangoes and kumquats, so it is not surprising that the former were regarded as 'better' exemplars of fruit than the latter. However, the results could not be explained away solely on the basis of word frequency. On the furniture list, rare items of furniture such as *love seat*, *davenport*, *ottoman* and *cedar chest* came out much higher than *refrigerator*, which is a standard part of every American household. On the vegetable list, *pea*, *carrot* and *cauliflower* came out higher than *onion*, *potato* and *mushroom*. And on the clothes list, *pyjamas* and *bathing suit* came out higher than *shoe*, *tie*, *hat* and *gloves*. So people genuinely feel that some things are better exemplars of a category than others, a feeling which is not simply due to how often one comes across the word or object in question.

Furthermore, these judgements were not made primarily on the basis of appearance. Peas, according to Rosch, are prototypical vegetables. If people were simply comparing other vegetables to a visual image of a pea, then we would expect carrots to come out near the bottom of the list. In fact, they come very near the top. And if visual characteristics were important, we would also expect vegetables which look similar, such as carrots, parsnips and radishes, to be clustered together. But they are not. Nor were judgements made purely in terms of use. If this was so, one would expect benches and stools to come out near the top, since they are closest in function to the prototypical piece of furniture, a chair. But in fact bookcases rank higher than either benches or stools. It is not immediately obvious, therefore, how people came to their conclusions. They were making some type of analysis, though its exact basis was unclear, as the criteria used seemed to be heterogeneous.

To summarize, Rosch's work suggests that when people categorize common objects, they do not expect them all to be on an equal footing. They seem to have some idea of the characteristics of an ideal exemplar – in Rosch's words, a 'prototype'. And they probably decide on the extent to which something else is a member of the same category by matching it against the features of the prototype. It does not have to match exactly, it just has to be sufficiently similar, though not necessarily visually similar.

Prototype theory is useful, then, for explaining how people deal with untypical examples of a category. This is how unbirdy birds such as pelicans and penguins can still be regarded as birds. They are sufficiently like the prototype, even though they do not share all its characteristics. But it has a further advantage: it can explain how people cope with damaged examples. Previously linguists had found it difficult to explain why anyone could still categorize a one-winged robin that couldn't fly as a bird or a three-legged tiger as a quadruped. Now one just assumes that these get matched against the prototype in the same way as an untypical category member. A one-winged robin that can't fly can still be a bird, even though it's not such a typical one.

Furthermore, the prototype effect seems to work for actions as well as objects: people can, it appears, reliably make judgements that *murder* is a better example of killing than *execute* or *commit suicide*, and that *stare* is a better example of looking than *peer* or *squint*.[5]

However, so far we have dealt only with assigning objects and actions to larger categories. We now need to consider whether this is the way in which humans cope with individual words.

Degrees of Lying

'Can you nominate in order now the degrees of the lie?' asks a character in Shakespeare's play *As You Like It* and the clown Touchstone responds by listing seven degrees of lying.[6] Obviously the idea that some lies are better lies than others has been around for a long time, and still seems to be relevant today.

A 'good' lie, it transpires, has several characteristics.[7] First, the speaker has to assert something that is untrue. However, people often utter untruths without being regarded as liars, particularly in cases of genuine mistakes: a child who argued that six and four make eleven would not be thought of as lying. So a second characteristic of a good lie is that a speaker must believe that what he is saying is false. But even this is insufficient, because a person can knowingly tell untruths without being a liar, as in: 'You're the cream in my coffee, you're the sugar in my tea' (metaphor), 'He stood so still, you could have mistaken him for a door-post' (exaggeration or hyperbole), 'Since you're a world expert on the topic, perhaps you could tell us how to get the cat out of the drainpipe?' (sarcasm). A third characteristic must therefore be added for a good lie: that the speaker must intend to deceive those addressed. In brief, a fully-fledged or prototypical lie occurs when a speaker:

1   asserts something false
2   which they know to be false
3   with the intention of deceiving.

A prototypical lie, therefore, might be when a child denies having eaten a jam tart which it knows full well it has just scoffed. But consider a situation such as the following: 'Schmallowitz is invited to dinner at his boss's house. After a dismal evening enjoyed by no one, Schmallowitz says to his hostess, "Thanks, it was a terrific party." Schmallowitz doesn't believe it was a terrific party, and he isn't really trying to convince anyone he had a good time, but is just concerned to say something to his boss's wife, regardless of the fact that he doesn't expect her to believe it.'[8]

Did Schmallowitz lie? The 71 people asked this question were quite unsure. They had been told to grade a number of situations on a seven-point scale, from 1 (very sure non-lie) to 7 (very sure lie). For many people, Schmallowitz's situation lay just in the middle between these two extremes, at point 4, where they were unable to decide whether it was a lie or not. Another situation which lay in the middle was the case of Superfan, who got tickets for a championship game, and phoned early in the day to tell his boss that he could not come to work as he was sick. Ironically, Superfan doesn't get to the game, because the mild stomach-ache he had that morning turned out to be quite severe food poisoning.

Both the Schmallowitz and Superfan cases broke one of the conditions of a good lie, though each broke a different condition. Schmallowitz was not trying to deceive his hostess, he was merely trying to be polite. Superfan did not tell an untruth. Lies, then, like birds, can be graded. Lies can still be lies even when they are not prototypical lies, and they shade off into not being 'proper' lies at all.

The realization that individual words need not be used in their prototypical sense can explain a number of puzzling problems, especially cases in which people are unsure of whether they are dealing with the 'same' word or not. Consider the following sentences:

> I must have seen that a dozen times, but I never noticed it.
> I must have looked at that a dozen times, but I never saw it.[9]

Some people have argued that there are two different verbs *see*, one meaning 'my gaze went to an object', as in the first sentence, and the other containing in addition the meaning 'something entered my awareness', as in the second. But in a prototypical use of the verb *see*, both conditions are present: one's gaze goes to an object *and* the object enters one's awareness. If awareness is missing, one can stare at something without noticing it. Alternatively, something may enter a person's awareness, such as a dream or a hallucination, even though their gaze has not gone anywhere. These are both 'ordinary' uses of the word *see*, but not prototypical ones.

To take another example, look at the following sentences:

> The janitor goes from top to bottom of the building.
> The staircase goes from top to bottom of the building.

The janitor is clearly moving, but the staircase is not. So are these both instances of the same word *go*? A prototype approach allows *go* to be treated as a single word.[10] In its prototypical use, *go* involves movement, with the mover starting at one point, ending at another, and traversing the distance in between. However, *go* can be used untypically, with the 'movement' condition omitted, as happens with staircases and roads. This is a better solution than assuming that two different words *go* are involved, because it avoids the need to make difficult decisions as to which use of *go* is found in sentences such as:

> The river Ganges goes from the Himalayas to the Indian Ocean.
> The power of prayer goes round the world.

The verb *climb* provides a further example.[11] Consider:

Peter climbed a ladder.
The plane climbed to 30,000 feet.
The temperature climbed to 40°C.
The price of petrol climbed daily.
Mavis climbed down the tree.
Brian climbed into his clothes.

These various uses all sound 'normal', even though they differ quite considerably from one another. Prototype theory provides a simple explanation. A prototypical or 'default' use of *climb* involves upwards movement and clambering – effortful use of limbs, as when Peter shinned up the ladder. If one of these conditions is absent, the result is still a normal use of *climb*, though not a prototypical one. Planes, temperature and the price of petrol can climb because they are moving upward, even though they are not using any limbs. In contrast, Mavis can climb down the tree, and Peter can climb into his clothes because they are effortfully using their limbs, even though they are not going upward.

But when both upward movement and clambering are absent, the result is weird (an exclamation mark notes oddness):

!The plane climbed down to 20,000 feet.
!The temperature climbed down to 10°C.
!Marigold climbed down the stairs.
!The snail climbed along the drainpipe.

Judging something against a prototype, therefore, and allowing rough matches to suffice, seems to be the way we understand a number of different words. Furthermore, a general realization that this is how humans probably operate could be of considerable use in real-life situations, as in the example below.

Mad, Bad and Dangerous to Know

Some years ago a man who specialized in brutal murders of women was brought to trial. The Yorkshire Ripper, as he was called, divided public opinion sharply. Some people argued that he was simply bad, and therefore ought to be punished with a long term of imprisonment. Others claimed that he must be mad, in which case he should be admitted to a hospital and treated as someone who was not responsible for his actions.

Was he mad? Or was he bad? According to newspaper reports, the judge asked the jury to consider whether the Ripper had told the truth to the psychiatrists who examined him. The discrepancies and alterations in the Ripper's story made them conclude that he had told a considerable number of lies. This led them to classify him as 'Guilty' – bad, not mad. This judgement implies, therefore, that anyone who lies cannot be mad, a somewhat strange conclusion. Perhaps the situation would have been less confusing if the terms *mad* and *bad* had been considered in terms of prototypes.[12]

'To define true madness, What is't to be nothing else but mad?' asks Polonius, on observing the deranged Hamlet.[13] But contrary to Polonius's opinion, madness is not an all or nothing state. A prototypical mad person has several different characteristics. A mad person is, first, someone who thinks and acts abnormally. But this is insufficient, as it would categorize as mentally deranged such people as chess champions. Someone truly mad would, in addition, be unaware that he was thinking and acting abnormally, and furthermore, be unable to prevent himself from behaving oddly. A prototypical lunatic, therefore, might be someone who covers his head with tin-foil because he fears that moon men are about to attack, or someone who walks on her hands because God has supposedly told her not to wear out her feet. On this analysis, the Ripper was partially mad, because he acted strangely and seemed unable to prevent himself from doing so. Yet he was not prototypically mad, because he was perfectly aware that his actions were abnormal.

To turn to badness, someone bad commits antisocial acts, is aware that their actions are antisocial and could control their behaviour if they wished. So a protypical villain might be the pirate Captain Hook in Peter Pan or Shakespeare's character Iago. On this reasoning, the Ripper was partially bad, in that he acted antisocially and was aware of it, but not entirely bad, since he apparently could not control his actions.

To modify Caroline Lamb's statement about Lord Byron and reapply it to the Ripper, one could say that he is 'Around two-thirds mad, two-thirds bad and certainly dangerous to know'. No wonder the jury took so long to decide whether he was mad *or* bad, when he was neither prototypically mad nor prototypically bad.

This example shows that the notion of prototype can be extended beyond nouns and verbs – in this case to the adjectives *mad* and *bad*. But it also hides a problem, that the meaning of adjectives may vary, depending on the noun. Our account of *mad* is fine when accompanied by the word *man* or *woman*, but a *mad dog*, a *mad idea*, or a *mad evening* would require an amended analysis. Such examples suggest that the notion of prototype is not always as straightforward as has been suggested so far. Let us go on to consider this issue.

Muzziness of Multiple Meanings?

Pig: 'short-legged and typically stout-bodied mammal . . . with a thick bristly skin and long mobile snout'; 'shaped mass . . . of cast crude metal'. Both these defini-tions appeared under a single entry in a well-known dictionary.[14] The dictionary assumes that both are instances of the 'same' word *pig*, as opposed to another type of *pig* which is given a separate entry: *pig* 'an earthenware vessel; a crock'. But how is a plump farmyard animal related to a lump of metal? Above all, how many words are involved?

Ideally, prototype theory allows us to cut down on the multiple meanings found in many dictionaries, and to say that an understanding of the prototype allows other senses to be predicted. But how does anyone distinguish between one word with non-prototypical usages, such as *climb*, and more than one word, as perhaps with *pig* 'farmyard animal' and *pig* 'lump of metal'? A word such as *fork* provides a further problem. Is a *fork* you eat with the same word as the *fork* you dig with?

Polysemy – 'multiple meanings' – is an age-old problem which has been helped by prototype theory, but by no means solved. Ideally, there should be some agreed test to decide whether a word has more than one meaning (polysemy) or is simply muzzy in its coverage (vagueness). But no one can find one which works.

Various suggestions have been put forward,[15] but none of them are foolproof. Dictionaries often rely on history, and combine items in a single entry if they are descended from the same original word – as seems to be true of *pig*. But this is not very helpful when considering how current-day speakers handle words in their minds.

A *so did* test is sometimes used to distinguish items: 'The farmer watched the pig feeding its piglets, and so did the foundry foreman' would be very odd if the foundry foreman was looking at a metal pig.[16] But used on *fork*, this test gets weird results. Intuitively, a *fork* is a 'pronged implement'. Yet the *so did* test would split it up into more than one 'word': it would be very odd to say 'The glutton used a fork to shovel his potatoes, and so did the farmer' if the glutton was shovelling potatoes into his mouth, and the farmer was digging them out of the ground. Similarly, *sad* in 'a *sad* book' would probably be regarded as a different word from *sad* in 'a *sad* woman'. Each case therefore has to be considered on its merits. Let us look at two puzzling words, *over* and *old*.

Mulling over *Over*

Mulling over *over* has taken up a lot of research time.[17] First, it's hard to identify proto-typical *over*. Second, it's unclear how many separate meanings *over* has. Consider:

Virginia's picture is over the fireplace.
The clouds floated over the city.
Doreen pulled the blanket over her head.

Virginia's picture is stationary, but the clouds are moving. The clouds are unlikely to be touching the city, but the blanket is in contact with Doreen's head. Which of these meanings is basic?

There is no agreed solution. Some people argue that Virginia's static picture represents prototypical *over*, others the moving clouds. Still others suggest that *over* is by nature a muzzy word with vagueness built into it: that it means 'above, on top of', versus *under*, but does not specify whether the 'over' item is stationary or moving, in contact with or separated from what's underneath. In this case, all the sentences quoted could be regarded as prototypical. However, all three uses are clearly instances of the same word, even if the prototype is not obvious.

But now look at:

The cow jumped over the moon.
The water flowed over the rim of the bathtub.
Fenella pushed Bob over the balcony.
Sam walked over the bridge.

In all these, there is successful movement to a new location. This cannot easily be accommodated in the primary meaning of *over*. But neither is it completely separate. There seem to be at least two overlapping meanings of *over*: a basic one in which location above is specified and an extended one in which successful movement across occurs (figure 5.2).

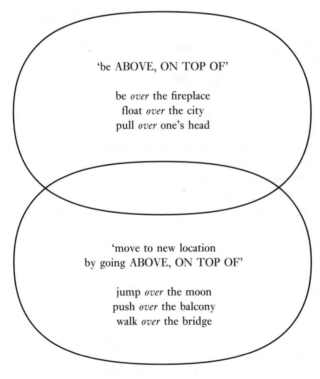

'be ABOVE, ON TOP OF'

be *over* the fireplace
float *over* the city
pull *over* one's head

'move to new location
by going ABOVE, ON TOP OF'

jump *over* the moon
push *over* the balcony
walk *over* the bridge

Figure 5.2   Over

Over therefore shows that polysemy is a complex affair, in that different senses of a word may overlap. They cannot easily be related to a prototype, nor do they split neatly into different domains. Let us go on to consider another problem of this type.

Old Problems

The word *old* is an old problem.[18] Consider:

> Pauline was astonished to see –
>   – an old woman (an aged woman)
>   – an old friend (a long-standing friend)
>   – her old boyfriend (a former boyfriend)
>   – old Fred (Fred whom she knew well).

The old woman is aged, but the others may be young. The old friend is still a friend, but the old boyfriend might now be an enemy. Is there a basic usage which can link the others together?

'Aged' in the sense of 'in existence for longer than the norm' is arguably the default meaning of *old*. This sense stays the same when the sentence is switched around: *Old* before the noun – 'attributive' position' – still means the same when moved to after *is*, 'predicative position'.

> Pauline saw an old woman: the woman is old.

This meaning also works with various other words, such as *building, tradition* – though a minor complication is that in some cases the opposite of *old* is *young*, as in *young woman*, in others *new*, as in *new building*. The sense 'long existence' can also cover *old friend*, though *old* cannot be moved about in the sentence, because the friendship, rather than the friend, is old.

But *old* 'former' as in *old boyfriend* does not fit this pattern. Nor does *old Fred*. These have to be regarded as separate, though linked meanings. So how do people know when *old* is used in these funny ways? They have to look for extra clues. A common clue that old means 'former' is a mark of possession:

> Steve's old girlfriend went to Brazil.
> An old boyfriend of mine sailed round the world.
> Our old house is now divided up into apartments.

In the case of *old Fred*, English speakers have to know that *old* attached to proper names is a mark of friendly affection.

In some cases, then, a basic meaning can be detected by a lack of restrictions on the surrounding syntax, as with *old* 'aged'. This default meaning can with minor adaptations be extended to other, less prototypical usages, as with *old* 'long-standing'. But it is impossible to incorporate all meanings under the one prototype. *Old* 'former' and *old* 'term of affection' need to be recognized as separate words. Their distinctness is signalled by the words which accompany them. This situation is shown in figure 5.3.

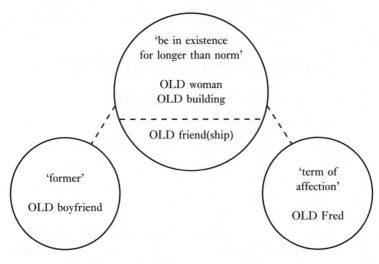

Figure 5.3   Old

Old and *over* show that prototypes reduce the polysemy problem, but do not solve it. They also show that prototypes cannot always be handled by looking at words in isolation.

Summary

In this chapter we have looked at how people are able to cope with word meaning when it is so fuzzy and fluid. They appear to analyse a prototypical exemplar of a word, and then match any new example against the characteristics of the prototype. It does not have to be a perfect match, merely a reasonable fit. This explains how words can be used with slightly different meanings, and how people can recognize new or damaged examples of a category. It also explains how people can deal with verbs.

However, prototype theory only partially solves the polysemy problem – that of cutting down on the apparent multiple meanings of a word. A full understanding of the meaning of many words requires a knowledge of the words which are found with it or related to it. This, and further problems associated with prototypes will be the topic of the next chapter.

6

Whispering Chambers of the Imagination
— Mental models —

'Mind and matter', said the lady in the wig, 'glide swift into the vortex of immensity. Howls the sublime, and softly sleeps the calm Ideal, in the whispering chambers of the Imagination.'

Charles Dickens, *Martin Chuzzlewit*

Prototypes explain a lot. They show how people deal with the fuzziness of word meaning, and how new or damaged examples can be understood. Something can still be labelled a parrot if it is sufficiently like a prototypical parrot, even if it has only one leg, pink and blue stripes, and carries an umbrella. Prototypes work with whole categories, such as birds or fruit, and with individual examples, such as dove or orange. They work with verbs as well as nouns, and sometimes with adjectives.

But the nature of prototypes remains mysterious. The 'calm Ideal' in the 'whispering chambers of the Imagination' leads to inconsistencies. The more closely prototypes are examined, the more elusive they seem to be. Let us consider the matter further.

The Oddity of Odd Numbers

'The oddity of odd numbers' is perhaps the most puzzling problem. A group of researchers found that some odd numbers were felt to be 'better' odd numbers than others.[1] The subjects they quizzed thought that 3 was a better example of an odd number than 23, which was in turn better than 57 or 447! How could people possibly think that 3 was better than 23, when both are equally odd? Furthermore, this result had nothing to do with the ambiguity of the word *odd* which can mean either 'uneven' or 'peculiar', because the researchers found a very similar result for even numbers: 4 was considered a better example than 18, which was in turn better than 34 or 106! So what's going on? Surely when they judge whether 57 is a good example of an odd number, people are not matching it against a prototypical odd number such as 3? Can we explain all this away, or is there some fatal flaw in prototype theory?

People are still arguing about these results. But a plausible explanation is that we need to make a distinction between identification criteria and stored knowledge.[2] In judging whether something is a good example of an odd number, people may be using easy recognition as their yardstick, rather than basic knowledge. A clash between identification and knowledge is common in some areas. Take bulls. A farmer had trouble with people breaking down fences so that his cattle escaped, according to a newspaper report.[3] He therefore put a ring through the nose of one of the cows. Since a ring usually signifies a bull, which might be dangerous, he reckoned it would sucessfully keep people away. Within two days he had a telephone call from the local police:

Police: You've got a bull in the park – it's illegal.
Farmer: I'm sorry but we have no bull in the park.
Police: I've seen it myself – I saw the ring in its nose.
Farmer: You'd better go and look at the other end.

The moral is obvious. People know that bulls are male, but they do not normally identify them by checking their genitalia: they identify them by something which could be quite extraneous to their basic make-up. The problems such cases raise in relation to prototypes is that we do not know exactly how identification criteria are interwoven with stored knowledge in the minds of speakers.

Of course, with many words, identification criteria and stored knowledge might be the same, as perhaps with *rainbow* or *lamppost*. But in a large number of others there may be a difference, even though the two will probably overlap to a considerable extent. How we perceive and identify things cannot be entirely removed from our stored knowledge of them: 'Any sharp division between perception and conception seems questionable,' note two psychologists.[4] A further complication is that people sometimes have to interweave their own observations with information presented by others, since biological taxonomies and cultural beliefs may clash with instincts. Children often find it hard to believe that a spider is not an insect, a whale is not a fish, and a bat is not a bird. And in Papua New Guinea, the Karam people of the upper Kaironk valley do not regard the cassowary as a bird, even though to us it obviously is one.[5] It is unclear how such 'facts' gets integrated into a person's overall view of a word's meaning. This indicates that finding out the characteristics of a prototype is enormously difficult.

Birdy Birds versus Reddy Reds

'We remember objects at their most personable,' commented one television presenter. 'Legs are leggy, fruits are fruity, newspapers are newspapery.' This true but empty comment hides another problem, that of the diversity of prototypes. Leggy legs are rather different from fruity fruits or birdy birds or reddy reds.[6]

A birdy bird involves a cluster of typical characteristics, relating to its appearance and behaviour: it will have feathers, wings and a beak, it will fly, and it will lay eggs in a nest. And people are reasonably reliable at judging whether something is a bird.

But a reddy red is somewhat different, unless one happens to be a physicist, who can analyse the various properties of colours. For most people, a reddy red is characterized by its centrality – it will have a central place within a range of reds, probably because it is the most perceptually salient. Similarly, the term *adult* is usually understood with reference to a central example: a man of 25 would be a more adultlike adult than a 17-year-old. For both *red* and *adult* there is no abrupt cut-off point, but a gradual fading away at the edge of the category. A major task therefore is the sorting out and comparing of 'the diverse phenomena that have been lumped together under the label of prototypicality'.[7]

Other prototypes may be the convergence point for a cluster of overlapping meanings. The word *vegetable* in its broadest sense is 'something which grows', as in the phrase 'animal, vegetable and mineral'. In a narrower sense, it is an edible plant, as when a restaurant offers 'meat and two veg.', one of which is usually potatoes. More narrowly still, potato can be excluded, as in eating places which offer meat, a vegetable, and either rice or potatoes. A prototypical vegetable such as peas or carrots fits all of them (figure 6.1).

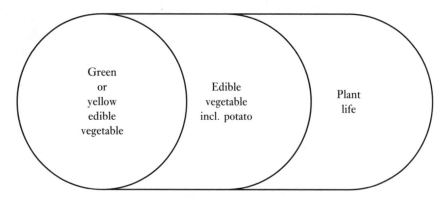

Figure 6.1   Overlapping meanings: vegetables

Or take the Dutch word *vers* 'fresh'.[8] This can mean 'new, or recent' of news or information, and 'in good condition, pure' when applied to air. Its prototypical use is then one which combines newness and good condition, as in 'fresh fruit', 'fresh fish' (figure 6.2).

Something of high cultural value is an occasional source of a prototype. Many Indians claim that a *peacock* is a prototypical bird. Some English children think of *potato* as a prototypical vegetable, perhaps because of their fondness for French fries and potato chips. And some European adults rank *cupboard* highly as a piece of furniture, perhaps because of the valuable carved family heirlooms found in

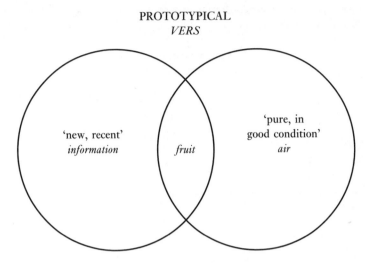

PROTOTYPICAL
VERS

'new, recent'
information

fruit

'pure, in
good condition'
air

Figure 6.2   Overlapping meanings: Dutch *vers* 'fresh'

some houses.[9] It is unclear whether people truly regard such unusual examples as prototypical. They may have misunderstood the request to choose a 'best example', and instead have selected a 'high quality' or 'favourite' specimen. In ranking items, high quality, personal preference, well-formedness and typicality may be confused.[10]

The diversity of prototypes has evoked two main responses. The whole notion of prototypes has become overbroad, according to some researchers. They claim that prototypes work only for categories such as *birds* or *flowers*, and at a 'basic level', defined as the highest level at which a visual image can be formed.[11] It is pointless to go further. Bundling together the things found in a house, calling them furniture, and trying to rank them is simply absurd.[12]

Other researchers – possibly the majority – accept that prototypes are by nature heterogeneous.[13] Prototypes are somewhat like *games* (chapter 4). They have a family resemblance, but no single definition covers them all: 'The concept of "prototype theory" as used in linguistics has itself a prototypical structure.'[14]

Because of the disparate nature of prototypes, it may be wiser to speak of *prototype effects* rather than straight prototypes. The possible causes of these effects have become a major research topic.[15] Let us consider the matter further.

A Mixture of Mind and Matter

A penguin is a bad bird, an owl is a better bird, and a robin is an excellent bird. Almost everyone agrees on this. But what underlies this judgement? It's hard to say (chapter 5).

It is probably fairly important for a bird to have feathers. As the humorous poet
Ogden Nash once noted:

> All I know about the bird:
> It is feathered, not furred.

But what comes next? Perhaps having wings. What then? Ability to fly? Egg-
laying? Nest-building? There are unlikely to be clear answers, as suggested by the
argument between the bird and the duck in Prokofiev's *Peter and the Wolf*:

> Seeing the duck, the little bird flew down upon the grass, settled next to her and
> shrugged his shoulders:
>   'What kind of a bird are you, if you can't fly?' said he.
> To this, the duck replied:
>   What kind of a bird are you, if you can't swim? and dived into the pond.
> They argued and argued. . . .

Furthermore, where does one stop? Does it matter that prototypical birds have
twig-like legs and small beady eyes?

Pulling things apart in this way raises insuperable problems. It's far easier to
consider prototypes as a whole. People look for bundles of properties: feathers,
wings, beak, nest-building and flying ability together constitute a 'good' bird.
What then do these bundles tell us about words in the mind? There are several
theories.[16]

According to one view, humans prefer their thoughts to be neat and tidy. The
messiness of natural categories causes 'cognitive dissonance', a mental clash which is
hard to handle. People therefore subconsciously pick on a clear example, and pretend
that it represents the 'proper' meaning of something. Prototypes may therefore be
an unconscious attempt to reconcile natural variability with a 'checklist' approach
to meaning (chapter 4).

Alternatively, prototypes may represent the inevitable outcome of numerous
exposures to creatures with feathers, wings, beaks and flying ability. This cluster
of properties pops up in real life each time a blackbird, robin, parrot, or dove is
viewed, and these birds are seen more often than untypical ones, such as emus or
toucans. On each viewing, the connections between the associated characteristics
become stronger, and this is how categories are formed in the mind. This
connectionist viewpoint is highly fashionable at the moment.

Unfortunately, each of these viewpoints works only for a small number of
prototypes. Neither of them explains why peas and carrots come out top on the
American vegetable list, or why tables and chairs come out together at the top of
the furniture list.

A third view is winning the day: that prototypes represent internal theories.
People subconsciously construct 'mental models' for themselves in order to handle
their lives and everything in them. These models are an inextricable mixture of
acute observation, cultural brainwashing, fragments of memory and a dollop of

imagination. They embody a person's assumptions about the world, including naïve beliefs as to how it works, some learned, some invented.

Take the word *week*.[17] Dictionaries usually define it as a seven-day cycle. But this underrepresents what most people know about a week: in England, it is thought of as five working days, labelled Monday, Tuesday, Wednesday, Thursday, Friday. These are followed by 'the weekend', Saturday and Sunday, a sequence of two days off. People maintain this model, even if does not correspond to their own personal week. The model is an intangible cultural artefact – and does not even agree with the 'official' week, which starts on Sunday. Compare it with an Inca week: this contained nine working days, followed by market day, when the king changed his wives (figure 6.3).

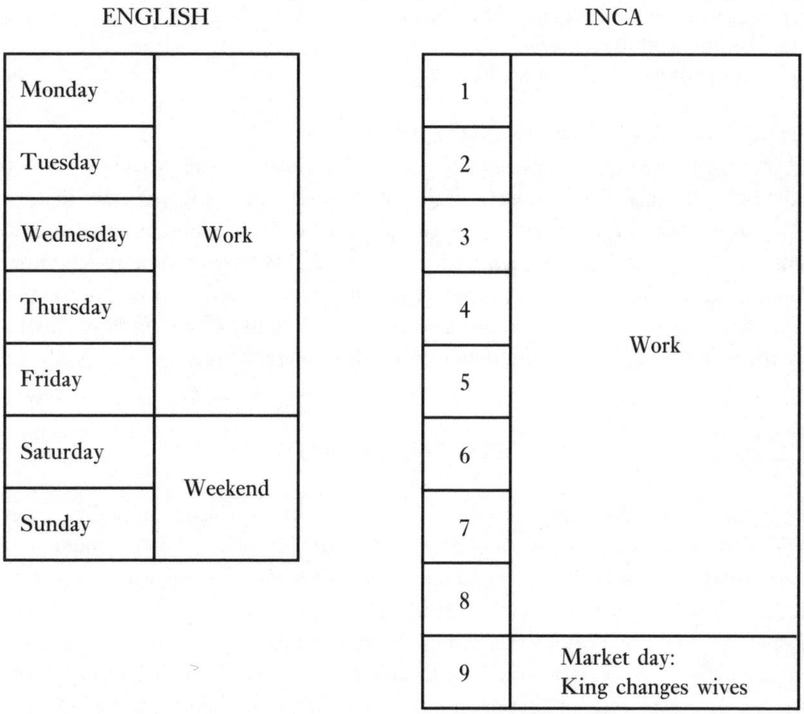

ENGLISH   INCA

Monday			1	
Tuesday			2	
Wednesday	Work		3	
Thursday			4	Work
Friday			5	
Saturday	Weekend		6	
Sunday			7	
			8	
			9	Market day: King changes wives

Figure 6.3   Prototypical weeks: English and Inca

Mental models can be very persistent, and may even influence behaviour, as with the term *working class*. Many British citizens have a mental image of a 'layer-cake' society, with rich upper class at the top, comfortably-off middle class in the middle, and poor working class at the bottom. Numerous socio-economic publications have shown that the middle-class versus working-class divide is largely one of differing lifestyles, rather than position in an economic hierarchy.[18] Yet the cultural stereotype of Britain as a layer-cake, class-ridden society remains.

Or consider the word *mother*, which may be used in several different senses.[19] A mother is someone who gives birth to a child, but can also be a nurturer, someone who looks after a child: 'Alison's mother chose her from twenty orphans because she had a cute snub nose.' Or a mother may be the person who is married to the father: 'Marigold's father has married again: now she's got a mother.' A prototypical mother is one who fulfils all of these: she gave birth to the child, looks after it, and is married to the father. This model of a 'proper' mother permeates British society, and may account for why child-care facilities are so bad for mothers who would like to work.

The subconscious metaphors which may govern our thoughts are another powerful source of mental models, as in the notion that 'argument is war':[20]

> He attacked every weak point in my argument.
> He shot down all my answers.
> His criticisms were right on target.

This topic will be discussed in chapter 14.

Prototypes, therefore, represent the mental models of the world we live in, models which are private and cultural architectures, and only partially in touch with 'reality'. Such models are referred to under various names: mental models, frames, scripts, internalized cognitive models or ICMs, cognitive domains, image schemas.[21] The word *frames* is perhaps the most widely used, but is also the most confusing, since it is employed in several different senses. Let us now consider how the mind might call up models in everyday conversations.

Salads and Monks

Words considered alone are deceptively simple, as we have seen. In reality, even a single word may evoke a complex mental structure. Consider Gus, a character in Pinter's play *The Dumb Waiter*, who seems to have a clear idea of what a prototypical salad bowl is like: 'They've probably got a salad bowl up there. Cold meat, radishes, cucumbers. Watercress, roll mops. Hardboiled eggs.' Gus's mental model of a salad bowl goes way beyond the 'meaning' of the word. His mind has flipped up a whole 'salad bowl situation', with particular ingredients in the bowl. Or consider the conversation between Ackroyd and Boothroyd, two characters who visit a ruined abbey in Alan Bennett's play *A Day Out*:

> *Ackroyd*:   They were Cistercian monks here . . .
> *Boothroyd*: It's an unnatural life, separating yourself off like that. . . . There wouldn't be any kids, would there? And allus getting down on their knees. It's no sort of life. . . .

Here, the word *monk* has triggered not just the basic 'meaning' of the word, but a whole situation, in which Boothroyd imagines silent corridors and monks praying.

Are all these associated scenes part of our knowledge of a word? To some extent, yes. In our memory, we seem to have a stack of mental models – sets of stereotypical situations, 'remembered frameworks',[22] which we call up as necessary. These provide a background into which the details of the present situation are fitted.[23]

From the point of view of the mental lexicon, such stereotypical situations may be optional back-up material which is accessed if required. If a person was asked to define a *zebra*, they could do this quite efficiently without calling up a whole 'zoo' or 'safari' frame. But if they overheard someone talking about a zebra seen in London earlier in the day, then they could go deeper into their memory, and call up a zoo frame, which would allow them to fit the narrative into a predicted set-up, and be prepared for mentions of turnstiles, monkeys, and elephant rides.

This back-up information may work in two ways. Either the mental lexicon is organized so that the most important things pop up first. Or, alternatively, the mind may automatically flip up considerably more information than is necessary, and humans may be very good at discarding or suppressing information that is not required. Or perhaps these two mechanisms work together.

But whatever the mechanism involved, the activation of whole frames in the mind makes it even harder to specify the characteristics of individual prototypes, since they interact with other elements present in the scene, and involve the optional use of a seemingly endless supply of back-up material from a person's memory – or even the temporary invention of new models, as will be discussed below.

Fixed or Temporary?

Some mental models turn out to be fairly fixed. A *car* is usually regarded as a prototypical vehicle, and people expect it to have four wheels, a steering wheel, an engine and so on. They have a car 'frame' in their minds, into which they slot the details of the particular car they are discussing, with a frame here defined as 'a fixed set of named slots whose values vary across applications'.[24]

But others are temporary, thought up for a particular occasion, such as 'what to take on vacation'. This has been called a 'goal-derived' category,[25] because all the various objects – suitcase, suntan lotion, plane tickets – are there for a common goal, the vacation. Such categories are probably formed as needed. Yet they exhibit a structure similar to that found in more permanent categories, such as furniture, in that items in them can be ranked, with a suitcase being more important than a camera, and a camera ranked above a sewing kit. And ranking is found even in hotch-potch categories which are invented on the spur of the moment, such as 'things to hold a door open with'.[26]

The baffling fact remains that humans can set up frames either on a fairly permanent basis or on a temporary one. And it is not easy to tell which is which. Mixed prototypes are a further problem, as in 'the guppy effect'. A guppy is a small tropical fish, popular in household aquariums. It is a prototypical pet fish.

But how is a combined prototype such as 'pet fish' formed? It cannot be a straight combination of prototypical fish and prototypical pet, because the latter probably includes being cuddly and playful, and a fish can't easily be cuddled or played with. A composite prototype therefore needs to be set up, somehow relating to pets, fish and guppies.[27] Exactly how this is done is disputed. But one thing is clear. Mental models of this type are an inextricable mix of ready-set structure and on-line adaptation.

The human mind therefore is forever active, taking stored outline information which it then uses as a basis for constructing the model required at any given moment. As one researcher notes: 'Frames are finite generative mechanisms. A modest amount of explicit frame information in memory enables the computation of a tremendously large number of concepts.'[28]

The word *frame* suggests a static set-up, as if humans had a mental snapshot of a situation. But real life behaves more like an ongoing movie than a series of freeze-frames. Humans have expectations of what will happen, reconstructed from past memories. Anyone going to a restaurant will expect to be led to a table, to be presented with a menu, to order food, to eat that food, then to pay for it. Anyone having a bath will expect to turn on the taps (faucets) and watch water gush out until the tub contains several inches of hot water, to step into that bath, then sit down, wash, and so on. These predictable sequences are sometimes known as *scripts*.[29]

Summary

Prototype theory solves many problems, but prototypes themselves are elusive. Identification criteria are interwoven with stored knowledge, and many prototypes involve inextricable clusters of properties. Prototypes are heterogeneous in nature, and prototype theory itself has a prototypical structure. Prototype effects can therefore have several causes. But above all, prototypes probably represent naïve models which humans build for themselves of the world and how it works. They are therefore an inextricable mixture of observation, cultural beliefs and personal interpretation.

Some of these models involve a fixed framework, with empty slots into which items are inserted – but other frameworks are built up on the spur of the moment. The exact specification of the mental models which apparently exist in a person's mind is still a long way beyond our current ability.

Above all, this chapter has shown that humans do not very often deal with isolated words. We therefore need to find out how words relate to each other in the mental lexicon. This is the topic of the next chapter.

7

The Primordial Atomic
Globule Hunt
— The search for semantic primitives —

> I can trace my ancestry back to a protoplasmal primordial atomic globule. Conse-
> quently, my family pride is something inconceivable.
>
> W. S. Gilbert, *The Mikado*

Words cannot be treated as if they were a swarm of bees – a bundle of separate items attached to one another in a fairly random way. They are clearly inter-dependent. In some cases it is difficult to understand a word without knowing the words around it: *orange* is best understood by looking at it in relation to *red* and *yellow*, or *warm* by considering it as the area between *hot* and *cold*. How, then, do humans fit words together in the mental lexicon?

As a preliminary guess, one might suggest that words are stitched together in one's mind like pieces on a patchwork quilt. The shape and size of the patches would differ from language to language, but within each language any particular patch could be defined with reference to those around it. But this simple idea will not work. Words do not cover the world smoothly, like a jigsaw with interlocking pieces. The whole situation is more like badly spread bread and butter, with the butter heaped up double in some places while leaving bare patches in others. Some words overlap strongly, as with *chase* and *pursue*, or *plump* and *fat*, while elsewhere there are inexplicable gaps: there is no generally accepted term for 'live-in lover' or 'dead plant'.

Perhaps the biggest problem for the patchwork quilt idea arises from words which overlap, as with *hog*, *sow* and *piglet*, which are all pigs, or *sow*, *hen* and *princess*, which are all female, or *piglet*, *chick* and *princeling*, which are all youngsters. Every word in the language has similar links with numerous others, reminiscent of the character in Gilbert and Sullivan's opera *HMS Pinafore* who had dozens of relatives:

> His sisters and his cousins,
> Whom he reckons up by dozens,
> And his aunts!

How, then, does the mind cope with these relationships? There have been a number of different proposals. As two psychologists warn: 'In approaching the question, how are words related to one another, we must take care not to drown in the diversity of answers.'[1]

The diversity of answers is not, however, totally unmanageable, since the theories put forward tend to fall into two broad categories, which we may call the 'atomic globule' viewpoint on the one hand and the 'cobweb' viewpoint on the other (figure 7.1). Atomic globule supporters argue that words are built up from a common pool of 'meaning atoms' and that related words have atoms in common. Cobweb supporters claim that words are recognized as related because of the links which speakers have built between them. On the one hand, then, words are viewed as an assemblage of bits. On the other, they are regarded as wholes which have various characteristics and enter into relationships with other words. Both these viewpoints are compatible with prototype theory,[2] though the proponents of each have a different view of the way in which people deal with a prototype. Let us therefore consider these opposing ideas. In this chapter we will discuss atomic globules, and in the next, cobwebs.

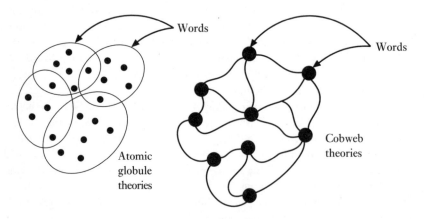

Figure 7.1   Atomic globules versus cobwebs

Primordial Atoms

'But numerous primordial atoms, whirled around in numerous ways from time immemorial, kept in motion by collisions and their own weight, have finally come together in every possible way and tried out everything that could be formed by their various combinations.' This sentence comes from the ancient Roman poet Lucretius,[3] who is describing how the world may have come into existence according to a theory current in his time. But it could equally well describe one recurring viewpoint in linguistics, that there is some universal set of basic atoms of meaning known as 'semantic primitives' which are combined in different ways in different languages: 'Semantic features cannot be different from language to language, but are rather part of the general human capacity for language, forming a universal inventory used in particular ways in individual languages.'[4]

The atomic globule idea dates back at least to the seventeenth century, when the German philosopher Leibniz argued that humans were born with a basic 'alphabet of human thoughts', which is 'the catalogue of those concepts which can be understood by themselves, and by whose combination all our other ideas are formed'.[5] This viewpoint was particularly dominant about 20 years ago. 'The very notion "lexical entry" presupposes some sort of fixed universal vocabulary in terms of which these objects are characterized,' according to the influential American linguist Noam Chomsky.[6]

However, at least two different levels of semantic primitives need to be distinguished. On an underlying level, the human mind may single out certain concepts, such as *things* as in 'That's a panda', or *events* as in 'The panda escaped'. Finding out about these is an interesting though as yet unsolved matter.

On a more superficial level, some researchers have wondered whether humans treat words like jigsaw puzzles, assembling and disassembling them into their component parts whenever they use them. If so, then there should be a stock of component parts in each person's mind, ready for use. At the very least, words should be like a garment whose various component pieces have been sown together, but with the seams still visible.

Some early work on the topic did not distinguish clearly between the underlying and the surface levels, possibly hoping that their research would identify both levels together. Let us consider two well-known early attempts to do this, and the problems they raised. The aim of the first was to seek out the primitives underlying common verbs.[7] The other sought to link semantic primitives with human perception.[8]

Approximately a dozen semantic primitives formed the basis of all the verbs we ordinarily use, according to Roger Schank, a researcher in artificial intelligence.[9] Some of these primitives were physical acts, such as MOVE, INGEST, GRASP. Others were mental, such as CONC, which means roughly 'to think about', or MTRANS, which involved the transfer of mental information. And others were more general, such as ATRANS, which dealt with the transfer of possessions. For example, verbs such as *breathe*, *drink*, *eat*, *inhale* and *sniff* all had a component INGEST in common. *Buy*, *sell*, *give*, *take*, *steal* all had ATRANS in common. But a number of problems arose.

First, Schank and his colleagues found it quite difficult to specify exactly how many of these primitives there were, and what they should be. They changed their minds several times, and they never reached an entirely satisfactory conclusion. Therefore they were unable to claim that they had actually found the components out of which these verbs were made. This is perhaps a minor problem, because it often takes some time to specify things exactly. A more serious problem is that it is hard to see why several of these components are 'primitives', since each one is in fact decomposable into more basic elements: INGEST, for example, is a complex notion which could be broken down into several subcomponents. A third problem is that most verbs contain far more in their meaning than the components specified in these 'primitives', which form only the rough framework on to which more detailed specifications need to be added – yet a major claim of the atomic viewpoint approach is that the meaning atoms cover the whole meaning of the word.

In view of these problems, it seems unlikely that Schank had specified 'primitives' in any psychological sense. He had simply found a convenient way of describing 'family resemblances' between the groups of words he was dealing with. As we noted in chapter 3, it is important to distinguish between useful ways of describing things and structures which are likely to exist in speakers' minds. Judging from the work of Schank, there is no reason to believe that verbs are assembled out of pieces in the human mind – even though we might well adopt his system if we were trying to write a computer program which explained relationships between words in a helpful, though non-realistic way. And the problems found with Schank's primitives – difficulty of deciding what they are, their decomposability and their incompleteness for specifying meaning – occur in most other attempts to identify primitives.

An impressive exploration of the topic was made by two psychologists, George Miller and Phil Johnson-Laird, who tried to link semantic primitives to perceptual primitives.[10] They attempted to anchor them to some kind of observable human experience, to things people can see, hear or feel. This seems a useful enterprise, since a number of people have suggested that humans start out by dealing with the world which they perceive, and then generalize from this to more abstract matters.

Their book ran to almost 800 pages, and presented a thorough investigation of the subject, even though, as they admit, the whole project was based on somewhat shaky foundations, since psychologists have not yet produced an agreed, fully worked-out theory of perception: 'Not having an explicit perceptual theory means that we cannot be sure what the primitives of the system are . . . The best we can do, therefore, is to limit ourselves to judgments that seem to be likely candidates as primitives. In a sense we are building on sand, but it is better to build on sand than on nothing at all.'[11]

Miller and Johnson-Laird's proposals were quite specific. There turned out to be a lot of probable primitives. For object recognition alone they proposed almost 100, such as PLACE, SIZE, STRAIGHT, HORIZONTAL, VERTICAL, BOTTOM, TOP. For example, a *table*, which can be regarded as a connected, rigid object, with a flat horizontal top, supported by vertical legs, would involve at least the primitives OBJECT, CONNECTED, RIGID, TOP, FLAT FACE, HORIZONTAL, VERTICAL. However, as the researchers pointed out, these perceptual primitives are insufficient to deal with the meaning of *table*. All they do is specify the appearance of a table. Further specifications are needed in order to account for the fact that people also know what tables are used for – to eat off, work on, stand on to change a lightbulb and so on. In brief, they came to the conclusion that the concept behind the word *table* is not simply based on the way in which tables are perceived.

And when they moved on to less tangible items, they ran into even greater difficulties. How does one tie down verbs such as *promise*, *predict* or *disagree* to something one can perceive directly? It proved impossible. The words themselves did not contain perceivable components, and there were no obvious concrete words which could have served as a pattern. They comment: 'If a person knew only words whose meanings are given perceptually and related words interpretable by generalization from the perceptual words, his vocabulary would be severely limited.'[12]

In brief, they concluded, first, that even words for straightforward objects such as tables had elements of meaning which were not perceptually based. Second, there were an enormous number of vocabulary items whose meaning could not be tied down to a perceptual foundation. They therefore came to the reluctant conclusion that 'much of the lexicon is based on primitive concepts that are not perceptual.'[13] It seems, then, that even if semantic primitives exist, they cannot be based purely on perception.

A more recent attempt to find semantic primitives has been made by Anna Wierbicka,[14] of the Australian National University, Canberra. She quotes the seventeenth-century philosopher Leibniz, who maintained: 'We can say that we have understood something only when we have broken it down into parts which can be understood in themselves.' Her aim is to 'identify the shared core of all natural languages and build on this basis a "natural semantic metalanguage"'. She proposes doing this as follows: 'If by investigating as many diverse languages as possible we can establish a hypothetical shared core of all natural languages, we can then treat this shared core as a language-independent metalanguage for the description and comparison of all languages and cultures.' For example, concepts such as I, YOU, SOMEONE, SOMETHING, PEOPLE, THINK, KNOW, WANT, FEEL, SEE, HEAR, SAY, DO, HAPPEN, MOVE, LIKE, PART, PLACE, UNDER, ABOVE, INSIDE, FAR, NEAR, HEAR, GOOD, BAD, BIG, SMALL are among those considered as basic.

But this has the disappointing effect of making almost all definitions vague. For example, Wierbicka explicates *sad* as follows:

X feels something; sometimes a person thinks something like this: something bad happened; if I didn't know that it happened I would say: I don't want it to happen; I don't say this now because I know: I can't do anything; because of this, this person feels something bad; X feels something like this.

This 'definition' could equally well apply to *unhappy*, *distressed*, *frustrated*, *upset*, *angry*, *annoyed*. At the most it captures the notion of a negative emotion.

Since these attempts at listing semantic primitives failed, does it mean that we should abandon the search for them? No, but we need to realize that any true primitives are likely to exist only at an underlying level. Consequently, future proposals need to be more abstract and wide-ranging than previous ones. For example, attempts have been made to look at the image schemata which underlie human thinking, with notions such as CONTAINER, OBJECT, NEAR–FAR, FULL–EMPTY.[15] These are arguably recurring patterns which influence our experience, but they cannot always be easily linked to particular lexical items.

To sum up so far, we are a long way from finding any 'semantic primitives'. Let us therefore go on to consider whether 'atomic globules' exist at a more superficial level, as part of the way humans store, produce and comprehend lexical items in their own language.

Hunting for Globule Effects

If atoms of meaning exist at the level of individual languages, they could be reflected in the way humans deal with words.

A number of psycholinguists have checked to see if word comprehension could give some clues to the existence of meaning components. Their reasoning was as follows: if small components of meaning exist, then words might be stored in the human mind in a disassembled state. If so, then it would be necessary to assemble them whenever they are used in producing speech and to disassemble them into their component parts in order to comprehend them. If this scenario is a reasonable one, then words which are likely to have a large number of components will take longer for the mind to process than words which have fewer. The word *kill* might be assembled out of CAUSE DIE, and so take longer to produce or comprehend than *die* alone. *Bachelor* might be assembled out of NOT MARRIED, and so take marginally longer to process than the phrase *not married*, since additional packaging and unpackaging would be required. Such experiments would not test directly whether these components were primitives. They might, however, show whether the comprehension of words required them to be disassembled into smaller pieces: if so, the notion that words are built up out of smaller fragments would be a point of view worth taking seriously.

In one experiment, researchers thought up a number of sentence pairs.[16] For example:

1   If practically all of the men in this room are *not married*, then few of the men in the room have wives.
2   If practically all of the men in this room are *bachelors*, then few of the men in the room have wives.

The first of each pair contained an explicit negative, such as *not married*. The second contained a word such as *bachelor* where the proposed semantic representation contained a negative. The experimenters jumbled up the order of the sentences so that the paired ones did not come together, and asked subjects to evaluate the validity of the argument in each. The result was that sentences containing the explicit negative took longer to evaluate – something which should not have happened if the subjects had had to spend time disassembling a word such as *bachelor* into its component fragments.

This experiment has been criticized because it asked subjects to perform a reasoning task which might have been carried out after the original processing of

the sentence. However, a similar result was found in an experiment which investigated sentences as they were processed.[17] The researcher used the technique of
'phoneme monitoring': 'Press a button as soon as you hear the sound [b].' As we
noted in chapter 2, subjects do this slowly if there is any problem with the word
preceding the one with the monitored sound. In this case, the experimenter again
worked with pairs of sentences. For example:

1   The dog sniffing round the yard stuck its nose into the *yellow* bucket.
2   The dog sniffing round the yard stuck its nose into the *empty* bucket.

The words *yellow* and *empty* are both the same length when spoken, and are
equally common. However, *yellow* seems to be fairly straightforward, at least when
compared with *empty*, which could be glossed as 'not containing anything'. If
empty had to be disassembled into smaller components such as NOT CONTAIN
ANYTHING, one would expect the reaction time to the [b] in *bucket* to be fairly
slow. In fact, there was virtually no difference between the monitoring times for
the two words, so there was no reason to claim that one had a more complicated
make-up than the other.

The experiments discussed so far all involve negatives, and negatives behave
somewhat oddly, as psycholinguists have known for a long time.[18] So perhaps one
should pay more attention to experiments which have avoided negatives and tested
to see if a word such as *kill* involved the assemblage of CAUSE DIE, or *chase* the
piecing together of TRY CATCH.[19] But once again the experiments failed to show
that the word which supposedly had more components took longer to process.

These results lead us to one of several possibilities. Either the words which
have been tested have been wrongly analysed, in which case we cannot draw any
conclusion. Or assemblage is so amazingly fast that it is unmeasurable by current
techniques. Or people do not assemble words when they comprehend them – they
are already pre-packaged.

So far, then, we have noted, first, that a number of linguists believe in the
existence of a universal store of 'semantic primitives', small components of meaning out of which words are built. Second, no one agrees what these components
are, and no one has been able to find them. Third, experiments have not revealed
any trace of assemblage procedures when people comprehend words. All this is
still not proof that semantic primitives are non-existent: 'The problem is that it is
very difficult to show conclusively that something does not exist.'[20] And some
people still persist in the claim that there are meaning globules in the mind. Let us
now consider why this might be so.

Atomic Globule Faith

Many people believe in things because they seem to provide the 'best' explanation
amidst a group of not particularly satisfactory ones. And atomic globules, it is

claimed, provide a possible explanation for a number of puzzling phenomena, as well as fitting in with intuitions about the way the world works.

A common reason for proposing the existence of meaning atoms is, as we have noted, that they provide a convenient explanation for why certain words overlap in meaning. A group of related words such as *mother*, *aunt*, *mare*, *waitress* could all be regarded as sharing a common basic component, that of FEMALE. Or *hop*, *skip*, *run* and *jump* might all share a component MOVE. A word such as *cow* might be decomposed into BOVINE, ADULT, FEMALE, as opposed to a *bull*, which could be BOVINE, ADULT, MALE, and a *calf*, which might be BOVINE, NON-ADULT. In brief, according to this view, words may overlap because they share one or more components. But, as we shall see, there are other ways of explaining overlaps, so it is not conclusive.

A second reason for adopting the atomic globule viewpoint is that it fits in with the way the world appears to work. In chemistry, for example, chemicals can be decomposed into more basic elements, and some scholars have explicitly suggested that there are parallels between the breakdown of chemical structures and the decomposition of words.[21] In the realm of linguistics, a number of researchers have drawn attention to a possible parallelism between the sound structure of words and their meaning structure.[22] Since the sounds of language can be broken down into more basic components such as labiality (use of lips), voice (vibration of vocal cords) and so on, which might be universal, it seems plausible that word meanings should also be broken down in this way. There is, however, no convincing evidence that mental phenomena such as word meanings behave identically to physical elements which can ultimately be identified and measured.

A third reason for proposing semantic primitives is wishful thinking. Their existence would make life easier for anybody working with problems of meaning, since they solve the problem of where definitions stop. Without semantic primitives one simply defines words in terms of each other in an endless chain. If a person asks about the meaning of *bachelor*, the reply 'unmarried man' is not particularly helpful unless the components UNMARRIED MAN are in some sense more basic than the word *bachelor*. Even if we agreed that *unmarried man* was more basic than *bachelor*, we would still need to know the meaning of *man* and *unmarried*. If the reply was that a *man* is MALE, ADULT and HUMAN, then one would want to know what was meant by *male*, *adult* and *human*, and so on. Unless we are going to come to a halt somewhere, we would go on for ever. As one group of scholars noted: 'Definitions typically apply in chains, and the further along a chain we go, the closer we get to expressions couched in the vocabulary of the primitive basis. The primitive basis is where definitions stop.'[23] However, wanting definitions to stop in this way does not mean that they necessarily do so.

A further reason for the appeal of 'lexical decomposition' may be that it is fairly familiar: many dictionaries work on this principle. It is in line with 'a time-honoured maxim of lexicographers "a word should be defined by using words simpler than itself " . . . In this sense, simpler should be taken to mean "of a higher order of generality".'[24] For example, a *mare* is defined by the *Concise Oxford Dictionary* as 'female of equine animal', and a *sow* as 'adult female pig'.[25] The *Longman Dictionary of Contemporary English* defined the meanings of 55,000 words using a total vocabulary of only 2,000.[26] However, we are concerned not with writing dictionaries, but with analysing the mental lexicon. Are all humans qualified lexicographers, at least subconsciously? It seems unlikely.

We are left, then, with the conclusion that there is no convincing evidence to support the proposal that humans split words up into 'atomic globules' in the mind. All the arguments that we have discussed in favour of this viewpoint have been quite inconclusive, and mostly based on descriptive convenience and wishful thinking.

Of course, human beings can perfectly well *analyse* the words they use, by identifying critical characteristics, such as the properties of upward movement and clambering involved in *climb*. But identifying different characteristics does not involve splitting the words up into a finite number of component parts, and then gluing them back together again. The old idea that words would be divided into a fixed number of pieces may be an unwanted hangover from the days of the 'checklist' view of meaning, when all members of a category were assumed to have the same basic make-up, which could be specified.

We conclude, therefore, that atomic globules do not exist in the mind.

Summary

This chapter has dealt with the way in which words might be related to one another in the mental lexicon. It examined the atomic globule viewpoint – the suggestion that there is a stock of semantic components out of which all words are composed.

This theory ran into insuperable problems: no one has been able to specify what these atomic globules are, and they leave no trace in the processing of words. The arguments in favour of this viewpoint are based mainly on descriptive convenience and wishful thinking. Our overall conclusion was that they are useful descriptive devices for people such as lexicographers who need to describe things in a succinct and orderly way. But they are unlikely to exist in the mental lexicon.

Our next chapter therefore looks at 'cobweb theories' – an alternative view of how words might be related to one another.

8

Word-webs
— Semantic networks —

Experience is never limited, and it is never complete; it is an immense sensibility, a kind of huge spider-web of the finest silken threads suspended in the chamber of consciousness, and catching every airborne particle in its tissue.

Henry James, *Partial Portraits*

Words are not assembled out of a common store of semantic primitives, we decided. So how are they related to one another? Perhaps we should imagine them as linked together in a gigantic multi-dimensional cobweb, in which every item is attached to scores of others. Or, to use a more sophisticated image: 'Suppose the mental lexicon is a sort of connected graph, with lexical items at the nodes with paths from each item to the other.'[1] Theories of this type are known as network theories.

A network, according to the eighteenth-century lexicographer Samuel Johnson, is 'anything reticulated or decussated at equal distances, with interstices between the intersections'. Johnson was presumably thinking of something like a fishing net, in which the intersections must be equidistant. A network in relation to the mental lexicon simply means 'an interconnected system'. Researchers mostly agree that a network of some type is inevitable, but they disagree as to how it is organized and how to explore it.

In general, early work on the topic concentrated on finding out the strength of a link between one particular word and another. The findings laid the groundwork for later research, which has spent more time on trying to ascertain the overall structure underlying the individual connections. In this chapter, therefore, we will consider the outline conclusions of some early researchers, and then try to specify the probable overall organization more carefully.

Linguistic Habits

Early work on meaning networks suggested that links between words were formed by habits: if words often cropped up together, such as *pen* and *pencil*, *envelope* and *postage stamp*, or *moon* and *stars*, then these frequently associated items were thought to develop extra strong ties. The close links forged by these habits could be revealed quite easily, it was suggested, by means of simple word association experiments.

'Give me the first word you think of when I say "hammer".' This, as we saw in chapter 2, is the standard procedure for word association experiments. The experimenter draws up a list of words, and for each item asks a subject to name the first word which comes to mind. In such experiments, different people generally give rather similar responses. For example, out of 1,000 subjects, over half said *nail* in response to 'hammer', *low* to 'high' and *black* to 'white'.[2] And for some other words the probability of a particular response was much higher: over three-quarters of the subjects responded *queen* to 'king', *girl* to 'boy' and *short* to 'long'. Moreover, in cases where there was no overwhelming single response, there were usually several very common ones: *water*, *sea* or *blue* accounted for around two-thirds of the responses to 'ocean'. The consistency of the results suggested to psychologists that they might therefore be able to draw up a reasonably reliable 'map' of the average person's 'word-web.'

At least three important findings emerged. First, people almost always select items from the semantic 'field' of the original word. Nobody said *nail* or *poker* in response to 'needle', even though these are also thin pointed objects. The majority mentioned some aspect of sewing: *thread*, *pin(s)*, *eye* and *sew* were the words mentioned most often. Sewing items seemed to trigger one another off, suggesting that clusters of words relating to the same topic are stored together. The second finding was that people nearly always pick the partner if the item is one of a pair, as in *husband* and *wife*, or has an obvious opposite, as in *big* and *small*. The third finding (which will be discussed in a later chapter) is that adults are likely to respond with a word of the same word class: a noun tends to elicit a noun, an adjective another adjective, and so on.

Can we build up a detailed mental map from these responses? Unfortunately not, in spite of the enormous amount of information available from word association experiments.[3] There turn out to be a number of problems. First, thinking up an immediate response to just one word is a somewhat unnatural kind of activity, so may not reflect ordinary speech processes. Second, the standard results can be altered quite dramatically by presenting a word in a group, rather than alone. People normally respond to the word 'moon' with items such as *sun*, *night* and *star*. But if 'moon' is presented alongside words such as 'elephant, hall, whale, stadium', subjects tend to reply with the word *big*.[4] If a word's associations can be changed so easily by the context, then it is possibly wrong to assume that we can ever lay down fixed and detailed pathways linking words in the mental lexicon.

But the most serious shortcoming of word association experiments is that they cannot tell us about the probable structure of the human word-web. This is partly because each person is asked for only one response to a particular word, and partly because the links between words are multifarious. For example, the ten most common responses to 'butter' were *bread* (the commonest), then *yellow*, *soft*, *fat*, *food*, *knife*, *eggs*, *cream*, *milk*, *cheese*.[5] These responses represent several different types of link: *bread* is eaten alongside butter, *yellow* and *soft* describe 'butter', whereas *cream*, *eggs*, *milk* and *cheese* are other kinds of dairy food. One would expect the mental lexicon to treat these various connections differently from one another. Let us consider this problem more carefully.

Listing the Links

The ten commonest responses in word association tests to the words *butterfly*, *hungry*, *red* and *salt* are listed in figure 8.1.[6] As with *butter*, these replies encompass a number of different types of link between the stimulus word and the response.

	BUTTERFLY	HUNGRY	RED	SALT
1	moth	food	white	pepper
2	insect	eat	blue	sugar
3	wing(s)	thirsty	black	water
4	bird	full	green	taste
5	fly	starved	colour	sea
6	yellow	stomach	blood	bitter
7	net	tired	communist	shaker
8	pretty	dog	yellow	food
9	flower(s)	pain	flag	ocean
10	bug	man	bright	lake

Figure 8.1   Word association responses

Let us consider the four which may be the most important:

1 COORDINATION. The commonest response involved coordinates, words which cluster together on the same level of detail, such as *salt* and *pepper*; *butterfly* and *moth*; *red*, *white*, *blue*, *black*, *green*. Opposites come into this category, as they are coordinates in a group consisting of only two members, as with *left* and *right*, or they are the two commonest members in a larger group, as with *hot*, *cold*, *warm*, *cool*.
2 COLLOCATION. The next most common response involved a word which was likely to be collocated (found together) with the stimulus in connected speech, as with *salt water*, *butterfly net*, *bright red*.
3 SUPERORDINATION. Less often, a superordinate occurred, the cover term which includes the stimulus word. For example, *insect* was elicited by 'butterfly', and *colour* was a response to 'red'.
4 SYNONYMY. Occasionally, a rough synonym was found, a word with the same meaning as the original word, as with *starved* beside 'hungry'.

Names for these links vary. Superordinates are sometimes referred to as 'hyperonyms'. The items included under a superordinate are usually known as 'hyponyms'. *Red*, *blue* and *green* are therefore hyponyms of the superordinate or hyperonym *colour*. Coordinates are sometimes referred to as 'co-hyponyms', on the grounds that they may be hyponyms (subordinates) of a single hyperonym (superordinate).

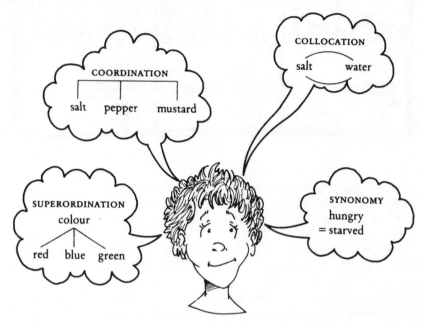

Figure 8.2   Types of link in the word-web

How, then, do all these connections (figure 8.2) intermesh in the mental lexicon? And are some links stronger or more permanent than others? Let us consider these questions by examining each kind of link in turn, starting with coordination.

When Left means Right

The secret of good communication is to know when *left* means 'right', according to a newspaper cartoon. Muddling up *left* and *right* is possibly the commonest semantic tongue-slip of all, closely followed perhaps by the confusion of *yesterday*, *today* and *tomorrow*. And other similar examples can be heard daily. People say *Tuesday* when they mean 'Wednesday', *blue* instead of 'green' and *brother* instead of 'sister'. And there are numerous others, as in:

The picture on the front was the *whale* (shark) from Jaws.
Ask (tell) me whether you think it'll do the job.[7]

In addition, people sometimes blend together similar words, such as:

COUPLES   by Calman

I went to *Noshville* (Nashville + Knoxville, Tennessee towns).
I'd like some *taquua* (tequila + kahlua, Mexican drinks).
He's a born *sailure* (success + failure).

These errors confirm the results of word association experiments, that words are
stored in semantic fields and that coordinates are closely associated. Word searches
provide additional support. When looking for an elusive word, people frequently
fumble around not only in the same general semantic area but often within a group
of coordinates. Freud, when he could not remember the name 'Monaco', ran
through a whole series of place-names: *Piedmont, Albania, Montevideo, Colico,
Montenegro* (chapter 2).[8] In the 'tip of the tongue' experiment (chapter 2), subjects
who could not remember the word *sextant* recalled other navigational instruments,
such as *compass* or *astrolabe*.[9]

Furthermore, aphasic patients often produce a coordinate or close relative of the
target, as in *orange* for 'lemon', *table* for 'chair' and *diving* for 'swimming', and they
may make this type of mistake in comprehension also:

Mrs P.:   Do you want rice crispies?
Mr P.:   Yes.

When the rice crispies arrived in front of him, Mr P., who had recently had a
stroke, was surprised and angry, and Mrs P. became upset at his unreasonable
behaviour. It seems that poor Mr P. could no longer remember which sound sequence
paired with *rice crispies*, and had perhaps thought Mrs P. meant 'cornflakes'.[10]

Such episodes suggest that some coordinates are so closely linked that brain-
damaged people may have difficulty in distinguishing between them. A particular
sound sequence may lead into the general area of the lexicon required, at which
point the matching procedure needed to pinpoint the exact word fails. This was
suggested by an experiment in which aphasics were asked to single out one item in

a picture showing several objects. If the instruction was 'Point to a lemon', patients were likely to succeed if the other objects were things quite different from it, such as a boot, an armchair, a cup or a pig. But many of them found it much more difficult to pick out the lemon from among other pieces of fruit.[11]

Moreover, ties between coordinates tend to be retained even after serious brain damage. Aphasics were asked to squeeze a rubber ball if they recognized a relationship between pairs of words which were read aloud to them.[12] They responded fastest if these words were coordinates, and their error rate was exactly the same as that of normal subjects. In addition, work with elderly patients indicates that these connections do not deteriorate in old age.[13] A number of young and old subjects were presented with two simultaneous strings of letters and asked to judge whether both were words. In general, the older group, whose average age was 70, took longer to respond than the younger group, average age 28. But if the strings were both words, and these were either coordinates (*rain–snow*) or contained collocational links (*rain–wet*), then the responses of both groups were speeded up equally. This result suggests that the first word was linked to the second word as strongly in the old group as in the young one.

Links between coordinates, then, are strong. According to one researcher,[14] all the examples in his collection of semantic slips fitted into three categories: contrasting coordinates, as with *apple* for 'pear', *red* for 'black', *Monday* for 'Tuesday'; opposites, as with *up* for 'down', *fat* for 'thin', *man* for 'woman'; and 'semantic cousins', as with *Saturday* for 'January', which are both dates but dates of a different type. Another researcher looked at errors in which a body part was supplanted by another word.[15] These indicated 'a strong constraint of field boundaries on the substitution patterns'.[16] Out of 32 errors, 28 were other body parts, such as *shoulder* for 'elbow', *finger* for 'toe'. And the four that did not fit this pattern were probably sound pattern errors, such as *soldier* for 'shoulder'. A similar pattern was found with other fields, such as foods, clothing and colours.

The strength of links within fields, and the possible weakness of links between fields is also shown by the strange behaviour of some aphasic patients. 'I've forgotten,' said one, when asked to define a *needle*. Asked about the word *carrot*, he said, 'I must once have known,' to *mosquito* his reply was 'It sounds familiar,' and to *geese*, 'An animal, I've forgotten precisely.' But the same patient defined a *pact* as 'friendly agreement', *supplication* as 'making a serious request for help' and *knowledge* as 'making oneself mentally familiar with a subject'.[17] He was able to cope with certain types of topic but not others. At first sight one might suspect that he simply had a neurotic block about some kinds of words. But an ability to handle some semantic fields and not others has now been reported in quite a few patients. One of the earliest studies on the topic tested the vocabulary of 135 patients within a number of general areas, such as colours, actions and numbers.[18] The researchers found that in several of these patients the performance across these different areas was quite uneven.

One possibility is that these patients had lost the ability to deal with certain types of lexical organization: the first patient could cope with abstract words but not concrete objects; the other patients might have had difficulty with colours because of their graded nature. But this explanation cannot account for the problems of every aphasic of this type, some of whom have deficits in quite precise areas. One man knew the names of kitchen utensils but not the names of fruit. He could name items of clothing but not types of cloth. And he could name tools but not kinds of metal. One woman was significantly better on food words than on objects.[19]

Fruit and vegetables were a problem for another patient.[20] This 34-year-old male had a stroke in 1981, which at first left him almost totally speechless. But he gradually recovered, and after 18 months appeared to be better – apart from fruit and vegetables. He 'showed a striking inability to name such common items as Peach and Orange while able to name easily less frequent items such as Abacus and Sphinx'.[21] He was not entirely hopeless at dealing with these, and scored just over 60 per cent in a naming test. But this was a strange contrast to everything else in his world, which he apparently coped with just about normally – including other food items. And similar strange cases are coming to light all the time.[22]

These cases suggest that topic areas are stored to some extent independently, and that some semantic fields can be damaged without affecting others, even though in normal speakers one would not expect this degree of isolation between areas.

It is difficult to be precise about the detailed organization of coordinates within the mental lexicon, since the structure of a group is likely to depend on the type of word involved – objects, colours and actions might be treated rather differently. It seems probable, however, that for each group there is a nucleus of closely linked words, with other words attached somewhat more loosely round the edges (figure 8.3).

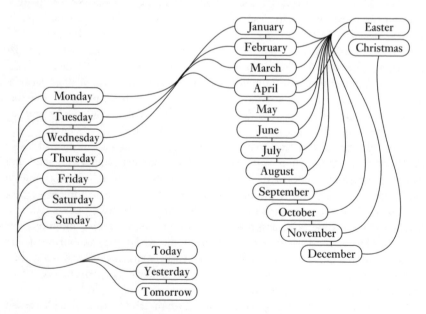

Figure 8.3   Clusters of coordinates

In some cases, as with colours, the words in the nucleus may overlap to some extent, since many words have fuzzy edges which merge into one another (chapter 5).

Stardust and Star Wars

A popular television quiz show was based on the idea that different people will come up with the same continuation for a word such as *star*: *stardust*, *starfish* or *star wars*, perhaps. Humans seem to be fairly sensitive to collocational links of this type, as word association experiments suggested. This finding is strengthened by evidence from tongue-slips, where people sometimes start out with one phrase and then get 'derailed' on to a familiar routine, as in *Hungarian restaurant* for 'Hungarian rhapsody'. Aphasics also preserve collocational links well.[23] Futhermore, the experiment involving old people mentioned earlier in this chapter showed that links such as *rain–wet* were as strong in the old subjects as in the younger ones.[24]

Word meaning is probably learned by noting the words which come alongside. Take the relatively new word *wimp* (chapter 1). Most people discovered its meaning of 'feeble, timid or ineffectual person'[25] because of its neighbours, as in *pale-faced wimp, craven wimps, pathetic wimps a wimp and a coward*.[26]

Collocational links cover a wide spectrum. At one end of the range there are words which are optionally, but commonly associated: *fresh-faced youths*, *buxom barmaids*, *rude adolescents*, *unruly hair*. These frequent associations merge into habitual connections or clichés: *agonizing decision*, *astronomically expensive*, *blissfully ignorant*, *wide awake*. There are also numerous 'freezes', pairs of words which have been frozen into a fixed order, such as *knife and fork*, *bride and groom*, *bread and butter*.[27] Clichés and freezes overlap with idioms, phrases whose overall meaning cannot be predicted from the sum total of the individual words: *keep tabs on, call it a day, fall into place*.

Idioms spread over a broad range, and thousands of them are found – over 4,500 according to one dictionary of idioms.[28]

There are 'many dimensions of idiomaticity'.[29] Some idioms resist being altered: *Bill kicked the bucket* in the sense 'Bill died' cannot be changed to *The bucket was kicked by Bill*, nor can words be added: *Bill kicked the filthy* bucket or *Bill kicked the bucket noisily* would be impossible. Other idioms allow changes in word order. *They pulled Tom's leg* in the sense 'they teased Tom' might equally well be found as *Tom's leg was pulled*.

Other idioms allow words to be inserted: 'To leave no stone unturned' could appear as 'leave no *legal* stone unturned', and 'The President doesn't have a leg to stand on' could be modified to read 'The President doesn't have an *economic* leg to stand on.'[30]

Sometimes words can be interchanged, as in 'Add fuel to the *fire*' where *flames* could replace *fire*, and 'Hold a *gun* to his head,' where *pistol* could be substituted for *gun*. Certain vague verbs occur repeatedly, as *take* in *take a dim view of, take a back seat, take note of*, or *make* in *make fun of, make a go of, make the best of*.[31]

Given this wide range of variation, what truly counts as an idiom? Should it include two-word phrases such as *plastic flower* where the hearer has to interpret this as 'artificial flower that is made of plastic', since real flowers cannot literally be made of plastic? Or *stuffed tiger* which has to be interpreted as 'dead tiger that has been stuffed'?[32]

And how does one draw the line between a *phrase* and an *idiom*? So called *phrasal lexemes*, defined as 'multi-word expressions', are very numerous in all known languages: they have been claimed to outnumber words by about ten to one.[33] Phrasal lexemes are so common that a new branch of lexicography known as *phraseology* has arisen, which is loosely defined as 'the study of conventional phrases'.[34]

The boundary between idioms and phrases is hazy, so is the boundary between genuinely 'new' utterances and ready-made sequences. These topics will be explored further in the next section.

What's this Fly Doing?

Diner: 'Waiter, what's this fly doing in my soup?'
Waiter: 'Madam, I believe that's the backstroke'.

This old joke highlights a linguistic problem.[35] The waiter had apparently understood the question as: 'What action is that fly performing in my soup?', in line with the commonest dictionary definition of the verb *do*. Yet the diner was asking with indignation and surprise: 'How come there is a fly in my soup?'

This usage, sometimes known as the '*What's X doing Y?* construction' presents a difficulty. It's an idiom, but not one that can be simply be listed as a repeated, one-off phrase, as could *Keep your shirt on* meaning 'Calm down.' Instead, it's found reasonably often, in a variety of contexts, for example:

What is this scratch doing on the table?
What's a nice girl like you doing in a place like this?
What am I doing reading this junk?

This construction always contains the verb *do* with *-ing* on the end, it always follows part of the verb *be*, and neither *be* nor *do* can have a negative added. The construction would have a quite different meaning if anyone said:

What's this fly done in my soup?
What will this fly do in my soup?
*What isn't this fly doing in my soup?
*What is this fly not doing in my soup?

But listing the words and syntax needed in the *what's X doing Y?* construction is not enough: a meaning element must be included. The construction always highlights some type of incongruity which needs to be explained.

The *what's X doing Y?* construction is not alone. Several groups of words don't fit easily into traditional grammars as either idioms or full constructions. Another example is:

> We're twistin' the night away
> Fred drank the evening away
> Bill snored the afternoon away.[36]

This has been labelled the 'time-away' construction. It has a number of requirements. The verb needs to be be intransitive, that is, it cannot have an object. The noun phrase preceding *away* is not a proper 'linguistic object' – but it seems to prevent a proper object from occurring. So you couldn't say:

> *Fred drank the whisky the night away.

If you wanted to specify what Fred drank, you'd have to say, perhaps:

> Frank drank the night away with a bottle of whisky.

The performer of the action must be acting under his/her own volition, you couldn't say:

> *The lighthouse flashed the night away.

And the verb requires some type of activity, so you couldn't say:

> *Paul waited the afternoon away.

The meaning insinuation is that the 'time-away' activity involves heedless pleasure. You could say:

> Linda frittered the week away.

But it would be quite odd to say:

> !Linda worked the week away

Both the *what's X doing Y?* and the 'time-away' constructions seem to be idiomatic expressions which have their own syntax and whose semantic content goes beyond the lexical items which make them up. They have been plausibly labelled *constructional idioms*.[37] They are midway between 'real' idioms, which have to be learned, and fully productive grammatical rules. To cope with this phenomenon, a new type of grammar may be needed, provisionally known as *construction grammar* 'in which the particular and the general are knit together seamlessly'.[38] Construction grammar contains general rules, but in addition, restricted, local versions of these to deal with semi-idioms. Then constructions such as *what's X*

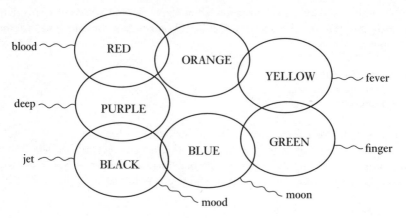

Figure 8.4   Strong links in the word-web

doing Y? and 'time-away' can be said to *inherit* the general rules, but with added restrictions. Such a grammar, when it is fully developed, will be a useful way of relating words and syntax.

So far in this chapter, coordinate links and collocational links have been discussed (figure 8.4). These are powerful and long-lasting, though as the discussion above has suggested, they interact in complex ways. The next sections will consider further types of link, synonymy and superordination.

Chasing or Pursuing Shadows

Humans have a pretty good idea as to which words are interchangeable. Perfect synonymy – total overlap of meaning – is somewhat rare, but many words are intermittently interchangeable. Shadows are *chased* in Matthew Arnold's poem 'The Buried Life':

> A man . . . doth forever *chase*
> That flying and elusive shadow, rest.

But they are *pursued* according to the orator Edmund Burke:

> . . . what shadows we are, what shadows we *pursue* . . .

Yet this interchangeability is not general. It's possible to *pursue* knowledge, but not to *chase* it. You can *chase* a wasp out of the plum jam, but would be unlikely to *pursue* it out of the plum jam.

In actual usage, *chase* and *pursue* overlap relatively little, even though the meaning 'follow after' is given for both in some dictionaries.

English speakers *chase* physical objects, such as runaway horses, burglars and balls:

> More frigging football! Bunch of tarts going round a field *chasing* a ball!

But they *pursue* concrete objects only occasionally. Mostly, they *pursue* figuratively, following abstract aims, issues, strategies and targets, as:

> We need to take the initiative in *pursuing* a strategy for employment and growth.

Such figurative journeying along a path accounted for the majority of examples of *pursue*, but no examples of *chase*.[39]

Other English synonyms also turned out to be more distinct than their dictionary definitions suggested. For example, *wide* and *broad* sometimes overlapped, but they also had their own non-overlapping contexts.[40] *Wide* was found in measurements, often alongside *long* and *deep*:

> The dish is about this *long*, this *wide*, and about that *deep*. And I make it on Thursdays, nice big lasagna. And I ate it all!

No examples of measurements were found with *broad*.

Broad, but not *wide*, was used to mean 'lacking detail'. It occurred in phrases such as *broad outline*, *broad spectrum*, *broad sweep*, *broad terms*, as:

> In *broad* terms, the master plan is unchanged in concept but we think improved in detail.

However, both *broad* and *wide* overlapped strongly when used for figurative extension, as in *broad/wide choice*, *broad/wide support*, *broad/wide view*, as in:

> A *wide choice* of sites can be made available.
> You pick the ones you like, there is that sort of *broad choice*.

This type of partial overlap shows that speakers need to be permanently 'tuned in' to the usages of their language.

The Old Man with a Beard

> There was an Old Man with a beard,
> Who said, 'It is just as I feared!
>   Two Owls and a Hen,
>   Four Larks and a Wren,
> Have all built their nests in my beard!'

Try reading Edward Lear's limerick about the Old Man with a beard to a friend. Then ask the friend to summarize the content of the poem. The reply is likely to be something like: 'There's this old chap with a beard, and a whole lot of birds come and build nests in it.' Almost everybody uses the word *bird* in their reply, even though it is not explicitly mentioned in the original. People, then, know that *owls*, *hens*, *larks* and *wrens* are 'hyponyms' of the cover term or 'superordinate' *bird*. Does this imply that words are always kept in bundles, labelled with the superordinate term?

There are several problems with assuming that the labelling of bundles is an inevitable procedure. First, superordinate terms do not crop up very often as errors in slips of the tongue,[41] although they are commoner in aphasia. It may be that such slips are not noticed: 'That wretched *animal*'s been digging up my bulbs again' sounds quite normal, and would not be categorized as an error, even though the speaker might have intended to say *cat*. But the rarity of this type of error may also be because a superordinate term is not always readily available.

It is often quite difficult to think up a suitable superordinate. Take *hail*, *rain* and *snow*. The technical term *precipitation* is restricted mainly to weather forecasters. Or how about *cough* and *sneeze*? Is this 'noise indicating respiratory distress'? And what about *baths* and *basins*? Are these bathroom fixtures? Or sanitary fitments? Or take the tongue-slip *tin-opener* for 'nutcrackers': are these 'kitchen gadgets for opening things which are going to be consumed'? Although people appear to link groups of items together, they may not give the resulting bundle a label.

Even when it exists, a superordinate may be quite rare. English speakers often choose two coordinates to describe a set of items in preference to a technical-sounding hyperonym. They say 'Do you have any brothers and sisters?' rather than 'Do you have any siblings?', and 'Where are the knives and forks?' instead of 'Where is the cutlery?'

Only in a few clear-cut cases, such as *bird* for owl, wren, lark, hen, can a superordinate label be confidently attached. And even here, the number of possible layers presents problems. Daisy, dandelion, rose, tulip are all flowers. But should daisy and dandelion be bracketed under the label 'wild flowers', and rose and tulip under 'garden flowers', as an intermediate stage before the generic label *flower*?

Furthermore, superordinates change, depending on a group's make-up: shoes, slippers and gumboots would presumably be *footwear*, but gumboots, rainhat and mackintosh might be *rainwear*. These observations suggest that superordinates are often thought up on the spur of the moment.

And not all members of a category are on an equal footing (chapter 5). It's easier to categorize a prototypical bird such as *robin* as a *bird* than a slightly odd one such as *pelican*. Perhaps because of this problem, almost all experiments which have tried to find out about the relationship between hyponyms and their superordinates have been somewhat unsatisfactory. Let us consider some of these.

The process of grouping and labelling can often be repeated several times, because each item in a group can usually be subdivided. *Owls* can be split into *barn owls*, *snowy owls*, *screech owls* and so on. And a superordinate is also likely to be included in a still higher category: *birds* form a group with *fish*, *insects* and so on,

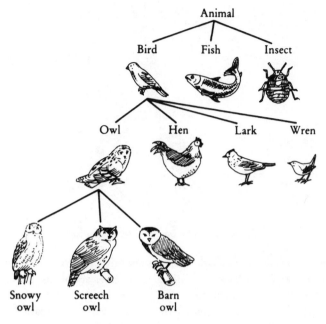

Figure 8.5 Levels of superordinates

within a category of *animal*. This progressive layering can be envisaged as a type of upside-down tree (figure 8.5).

In the late 1960s and early 1970s a number of researchers proposed that this was how the mental lexicon might be organized – in hierarchical structures of the type described above. One of the earliest papers on the topic was by Collins and Quillian (1969). They suggested that one could test this idea by asking subjects to verify sentences such as 'A canary is a canary' or 'A canary is a bird' or 'A canary is an animal,' and timing how long they took to do this. They assumed that the further a person had to travel on the tree in order to verify a sentence, the longer it would take. According to this theory, 'A canary is a canary' should be verified very fast, as there is no need to travel at all. 'A canary is a bird' should take a little longer, as an adjacent node has to be reached. 'A canary is an animal' should take longest of all, since it involves travelling from *canary* to *bird*, then from *bird* to *animal* (figure 8.6).

These predictions turned out to be correct. However, their findings do not conclusively prove the existence of upside-down trees, since there are a number of other possible explanations of the result. First, *canaries* and *birds* are associated much more frequently than *canaries* and *animals*, so the effect could be caused by a strong habitual association rather than a hierarchy. Second, there are many more possible animals than possible birds, so maybe the difficulty of assessing 'A canary is an animal' is due to the large number of items in the category *animal*. Third, the word *animal* is ambiguous: sometimes it is used in contrast to *bird*, as in 'An owl is

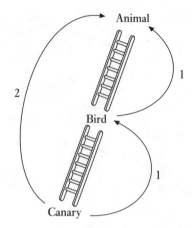

Figure 8.6 The canary–bird experiment

a bird, but a dog is an animal,' whereas at other times it includes the word *bird*, as in 'Owls and dogs are animals, but roses and oak-trees are plants.' This ambiguity might have delayed assessment time.

This last problem can be avoided by testing people on creatures which are more usually thought of as animals, such as *dogs*.[42] The psychologists who tried this incorporated a subtle but significant difference into the task. They noted that almost all previous experimenters had contrasted the time taken to verify a link from one word to its immediate superordinate, as in 'A poodle is a dog,' with the time taken to verify a link to an even higher superordinate, as in 'A poodle is an animal.' No one seemed to have checked whether 'A dog is an animal' (one step) also took less time than 'A poodle is an animal' (two steps), as the theory would predict. The researchers were unable to find any reliable difference. Subjects in general took as long to verify 'A dog is an animal' as 'A poodle is an animal.' This result suggests that even if people organize words in clumps, it is unlikely that they climb nimbly up and down lexical trees as if they were fixed scaffolding.

To summarize, superordinate labels may be easily available when the contents of a group are fairly prototypical and the label is a commonly used one. But this vertical movement, as it were, between different levels of generality seems to require somewhat more effort than horizontal movement among coordinates. In a number of cases, creative decision-making may have to be carried out. Faced with a question such as 'Is a tadpole an animal?', a person might well have to think this out. They might be quite sure that a *tadpole* is a small frog, and also that a *frog* is a kind of animal, but they might have to actively deduce that a tadpole is therefore an animal from these two separate pieces of knowledge.

In some cases, then, vertical links are likely to have been pre-established, and no further reasoning will be required. In other cases, humans have to make inferences on the spot. Similar active computation may also be required when one superordinate links words from different areas, such as *female*, which links *sow*, *princess* and *mare*.

Humans can compare different words and decide what they have in common quite easily. However, unless the link is a commonly used one, it seems likely that humans work out the connection by performing a quick analysis rather than by simply consulting a fixed chart in their mental lexicon. In brief, the treatment of superordinates suggests that firm connections, such as those between coordinates and those between common hyponyms and superordinates, are used in conjunction with our reasoning ability to make other temporary links as we need them.

But how does this reasoning ability work? Let us consider the matter further.

Is the Lexicon Logical?

Babies are illogical.
Nobody is despised who can manage a crocodile.
Illogical persons are despised.
Answer: Babies cannot manage crocodiles.

This whimsical puzzle by Lewis Carroll[43] raises an important question. Do humans work things out or look things up? And when they work things out, do they do this in terms of 'ordinary' logic? This section assesses the role of logic in the mental lexicon.

Several logical relationships recur in discussions of the lexicon.[44] The following are important ones, some of which have already been mentioned in this chapter (figure 8.7):

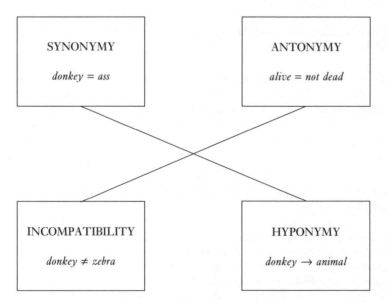

Figure 8.7   Some logical relationships

ANTONYMY: If it isn't alive, it must be dead.
HYPONYMY: A donkey is an animal.
INCOMPATIBILITY: If it's a donkey, it can't be a zebra.
SYNONYMY: A donkey is an ass, an ass is a donkey.

Let us now summarize their value.

An antonym is usually defined as 'a word of opposite meaning'. But this is an over-simplification, because it commonly includes several different types of opposites.[45] In an *either–or* type, the negation of one implies the other:

If it's not *dead*, it's *alive*.
If it's not *alive*, it's *dead*.

In a hidden scale type, the opposites are not absolute, but are relative to some norm: 'What a *large* bumblebee!' means large in comparison to the normal size of bumblebees, and 'What a *small* rabbit!' means small in comparison to the average rabbit. In absolute terms, the small rabbit would undoubtedly be bigger than the large bumblebee. Differing viewpoint opposites depend on the angle from which something is viewed: 'Meg *bought* the bicycle from Peter' implies 'Peter *sold* the bicycle to Meg'.

So different types of antonymy need to be distinguished,[46] as logicians admit. But even this oversimplifies the situation, because many opposites depend on the context. The opposite of *short* varies, and may be hard to find:

A *short* life versus a *long* life
A *short* man versus a *tall* man
A *short* temper versus a *good* temper.
In *short* supply versus in *plentiful* supply

Furthermore, if logic were all-powerful, opposites should always be interchangeable, as in: 'Paul found himself in a *better* (or *worse*) situation.' But sometimes the interchange is impossible. You can say: 'Peter's illness was *worse* than Paul's', but not !'Paul's illness was *better* than Peter's' (with an odd sentence marked by an exclamation mark). You would have to say: 'Paul's illness was *less serious* than Peter's.'

People learn these illogicalities, because opposites often co-occur. Antonymous adjectives are used together in the same sentence more frequently than chance would allow,[47] as in:

She didn't look forward to Cathy's visit, *short* or *long*.
You'll have to take the *rough* with the *smooth*.
Don't mix *clean* clothes with *dirty* ones.
I can't decide whether I *love* him or *hate* him.
The great transitions of *life* . . . and the certainty of *death*.

Antonymy, then, is not a true logical relationship within language.

Synonymy presents similar problems for logic. The choice of synonym is primarily dictated by the surrounding context. *Wide* may be more closely linked to *road*, and *broad* to *mind*, than *wide* and *broad* to each other. Similarly, *gallop* may be more closely attached to *horses*, and *sprint* to *humans*, than *gallop* and *sprint* to each other.

Hyponomy is even trickier. Only a few words have obvious superordinates, as already noted. Links such as *owl* to *bird*, *cabbage* to *vegetable* and *yellow* to *colour* may be in the minority. Often a superordinate has to be selected by the speaker as the situation demands.

And incompatibility is messy too. It occurs primarily between coordinates: *Monday* cannot be *Tuesday*, a *rose* is not a *tulip*, and a *plant* is not a *metal*.[48] But incompatibility breaks down in the case of virtues, vices and emotions. *Sincerity* and *honesty* are both virtues, yet they are neither synonyms nor incompatible. They overlap. So do the vices *greed* and *selfishness*. So do the emotions *hate* and *anger*. Incompatibility therefore works selectively. It is useful with some groups of words, but not with others.

Logical relationships therefore present a problem. They sometimes work, but often they don't. And some important relationships cannot be handled by logic. *Meronomy* or *partonomy* – parts of things which make up a whole – is important for speakers of a language.[49] A tree has a trunk and branches, branches have twigs and leaves, and so on, as will be discussed in chapter 9.

This section has shown that logical relations cannot be applied as automatic routines. In some cases, they are useful, but in others, they are not. They interweave with other types of information in ways that are still unclear. Crucially, they interact with parts of speech (word classes), as will be discussed in the next chapter.

Summary

In this chapter we have examined the human word-web – the way in which humans link words together in their minds. We noted that words seem to be organized in semantic fields, and that, within these fields, two types of link seem to be particularly strong: connections between coordinates and collocational links.

Links between hyponyms and their superordinates are overall somewhat weaker. Some are more firmly established than others. Humans then use these firm connections in conjunction with their reasoning ability to make other, temporary links as they are needed. In this, logical relationships are only partly useful.

The general picture of the mental lexicon so far is one in which there are a variety of links between words, some strong, some weak.[50] These provide a general framework within which further links can be made as the situation requires.

However, the pre-existing links interact with parts of speech. This will be the topic of the next two chapters.

9

Lexical All-sorts

— Parts of speech —

Above all the noise and tumult of the crowd could be heard the merchants' voices loudly advertising their products.

'Get your fresh-picked ifs, ands and buts.'

'Hey-yaa, hey-yaa, nice ripe wheres and whens' . . .

'Step right up, step right up – fancy, best-quality words right here', announced one man in a booming voice. 'Step right up – ah, what can I do for you, little boy? How about a nice bagful of pronouns – or maybe you'd like our special assortment of names?'

Milo had never thought much about words before, but these looked so good that he longed to have some.

'Look, Tock,' he cried, 'aren't they wonderful?'

Norton Juster, *The Phantom Tollbooth*

In the quotation above, Milo and his dog Tock find the various types of words packaged separately in the market-place at Dictionopolis: 'ifs, ands and buts' can be bought quite independently of 'a nice bagful of pronouns' or 'our special assortment of names'. This is not surprising. All languages divide words up into 'parts of speech', or word classes, which are conventionally given labels such as noun, adjective, verb and so on, each of which has its own special role to play in the sentence: 'Think of the tools in a tool-box,' suggested the philosopher Wittgenstein. 'There is a hammer, pliers, a saw, a screwdriver, a rule, a glue-pot, glue, nails and screws. The functions of words are as diverse as the functions of these objects.'[1]

The tool-box analogy is a useful one, in that it expresses the fact that each 'part of speech' behaves differently. However, an alternative way of viewing the situation is to regard word classes as building materials out of which a sentence is constructed. These materials are of two broad types: bricks on the one hand, and mortar or cement on the other. The bricks can be equated with 'content' words, those which have an independent meaning, such as *rose, queen, jump*. The mortar represents the 'function' words, those whose role is primarily to relate items to one another, as in 'Queen *of* Hearts', 'work *to* rule', 'eggs *for* breakfast'.

This book is concerned mainly with content words, which are regarded by many people as constituting the 'lexicon proper'. Within content words we shall discuss primarily nouns, verbs and adjectives, which constitute the major building blocks of English. The most important task in this chapter is to find out how these are dealt with within the mental lexicon. We can then move on to other topics: in particular, problems with deciding how many word classes there are, and psycholinguistic evidence for the divide between 'bricks' and 'mortar'.

An Eye for an Eye

When people pick one word in mistake for another, the errors almost always preserve the word class of the target, whether they are based on meaning, sound, or both meaning and sound. Nouns change place with nouns, verbs with verbs and adjectives with adjectives, as in the examples below:

> It's called the *Quail* (Lark) and Dove.
> I looked in the *calendar* (catalogue).
> It's a good way to *contemplate* (compensate).
> The book I just *wrote* (read) was awful.
> That model is *extinct* (obsolete).
> The tumour was not *malicious* (malignant).

This characteristic of speech errors has been reported by just about every researcher on the topic. It is a feature which the playwright Richard Sheridan was unaware of when he created his fictional Mrs Malaprop. She sometimes gets her word classes confused, as in:

> You will promise to forget this fellow – to *illiterate* (obliterate) him, I say, quite from your memory.

A confusion between *illiterate* (adjective) and *obliterate* (verb) would be unlikely in spoken speech in real life.

The finding that word selection errors preserve their part of speech suggests that the latter is an integral part of the word, and tightly attached to it. The phenomenon cannot just be accidental, nor can it be solely due to syntactic selection procedures. According to some researchers, speakers select a syntactic 'frame' for a sentence, such as noun–verb–noun, then put appropriate words into the slots.[2] The choice of a correct word class is then due to a syntactic checking device which monitors the process. But this cannot be entirely true, because words often dictate the frame: a choice of *put* (Martha *put* the car in the garage) involves a longer frame than, say, *park* (Martha *parked* the car). You cannot say *'Martha *put* the car' (an asterisk indicates an impossible word or sentence). Furthermore, even if words are put into appropriate pre-planned slots, they would still have to be 'labelled' with a word class in order to be picked for the slot. It seems likely therefore that the abstract meaning of a word is tightly attached to its word class.

A connection between the abstract meaning of a word and its part of speech is perhaps to be expected. Word class categorization is not arbitrary, and in origin arose out of semantic categories. Prototypical nouns tend to be people and things, and prototypical verbs tend to be actions. This correlation appears to be universal[3] – even though the link between a particular word and its part of speech prototype can be quite obscure: for example, verbs such as *exist, know, believe* do not involve obvious actions. Semantics and syntax therefore overlap, and linguists spend a good deal of time arguing where the boundary between them should be located. From the point of view of the mental lexicon, this suggests that we should not regard meaning and word class as separate ingredients which need to be attached, but as integrated. In brief, we should regard words as coins, with meaning and word class together on one side, a combination sometimes called the *lemma*,[4] and the sounds on the other. So, for example, choice of a word meaning 'daisy' automatically brings with it a metaphorical label of noun, and selection of a word meaning 'jump' inevitably involves a label of verb.

Like with Like

'A place for everything, and everything in its place.' This comment by the nineteenth-century writer Samuel Smiles describes the words in different word classes: they are diagnosed as different from one another, primarily because each has its own appointed 'slot' in the sentence. Nouns (N), verbs (V) and adjectives (A) cannot be randomly jumbled up:

> Grey (A) rabbits (N) eat (V) green (A) grass (N)
> Tall (A) trees (N) hide (V) young (A) birds (N)

make sense, but the same words jumbled up do not:

> *Green eat rabbits grass grey
> *Young hide trees birds tall.

This slotting into place raises another important question. Are words from the same word class linked particularly closely together, so that a verb such as *shout* is more tightly connected to other verbs such as *yell* and *bellow* than to its own noun *shout*? Probably, yes. There are indications that, on the one hand, words from the same word class are closely connected in the mind, and that, on the other hand, those from different word classes are more loosely attached. Let us consider these.

Close connection within word classes is suggested by bonds between coordinates, as in *red, yellow, blue* (adjectives), *tulip, daffodil, rose* (nouns) (chapter 8). Similarly, the part of speech is mostly maintained in 'tip of the tongue' guesses.

According to one researcher, nouns and verbs retain their word class strongly (90 per cent of the time), whereas adjectives do so to a lesser extent (60 per cent of the time), mostly eliciting nouns when the word class is disturbed.[5] Word association experiments provide further evidence, where the commonest adult response is a word from the same class. Nouns elicit nouns around 80 per cent of the time, whereas verbs and adjectives do so somewhat less strongly, with a figure of just over 50 per cent.[6]

On the other hand, loose attachment between word classes is shown in some types of aphasia, where verbs seem to be less accessible to the patients than nouns:[7] 'Water . . . man, no woman . . . child . . . no, man . . . and girl . . . oh dear . . . cupboard . . . man, falling . . . jar . . . cakes . . . head . . . face . . . window . . . tap. . . .' This is an attempt by a stroke victim to describe a busy kitchen scene, depicting a woman by an overflowing sink, a boy about to topple off a stool as he reaches for a jar of biscuits, and a girl looking on. Yet to deal with this action-packed picture, mainly nouns spring to the patient's mind. And this has been confirmed in a number of other studies. The preference for nouns shown by aphasics is not just because there are more nouns than verbs. It is more likely because nouns are relatively free of syntactic restrictions. Verbs, on the other hand are somewhat more tricky, perhaps because they are inextricably entangled with the syntax of the sentence.[8]

Further evidence for the relative separation of verbs from nouns is their apparent rarity in semantic selection slips, even though there are plenty of verbs in all other types of tongue-slip.[9] In one collection, out of 101 semantic errors in English, there were only three verbs, compared with 81 nouns, and 17 adjectives and adverbs. Yet judging by the proportion of verbs in English as a whole, one would have expected about 30 errors involving verbs. And in a collection of German errors, nouns, adjectives and adverbs accounted for over 90 per cent of the semantic errors, and verbs less than 10 per cent. The explanation for this may be that when speakers produce a sentence, they pick the verb very early from a special verb store which gives the syntactic framework for the rest of the sentence, then the other words are slotted in around it.

Differences between word classes are therefore important for speakers of the language. However, the most powerful argument for the separateness of word classes is that words within each part of speech appear to be organized in different ways.

Nouns versus Adjectives versus Verbs

Shoals of fish, swarms of bees, and flocks of sheep all cohere – but in very different ways. And the same is true of parts of speech. Nouns relate to nouns differently from adjectives to adjectives and verbs to verbs. This is not easy to see from standard dictionaries – though it is built into a pioneering electronic dictionary, *WordNet*, developed by George Miller and his colleagues at Princeton University.[10]

Potential layered structure is a key characteristic of nouns:[11] a Shetland pony is also a pony, a horse, an equid, an odd-toed ungulate, a herbivore, a mammal, a vertebrate, an animal, an organism and an entity – eleven levels. Layers can be diagnosed by a *kind of* test: a Shetland pony is a kind of pony, a pony is a kind of horse, and so on.

These tiers are *potential* rather than inevitable. Levels are usually few in number, and names are often missing, especially at the superordinate level (see chapter 8). The lack of layers for most words indicates that within the mental lexicon information is probably repeated at each level in most cases, rather than assuming an 'inheritance' system in which a low-level layer (such as Shetland pony) 'inherits' the properties of higher layers. But not all researchers agree with this conclusion.[12]

A 'basic level' layer of nouns outstrips the others in importance.[13] This is the highest level at which a composite mental image can be formed, and contains items such as *dog*, *shirt*, *tree*, *book* – even though there is some argument as to just what is meant by 'basic level'.

Meronomy or partonomy (parts of things) is an important relationship for nouns (see chapter 8). When quizzed about basic-level objects, people frequently list their component parts.[14] They mention the *sleeves*, *front*, *back* and *collar* of a *shirt*. They note that a *body* has a *head*, a *trunk*, *legs* and *arms*. And the parts themselves have parts, so a *leg* has a *thigh*, a *knee*, a *shin*, and a *foot*; and a *foot* has *toes*, and so on (figure 9.1). Parts, it seems, 'form a conceptual bridge from appearance to behaviour'.[15] Take a hammer: it has a *head* which you hit with and a *handle* which you grasp. And people identified as 'good parts' those which were both noticeable and useful, such as the *blade* of a *saw* and the *keys* of a *piano*.

The range covered by meronomy is unclear. A strict view adopts a test: 'The parts of this thing include X Y Z.'[16] This strict view includes members of collections

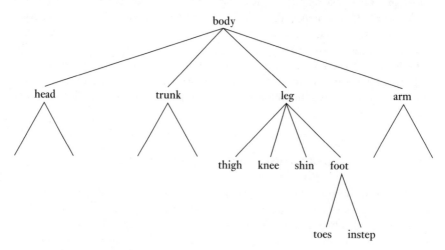

Figure 9.1 Meronomy: parts of a whole

– 'A fish is part of a shoal' – and portions of a whole – 'A slice is part of a cake.' But is a month a part of a year? Is a punch line part of a joke? Some researchers think meronomy should include these things,[17] others that it should exclude them.[18] In short, meronymy is an important relationship of nouns, but one whose properties are still being explored.

Nouns involve not only parts: a *canary* has a *beak* and *wings*, but also attributes: a canary is *small*, is *yellow*, and functions: a canary *sings, eats birdseed, can fly*[19] – though how these are all integrated is unclear, and leads back to a discussion of prototypes (chapter 5). Nouns therefore are characterized above all by potential layers, and within the basic level, layers of parts.

Adjectives are rather different. They are less independent, and often rely for their interpretation on the noun to which they are attached (chapter 5): a *rich cake* is rather different from a *rich businessman*.

Adjectives are of two main types, according to *WordNet*:[20] the *heavy suitcase* type and the *mathematical genius* type.[21] The first ascribes a value such as *heavy* to a noun such as *suitcase*, and so can be called an 'ascriptive adjective'. Such adjectives are usually graded, so *heavy* here means *heavy* in relation to the normal weight of suitcases. *Heavy*-type adjectives almost all have an opposite, though this may vary, depending on the noun (chapter 8):[22] *heavy* versus *light* for a suitcase, versus *slight* for a cold, versus *calm* for a sea.

The other type of adjective can be glossed by the phrase 'pertaining to', and these have been labelled 'pertainyms': so a *mathematical genius* is a genius in the field of mathematics, and a *musical cat* is a cat which likes music (figure 9.2).

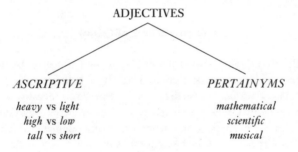

ADJECTIVES

ASCRIPTIVE

heavy vs light
high vs low
tall vs short

PERTAINYMS

mathematical
scientific
musical

Figure 9.2 Types of adjective

Verbs often come in a double layer: a hyponym and a superordinate, though the relationship is different from that in layered nouns. The lower-level verb carries out the action of the superordinate in a particular way: to *lisp* or *stutter* is to 'talk in a particular way', to *limp* or *amble* is to 'walk in a particular way', to *munch* or *chew* is to 'eat in a certain way' (figure 9.3). This has been dubbed *troponymy* in *WordNet*[23] – even though not all verbs fit into this pattern. Bodily function words, for example, such as *snore, faint, shiver* are difficult to handle. Is to *snore* to breathe in a particular way, or to *faint* to fall in a particular way, or to *shiver* to tremble in a particular way?

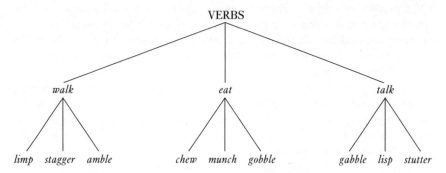

Figure 9.3 Troponymy: acting in a particular way

Nouns, verbs and adjectives therefore all have their characteristic organization within word classes, giving support to the conclusion that word classes are fairly separate in the mental lexicon.

But what about other word classes? So far, only nouns, adjective and verbs have been discussed, yet most grammar books list more parts of speech than this. Adverbs in particular figure strongly in English dictionaries. Let us therefore briefly mention some of the problems raised by adverbs, and explain why it is impossible to give a definitive list of the word classes in the mental lexicon.

The Adverbial Rag-bag

There is a deeply ingrained belief among many well-educated English speakers that there are eight parts of speech in English, a belief usually derived from schooldays. School textbooks usually pick on this figure because eight was the number decided on by Greek grammarians for ancient Greek – and until relatively recently descriptions of English were based on Latin grammars, which were them-selves based on Greek ones. Greek is not entirely useless as a model, since Greek and English are ultimately descended from the same language, so some of the categories – noun, verb, adjective, preposition – work quite well. But the fit is bad in some other respects: for example, there is no obvious category for 'determiners', words such *a, the this, that*.

Furthermore, according to some linguists, eight word classes may be too few, reflecting a 'common prejudice that the number of "parts of speech" should be small . . . That prejudice, of course, is as baseless as the once equally common prejudice that the number of chemical elements should be small.'[24] The number eight is largely preserved by treating the category adverb as a rag-bag containing a heterogeneous collection of words, many of which are there principally because they do not fit into any other category.[25] For example:

The parrot has *presumably* been taught *not* to swear.
The bird *nevertheless* swore *fluently* at Aunt Jemima.
Aunt Jemima was *really quite* upset.
Astonishingly, she was *almost completely* speechless.

The words italicized are all traditionally classified as adverbs. Yet they behave quite differently from one another. Words from the same word class can often be interchanged without altering the basic structure. But hardly any of the adverbs can change places with one another. If we try this kind of switching around, we get a quite unacceptable result:

*The parrot has *really* been taught *quite* to swear.
*The bird *presumably* swore *not* at Aunt Jemima.
*Aunt Jemima was *completely astonishingly* upset.
*Almost, she was *fluently nevertheless* speechless.

In the case of adverbs, then, words which behave somewhat differently are lumped together under the same label – though it is possible to identify some 'core' adverbs, often regarded as manner adverbs, meaning 'in a particular manner', such as *fluently*, 'in a fluent way'.

However, the whole set of words labelled adverbs shows, first, that care should be taken in assigning words to word classes; and second, that we are unlikely to be able to work out with any accuracy how many different word classes are distinguished by the mental lexicon. In particular, it is not clear whether one should regard a clump of words which behave partially like another clump as a subcategory within an overall category or as a category in its own right. In spite of these cautions, however, a large number of English words can be readily identified as nouns, verbs or adjectives,[26] on the basis of both their position in the sentence and their general make-up. This is why we have kept mainly to these categories, dealing with clear-cut cases as far as possible.

Finally, let us look at the division mentioned at the beginning of the chapter, between content words as 'bricks' and function words as 'mortar', and assess the psycholinguistic evidence for this division.

Bricks versus Mortar

Dim was a lot more *starry* and grey and had a few *zoobies* missing as you could see when he let out a *smeck*, *viddying* me, and then my *droog* Georgie said, pointing like at me: 'That man has filth and *cal* all over his *platties*,' and it was true.

These lines from Anthony Burgess's novel *A Clockwork Orange* illustrate the main distinction between the bricks and the mortar. Word classes comprised of content words are mostly 'open' in the sense that they readily allow newcomers: any number of new nouns, verbs and adjectives can be invented without any problem, as shown by the passage above. In contrast, word classes containing function words are mostly 'closed', in that they keep out intruders.

One would expect to find an identifiable difference between open and closed word classes in the mental lexicon, correlating roughly with the content–function distinction. And this turns out to be true, even though some of the evidence for differential treatment is disputed.[27] There are two main reasons for this controversy: first, the divide between open and closed word classes is not absolute, nor is that between content and function words. Second, some of the evidence comes from brain-damaged patients, whose speech might not represent that of normal speakers.

Prepositions – words such as *from*, *into*, *out* – show the difficulty of making sharp divides. They are usually regarded as a closed class, but are marginally more welcoming to new members than the other closed classes. *Upsides* 'up alongside, up beside' can be heard in horse-racing circles: 'Phantom Kipper has come *upsides* Happy Cheese,' and people can fall *overside* the boat when sailing.

The small word *to* illustrates the preposition problem. This behaves in two rather different ways and brings to mind Wittgenstein's analogy: 'It is like looking into the cabin of a locomotive. . . . We see handles all looking more or less alike. . . . But one is the handle of the crank . . . another is . . . the handle of the brake lever.'[28] Sometimes, *to* appears to be quite empty of meaning, serving only to show the relationship between the words on either side of it, as in: 'The wart-hog wanted *to* eat.' But at other times, it has an independent meaning, as in: 'The wart-hog trotted off *to* the forest.' Here *to* can be glossed as 'towards', 'in the direction of', so qualifies as a content word.

But aphasic patients – people with severe speech problems – are at the centre of the bricks versus mortar discussions. At first sight, they provide excellent evidence. Not surprisingly, perhaps, many find it easier to produce prepositions in their speech if they have intrinsic meaning,[29] and handle *to* 'towards' better than the meaningless *to*.

A more dramatic content–function divide is found in the speech of some patients. They appear to lose function words, but retain content ones, as in the following conversation:

Interviewer: What happened to make you lose your speech?

Patient: Head, fall, Jesus Christ, me no good, str, str . . . oh Jesus . . . stroke.

Interviewer: I see. Could you tell me, Mr Ford, what you've been doing in the hospital?

Patient: Yes, sure. Me go, er, uh, P.T. nine o'cot, speech . . . two times . . . read . . . wr . . . ripe, er, rike, er, write . . . practice . . . get-ting better.

Interviewer: And have you been going home on weekends?

Patient: Why, yes . . . Thursday, er, er, er, no, er, Friday . . . Bar- ba-ra . . . wife . . . and, oh, car . . . drive . . . purnpike . . . you know . . . rest and . . . tee-vee.

The patient in this dialogue[30] is suffering from a disorder usually labelled 'Broca's aphasia', after the nineteenth-century neurologist Broca, who tried to pinpoint the area in the brain affected in patients who showed symptoms such as those of Mr Ford. Their speech is slow and effortful, they have difficulty thinking up the words they want and problems in pronouncing those they do find. But their most noticeable symptoms are a lack of word endings and a dearth of the 'little' words which normally hold content words together: there appears to be no mortar between the bricks, as it were.

Some researchers have regarded such symptoms as evidence that the content versus function word distinction is valid: patients still have access to the main portions of the mental lexicon, but they are mostly unable to cope with the syntax of sentences, the processes which tie words together. This viewpoint has been around for quite a long time.[31] If this interpretation is correct, then it is reasonable to assume that the 'lexicon proper' is separate from function words.

However, this is not the only possible explanation. A second possibility is that the missing words are just too small and insignificant to be retrieved easily. Maybe the aphasic described above is perfectly aware of what the sentence should be like, but something has gone wrong with their retrieval mechanism for sounds, and short unstressed items are just too small to get hold of. Metaphorically, such a patient is like a short-sighted person who knows quite well that a shirt needs buttons sewn onto the front and cuffs, but may be entirely unable to locate and select such tiny items as buttons. In linguistic terminology, this theory suggests that 'the manifested linguistic deficits of Broca's aphasics can only be accounted for in terms of the interaction between an impaired phonological capacity and otherwise intact linguistic capacities.'[32] Supporters of this hypothesis point out that the items affected are linguistically quite varied in character. The main thing they have in common is their insignificance from a phonological point of view. If this viewpoint is correct, then there is no reason to believe that the function words are separated off from the content words. They are just written in more faintly, as it were, because of their lack of stress.

In this controversy, both sides may be right to some extent, in that patients with these symptoms could be suffering from a mixture of disorders.[33] However, there is further evidence to support the content–function divide. In speech errors, words can change places with one another, as in: 'We have a *laboratory* in our *computer* (computer in our laboratory).' When these exchanges involve content words, the rhythmic pattern of the sentence is unaffected, as above. But closed class words tend to take their accent with them,[34] as in: 'Can I turn *off this* (this off).' And closed class words retain their accent in slips of the tongue such as: 'Well I *much would have* (would have much) preferred the owl.'

Lexical decision tasks provide a further slim strand of evidence for an open versus closed word class division.[35] These researchers argue that normal speakers treat open and closed class words differently in lexical decision tasks, whereas aphasics apparently do not. When normal speakers are asked to judge whether a string of letters such as CAT or PUDDLE or CUG or PLIGN is a word or not, they say 'Yes' faster to a real word if it is a common one. This is a well-known effect for open class words. Closed class words differ in frequency of usage, just as open class ones do, so one might expect the same frequency effect to be found. But this seems not to be the case. All closed class items are reportedly responded to in approximately the same time. This suggests that they are perhaps treated differently from the open class items, and stored separately. Broca's aphasics, however, did not show this difference. They seemed to treat closed class items on a frequency basis, as they did open class words, suggesting that a whole area of their brain, that dealing with syntax, had been disconnected.

These findings have been disputed by researchers who were unable to replicate this result.[36] However, some work done on German words partially supports the original claim[37] – though it is not definitive, since care must be taken in generalizing from one language to another. Subjects were asked to press a button as soon as they heard a target word, such as *Geld* 'money', as they listened to a couple of sentences. The speed with which open class items were responded to depended on whether or not the previous sentence had involved the general area of the target word. For example, when a casino was mentioned in the sentence preceding *Geld*, the listeners spotted the word for 'money' more quickly. But the speed with which closed class items were accessed remained the same, whatever the previous context. This finding was true for both normal speakers and aphasics, though the responses of the latter were much slower, especially for closed class words.

These various strands of evidence suggest that for most speakers, words are divisible into two major categories: content words, which constitute the 'lexicon proper', and function words, which are linked to syntax[38] – though further work is still needed to clarify the details.

Summary

This chapter has examined how the human mind copes with the different 'parts of speech'. Word class 'labels' are tightly bonded on to the abstract meaning of a word, so much so that these two ingredients can be regarded as integrated into a single whole, the *lemma*.

Words within each of the three major word classes in English – nouns, verbs and adjectives – are closely bonded, and each word class has its own characteristic organization.

It is impossible to say exactly how many word classes exist in the mental lexicon, especially as adverbs in English form a 'rag-bag' category, covering different types of word. But there is evidence for a broad distinction between content words and function words, with the former constituting the 'lexicon proper'.

The next chapter will deal with verbs, whose important role in sentences needs to be discussed.

10

Verb Power
— The role of verbs —

The word, it's the Verb, and the Verb, it's God.
Victor Hugo, Contemplations (1856)

The French writer Victor Hugo is not alone in thinking verbs are all-powerful. Humpty Dumpty thinks so too, when lecturing Alice on the topic of words in Looking-Glass Land: 'They've a temper, some of them – particularly verbs: they're the proudest – adjectives you can do anything with, but not verbs – however, *I* can manage the whole lot of them!'[1]

The belief that verbs are super-powerful is shared by those who work on language, for whom 'Verbs are arguably the most important lexical category of a language.'[2] Every independent English sentence must contain at least one verb, but need not contain a 'real' noun, as shown by: *Hurry!*, *Run!*, *It's raining!* Yet there are around three times as many nouns as verbs. One well-known dictionary lists just under 45,000 nouns, but fewer than 15,000 verbs.[3] This chapter will therefore explore the role and power of verbs.

The Pump of the Sentence

We use a VERB for what they do.
My pussy *sleeps* the whole night through.
She *laps* her milk; my rose tree *grows*.
When winter *comes* I hope it *snows*.

This rhyme from a children's grammar book[4] encapsulates a general belief about verbs, that they describe actions. This is true of prototypical verbs, such as *hit*, *run*, *eat*,[5] but it oversimplifies the situation. Verbs such as *elapse*, *seem*, *prefer* do not describe actions. And the children's rhyme fails to capture the most important aspect of verbs: that verbs are the pump which drives sentences along.

The verb dictates how many other words are required, as in the following advertisement: 'It's quite simple really . . . You connect the whatsisname to the thingumajig. O first remember to plug in the whatchamacallit.'[6] This makes (relative) sense, because the writer knows the structure associated with the verbs *connect*, *remember* and *plug in*: it would have been quite confusing if this had been inappropriate: 'You connect for the thingumajig. O first remember for plug in.'

Verbs are inextricably linked with the syntactic structure, which may be why people with language disorders often find them harder to handle than nouns (chapter 9). In one study, a normal person and a stroke patient were asked the same set of questions about their life and interests. In her replies, the normal speaker used 67 different nouns and 56 different verbs. The aphasic, on the other hand, used 80 different nouns but only 28 different verbs.[7] She had developed a number of strategies in order to cope with the unavailability of verbs. She tended to re-use the same verb repeatedly: 'I love the sailboat,' 'I love the music,' 'And I love hiking,' 'I love mother,' 'I love outside.' She also used a general all-purpose verb *did* several times: 'I did the sailboat,' 'I did the line,' 'I did the kitchen and kitchen and kitchen.' But mostly, she used the phrase *this is* or *it was* in place of the appropriate verb: 'It was Charlton Avenue' (= I lived on Charlton Avenue), 'And then it was the stroke' (= And then I had a stroke), 'And right here this is Eddie the telephone' (= Eddie worked for the telephone company). At other times she omitted the verb entirely, which made her speech difficult to understand: 'And the cookies jam cookie jam', 'And the arts Susie', 'Right here and me boom boom boom boom'.

The apparent rarity of verbs in semantic selection slips (chapter 9) is further evidence of the special status of verbs. This may be because the verb is selected early, in order to provide a frame for the rest of the sentence.

Textbooks traditionally distinguish three types of verbs, depending on the number of noun phrases which follow:

INTRANSITIVE: Mavis *snores*.
TRANSITIVE: Henry *thumped* Mavis.
DITRANSITIVE: Angela *gave* some socks to John.

But speakers know a lot more than this about each verb. For example, you can't say: *'Marigold *crept*'. You have to add an extra phrase saying where Marigold crept: 'Marigold *crept* along the tunnel,' 'Marigold *crept* past the sleeping monster.' And you can't say: *'Stella *put*'. You have to state what Stella put, and where she put it: 'Stella *put* the goldfish in the bath,' 'Stella *put* the owl on the shelf.'

However, the structures attached to verbs may not be as haphazard as appears at first sight. There is a slim but tantalizing link between a verb's structure and its meaning. Let us consider the matter further.

Interpreting the Wimbush

What did the wimbush do?

The wimbush *grinched*.
The wimbush *glipped* the rolkin.
The wimbush *wollached* along the snat.

Ask a friend to interpret the 'words' *grinched*, *glipped* and *wollached*. There is likely to be broad agreement. *Grinched* tends to be bodily behaviour, perhaps *grinned*, *wept* or *snorted*. *Glipped* may be rendered as *caught*, *bit* or *scratched*, usually an attack on something else. *Wollached* will probably be movement, such as *walked*, *swam* or *crawled*. This occurs even though the 'translation' of *wimbush* may differ widely, from 'a kind of mole', to 'duck', 'wombat', 'walking bush' or even 'space-man'.[8] In short, 'there is much evidence that the relationship between the meaning of verbs and their syntactic behaviour is governed by quite general principles'[9] – although these are infuriatingly difficult to discover.

Native speakers of English handle verbs in clumps. They know that all grooming verbs – *bathe*, *change*, *wash*, *shower* – behave in a similar way.[10] You are grooming *yourself* unless an external object is specified:

Tim *bathed*, and Helen *washed*.
Tim *bathed* the baby, and Helen *washed* the dog.

On the other hand, there is a group of activity verbs – *cook*, *sew*, *read* – where you know that you couldn't be eating, sewing or reading yourself, even when no object is mentioned: 'Tim *cooked*, and Helen *sewed*' must mean something like: 'Tim *cooked* dinner, and Helen *sewed* a skirt.'

A critical challenge therefore, is to find valid clumps of verbs. In some cases, this is fairly straightforward. For example, verbs of sound emission – *whistle*, *grunt*, *buzz*, *bleep* and so on – have a clear meaning connection, and behave similarly, with the source of the emission as the subject of the sentence: *the train whistled*, *the pig grunted*, *the bee buzzed*, *the bleeper bleeped*.[11] Verbs of light emission behave in a parallel way: *the lightening flashed*, *the flame flickered*, *the sunset glowed*.

But in other cases, high-level detective work is needed to discover linguistically relevant verb clumps. Consider:

Pam *cut* the cake with a nail-file.
Alexander *tickled* Penelope with a straw.
Penelope *hit* Alexander with a saucepan.

These all involve contact, and superficially have a similar structure.[12] One might therefore suggest a category of contact verbs, which would also include *hack*, *scratch*, *bash*, *kick*, *touch*, *stroke* and so on.

But on closer inspection, this is not subtle enough. You can say:

The cake *cut* easily.

but not:

*Penelope *tickled* easily.
*Alexander *hit* easily.

The 'middle' construction allowable with *cut* suggests a distinction between contact verbs which bring about a change of state, as with *cut, slice, chop,* and those which do not.

But in another structure, *cut* and *hit* side together against *tickle*:

Penelope *hit* at Alexander.
Pam *cut* at the cake.
*Alexander *tickled* at Penelope.

Hit and *cut* allow unsuccessful contact, to *hit at* or *cut at* something, but *tickle* and *touch* do not.

Contact verbs therefore cover at least three different sub-categories:[13] *touch* verbs (*touch, stroke, tickle*) are pure verbs of contact; *hit* verbs (*hit, bash, kick*) are verbs of contact by motion; *cut* verbs (*cut scratch, hack*) are verbs which produce a state via contact (figure 10.1).

		A X *with* Y	B 'middle'	C unsuccessful
change of state via contact	*cut*	✓	✓	✓
contact by motion	*hit*	✓	×	✓
pure touch	*tickle*	✓	×	×

A. Betty *cut* the butter with a penknife.

B. The butter *cut* easily.

C. Betty *cut* at the butter.

Figure 10.1   Types of contact verbs

These examples show that careful analysis is required. And in some cases, verbs may disguise their true affinities, as will be discussed below.

Cleaning the Bath

Doug *cleaned* the mud from the bath.
Kay *wiped* the custard from the wall.
Augustus *stole* the pie from the cupboard.

At first sight, these are all removal verbs,[14] in which you remove a thing from a location – and *brush, clear, dislodge, extract, mop, steal, sweep, steal* and so on superficially behave in the same way.

But differences can be spotted almost immediately:

Doug *cleaned* the bath.
Kay *wiped* the wall.
Augustus *stole* the cupboard!!

Clean and *wipe* can be followed directly by the location, without altering the basic meaning. But *steal* is different. So as a first step, *clean* and *wipe* verbs need to be separated from *steal* verbs.

But *clean* and *wipe* also differ:

Doug *cleaned* the bath: The bath was *clean*.
Kay *wiped* the wall: *The wall was *wipe*.

A hunt through the lexicon shows that *clean*-type verbs fit with verbs such as *open*, *shut*, *cool*, *warm*: they are basically change-of-state verbs, as in:

Meg *warmed* the soup: The soup was *warm*.
Sandy *shut* the door: The door was *shut*.

Wipe verbs, on the other hand, fit in with *brush*, *polish*, *rub*, *spread*. They describe surface contact through movement, as in:

Pam *rubbed* the ointment onto her leg.
Peter *wiped* the oil over the baby's chest.

To conclude, of the three verbs we started with, only *steal* verbs are true removal verbs – although *wipe* verbs and *clean* verbs sometimes masquerade as removal verbs (figure 10.2).

		A X *from* Y	B location	C change of state	D movement
change of state	*clean*	✓	✓	✓	✗
contact via movement	*wipe*	✓	✓	✗	✓
removal	*steal*	✓	✗	✗	✗

A. Doug *cleaned* the mud from the bath.

B. Doug *cleaned* the bath.

C. The bath was *clean*.

D. Pete *wiped* oil over the baby's chest.

Figure 10.2   Removal verbs and pseudo-removal verbs

Many verbs, it seems, acquire extended meanings, and take on the behaviour appropriate to another verb clump. From the point of view of the mental lexicon, it's important to identify not only valid groups of verbs, but also how these groups can affect one another, since 'knowledge of possible extended senses and the factors that licence them are an important part of the lexical knowledge of a speaker of English.'[15] Speakers, then, can often predict the link between verb syntax and verb meaning. Let us now go on to consider another aspect of this interaction.

Framing the Picture

The fashionable word *frame* is found in several overlapping senses, the most widespread being a set of slots into which varying values are inserted. Frames provide an outline, which humans adapt to fit different situations. A small amount of firm information forms the basis of a huge amount of on-the-spot creativity (chapter 6).

This concept can be extended to verbs, to show how semantic and syntactic information can be packaged together. Take the word *buy*.[16] It requires a buyer, goods and (optionally) a seller and a price, each with its own place in the sentence (figure 10.3). Verbs with related meanings are likely to have the same meaning slots, but in a different order (figure 10.4).

BUYER	*buy*	GOODS	(SELLER)	(PRICE)
subject		object	*from*	*for*
Angela	bought	the owl	from Pete	for $10
Eddy	bought	ten oranges		for £1
Penny	bought	a bicycle	from Stephen	

Figure 10.3   Buy frame

SELLER	*sell*	GOODS	(BUYER)	(PRICE)
subject		object	*to*	*for*
Pete	sold	the owl	to Angela	for $10
Stephen	sold	the bicycle	to Penny	

Figure 10.4   Sell frame

A whole 'commercial transaction' frame can therefore be set up.[17] A relatively simple outline with buyer, seller, goods, money and associated syntax can form the basis of an enormous number of different transactions, with further additions possible, such as the place of the transaction – at Harrods, at the market and so on (figure 10.5). And such frames may be valid across cultures.

VERB	BUYER	GOODS	SELLER	MONEY	PLACE
buy	subject	object	*from*	*for*	*at*
sell	*to*	object	*subject*	*for*	*at*
cost	i-object	subject	–	object	*at*
spend	subject	*on*	–	object	*at*

Figure 10.5 Commercial transaction frame

Or consider the *risk* frame.[18] Words such as *risk, threaten, endanger, gamble* all involve uncertainty about the future. At first sight, sorting out the associated roles is difficult, because of the variety involved. You can risk something valuable, risk harm or risk a deed:

VALUABLE: Pauline *risked her life*.
HARM: Alan *risked a bad cold*.
DEED: Angela *risked a phone-call*.

But on inspection, the same participants recur: RISK-TAKERS risk VALU-ABLES or HARM, for GAIN or a BENEFICIARY, by or through a DEED:

Pauline risked her job for a bottle of whisky.
Marion risked her life for her cat by climbing on the roof.
Alan risked a bad cold by jumping in the river.
Angela risked her mother's fury by staying out all night.

Other risk-taking verbs require similar participants, though not necessarily in the same order. A RISK-TAKER *endangers* a VALUABLE by or through a DEED:

Pamela *endangered* her health by drinking the water.

Or HARM *threatens* a VALUABLE:

Drought *threatened* the rice crop.

Or a VALUABLE may *be in danger* of HARM:

The castle *was in danger* of collapsing.

In short, a few participants are associated with a large number of different lexical items within a frame, though these may be arranged differently (figure 10.6).

	RISK–TAKER	VALUABLE/HARM	DEED	GAIN/ BENEFICIARY
risk	subject	object	*by*	*for*
endanger	subject	object	*by/through*	
threaten	object	subject		

Figure 10.6   Risk-taking frame

In the past, the importance of frames was not sufficiently recognized. But this is changing. Active research is in progress, and some dictionaries now include frame-type information.[19]

The links between meaning and syntax which we have looked at are fairly 'surfacey' ones. However, some may be more deep-seated, as outlined below.

Primitive Roles

Consider:

The windscreen (windshield) *shattered.*
The kangaroo *shattered* the windscreen with its feet.
The kangaroos's feet *shattered* the windscreen.

Or:

We *loaded* the kangaroos into the ambulance.
We *loaded* the ambulance with kangaroos.

Speed of comprehension suggests that people can easily handle the differing uses of verbs such as *shatter* and *load*,[20] but have much greater difficulty with pairs of sentences containing a homonym such as *pass*:

Bill *passed* the test to his great surprise.
Bill *passed* the test to his great friend.

This finding makes sense if, at some underlying level, speakers work with a set of deep semantic roles, such as AGENT 'the doer of the action', PATIENT 'the sufferer of the action', and so on.[21] Efficient handling of the shattered windscreen sentences could then be due to the windscreen having the same role, that of PATIENT in all of them.

The primary difficulty lies in deciding how many roles there could be. Some researchers propose dozens, others make a few go a long way. Some roles are fairly uncontroversial. For example, an AGENT has the capacity for voluntary action:

The cow ate the grass.

LOCATION specifies where something is found, and may include ownership:[22]

Peter clung to *the windowsill*.
The book belongs to *Alphonse* ('The book is at Alphonse').
Max kept a rabbit ('At Max is a rabbit').

GOAL expresses an arrival point:

Leonora put the carrots into *the saucepan*.
Mick received the message.
Pam sold her car to *Len*.

SOURCE handles the point of origin:

Tim fetched the suitcase from *the attic*.
Harry bought the bike from *Max*.

Such roles have been given various names, the most general being 'semantic roles' and the most fashionable 'thematic roles'. This last term was popularized by a pioneering researcher,[23] who argued that in every sentence there is a THEME, defined as the noun phrase which moves or is located:

Little Jack Horner sat in a corner.
The cow jumped over the moon.
The ship floated across the sea.
Bill floated *the boat* on the pond.
Alison posted *the letter*.

However, the sentences above reveal a major problem. How many roles can a noun phrase have? Is the cow jumping over the moon both a THEME and an AGENT? Some researchers say that only one role is allowed.[24] Others say that many noun phrases must have more than one.[25] Consider:

The bath *filled*.
The chimney *smoked*.

In the first, the bath is both the PATIENT and the GOAL. In the second, the chimney is both an ACTOR and a SOURCE. If noun phrases have more than one role, it becomes necessary to set up a hierarchy of roles, crucial ones and secondary ones, and to allow noun phrases to pick a role from each level of the hierarchy. How many roles there are, and the kind of layers they might be organized into, are still under discussion.

These arguments are interwoven with disputes about whether the roles are basically part of the syntax or the semantics, as in what can be called the 'Humpty Dumpty' problem. Let us consider this.

A Humpty-Dumpty Problem

> Humpty-Dumpty sat on a wall
> Humpty-Dumpty had a great fall.

This well-known children's rhyme hides a mystery. What caused Humpty-Dumpty to crash down from his wall? Did he intentionally jump, or accidentally fall? Either way, the result is the same: Humpty-Dumpty broke into pieces, and couldn't be mended. So perhaps it doesn't matter.

Linguistically, however, it matters a great deal. If Humpty-Dumpty jumped, he actively initiated the action of the verb. If he fell, he was an inactive sufferer. According to a recent theory, traditional intransitive verbs split into two types – a so-called split intransitivity hypothesis.[26] Active initiators are found with one type, inactive sufferers with the other.

ACTIVE INITIATOR: Humpty-Dumpty *jumped*.
INACTIVE SUFFERER: Humpty-Dumpty *fell*.

Some researchers suggest that the active versus inactive distinction might exist at a deep syntactic level. Down there, perhaps verbs such as *jump* have a subject, but no object, whereas verbs such as *fall* have an object, but no subject. The sentences could be analysed as:

Humpty-Dumpty jumped
        fell   Humpty-Dumpty

At the surface level, Humpty-Dumpty is moved into the subject position. The advantage of this suggestion is that it can be extended to explain the differing behaviour of verbs such as *shatter* in the kangaroo and windscreen sentences.

The Kangaroo shattered the windscreen.
The windscreen shattered.

In both sentences, the windscreen is the underlying object, which gets brought to the front in the surface structure:

> The kangaroo shattered the windscreen
> shattered the windscreen.

However, linguists argue as to whether these differences are part of the syntax or part of the semantics. Increasingly, people lean towards a semantic viewpoint.[27] And a further difficulty in the Humpty-Dumpty problem is finding tests to distinguish between active initiation and passive suffering, as with verbs such as *cough, sneeze, snore*.[28] And other verb complications will be outlined below.

Floating Ducks versus Burbling Brooks

The duck floated in the bath (intransitive, 1-place)
Marmaduke *floated the duck* in the bath (transitive, 2-place)

Many intransitive verbs (verbs without an object, sometimes called 1-place verbs) have a transitive counterpart (verb with an object, or 2-place verb), as in the *float* examples above. Consequently, many linguists assume that intransitives are basic, and that transitives come about because extra information about the person causing the action has been added.

But a problem arises. This transitive/intransitive pairing does not extend to all verbs. Take *bloom* or *burble*. These can only be intransitive, as in:

> The bluebells *bloomed*
> The brook *burbled*.

You can't say:

> *The gardener *bloomed the flowers*.
> *The pebbles *burbled the brook*.

Other verbs, such as *hit* or *crush*, can only be transitive:

> Tom *hit the wasp*
> Felicity *crushed the plum*

You can't say:

> *The wasp *hit*
> *The plum *crushed*.

In short, some intransitive verbs lack a transitive partner, and some transitive ones lack an intransitive. So the assumption that intransitives are basic, and that an agent is added to form a transitive does not work for all verbs.

Perhaps the *type* of cause is important, it's been suggested.[29] Perhaps *internally* caused verbs such as *bloom* or *burble* are inherently 1-place. No external agent causes the blooming or burbling. But *externally* caused verbs such as *hit* or *crush* may be inherently 2-place. These are cases when an external agent causes the hitting or crushing. Someone or something else has to be involved: an animate, intentional, volitional agent is required. Other examples are *murder*, *steal*, *remove* or verbs of creation such as *write*, *build*, *paint*.

But verbs such as *break*, *float* can on the surface be either intransitive or transitive:

> The window *broke*
> Alphonse *broke* the window

Yet windows do not normally break by themselves; somebody shatters them. *Break*-type verbs therefore seem intuitively to be more complex than *bloom*-type ones. They require hearers to understand that somebody must have caused the breaking. Perhaps these are really transitive verbs which have undergone a process of 'detransitivization'[30] – a solution which calls into question the 'standard' idea that all verbs are basically intransitive (figure 10.7).

INT. CAUSED 1-place	EXT. CAUSED 2-place → 1-place	EXT. CAUSED 2-place
bloom burble	break float	hit murder

Figure 10.7   Internally and externally caused verbs

But there's a problem: some verbs seem to be both internally and externally caused. Take 'The pipes *rusted*' and 'The salt water *rusted the pipes*.' In the first, the pipes have apparently rusted away by themselves. In the second, the pipes rusted due to a specific external cause. A study which looked at these verbs that are difficult to classify found that verbs such as *rust*, *erode* were mostly internally caused. But when they were externally caused, they had a few predictable causes, usually natural entities, such as water, wind or heat. This was in contrast to the vast body of primarily externally caused verbs, which had a very wide range of agents. In short, internal and external causation verbs differ significantly in the range of entities that appear as their transitive subjects. This was confirmed with both studies of linguistic corpora and psycholinguistic experiments.[31] It shows that verbs cannot be rigidly categorized; their meaning has to be taken into account as well.

Events

Attention to verbs has gone in waves. First, the verb's syntax attracted interest. Then, the relationship between the syntax and the semantics was the main focus. Recently, the semantics has become prominent, as the type of event described by the verb has come to the forefront, the verb's so-called *event structure*.

The children's grammar book mentioned at the beginning of the chapter claimed that verbs were used for what people *do*. Yet 'doing' best describes verbs which deal with a completed event, such as 'Peter *killed* the wasp.' Other verbs represent a state, as in: 'Pamela *sat* motionless,' others an ongoing activity, as in: 'Marigold *jumped up and down*.' These distinctions have been around for a long time.[32] Recently, the notion of 'event structure' – the overall label assigned to verbs when sorted by their type of meaning – has begun to be re-examined. Verbs have been classified into types, and also into sub-types – though the details are still under discussion.[33]

Summary

This chapter has looked at verbs. Verbs dominate a sentence and dictate its structure. There is an elusive link between meaning and syntax, and some verbs with similar meanings seem to behave in similar ways. An important but still unsolved problem is the nature of the primitive roles which may underlie verb–noun relationships. The chapter also looked at how different types of verb, in particular transitive and intransitive ones, might relate to one another.

The next chapter will consider whether words should be regarded as wholes or split into pieces.

11

Bits of Words
— The internal architecture of words —

Are your pillows a pain in the neck?
Are they lumpy, hard, or torn?
Are they full of old influenza germs?
Are the feathers thin and forlorn?
Bring 'em to us,
We do the trick;
Re-puff,
Replenish,
Re-curl,
Re-tick,
We return your pillows, spanned-and-spicked,
Re-puffed, replenished, re-curled, re-ticked.
　　　Ogden Nash, 'Any millenniums today, lady?'

From the point of view of internal architecture, there are two kinds of English words. On the one hand, there are words such as *owl*, *wallaby* or *giraffe*, which seem to exist as wholes. On the other hand, there are items such as *replenished*, *uncaring* and *disagreement*, which are internally complex, in that they can be divided into chunks which they share with other words. *Disagreement*, for example, can be split into three sections: a base *agree*, with a prefix *dis-* tacked on to the front and a suffix *-ment* attached to the end (figure 11.1). Each of these components figures in other words also, such as *disintegrate*, *agreeing*, *merriment*, and so can be categorized as a morpheme, which is sometimes defined as 'the smallest grammatical unit'.[1]

PREFIX	STEM	SUFFIX
dis-	*agree*	*-ment*

Figure 11.1　Bits of a word

Are these bits of words relevant to the mental lexicon? This is a matter which has been much discussed: 'A central question in the psychology of language is whether the mental lexicon – the dictionary in our heads – is a lexicon of words.'[2] Are words stored as single items ready for use? Or are they stored disassembled into morphemes, and then put together when needed, as some people have suggested?[3] And if they are disassembled, how does one find the word one wants? Would *disagreement* be listed under *dis-*, or under *agreement*, or under *agree*, or under all three? These are fundamental questions which need to be answered in order to understand how humans cope with words.

'Common sense' can provide the answer, according to some people. The common-sense viewpoint claims that if a prefix or suffix can be added on to a stem by a regular rule, then it is unlikely to be already attached in the lexicon: 'Regular variations are not matters for the lexicon, which should contain only idiosyncratic items.'[4] This may be a useful guideline for a written grammar, but it is not inevitably true of the mental lexicon, where a common-sense view of speech processing would allow us to argue either way.[5] On the one hand, listing each word separately puts a heavy load on human memory, especially when the forms are predictable by a regular rule. On the other hand, attaching suffixes each time they are needed adds considerably to the burden of 'on-line processing'. Since humans have so much to cope with when they speak, perhaps they minimize the amount of on-the-spot assemblage.

Of course, even if words are stored as wholes, humans are still likely, on consideration, to be able to analyse them into sections, just as a car-owner can recognize that her car engine has a number of different components when she peers under the bonnet (hood). The point at issue, then, is not whether humans *can* analyse words, but whether these words are normally stored in a disassembled state. This is the topic of this chapter.

Various Attachments

There may not be a blanket answer to the assemblage question: some morphemes may already be attached to stems, others not, depending on their type. Lines from Ogden Nash's poem 'The joyous malingerer' illustrate a fundamental distinction, that between *inflection* and *derivation*:

> If faced with washing up he never *gripes*,
> But simply drops more dishes than he *wipes* . . .
> Stove-wise he's the perpetual backward *learner*
> Who can't turn on or off the proper *burner* . . .
> He can, attempting to *replace* a fuse,
> Black out the coast from Boston to Newport News.

The words *gripes* and *wipes* at the end of the first two lines illustrate the process of inflection: an ending (in this case -*s*) adds extra information to an existing word (*gripe*, *wipe*) without fundamentally altering it. *Dishes* in the second line is another example, consisting of *dish* + plural ending.

Learner and *burner* at the end of the middle two lines exemplify derivation: a morpheme (in this case *-er*) is attached to an existing word (*learn*, *burn*), and the result is a new word. *Replace* in the next to last line is another example of derivation, though in this case via a prefix: *re-* is added to *place* to form a new word, *replace*.

For the most part it's fairly easy to distinguish inflection from derivation. A rough rule of thumb for telling them apart is that you can add inflectional endings after derivational ones, but not vice versa. You can say *comput-er-s* (derivational *-er*, then inflectional *-s*), but not *compute-s-er. You can say *comput-er-ize-ed* (derivational *-er* and *-ize*, then inflectional *-d*), but not **comput-er-ed-ize.*[6] This suggests that derivational endings may be more firmly attached than inflectional ones – as turns out to be the case. We will deal with the matter in the order indicated in figure 11.2: inflectional suffixes, then derivational prefixes, then derivational suffixes.

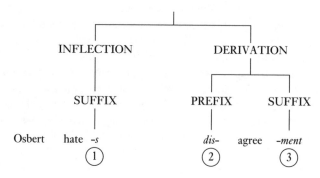

Figure 11.2　Inflection and derivation

Wash Upping the Dishes

An amalgam of smallish clues suggests that inflectional suffixes are quite often added on in the course of speech. First, consider slips of the tongue, as in the following:

> He *go backs* (he goes back).
> They *point outed* (pointed out).
> She *wash upped* the dishes (washed up).
> She *come backs* tomorrow (comes back).
> Stop him *go offing* (going off) and doing that.
> I'd *forgot abouten* (forgotten about) doing that.

These tongue-slips provide strong evidence that at least some inflectional endings are added on as needed. The examples listed involve phrasal verbs – verbs which consist of more than one word, such as *pick up*, *go back*, *point out*. If endings were already attached, one would always get *picks up*, *goes back*, *points out*. But if the ending needs to be attached in the course of speech, then it is quite probable that someone in a hurry might accidentally attach it at the end of the whole sequence, and say things such as *pick ups*, *go backs*. Furthermore, since these slips sometimes produce non-existent words, such as *abouten*, *outed*, these cannot be examples of wrong lexical selection – they must be examples of an ending added in the wrong place.[7]

Care must be taken, incidentally, as to which kind of errors we use as evidence. Sometimes stems change places, resulting in wrongly attached suffixes, as in *It waits to pay* (It pays to wait), *I want to get a cash checked* (I want to get a check cashed).[8] But since this type of switch-over also occurs with unsuffixed words, as in *Fran Sanisco* (San Fransciso), *The scan is a Sundal sheet* (The *Sun* is a scandal sheet), the detachment of suffixes is in this case probably a late error, which occurred as the phrases were about to be uttered, rather than a misplacement of suffixes during the planning process.[9]

On-the-spot attachment of suffixes is also suggested by the occasional accidental regularization of irregular forms:

All the men who *fighted* in it (fought).

Further examples occur in the plurals of complex lexical items such as *mother-in-law*. Is the plural *mothers-in-law* or *mother-in-laws*? Some people are uncertain and fluctuate between the two. All these examples suggest that, at least in some cases, inflectional suffixes are added on when needed, rather than being already glued to words in the mental lexicon.

Some people with speech disorders provide additional support for the attachment of suffixes as speech proceeds, especially those aphasics who produce strings of words with very little syntax: 'Jar . . . cakes . . . head . . . face . . . water . . . tap' (chapter 9). In severe cases, the only inflectional endings found are in rote phrases, such as 'I don't know what happened,' or forms which are more usually plural, as in *arts*, *crafts*, *bircuits*. Such patients indicate that inflectional endings are usually added on in the process of speech production, apart from some common phrases or words which are habitually inflected.[10]

In another kind of aphasia, patients produce fluent speech, but have difficulties with both comprehension and word-finding. In their struggle to remember words, such patients sometimes utter non-existent ones. In chapter 1, a brain-damaged man was unable to remember the name for a box of matches: 'Waitresses. Waitrixies. A backland and another bank. For bandicks er bandiks I think they are, I believe they're zandicks, I'm sorry, but they're called flitters landocks.' He also talks about a *pidland* – possibly a telephone dial – and then comments, 'Each of the pidlands has an eye in, one two three and so on.' In these examples he appears to be putting plural -*s* on to nonsense words. Elsewhere, he adds on verb endings: 'She wikses a zen from me,' 'He mivs in a love-beautiful home.' The fluency with which he does this suggests that the addition of inflectional suffixes in something which he is used to coping with routinely – much as normal speakers easily add endings onto new words, as in *blanded out* 'became conformist', *fragranced* 'scented'.[11]

The inconsistent behaviour of some normal speakers points to a similar conclusion. For example, teenagers in Reading frequently attach a non-standard *-s* to verbs which are typical of their subculture, as in the sentences below:[12]

> We fucking *chins* (hit on the chin) them with bottles.
> I *legs* it (run away) up Blagdon Hill.
> We *kills* (beat in a fight) them.

They also attach this *-s* to other verbs, but not so often, and they do this more often in casual than in formal speech. This suggests that *-s* is variably added most of the time, but there may be a few verbs to which it is already firmly attached in the mental lexicon.

A number of experimental psychologists have come to the conclusion that regular inflections are added in the course of speech.[13] Several experiments have found that prior exposure to a regularly inflected form of a word such as *jumps* appeared to speed up recognition time of the base *jump* as much as prior presentation of the word itself.[14] Irregular forms of the same verb, such as *hung* and *hang*, did not produce the same effect. The experimenters interpreted the result as indicating that *jumps* and *jump* led subjects to the same lexical entry *jump*. This particular type of experiment is controversial, and the reverse result was found by another group of researchers.[15] But overall the results support the other pieces of evidence. All indicate that regular inflectional suffixes are commonly attached as speech proceeds, whereas irregular forms are fully listed. And other experimenters have come to a similar conclusion.[16]

Our general conclusion, then, is that regular inflections are mostly added to words as we speak. However, they may already be attached to a few words used commonly in their inflected form, such as *peas*, *eyes*, *happened*, *needed*, having become welded on over the years. Humans develop routines for common procedures which gradually become automatic, and adding on frequently used inflectional suffixes probably comes into this category of behaviour.[17]

Let us now move on to prefixes – noting also that the conclusions reached so far may relate only to English.

The *Pertoire Question

Suppose, in a lexical decision task, you found that the non-word **pertoire* was rejected faster than the non-word **juvenate*, what would you conclude? **pertoire* was dismissed fast because there was no sign of it in the mental lexicon, according to the researchers who reported the finding.[18] People did not link it up with *repertoire*, since the *re* in this word is not a proper prefix. But **juvenate* was rejected slowly, because it actually existed as an entry, though with a small re- attached under it, showing that it could not be used without a prefix. The time taken to read through the entry slowed down reaction time. According to this view, words are entered in the mental lexicon in their stem form, with the prefixes stripped off, and listed underneath the relevant stems:

JUVENATE   PLENISH
RE-   RE-

And this conclusion seemed to be supported by other experiments.[19] In the first of these, it took subjects longer to recognize 'pseudo-prefixed' words – words such as *precipice* which look as if they have a prefix but do not in fact do so – than either prefixed words or unprefixed words. Perhaps hearers mistakenly think that such words are prefixed, and so strip away the pseudo-prefix and look for a non-existent lexical entry under its presumed stem. So *precipice* would take a long time to find, because the subjects mistakenly spend time searching under **cipice*. The experimenter concluded: 'In summary, then, from the finding that pseudo-prefixed words are indiscriminately treated as prefixed words, it can be concluded that prefix stripping occurs in word recognition, and this, in turn, implies that prefixed words are accessed through a representation of their stem.'[20]

This claim is superficially supported by some slips of the tongue, such as *constraint* for 'restraint', *advice* for 'device'.[21] But the idea set off a major controversy, which has rumbled on for years, as to how firmly affixes (prefixes and suffixes) are attached.[22]

There are a number of criticisms which can be levelled at these findings. In the first experiment, **juvenate* is very like *juvenile*, so the presence of the entry for *juvenile* might have slowed down reaction time. The main stress has been stripped off in *(re)pertoire*, but not in *(re)juvenate*. Subjects may have adopted artificial strategies to deal with this rather strange task.[23] Above all, the experiment used written words, so perhaps did not reveal anything about the way spoken words are stored. The definition of a prefix was also unclear. At its broadest, a prefix can be defined as a recurring sequence which is attached to different stems: for example, *con-* and *de-* would count as prefixes on the basis of words such as *confer, defer, conduct, deduct, contain, detain* – but this may be too wide a definition.

In answer to the 'prefix strippers', proponents of 'ready-made' words put forward a number of counter-claims. In cases such as *con-* and *de-* there is no consistency in the meanings of either prefixes or stems.[24] There is no discernible semantic link between *con-* in *consume, confer, conceive, condemn*, and there is no obvious connection between the various occurrences of *-fer* in *confer, defer, infer, prefer, refer*, unless you happen to know Latin. It is therefore most unlikely that such 'prefixes' are stored separately from their stems. If words were really stored in arbitrary fragments, one would expect there to be far more confusion than in fact exists, with wrong assemblies such as **desume* or **dedemn* as a common phenomenon. In fact, even apparently meaningful prefixes sometimes resist detachment from their base: *uncanny* and *uncouth* do not mean *non-canny* and *non-couth*.

Slips of the tongue confirm that *con*-type 'prefixes' are glued to their stems, because they are freely interchanged with unprefixed words:[25]

The emperor had many *porcupines* (concubines).
Those lovely blue flowers – *concubines* (columbines).

Con-type prefixes also preserve their beginnings as often as unprefixed words in speech errors,[26] something which one would not expect if prefixes were easily removable: 'He's a very *combative*, I mean, *competitive* man.' The same is true in word searches, as in the following rooting around by someone who was mildly drunk: 'I met a man at the party who said he'd written an article on the IRA, on its *contemplation*, no *combination*, I think I mean its *construction*, not quite, it's something like *consistency* or *constitution*, it's make-up, ah, *composition*!' These findings suggest that the prefix is an aid in remembering the word, not an appendage to be added later.

The strong attachment of such 'prefixes' is confirmed by a 'gating' experiment, using a technique which chops off increasing portions of a word until a 'recognition point' is reached. The researchers concluded that hearers recognized words long before they had heard all of the stem.[27]

How, then, are we to account for examples such as *advice* for 'device'? When the overall context is examined, it turns out that many of them are blends:[28]

I don't *expose* (expect + suppose) anyone will eat that.
At the moment of *compact* (impact + collision).
Plastic bags are *dispendable* (disposable + expendable).
The numbers aren't *consequential* (consecutive + sequential).

Most of those that are not obviously blends have unstressed prefixes, as in a most *extinguished* (distinguished) professor, suggesting that unstressed syllables are less prominent in storage, and perhaps cannot be retrieved as fast as stressed ones (to be discussed in chapter 12).

All this suggests that prefixes and stems are epoxied together in the mental lexicon, at least when stems obligatorily require a prefix, as in *rejuvenate*.

It is more difficult to decide in cases where a prefix with a clear meaning is attached to an otherwise independent word, as with *happy* and *unhappy*, though one suspects that the prefix is already added for common words – otherwise there would be far more cases of wrong attachment, such as **dishappy*, **non-happy*. Speakers are undoubtedly aware of the joins in such words, and they can often use this knowledge to detach elements in order to coin new words, as in 'I wish I could *unsay* that'. This ability will be discussed in chapter 15.

Prefixes, then, are normally attached to stems. But what about suffixes? There are many more of these in English, a language which like many others prefers suffixes to prefixes.[29] There is therefore no reason to expect them to behave identically in the minds of speakers.

Reproductive Furniture

It is possible that most individual and international social and economic *collisions*,
Result from humanity's being divided into two main *divisions*.
Their lives are spent in mutual *interference*,
And yet you cannot tell them apart by their outward *appearance*.

These four lines from Ogden Nash's poem 'Are you a Snodgrass?' encapsulate the problem of derivational suffixes. In a large number of cases, a derived form can be related to a more basic one, from which it was originally formed, as in the words at the end of each line: so *collision* was formed from *collide*, *division* from *divide*, *interference* from *interfere*, and *appearance* from *appear*. Some people regard this as a purely historical fact, of no relevance to the production of speech.[30] Others assume that these words are reassembled each time we use them: they claim that we store a base form of a word such as *appear* with an extra note about the possible suffix *-ance* and how to attach it.[31] Let us consider these points of view.

The lumping together of different types of suffixes is a problem in many studies. Some suffixes, such as *-ity* and *-al*, affect their stems fairly radically, as in *sanity*, *industrial*. Others, such as *-ness* or *-ism* have little effect, as in *goodness*, *alcoholism*. The difference between these types is sometimes indicated by using a plus (+) for *-ity*-type suffixes: *sane + ity*, *industry + al*, and a 'hash' (#) for *-ness*-type ones: *good # ness*, *alcohol # ism*.[32]

Plus-type suffixes are glued firmly onto their stems.[33] This is particularly clear for 'baseless derivatives', words such as *perdition*, *conflagration*, *probity* which have no base from which they could have been formed. In addition, the meaning link between a base and its derived form is often unpredictable, as in *comprehend/ comprehensive*, *revolve/ revolution*, *succeed/ succession*. And words with similar stems are fairly idiosyncratic as to which suffixes they allow: we find *induce*, *inducement* and *induction*, but *produce* and *production* only, with a gap where **producement* might have existed. These examples indicate the chaotic nature of the relationship between stem and suffix. This would make dismembered words extraordinarily difficult to remember. Words are therefore likely to be stored as wholes.

These observations are supported by slips of the tongue. In malapropisms (similar-sound errors), plus-type suffixes are usually maintained, as in *provisional* for 'provincial', *detergent* for 'deterrent', especially in long words.[34] Preservation of the end of the word occurs more often in suffixed words than in those without a suffix. Indeed, sometimes the suffix alone survives intact:

He has a terrible speech *predicament* (impediment).
She goes in for *pornographic* (hydroponic) gardening.

And when the suffix is changed, other portions of the word are usually changed as well, as in *malicious* for 'malignant', *prostitute* for 'protestant'. In a study of six common suffixes in a collection of malapropisms, the suffix was maintained in well over three-quarters of them. Out of nearly 200 errors, there were only eight examples of 'pure' suffix change[35] – cases in which only the suffix was altered and the rest of the word was retained, as in *reproductive furniture* for 'reproduction furniture', *indulgement* for 'indulgence', *industrial* for 'industrious'.

The sporadic cases of pure suffix error seemed to have three main causes. The first, as with prefix errors, is blending:

> It might be fun to *speculise* (speculate + surmise).
> It's a *contential* (contentious + controversial) matter.

The second reason is 'derailment' – cases where a speaker starts on a word, but, by not paying attention, gets 'derailed' onto another, more common word, just as someone who walks into the kitchen might, without thinking, put a kettle on to boil, even though she actually went into the kitchen for some quite different reason, perhaps as in: 'Bees are very *industrial* (industrious).' A final reason for wrong suffixes is the use of a fall-back procedure. If people cannot think of the word they want, they know methods of producing new ones, which might in any case produce the word they cannot think of, though sometimes it results in an error: 'Children use *deduceful* (deductive) rules.' Here, the speaker has temporarily forgotten the relevant word, and has attempted to recreate it afresh from its verb. Possibly 'speakers obtain lexical items by [at least] two distinct methods, either by finding them in the lexicon directly, or by building new items from existing bases . . . they pursue these two course simultaneously.'[36]

The arbitrary links between bases and suffixes and the preservation of suffixes in malapropisms suggest that words are entered into the mental lexicon as wholes, not as bits – though the evidence is less clear with hash-type suffixes such as *-ness*.[37] They are probably firmly fixed in common words, otherwise there might be far more errors, such as **goodism* instead of *goodness*. But, as with prefixes, speakers can see the joins and detach plus-type suffixes in order to create new words, as will be discussed in chapter 15.

So far, experimental evidence on this point has not been mentioned. Unfortunately, experiments which have tried to examine this question are somewhat inconclusive,[38] partly because they have failed to distinguish between different languages, different suffix types and differences in frequency of use.

On the whole, experiments have shown three facts: first, findings on English do not necessarily generalize to other languages, or vice versa. Second, in English, it does not take any longer to recognize a word with a derivational suffix such as *dust + y* than a word without, such as *fancy*.[39] This is a firm finding, because the experiment was repeated by other researchers after a gap of ten years with words ending in *-er*, such as *baker* 'someone who bakes', analysed as *bake + er*, and unsplittable words such as *timber* and *shoulder*.[40] These experiments support the 'whole words' view, though the devisers of the *baker* experiment point out a problem: since humans recognize words before they get to the end (chapter 1), the effect of a suffix might be unmeasurable.

A third finding is that people can split words up if they need to – something which may happen, but is not inevitable. When asked to judge whether two sequences were both words, it took longer if one was suffixed and the other not, as with *printer* and *slander*.[41] This slightly complicated task probably led subjects to attempt to disassemble them.

It seems clear, then, that people can decompose words into morphemes if they need to. They use this ability as a back-up procedure in order to construct a complex word if their normal memory for the word fails them, or if they are asked to perform a complex task. It is also probable that they disassemble a word if they are faced with a long, complicated one, whose meaning they are not quite sure about.

Alternatively, massive parallel processing may be the norm. Humans may automatically handle words on more levels than one at the same time.[42] They may subconsciously both deal with the word as a whole *and* split it up as they go along. If so, the back-up information is always there, whether they need it or not. Let us now consider how this back-up information might be stored.

Back-up Information

One possibility is that extra back-up information is kept (metaphorically) in a secondary store, attached to the lexicon proper. A human may be like a shopkeeper who keeps extra information about goods in a back room. Words which can be split up are linked to others with similar make-up, and this may involve a subsidiary network, attached perhaps between the 'lexicon proper' and the 'lexical tool-kit' – the procedures for making new words.

Some of the links in this subsidiary network are strong, others weak. Some are perhaps non-existent until the need to split up a particular word arises. The human mind is able to analyse and match elements continuously, as speech is processed. So it will automatically be reaffirming old links and creating new ones in the course of speech, and using the back-up information to do this. Words previously unanalysed will be moved into the back-up store as links with existing words are recognized. For example, it is quite possible to find adults who are unaware that the word *Plymouth* means 'at the mouth of the river Plym', even though they may have correctly analysed *Dartmouth* and *Exmouth* as towns at the mouths of the Dart and the Exe. When they come across the River Plym, perhaps on a map, *Plymouth* is moved to the back-up store (figure 11.3).

These back-up links are revised continuously. At a later stage, information from the back-up store may be incorporated into a firm 'rule' about how to form new words. We are dealing, therefore, with a triple process involving look-up (whole words), back-up store (words analysed into their component morphemes), and a lexical tool-kit (for making new words, to be discussed in chapter 15).[43]

Above all, this chapter has shown that the make-up of words is not a simple matter. And that it is essential to distinguish how people *store* words, sometimes known as

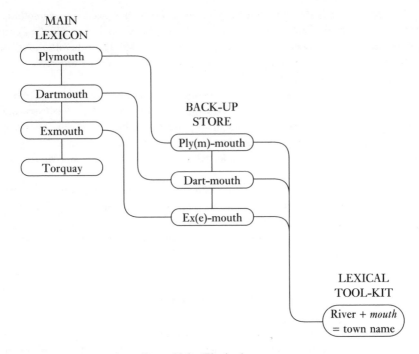

Figure 11.3   The back-up store

their *linguistic representation*, from how they retrieve that information when they are making use of that word, sometimes known as the *access representation*.[44]

But if words are stored as words, this means that people sometimes have to deal with quite long sequences. How then is their sound structure represented in the mental lexicon? This is the topic of the next chapter.

Summary

In this chapter we discussed whether the mental lexicon contained words or bits of words which have to be assembled when required. We concluded that inflectional suffixes are commonly added as needed in the course of speech, but that derivational prefixes and suffixes are already attached to their stems. However, even though words are already assembled in the main section of the mental lexicon, speakers can, if necessary, disassemble them, by using a back-up store attached to the 'lexical tool-kit', the procedures for making new words.

Meanwhile, we next need to discuss how the sound structure of words is stored in the mental lexicon.

12

Taking Care of the Sounds
— Dealing with the sound patterns —

'Ah, well! . . .' said the Duchess, digging her sharp little chin into Alice's shoulder . . . 'the moral of that is – "Take care of the sense and the sounds will take care of themselves".'

'How fond she is of finding morals in things!' Alice thought to herself.

Lewis Carroll, *Alice in Wonderland*

Most of us hope that if we think of the meaning of the word we want, then the sounds will take care of themselves by following immediately, like a train attached to an engine. This happens most of the time, but not always. This chapter considers how humans cope with the sound structure of words. In particular, what is an entry like in the mental lexicon from the point of view of sounds? And how are the various items organized in relation to one another?

For a printed dictionary, these questions could be answered quite straightforwardly by saying that each word consists of a sequence of units known as letters, and that all words are listed in alphabetical order, a conventional but arbitrary arrangement. As far as the mental lexicon is concerned, the answer is unlikely to be so simple, even though, at a superficial level, it is possible to characterize each word as a row of sound segments or phonemes, of which English has around 40. Speakers must subconsciously be aware of these: they know, for example, that [r] and [l] are different English sounds, because they distinguish words which are otherwise the same, such as *rid* and *lid*, or *rook* and *look* – though this is a distinction not made by some other languages, such as Japanese.[1]

Furthermore, each language has its own rules for permitted phoneme sequences: for example, English does not allow the combination [pt] at the beginning of a word, though this is common in ancient Greek, as shown by the spelling of borrowed words such as *pterodactyl*. Speakers subconsciously know these sequencing rules, since they can for the most part reliably judge if a nonsense word is a possible word, such as *scrad*, or an impossible one, such as **ptad*.[2]

However, the observation that humans 'know' the phonemes and phoneme sequences of their language does not necessarily imply that lexical entries are just a string of phonemes, all given equal value, like coaches on a train, especially as each English word has its own stress pattern, which intermeshes with the sounds. And compared with the entries in a written dictionary, words turn out to be stored somewhat unevenly, with some parts more prominent than others.

The Bathtub Effect

The 'bathtub effect' (my term) is perhaps the most commonly reported finding in the literature on memory for words. People remember the beginnings and ends of words better than the middles, as if the word were a person lying in a bathtub, with their head out of the water at one end and their feet out at the other. And, just as in a bathtub the head is further out of the water and more prominent than the feet, so the beginnings of words are, on average, better remembered than the ends (figure 12.1).

an_ _ _ _ _ _dote

Figure 12.1   The bathtub effect

The importance of beginnings and endings was first pointed out over 20 years ago by two Harvard psychologists.[3] As noted in chapter 2, they tried to induce a 'tip of the tongue' (TOT) state by reading out definitions of relatively uncommon words to around 50 students. This procedure resulted in over 200 'positive TOTs', situations in which the subjects, on later being told the target, claimed that it was the one they had in mind. The psychologists quizzed those in a TOT state about other items which came to mind in their search, and found a clear bathtub effect when the words judged to be similar-sounding – such as *sarong, Siam, sympoon* for 'sampan' – were matched against the target. This was not due to chance, since the effect was not repeated for similar-meaning words such as *houseboat, junk*,

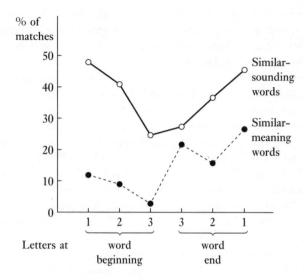

Figure 12.2 Similar-sounding versus similar-meaning words
(From Brown and McNeill, 1966)

for 'sampan' (figure 12.2). And the observation that people tend to recall the beginnings and to a lesser extent the ends of words they cannot otherwise remember has been confirmed by other researchers.[4]

In malapropisms – cases in which a similar-sounding word has been wrongly selected, as in *cylinders* for 'syllables', *anecdote* for 'antidote', *facilities* for 'faculties' – the effect is even stronger. The same bathtub-shaped curve was found in a study of around 200 errors involving numerous common words, such as *goof* for 'golf', *my* for 'me', *psychotic* for 'psychological',[5] which showed that the phenomenon did not relate only to low-frequency words. The data in subsequent studies showed over 80 per cent of word initial sounds and over 70 per cent of word endings as either identical or very similar to the target. The middles, however, do not show such a high level of agreement.[6]

Length of words has some influence in the bathtub. In a collection of almost 500 malapropisms, the initials of short words were marginally better remembered than those of long words, and memory for the ends of long words was considerably better than that for the ends of short words.[7]

	INITIAL CONSONANTS	· FINAL CONSONANTS
SHORT (1–2 syllables)	86%	70%
LONG (3 or more syllables)	82%	82%

The bathtub effect, then, suggests that particularly the beginnings of words, and to a lesser extent the ends, are prominent in storage. The effect is not just due to 'selective attention', paying attention to particular parts of the word when all sections are stored as equal, because words that get confused in memory show similar characteristics. When people forget the difference between two words and merge them in their mind, these items usually have similar beginnings and endings. A large proportion of the entries in a book of 'confusibles'[8] begin and end with the same sound, as in *flaunt/flout, fluorescent/phosphorescent, hydrometer/hygrometer, prodigy/progeny, hysterics/histrionics.*

How far along the word does the bathtub effect extend at each end? The bathtub starts sloping down almost immediately, it seems. In a study of around 500 TOT guesses,[9] the beginning phoneme was recalled in 51 per cent of cases, and the final in 35 per cent. Taking pairs of phonemes, the first two and the last two were each recalled 19 per cent of the time. Beyond this, the near misses had more segments in common with their targets than could be expected by chance, though these were not necessarily in the same order. The chunks remembered at the beginning and end did not correspond with either morphemes or syllables: CV (consonant + vowel) sequences tended to be remembered at the beginning of a word, and VC sequences at the end, as in *binomial* for 'bimodal', *rebuttal* for 'retrieval'. Vowels, it seemed, attached themselves either to consonants in front of them or to ones after them: 'Vowels are the swingers of the phonetic world.'[10]

Beginnings and ends of words, then, seem more prominent in storage, and are more likely to be remembered than other sections of the word which one might expect to be prominent, such as stressed vowels. Stressed vowels are moderately well recalled in short words, but match their target in fewer than 60 per cent of long words, according to one study of malapropisms.[11] In another, stressed vowels matched their target in 65 per cent of words, a retention rate that was less good than the first vowel in the word, after the elimination of cases in which the stressed vowel and the first vowel coincided.[12]

The bathtub effect relates to sequences of sounds. But words are a complicated amalgam of sounds and rhythm. Let us now consider how these two facets of a word are integrated.

The Skeleton Underneath

A word can be likened to a body: flesh (the sounds) covers an underlying skeleton which gives it its shape.

A basic feature of the skeleton is the number of syllables. TOT experiments show that people have a reasonable knowledge of word length when they try to recall words. When subjects were asked to make explicit guesses about the number of syllables in their unremembered words, they were correct more than half the time.[13] The percentage guessed correctly was the same as for guesses about initial consonants (57 per cent), though with syllables there are fewer possibilities to choose from. However, this figure is still considerably above the chance level, which is around 25 per cent.

Malapropisms – similar-sounding words – showed an even higher rate, though there is some disagreement between researchers over exact figures.[14] This is perhaps because shorter words retain the number of syllables better than longer ones, and the studies may have included different-length words. Interestingly, shorter words tend to get lengthened, and longer ones to get shortened, when syllable length is misremembered, and this happens in both TOTs and malapropisms. People were likely to remember both two- and four-syllable words as having three syllables, whereas three-syllable words move in either direction.[15]

However, a straight count of syllables is probably less important than the rhythmic pattern of the words. In spite of minor disagreements over the recall of the number of syllables, all studies agree that there is a close relationship between syllables and rhythmic pattern.

Figure 12.3   A rhythmic wave pattern

A word may be viewed as a complex wave formation, a series of peaks and troughs, with the most stressed syllable having the highest peak, and the weakest the lowest trough. Each syllable differs in strength, as shown by the number of asterisks assigned to it (figure 12.3). The strongest syllable has the greatest number of asterisks, and the weakest has the least – though this is relative. The relationship of strength between the various syllables is more important than the exact amount of stress on each one. A diagram showing the basic rhythmic pattern of strong and weak syllables is known as a 'metrical grid', though it is normally found with the asterisks underneath in linguistics texts[16] (see figure 12.4). Sometimes too people leave the weakest syllable unmarked, which reduces the number by one all along.

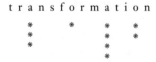

Figure 12.4   A metrical grid

More usually, however, the rhythmic pattern is represented by means of a diagram like an upside-down branching tree. This 'metrical tree' reveals the internal structure of the word clearly. It shows how syllables combine to form larger units, sometimes called 'feet', which in turn build up into words. The stronger branches on the trees are labelled S (strong) and the weaker ones W (weak). By

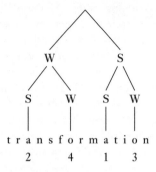

Figure 12.5   A metrical tree

following a syllable up through the various nodes – points at which branches join – it is possible to see the relative strengths of the different syllables (figure 12.5). (1) is the strongest (an S under another S), (2) is the next strongest (an S under a W), (3) comes next (W under S), and (4) is the weakest (W under W). The number underneath any particular syllable shows how strong or weak it is in relation to the others.

The exact way in which trees should be drawn is still under discussion.[17] Also under discussion are the 'rules' which specify how the rhythm alters when words come into contact: *hot*, *water* and *cylinder* will be rather different when they come together in *hot-water cylinder* than when they are pronounced separately.

However, in spite of minor differences, all researchers agree on one thing: that English words have a basic rhythm of alternating strong and weak syllables, and that this must be specified in the mental lexicon. As already noted, the exact amount of stress given to each syllable is irrelevant. The important point is the relationship of strong to weak along the whole length of the word.

The importance of metrical trees is shown by malapropisms. When they maintain the number of syllables, then they also retain the metrical structure, as in:

What are you *incinerating* (insinuating)?
Try *permeating* (permutating) the elements.

If a malapropism departs from this pattern, then a weak branch, an unstressed syllable, is liable to disappear, as in:

You need a *translation* (transformation).
The secret police *liquidized* (liquidated) him.

Sometimes also a weak syllable gets inserted, as in:

A *tactical* (tactful) person.
He was *castigated* (castrated).

Unstressed syllables, therefore, fade away easily, and get inserted easily.

Weak branches can cause problems even at the beginning of words – even though sounds in this position are normally recalled best of all. The biggest single category of word initial errors comprises those with unstressed first syllables, as in *fire distinguisher* (extinguisher), *a touch of vagina* (angina).[18] Meanwhile, middle sequences are better remembered if they involve the stressed syllable.[19]

A general rhythmic pattern appears to be tattooed onto speakers' minds, with the weakest syllables being the least well marked. This pattern is interwoven with the sound sequence, as shown by the errors in unstressed initial syllables. Indeed, one researcher who looked at the interaction between word shape errors and segmental errors commented: 'In general, an error at one level leads automatically to an error at the other.'[20] In addition, certain vowels tend to be stressed. For example, diphthongs – gliding vowels which slide from one vowel to another, such as *oi* in *ointment* – are almost always strong. If rhythm and segments were independent, one would not expect them to intermesh in this way. The rhythmic pattern and the segments are therefore intertwined, much in the way that flesh and bones are inextricably intermeshed in a body.

Our general conclusion so far is that certain outline features of a word are more prominent in storage than others, and that these are a mixture of word shape and segments. Above all, the beginning, to a lesser extent the end, and the general rhythmic pattern are salient, and people home in on these when they are selecting a word. This finding relates not only to normal speakers, but also to aphasics, who are able to make better than chance guesses about word beginnings and number of syllables,[21] though some types of aphasics do better than others.[22] Let us now look at another aspect of this rhythm and sound intermeshing, the structure of syllables.

Ducks and Bucks

Many syllables have a beginning, a middle containing the vowel, and an ending – sometimes called the onset, the peak and the coda, as in *fog* f-o-g, and *scratch* scr-a-tch. But these three portions do not behave like clothes spaced out on a clothes-line. Syllables may have their own internal structure, with some parts clinging together more closely than others.

Consider the speech errors *ducks* (dollars + bucks) and *shell* (shout + yell). Blends – two words which have been merged into one – usually share at least one sound, as in *tumber* (timber + lumber). But when they do not, breaks within syllables occur more often before the vowel than after it:[23]

D	ollars	SH	out
b	UCKS	y	ELL

This finding has been confirmed experimentally: a group of college students were given two made-up words, *krint* and *glupth*, and taught various ways of blending them. They found it easier to split the nonsense words before the vowel, making blends such as *krupth* or *glint*, rather than after it as in *kripth* or *glunt*. The researcher concluded: 'In tasks that require the active analysis of spoken syllables into smaller units and the manipulation of these units, people most readily divide syllables between the initial consonant or consonant cluster and the vowel.'[24] And this was also true when subjects unintentionally blended words in a word-learning experiment.

Spontaneous word games show a similar tendency: *Ets-lay alk-tay ig-pay atin-lay* sounds superficially like gibberish. But to many schoolchildren, it makes perfect sense, meaning: 'Let's talk Pig-Latin.' The first sound of each word has been removed, and attached to the end, together with the ending -*ay*, allowing schoolchildren to talk freely to each other without anyone else understanding – or so they hope.

These findings support the observations of linguists that there is a division between the onset and the remainder, sometimes known as the rhyme, in that there are very few restrictions between the onset and the vowel which follows, but quite a lot between the vowel and the consonants after it.[25] A beginning sequence of three consonants such as *str-* can precede almost any vowel, as in *strangle*, *strength*, *string*, *strong*, *strung*, *stroke*, *streak*, *strain* and so on. But there are restrictions on which vowels can precede a final clump of three consonants: English has a word *strength* but not **streength*, *glimpse* but not **gleemps*, *thinks* but not **thoonks*, and so on.

Subconsciously then, English syllables seem to be split into the onset and the remainder (figure 12.6). However, the rhyme is not always firmly glued together:

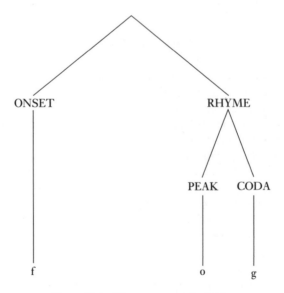

Figure 12.6   The structure of syllables

the extent to which the consonants at the end cling to the vowel depends on their type. [l] holds on tightly, so does [r] in American English. But other consonants are more easily detachable.[26]

Another problem, not fully solved, is where the syllable division comes. In a word such as *asparagus*, is it a-sparagus? Or as-paragus? Is *petrol* split as pe-trol or petr-ol? Or could *sp* and *tr* belong to both the first and second syllable? Different researchers give different answers,[27] perhaps because humans are themselves inconsistent.

Syllables, then, have their own structure, with some parts more closely associated than others. But there is another type of closeness which needs to be considered, the similarity of some sounds to others.

Natural Clusters

Just as A and B are near together in a book dictionary, so certain sounds are treated as close in people's minds – even though they need not be spatially close, just hooked up with strong connections. In slips of the tongue, certain errors recur more often than chance would allow, such as *par cark* for 'car park', indicating that the mind treats some sounds as similar to one another.

So far, sounds have been likened to flesh covering a rhythmic skeleton. But in some ways, they are more like clothes than flesh, in that, like garments, they fall into certain categories. Just as shirts and blouses fall together as opposed to jeans and shorts, so particular sounds can be grouped into 'natural classes'.[28] They are clumped together partly because they behave similarly, and partly because they share objective phonetic similarities. For example, [p], [t] and [k] are all pronounced with aspiration – a small puff of breath – at the beginning of English words, and they also have shared phonetic characteristics, such as late vibration of the vocal cords.

When malapropisms differ by only one segment from the target, these segments often come from the same natural class:

My *brain* (drain) is clogged.
A religious *profession* (procession).
Transcendental *medication* (meditation).

One study analysed the point at which malapropisms diverged from their targets, starting from the beginning of the word.[29] Almost half the malapropisms studied turned out to veer off onto a sound from the same natural class.

A natural clumping principle in the mental lexicon therefore replaces the arbitrary alphabetical system of a printed lexicon. The exact workings of this are unclear.[30] There is no overall agreement on how to categorize each sound, because the natural classes overlap. Sounds may therefore fall into more than one category. So [p] shares some characteristics with [b], others with [t], and others with [f].

Each segment can be regarded as having a composite structure. A few people have therefore suggested that the mental lexicon might store them disassembled, and gather them together as required.[31] This is somewhat unlikely. If segments had to be fitted together from a heap of components or 'features', one would expect numerous examples of incompetent bundling together, as in *tebestrian* for 'pedestrian', where a component of [p] has changed place with one belonging to [d]. In fact, such errors are extremely rare, and after extensive searching, two researchers concluded that 'features are not independent movable entities.'[32] Splitting sounds up into components is undoubtedly a useful descriptive device, a convenient way of characterizing similarities and differences between segments. But it is not the way in which sounds are dealt with in the mental lexicon, where whole segments only seem to be the rule.

Network Structure

In general, words which have similar beginnings, similar endings and similar rhythm are likely to be tightly bonded. 'Similar' in this context means either identical or coming from the same natural class. Words seem to be grouped in clumps rather than in a list, suggesting that, once again, we are dealing with a network (figure 12.7). Those that are most alike will be closely linked, such as *antidote* and *anecdote*, *hydrometer* and *hygrometer*, *musician* and *magician*. These are particularly likely to get confused. Those that are slightly less similar will be somewhat more loosely linked, such as perhaps *specialization* and *specification*,

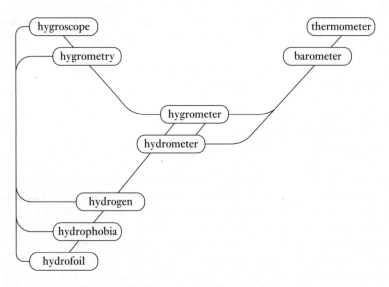

Figure 12.7   Network of similar-sounding words

tambourines and *trampolines*, *funicular* and *vernacular*, but still sufficiently near to get muddled up occasionally. As with other aspects of the lexicon, these links are not fixed and immutable. New ones are being created all the time, as existing words get shuffled into their place in the network, or as people get exposed to a new joke or rhyme in which they suddenly see a link between the sounds of words which they had not noticed before: '*Cleopatra*, Egypt's answer to *Montmartre*'.

These similar-sounding words sometimes aid recall of one another. But they can compete for selection, as shown by 'blocking' – a familiar, annoying experience when a required word gets pushed back by another like-sounding one. The name of the weather forecaster *Ian MacGaskill* remained elusive for one woman, because that of a colleague Don Mackenzie 'kept popping into its place' – a frequent phenomenon with names.[33]

A final point: what about the 'rules' which deal with the permissible sequences of sounds? Where do they fit in? These rules for permitted sound sequences do not appear to be particularly relevant for the storage of existing words. They may not be in the 'lexicon proper', but part of the back-up information attached to the 'lexical tool-kit' which speakers use for coping with new words (chapter 15). The extension of old words and the coining of new ones will be the topic of the next three chapters.

Summary

In this chapter we have considered the sound structure of words in the mental lexicon. It seems that some parts of words are more prominent in storage than others. They are, as it were, more deeply engraved in the mind. These are the sounds at the beginning and the end (the 'bathtub effect') and the general rhythmic pattern, which is inextricably linked with the sounds.

Words are possibly clumped together in groups, with those having a similar beginning, similar ending and similar rhythmic pattern clustered together. These similar-sounding words do not always aid recall of one another; they may also block it.

Within words, syllables have their own structure, with the first consonant less firmly attached. This may affect blends, when two words are accidentally mixed together. For sound segments, being 'similar' means coming from the same natural class. It is unlikely that segments are split into smaller atoms in people's minds.

So far, only existing words have been discussed. We now need to consider how these can be extended, and how new words are formed.

Part III
Newcomers

13

Drifting Words

— Layering and meaning change —

Words will often ride very slackly at anchor on their etymologies, will be borne hither
and thither by the shifting tides and currents of usage . . .

Richard Chenevix Trench (1855)

Words, unlike numbers, do not have fixed, absolute values. An understanding
of how and why words change meaning can provide valuable insights into the
mental lexicon. Yet, perversely, meaning change has often been considered a
sign of weakness and decline. Lord Byron (1811) speaks of words 'fading' and
'dwindling':[1]

As forests shed their foliage by degrees,
So fade expressions which in season please;
And we and ours, alas! are due to fate,
And works and words but dwindle to a date.

In the nineteenth century, words in the real world were assumed to have a
'proper, meaning, and some writers became quite agitated about 'wide, vague,
loose' usages:

This tendency of words to lose the sharp rigidly defined outline of meaning which
they once possessed, to become of wide, vague, loose application instead of fixed,
definite, and precise, to mean almost anything, and so really to mean nothing,
is . . . one of those tendencies, and among the most fatally effectual, which are at
work for the final ruin of a language, and, I do not fear to add, for the demoralization
of those that speak it,

thundered Richard Chenevix Trench in 1856.[2]

In Lewis Carroll's *Through the Looking Glass* (1872), Humpty-Dumpty claimed
boastfully: 'When *I* use a word . . . it means just what I choose it to mean – neither
more nor less.'[3] This arrogant assertion showed that he lived in a bizarre, back-to-front

world, where words could change their meaning at his whim, at a time when fixed meanings were presumed to be the norm.

In 1891, the German Georg von der Gabelentz suggested that words might be envisaged as employees of the state. First, they are hired, then promoted. Later, they are put on half-pay, and eventually retired. Forms grow pale (*verblassen*), and their colours are bleached (*verbleichen*). They sometimes die, and may be mummified.[4]

Worries about meaning change continued into the twentieth century. The trends of 'verbicide or weakening and distortion, were described as 'serious' by Geoffrey Hughes in 1988. 'The problem with verbicide is that words no longer die: having been drained of their vitality . . . they become zombies.'[5] He deplored 'liberties taken with the prime meanings of words . . .' and felt it to be unnecessary: 'Much verbicide seems to be an upper-class affectation. One cannot imagine coal-miners or crofters or shepherds complaining about "ghastly weather" or praising a "divine party". . .' But he provided no firm evidence that the upper classes are the main instigators of lexical change.

Cataloguing Changes

But, leaving unnecessary worries aside, why and how does meaning change happen? Writers at the end of the nineteenth century hoped to find 'laws'. In 1883, the Frenchman Michel Bréal claimed to have invented a new discipline, *semantics*, which would look at 'the laws governing changes in meaning, the choice of new expressions, the birth and death of idioms'.[6] Bréal was not in fact the earliest scholar to explore meaning change, though his work was perhaps the first to receive widespread attention. Bréal's term *semantics* has been retained, though it now includes all linguistic meaning, not just meaning change.

But the optimism expressed by Bréal withered, as the general laws he hoped to find proved elusive. For much of the twentieth century, meaning change was seen as an intractable problem.

Dismay was often expressed at the diversity of changes, at their huge number, and their apparent randomness:

> Semantic change is widespread and astonishing in its extent . . . One easily becomes overwhelmed in the fascinating diversity of the avalanche of verbal evidence,

commented one writer.[7]

Many of those who studied it simply catalogued changes. Types of change were identified and labelled, such as expansion, restriction, pejoration, amelioration, acceleration, retardation, association, differentation.[8] Word meanings appeared not so much to drift as to behave like exploding stars, shooting off in all directions.

A glance at any etymological dictionary confirms these unpredictable routes. Take the word *buff*.[9] This once meant 'buffalo', possibly from the French word *buffe* 'buffalo'. Then it came to mean 'leather', originally from buffalo hides. The association of 'hide' and 'skin' led to the expression *in the buff* 'naked'. In the eighteenth century, the colour of buff leather, a sort of dull yellowish-brown, led to its adoption as a colour term. In the nineteenth century, soft buff leather was used by silversmiths for polishing, leading to the word *buff* 'to polish'. In the 1820s, New York City volunteer firemen were known as 'buffs' from the colour of their uniform. Then anyone who was a volunteer or enthusiastic about something became known as a *buff*, as in *film buff*.

Causes of meaning change proved equally overwhelming to those who tried to catalogue them:

> Changes of meaning can be brought about by an infinite multiplicity of causes . . . no matter how fine a mesh of distinctions one may devise, there will always be some cases which will slip through it,

bemoaned Stephen Ullmann in 1962.[10]

A widely quoted, but restricted, enumeration of causes was proposed by the French linguist Antoine Meillet in the first decade of the twentieth century.[11] Words, he suggested, could alter their meaning for linguistic, historical, or social reasons. A recent linguistic reason is the increasing use of *of* (often spelled that way) in place of *have*. Fast pronunciation has led to *h*-dropping: 'I would *of* done it.' Social and historical causes are hard to disentangle, as with the word *soup*. This was borrowed from French *soupe* and originally, like the word *sop*, meant 'a piece of bread soaked in liquid'.[12]

Meillet's classification is still found in some books, often supplemented by 'psychological, reasons, such as taboo, when religion, superstition, or delicacy do not allow certain words to be spoken, as in a recent novel featuring American Indian beliefs:

> The Abenaki, when hunting Bear, do not call it Bear. This is considered unlucky. Instead, they call it Grandmother, or Cousin, or Chief's Daughter, or The One Who Owns the Chin.[13]

Lists of types and causes might be of use to historians. But they reduce semantic change to the level of a village fête, a collection of eye-catching trivia assembled to entertain and amuse. They do not provide any deep insight into the processes of change.

From Tadpoles to Cuckoos to Multiple Births

Historical linguistics – the study of language change – was one of the first branches of linguistics to get established. Consequently, it clung for decades to old beliefs promoted by the founders of the subject.

Gradual change, imperceptibly creeping through the language, was for a long time the image which linguists held of language alterations. Leonard Bloomfield, sometimes called 'the father of American linguistics', stated in his widely read book *Language* (1933): 'The process of language change has never been directly observed – we shall see that such observation, with our present facilities, is inconceivable.'[14] Sounds and words were assumed to 'change into' one another in a slow transformation which lasted decades, like a tadpole gradually acquiring legs and losing its tail as it became a frog.

But a breakthrough in understanding language change came in the second half of the twentieth century. Sociolinguists, and above all the American William Labov, began exploring changes in progress.[15] And they had a surprise. Sounds and words do not gradually 'turn into' one another, as had been assumed. Instead, a new sound or meaning creeps in alongside the old and coexists, sometimes for centuries. Eventually, the intruder takes over, like a young cuckoo pushing an existing occupant out of the nest.

The young cuckoo idea is not entirely new for word meaning. Coexistence followed by replacement was recognized by the German Hermann Paul at the end of the nineteenth century. In 1880, he pointed out that words had both 'normal meaning' (*usuelle Bedeutung*) and 'occasional meaning' (*okkasionelle Bedeutung*), and that the occasional meaning may sometimes become the usual one.[16] But Paul's insight was mostly forgotten.

Yet even the young cuckoo idea is now recognized as over-simple. Multiple births – several new meanings – may arise, and coexist semi-permanently, often with no loss of the original meaning. The different senses of the same word overlap, and may remain for centuries. Then eventually, some of the meanings may drop away.

Polysemy and Layering

Coexistence is the key to understanding word meaning. *Polysemy* – multiple meanings – is the norm. 'Meanings expand their range through the development of various polysemies . . . these polysemies may be regarded as quite fine-grained,' comment two researchers.[17]

A check through any dictionary shows that only a few words have one meaning, typically words which are long and not very common, as *pichiciago* 'a small burrowing south American armadillo', or *ticpolonga* 'a venomous serpent of India and Sri Lanka'.

But for less rare words, new meanings, sometimes several of them, creep in alongside the existing ones, and may last for centuries. Some words are particularly prone to splitting. Short, common words often have numerous different senses. The verb *jump*, for example, has a first meaning 'to spring off the ground' in a recent dictionary,[18] but fifteen other uses are also listed, such as to 'omit', as in *she jumped the next chapter*, and to 'pass through a red traffic light', as in *he jumped the traffic lights*, and so on.

Words therefore multiply, like ever-splitting amoebas, as new meanings creep in alongside the older ones. The process is known as *layering*.[19]

Multiple Meanings

Tourist: what a lovely colour that cow is!
Farmer: It's a Jersey.
Tourist: Oh, I thought it was its skin.

This joke illustrates a well-known fact, that many words have more than one meaning. 'Most words in a language have more than one meaning, but the ways in which words carry multiple meanings can vary,' it's been claimed.[20]

The simplest type of multiple meaning is *homonymy*, meaning literally, 'same nameness', when two quite different items share the same sound sequence, as in the Jersey/jersey case above where a type of cow, a Jersey cow, has the same name as a common item of clothing. This has also been labelled *contrastive ambiguity*, because the listener has to select one of two quite different meanings.

But consider:

Barbara shut the door.
Phyllis walked through the door.

Here, the word *door* has two different but linked meanings. In the first sentence it applies to an object, in the second to a space where the object sometimes stands. This has been called *complementary ambiguity*, since *door* refers to different aspects of the same object.

Look also at:

I managed to park outside.

Here the speaker does not mean that he parked *himself* outside, he intends to convey:

I managed to park *my car* outside.

This type of *sense extension* is a further aspect of polysemy, where the listener has to infer something that is not mentioned. Numerous other omissions are routinely mentally supplied by native speakers:

Peter began breakfast

generally means 'Peter began *to eat* breakfast', and

Paul began a book

usually means 'Paul began *to read* a book' – though the listener has to decide on the meaning. Consider *want*. If this had been substituted for the main verb in the sentences above, the meaning would remain the same for *eat*:

Paul wanted breakfast/Paul wanted to eat breakfast.

But 'Paul wanted a book' does not necessarily mean that Paul wanted to *read* a book, he might have wanted to buy it or to use it to prop up a defective chair-leg.

But the commonest type of polysemy is perhaps that in which different senses of a word coexist. This will be discussed below.

Utterly Devastated

'I was *devastated* when Sainsbury's discontinued Nature's Compliments hand and body cream in vanilla fragrance,'

ran a letter to a British Sunday newspaper. The upset suffered by this fashion-conscious lady seems trivial, compared with some other uses of the word, which may describe severe emotional distress:[21]

Nick P.... finished up dead after a street fight ... His family and friends are *devastated*.

Yet 'prostrated by grief' is still pale when contrasted with the word's older, but still current meaning of 'laid waste' of land:

An area nearly twice the size of Belgium was *devastated*.

These various meanings all occurred in British newspapers in the same few months. The related noun *devastation*, incidentally, had not layered to the same extent. It was mostly used for serious physical damage as:

A few half-timber houses still exist in Normandy: they have survived the *devastation* of the Second World War.

This verb–noun difference shows that any analysis must deal with the various word classes (parts of speech) separately.

As *devastated* shows, it's not only short, common words such as *jump* which split. Descriptions of those affected by shocking events, as *devastated*, *gutted*, layer easily, as do words for catastrophic happenings, such as *apocalypse*, *calamity*, *catastrophe*, *disaster*, *tragedy*.

Absolute Disasters

The word *disaster* is by far the commonest *disaster* word, judging from the British National Corpus (where a 'w-unit' is roughly, a word; see figure 13.1).

	BNC spoken	BNC written
Catastrophe	1.1	5
Disaster	22.3	32.1
Tragedy	6.3	19.3

Figure 13.1 Some disaster nouns (frequency per million w-units)

According to dictionaries, the main meaning of *disaster* is:

> a sudden event such as an accident or natural catastrophe that causes great damage or loss of life.[22]

And numerous examples of this usage are easily found, as:

> . . . the Hillsborough football *disaster* which killed 95 people.

Alongside this serious incident usage are numerous trivial ones, as:

> To get a panama hat wet is to court *disaster*. The hat becomes limp and shapeless.

A number of questions spring to mind. First, which meaning of *disaster* predominates? Are dictionaries right to assume that the main meaning is the most serious one? One study attempted to divide examples of *disaster* into various levels of seriousness.[23] An event which resulted in multiple deaths was classed as serious (S), one which caused severe environmental damage was listed as medium (M), and one which caused a social inconvenience was classed as trivial (T). For example:

> At least 62 people were killed and 3,000 missing last night after an underwater earthquake sent 50ft tidal waves crashing into the coast of Nicaragua. More than 227 people were injured in the *disaster*. (S)

> But if all 22 million gallons escape, the *disaster* will be twice as bad as the 1988 *Exxon Valdez* spill off Alaska. (M)

> All other efforts to lose the fat from the offending areas proved to be a *disaster*. If I lost weight below 54kg my bust disappeared, yet nothing went from my legs or posterior! (T)

The results are shown below in figure 13.2. These figures show that if the medium and trivial disasters are combined, they outweigh the serious ones.

	Serious	Medium	Trivial
Spoken n = 185	48%	14%	35%
Written n = 589	43%	20%	36%

Figure 13.2   Scale of disaster

So how do speakers use the wide-ranging word *disaster* appropriately? And how do hearers interpret it in the way intended by the speaker? This is at first sight a puzzle. But on closer examination, the surrounding context made clear the level of disaster intended, though not always in an obvious way.

Major disasters were the most straightforward. These were often named after the place where they had occurred: a geographical location was the main clue that a serious incident involving multiple deaths had taken place, as: *the Bradford football disaster, the 1986 Chernobyl nuclear disaster, the Hillsborough disaster, the Kegworth air disaster, the Lockerbie disaster, the Siberian pipeline disaster, the Stalingrad disaster, the Zeebrugge ferry disaster.*

If the disaster was not a major one, at a particular location, then the type of disaster was often noted, as: *ecological disaster, economic disaster, environmental disaster, financial disaster, industrial disaster.*

For trivial incidents, the cause of the problem tended to be specified immediately afterwards, as:

The gravy's a *disaster*. It's got too much fat in it.

New usages, particularly the trivial ones, tended to creep in by attaching themselves to certain general areas. A common one was cookery, as in the examples above and below:

There have been many *disasters* along the road, Yorkshire puddings you could sole your shoes with . . . and last Christmas a chocolate log that disintegrated, the proud little Santa on top sinking without trace in a sea of chocolate gunge.

Cookery *disasters* were always trivial, and this word was not interchangeable with other *disaster* words: presumably a cookery *tragedy* would have meant something more serious, perhaps food-poisoning.

Another common *disaster* area was sport:

The last wicket fell . . . So it was another blackwash, another *disaster* for England.

– though, unlike cookery, sport utilized all the *disaster* words interchangeably:

In a history of *disasters* stretching across 30 years, Scotland has been plagued by *calamity*, lapses in concentration and self-induced *tragedy*. The goalkeeper is always to blame and always will be.

Other collocating (adjacent) words sometimes signal whether the event is a genuine disaster or a social hiccup. Intensifiers, words such as *absolute*, *total*, often diminished the seriousness of the disaster:

The majority of dinners are very pleasant affairs, but some can be *absolute disasters*.

Figure 13.3   An absolute disaster

Similarly, the phrase *disaster strikes* or *disaster struck* typically referred to a minor, unimportant happening:

Even if *disaster strikes*, as it seemed to for one student of mine who dropped her nearly completed head on the concrete floor and an ear snapped off [the wooden rocking horse she was carving], don't let it worry you unduly. We simply glued the broken ear back in place.

Yet this is not the whole story: collocation (adjacency) indicated not only the seriousness level of an event, but also its factivity – whether it had actually taken place or not. Many disasters discussed are potential rather than actual. Only a proportion have actually happened, and the remainder are impending or hypothetical.

The hypothetical nature of disasters is shown by the linguistic expressions used with them, as: *avert, avoid, court, expect, face, foretell, head for, head off, predict, prevent, save from, warn of; imminent, impending, near, potential; brink of, chance of, doomed to, expectation of, fear of, recipe for; can be, could be, could have been, would be, would have been*. For example:

> When you rescue the old Christmas tree lights from the loft for the umpteenth time, remember that they *could be* the cause of an electrical *disaster*.

Since major disasters are relatively rare, the hypothetical use of the word *disaster* may have been responsible for its increasing use, which promoted layering.

The analysis of *disaster* shows, first, the importance of real language examples from an up-to-date database, one which includes examples from both written and spoken language. Second, that it may be possible to identify the source of layering. In the case of *disaster*, the areas of sport and cookery played an important role. Third, particular collocations signify to speakers/hearers whether the disaster is a serious or trivial one, as with the word *absolute* in the phrase 'absolute disaster' and *strike* in 'disaster struck', which indicate (usually) a minor event.

And the closer one looks, more details become clear. For example, singular and plural forms of words do not necessarily move together: more plural examples of *disaster* describe major incidents than singular ones. The intricacies of layering can be revealed only when such fine-grained differences are carefully charted.

The examples discussed in the last two sections showed some general characteristics of layering. But can studies of word meaning go further? This will be considered below.

Laws of Change and Meaning?

> There are universal laws of thought which are reflected in the laws of change and meaning . . . even if the science of meaning has not yet made much advance towards discovering them.[24]

These lines were written in 1925 by Otto Jespersen, a linguistic pioneer. Even today, linguists have not yet discovered firm 'laws of change and meaning', though they are beginning to comprehend some of the mechanisms behind meaning change, as with the layering discussed above.

Even if 'laws' are elusive, some of the directions of change are becoming clearer. Humans begin with the human body, and move outward to other parts of the physical world:

the *foot* of the mountain
the *ribs* of the ship
the *head* of the organization.

They also move inward, using everyday external bodily behaviour to describe internal events:

I *see* what Helen means
Peter *held on* to his point of view
Let's *go over* that plan again.

Humans also generalize from space to time:

from tree *to* tree → *from* day *to* day
in the wood → *in* the morning

and so on. And these tendencies were probably active right from the origin of language.[25] Language therefore reflects the interaction of humans with the world around them – and different nationalities may perceive the world differently, depending on their experience (as will be outlined in the last chapter).

Summary

In the past, meaning change has often been seen (wrongly) as a sign of decay and decline, possibly due to the difficulties earlier writers had in understanding such changes.

Much early work simply catalogued changes. Only recently have researchers realized that so-called 'layering' is the key. Words develop multiple meanings, and the various layers coexist, resulting in polysemy.

Certain types of word tend to layer fast: short, common words, and also words for catastophic events, such as *disaster*. Meanwhile, overall directions of change are also becoming clearer.

14

Interpreting Ice-cream Cones
— Extending old words —

> Your body is a mountain-chain, your bones
> Ridges of rock, your nipples ice-cream cones.
> Others have said the same, and others will,
> In rearranged comparisons, until
> The mountains have subsided to the plain,
> And the world's meanings have to start again.
> Laurence Lerner, 'Meanings'

Nipples are not ice-cream cones, nor are ice-cream cones nipples. Yet no one would be likely to suggest that the author of this poem was mentally deranged. Humans are amazingly good at extending the application of words: 'The lexical mosaic is constantly being stretched to cover more than it should.'[1] This stretching is not restricted to poetry: 'Cougars drown Beavers,' 'Cowboys corral Buffaloes,' 'Air Force torpedoes the Navy,' 'Clemson cooks Rice,' are all perfectly comprehensible headlines describing football games in American newspapers.[2] And in everyday conversation one is likely to hear numerous examples of superficially bizarre expressions: 'His new boss is a dinosaur!', 'A donkey is the car of the islanders,' 'The chimney provided a back-door to the cave,' 'The ham skated across the kitchen floor,' 'The brandy tobogganed down his throat.'

As these examples suggest, humans use words in creative and innovative ways, and this is an intrinsic part of a human's lexical ability (chapter 1). The mental lexicon contains equipment which enables a person to continually expand old worlds and coin new ones. In this chapter, we shall consider the extension of existing words, and in the next, the creation of new ones – although the distinction between these two processes is not always clear-cut. We shall be discussing what guidelines humans follow when they produce these novelties and how others manage to comprehend them. Our overall aim is to understand how this creative ability is integrated into the mental lexicon.

Metaphor will be our main concern in this chapter, a term which encompasses all the examples mentioned in the first paragraph. We shall then move on to metonymy, the use of a part for a whole, as in 'Do you have wheels?' meaning 'Do you have a car?' Finally, we shall turn to the type of creative extension involved in the instruction 'Please do a Napoleon for the camera,'[3] which listeners apparently interpret quite readily. Such usages provide a bridge between the word extensions of this chapter and the new formations to be discussed in the next.

Ice-cream Cones and Cabbages

Metaphor, according to the ancient Greek philosopher Aristotle, involves 'the application to one thing of a name belonging to another'.[4] One might expect humans to be puzzled by this apparent use of wrong labels,[5] such as calling nipples 'ice-cream cones'. But instead, they are amazingly good at thinking up plausible explanations when they encounter a metaphor: perhaps ice-cream cones and nipples have a similar shape, or they can both be licked or sucked. '*The mountain is a frog* . . . is interpretable . . . if given the visual image of a green mountain,' notes one group of researchers.[6] In fact, it is quite difficult to think up an inapplicable metaphor, because people are so good at finding potential explanations. Try out 'Her breasts were . . .' and then make a list of random objects. They almost all work. 'Her breasts were cabbages' (shape). 'Her breasts were rabbits' (perhaps soft feel). 'Her breasts were bricks' (feel again – perhaps she'd had a breast-enlargement operation). 'Her breasts were snow-drifts' (pale colour). 'Her breasts were doors' (perhaps the way in to deeper love-making). 'Her breasts were peas' (size). 'Her breasts were question marks' (perhaps symbols of tentative sexual exploration). These metaphors all work, to some extent, even though breasts are not cabbages, rabbits, bricks, snow-drifts, doors, peas or question marks, nor even particularly like them.

Interpreting a sentence such as 'Breasts are cabbages' might seem a complex task. Yet the basic mechanism behind metaphor is straightforward. It is simply the use of a word with one or more of the 'typicality conditions' attached to it broken. As we noted in chapter 5, words have fuzzy edges, in that for the majority of words it is impossible to specify a hard-core meaning at all. Humans understand words by referring to a prototypical usage, and they match a new example against the characteristics of the prototype. A tiger can still be a tiger even though it might have three legs and no stripes: it just wouldn't be a prototypical tiger. Seeing can still be seeing, even if your mind doesn't register what your eye fell on: it just wouldn't be a prototypical instance of seeing.

Use of words with broken typicality conditions happens all the time, in fact so often that one ceases to notice it. If anyone does, there is sometimes an argument as to whether a word is being used 'metaphorically' or not, as in: 'The price of mangos *went up*.' Is *went up* a metaphor, since the price did not literally travel up a hill? Or is this simply the use of *go up* with a typicality condition broken, since *going* typically involves travelling between two physical points and covering the distance in between? Similarly, what about:

Marigold is *coming out* of a coma.
Felix is *under* age.

Coming out typically involves physical movement, and *under* typically involves a physical position beneath. So are these metaphors, or ordinary uses with a typicality condition broken? As these examples show, the two are indistinguishable. One can therefore say either: 'Our ordinary conceptual system . . . is fundamentally metaphorical in nature,'[7] or: 'Metaphors . . . are in no sense departures from a norm.'[8] The two comments are equivalent and interchangeable.[9]

The necessity of breaking typicality conditions – or in other words, the inevitability of metaphor – is so high in some semantic fields that one cannot communicate without it. Music and art cannot be discussed intelligently without words such as *austere, balanced, charming, complex, empty, flamboyant, forceful, graceful, insipid, majestic, rough, soft, sweet, warm* – words which are also used for the description of wine.[10] Indeed, if one were restricted to only a prototypical use of words, wine would be undiscussable: 'You can talk about wine as if it were a bunch of flowers (fragrant, heavily perfumed); a packet of razor blades (steely); a navy (robust, powerful); a troupe of acrobats (elegant and well-balanced); a successful industrialist (distinguished and rich); a virgin in a bordello (immature and giving promise of pleasure to come); Brighton Beach (clean and pebbly); even a potato (earthy) or a Christmas pudding (plump, sweet and round).'[11] Quite often, if particular extended usages have become conventional, as in the wine examples, they are classified as 'dead' metaphors, on the assumption that they must once have been new and vivid but are now old clichés: 'The music flowed over her,' 'The evening staggered on,' 'Her heart drummed against her rib-cage,' and so on. Counting up metaphors is therefore difficult. But one survey estimated that there were, on average, over five examples of figurative language per 100 words spoken, almost a third of which were novel uses.[12]

Prototypical Metaphors

If every broken typicality condition is, in some sense, an example of metaphor, why do people make value judgements and say 'It's not a proper metaphor' for some extended usages, but 'That's a nice metaphor' for others? Some 'metaphorical' usages are less satisfactory because not all broken typicality conditions result in 'prototypical' metaphors. People seem to have some notion of what is a 'proper' metaphor, which is perhaps partly instilled by poetry lessons at school and partly by the ease with which they have recognized the speaker's intention. What, then, constitutes a prototypical metaphor?

At first sight, such an analysis might seem impossible. If breasts can be rabbits, and mountains can be frogs, it might seem a hopeless task to find any guidelines underlying the choice. Furthermore, the literature is confused, since some writers stress the similarity of the items that are compared and others stress the dissimilarity.[13] In fact, both similarities and dissimilarities must exist, but of different types.

First, the items must not be too similar, because then the metaphor will either be incomprehensible or it will not be a metaphor. One would not normally say: 'Wine is whisky,' or 'Cars are lorries,' or 'Jam is honey,' or 'Marmalade is jam.' In the first three of these examples the hearer is likely to be simply baffled, and in the last would probably regard 'marmalade' and 'jam' as being rough synonyms. In a good metaphor, therefore, the items compared should not share major characteristics. So 'Nipples are ice-cream cones,' 'Life is a subway train,' 'Women are thistles,' 'He posted the toast down to his stomach,' 'The brandy tobogganed down his gullet' would be far 'better' metaphors, in that the subject of the metaphor is compared to something which is quite different from itself, in the sense of coming from a different semantic field.

Second, although the items involved must not share major characteristics, they must share some. Statements such as 'His feet were stars,' 'Her cheeks were typewriters,' 'Her knees were penguins' are fairly unlikely and are difficult to interpret, even though humans can usually think up some kind of joint characteristic, given enough time to ponder. In a prototypical metaphor, the words involved share some fairly obvious characteristic, usually a minor one. In 'Her breasts were cabbages,' the hearer would probably interpret the metaphor as one of size or shape, even though when thinking of a breast or a cabbage separately the shape and size of each might not be the first thing which springs to mind. Similarly, 'His boss is a dinosaur' cannot refer to the most important characteristics of dinosaurs, that they are extinct and often enormous. It presumably relates to some additional piece of knowledge which people have about these animals, the fact that the species probably died out because it was slow-moving and failed to adapt to new conditions. In 'The brandy tobogganed down his gullet,' the drinker's throat cannot be lined with snow, a major typicality condition of tobogganing. It must instead refer to the speed and the downhill movement involved.

In a prototypical metaphor, then, the items compared are likely to be dissimilar, in that they come from different semantic fields, and similar in that they share obvious, minor characteristics. The dissimilarity of the semantic fields signals to the hearer that active matching has to be carried out in order to interpret the sentence. The listener sets about doing this because she routinely assumes that the speaker is trying to communicate intelligently,[14] unless there are clear indications that he is a lunatic. The computations required are no different in kind from those in 'ordinary' word interpretation (chapter 5), though some may require extra mental agility, since certain types of brain damage apparently limit a person's ability to deal with extended usages.[15]

Narrowing Down the Range

Unfortunately, matters are not always as simple as in the prototypical metaphor outlined above. Sometimes items may share more than one minor characteristic. The ice-cream cones and nipples metaphor could refer either to shape or lickability.

'Her eyes were coins' could refer to their roundness or their shininess. 'Mavis was a panda' could refer to her cuddliness, her large size, or a preference for black and white clothes, or even all three. How is the choice narrowed down? Sometimes speakers explicitly explain their metaphors: 'Life is a foreign language: all men mispronounce it' (Christopher Morley);[16] 'Hollywood money isn't money. It's congealed snow, melts in your hand' (Dorothy Parker).[17] 'Many people find it helpful to think of wines as having a shape . . . A round wine has its skeleton (the alcohol) adequately and pleasantly covered with flesh (the fruit) and is enhanced by a good skin (the fragrance)' (Pamela Vandyke Price).[18] But mostly the context will limit the possibilities, and allow the hearer to come to a plausible solution.

In some cases, however, it may not be possible to narrow down the metaphor to one exact comparison. This is particularly true of poetry, where the poet may intentionally have included several layers of interpretation. When Chaucer in *The Canterbury Tales* said that the prioress's eyes were 'greye as glas',[19] he overtly chose colour as the basis of the comparison. But he presumably intended other qualities of glass, such as translucence and brilliance, to be considered. 'Grey as rabbits' would hardly be as effective. Similarly, in the ice-cream cone example the reference to a mountain-chain and ridges of rock suggest very strongly that shape, rather than lickability, is the major comparison, though something deliciously edible in a peak-like shape is still more appropriate for a lover's body than, say, a pine-cone or a sun-hat.

Occasionally, there may be no obvious interpretation at all for a metaphor. The creator may intentionally have made understanding difficult, perhaps in order to force the hearer to think about the subject. For example, 'There is pleasure in exploring the metaphor of the Church as a hippopotamus even if we do not believe anything about the Church at the end that we did not believe at the beginning.'[20] Or take the following lines by Emily Dickinson:

> We barred the windows and the doors
> As from an emerald ghost;
> The doom's electric moccasin
> That very instant passed.

What on earth is an 'emerald ghost' or 'doom's electric moccasin'? Each time one thinks about these metaphors, some new idea about the links comes to mind: people wearing moccasins creep up stealthily, electric shocks make one tingle, and so on. But it would be hard to claim that one had finally interpreted it: the possible layers go on and on, as the poet perhaps intended.

The arousing of multiple associations raises another characteristic of some metaphors. Many of them go much further than a comparison of just two words. They require the activation of whole situations or 'frames' (chapter 6): Shakespeare's 'Sleep that knits up the ravell'd sleave of care'[21] requires the activation of a whole knitting scenario, and we imagine drunken dollars staggering about in Maynard Keynes's comment 'The recent gyrations of the dollar have looked to me more like a gold standard on the booze than the ideal managed currency which I hope for.'[22] Here, hearers have to pick out the relevant similarities in the whole situation, they cannot just compare two words. As we noted in chapter 6, humans continue to delve within their mental lexicons, activating more and more material, until they have acquired as much as they need for interpreting an utterance.

Ideas for Metaphors

Where do metaphors come from in the first place? A goodish number are based on conventional topics. In every century, even every decade, certain metaphors are prominent. The leading technology of the time tends to inspire metaphors. In the eighteenth century, watches were still a novelty:

> The human body is a watch, a large watch, constructed with such skill and ingenuity, that if the wheel which makes the seconds happens to stop, the minute wheel turns and keeps on going round.[23]

The most pervasive current metaphor may be the computer: it is standard to talk about topics in terms of software, hardware, input, output and so on. American politics in the 1960s were particularly characterized by repeated imagery of athletic competition: it was important to win, not lose, to be ahead, to defeat one's opponents. As Richard Nixon commented: 'This nation cannot stand still because we are in a deadly competition . . . We're ahead in this competition . . . , but when you're in a race the only way to stay ahead is to move ahead.'[24] And sport continues to inspire political metaphor today. The 'arms race' in particular is still with us.

Certain areas permanently attract a large number of metaphors. The human body is consistently the most frequent source, according to an analysis of figurative language over three centuries.[25] But the body is not only a source for the imagination: it also imprisons it. Our thought is channelled along pre-set grooves because of the ways we subconsciously think about our bodies, some of which may be technically quite inaccurate.[26]

Consider metaphors relating to anger. Anger is subconsciously regarded as heated liquid in a container.[27] The body is the container, and the liquid inside gradually gets hotter until the steam pours out. In severe cases, the lid comes off and the whole thing explodes:

> Marigold's anger welled up inside her.
> Henry was filled with rage.
> Pamela was brimming with fury.
> Peter had reached boiling point.
> Angela's just bursting with anger.
> Tony's just blowing off steam.
> Paul couldn't contain his rage.

> Fenella flipped her lid.
> Jonathan just blew up.
> Felicity exploded.

These images may go back to the writings attributed to the Greek physician Hippocrates in the fourth century BC. Hippocrates assumed that the body contained four humours (liquids), with *choler*, or yellow bile, being responsible for anger. Furthermore, the notion of anger as liquid in a container is envisaged even when thinking about idioms with no container mentioned, such as 'He hit the roof.' Students questioned on this idiom did not imagine people with springs on their heels banging their heads on the ceiling. Instead, they envisaged the contents of containers hurtling upwards.[28]

Of course, getting hot is a physical symptom of anger, so the heat is perhaps not surprising. And heat enters expressions of anger everywhere in the world. But the liquid is less important: in some Indian cultures, anger is thought of as dry heat which needs to be anointed with soothing oils.[29] Body metaphors are therefore partly based on genuine physical features, partly on convention, partly on imagination – the recipe for folk beliefs discussed in chapter 6. Any new metaphor is likely to follow the ready-made tramlines. Perhaps: 'The lava-flow of Pete's anger engulfed her,' 'Helen's pressure-cooked anger burst out.'

Anger has other metaphors: for example, a dangerous animal:

> Saul bared his teeth at her.
> Patricia was bristling with rage.

But the 'liquid in a container' metaphor predominates. And this may have consequences beyond the language. It may lead people to believe that it is normal and even socially acceptable to explode with anger, since explosion is an inevitable consequence of overheating a contained liquid. Some expressions of lust are parallel to those of anger:

> Max was really steamed up over Mary.
> Desire for Marigold welled up inside him.
> Paul was bursting with love.

In consequence, the high incidence of rape in America may, it has been suggested, be partly due to the way in which lust and anger are conceptualized.[30]

Universal and cultural aspects of metaphors are therefore intertwined. Any language selects one portion of the universal picture, and elaborates it. To take another example, fear triggers two opposing physical reactions: freezing or fleeing. Almost all common English *fear* metaphors involve the first reaction, with fear as freezing cold or an empty container:[31]

> Alan's limbs turned icy cold.
> Fear froze Angela to the ground.

> David was rooted to the spot.
> Pam's courage ebbed away.
> Paul's wits deserted him.

The only well-known 'fleeing' metaphor is the somewhat poetic 'Fear gave wings to his heels.' Yet in ancient Greek, the word for fear originally meant 'panic-stricken flight', showing that different cultures highlight different physical aspects of the world. Quite how the universal interacts with the cultural, and how it might affect behaviour is a question under active discussion.[32]

Specific cultural metaphors, such as anger as a heated liquid, fear as freezing cold, interact with possibly universal metaphors, such as the idea that life is a journey. A traveller, a route, and a destination is widely presupposed:

> Like pilgrims to th'appointed place we tend,
> The world's an inn, and death the journey's end.

said the seventeenth-century poet John Dryden.

This notion of a journey is incorporated not only into our poetry, but also into everyday metaphors of life:

> Belinda got off to a good start in life.
> Paul isn't getting anywhere.
> Anastasia seems to have lost her way.
> Herbert's plodding on.
> Angela's plodding on

Such universal metaphors overlap with more general 'image schemas' – outlined frameworks from which we subconsciously work, such as the 'ladder' image: an up–down scale or 'verticality schema' is implicit in much of our thought, with 'good' at the top and 'bad' at the bottom.[33]

> Sid's a high-minded individual!
> Betty's full of base thoughts.
> Marianna's spirits rose.
> Edward was feeling low.
> Simon's got a high opinion of her.
> Low self-esteem is Mandy's problem.

Such examples show first, the pervasiveness of metaphor, second, the impossibility of distinguishing metaphor from 'literal language', and third, the subconscious structuring of our thoughts by the folk images we have been brought up with.

When does use of metaphor start? Quite young, it seems. Youngsters use figurative language quite intentionally, and not simply because they do not know the word involved. For example, a young child asked to describe an Afro hairstyle said: 'Lots of snakes are coming out of his head.' When asked if this was truly so, the child said, 'Of course not, but his hair's all wiggly like snakes are.' This spontaneous use of metaphor decreases with age.[34] It fades fastest among children who attend reputedly good schools, and more slowly among those who go to supposedly bad ones. This suggests that education channels children towards conventional usages and less colourful speech.

However, although metaphor is perhaps the most noticeable form of extended word usage, it is by no means the only one. Let us now go on to consider metonymy.

Red Sails in the Sunset

> Red sails in the sunset
> Red sails on the sea
> Carry my loved one
> Back home to me.

These well-known lines[35] are superficially nonsense. How could red sails carry a loved one back home? The answer is obvious to any normal native speaker of English. The loved one is in a boat, and the boat has red sails. And in conversations, *metonymy*,[36] the use of a part to refer to a whole, is widespread:

> We need a strong *pair of arms* (a person who is strong)
> New *faces* (people) are always welcome
> Does he have *wheels?* (a car).

Superficially, metaphor and metonymy are dissimilar. In metaphor, a quite different entity is substituted for another, in metonymy the substitute is something close to the item for which it is exchanged, as *wheels* for 'car'. Metaphor involves two different domains, metonymy only one. Metaphor requires a comparison to be made between two fairly different things, metonymy only needs a substituted item to be understood for something found adjacent.

At first sight metaphor is more complex than metonymy, and involves more creative thought processes. On second sight, metonymy is not as simple as it first appears.

A key question is, what counts as metonymy? A part for a whole is prototypical metonymy. But what about an object substituting for people?, as in:

> The *buses* are on strike.

It's the people who drive the buses who are on strike, not the buses themselves. Similarly, a place could substitute for an event:

> *Pearl Harbour* is engraved on the mind of Americans.

Here an event which took place at Pearl Harbour is etched in the memory of Americans, not the place itself. A further complication is a part event substituting for a whole event. For example, in answer to the question, 'How did you come?' someone might say:

I found a taxi
I jumped on a bus.

Yet finding the taxi and jumping on the bus are only small parts of much longer journeys. All these examples suggest that metonymy may be complex, and that humans have to actively compute the meaning of what they are hearing. Furthermore, metonymy has interesting links with partonymy (meronymy) (chapter 9).

Let us now go on to consider another phenomenon which bridges the gap between the extension of old words and the creation of new ones.

Doing a Napoleon

'Suppose a friend, taking your photograph, asks you with a glint in her eye, "Please do a Napoleon for the camera." Most people to whom we have offered this scenario report imagining, quickly and without reflection, posing with one hand tucked inside their jacket à la Napoleon. Arriving at this sense is a remarkable feat.'[36]

The feat is remarkable, because Napoleon never had his photo taken, and he did a considerable number of things in his life, including dying from arsenic poisoning. Moreover, people do not habitually tuck their hands in their jackets for photos. This successful assessment of a new situation occurred not only with well-known figures such as Napoleon and Richard Nixon, but also, as we saw in chapter 1, when people were presented with entirely new characters about whom they had been given a few sentences of description. How do hearers arrive at the right conclusions? Can speakers just say anything and be understood, or are there pointers, as with metaphor, which lead listeners in the right direction?

A couple of experiments were devised to test this point.[37] In the first, students were read out sentences which included the name of a famous person, such as 'I met a girl at the Coffee House who did an Elizabeth Taylor while I was talking to her,' 'After Joe listened to the tape of the interview, he did a Nixon to a portion of it.' They were asked to interpret the sentence, and say how sure they were of their interpretation.

Hearers were fairly good at this. They seemed to utilize both knowledge of the character concerned and an assessment of the context. They were able to match a known and fairly obvious characteristic, possibly only a minor one, against the needs of the situation, much as people had when they interpreted metaphor. But they were much surer of their interpretations when they were pointed in the right direction by the speakers. If the context was vague and failed to help, people were puzzled.

In the second experiment, subjects were read out short descriptions of invented characters (as described in chapter 1): 'Imagine your friend told you about his neighbor, Harry Wilson. Harry Wilson decided that it was time to rejuvenate his house and property. He started by using his electric shears to carve his hedges into animal shapes – an elephant, a camel with two humps, and a fat seal balancing a ball on its nose. Then he decided to paint the exterior of his house. He painted the clapboard walls with bright white and the trim with royal blue. For the final touch, Harry moved his furniture out to the porch, so that he could enjoy the evening breezes. Later your friend told you, "This summer I plan to do a Harry Wilson."'

Once again, the students had to interpret these vignettes, and say how confident they were in their interpretation, though not all students were given the same ending. Others were presented with alternatives such as 'This summer I plan to do a Harry Wilson to the hedges' or 'do a Harry Wilson to a bar of soap'. And some stories were more complex than others.

People had no difficulty in picking out the unusual actions which typified the character in question, though they coped better if the context was narrowed down for them. So, in the example above, 'doing a Harry Wilson to the hedges' was the easiest to interpret, and the subjects felt fairly confident that their interpretation was correct.[38]

These experiments show that humans are prepared to make a guess at anything, but mostly their options are narrowed down by speakers, so that hearers are able to successfully select the relevant interpretation. A remarkable amount of active matching is involved, since existing knowledge has to be judged alongside the current situation, but it is matching in which the possibilities are not totally wide open. Humans are able to exploit the clues given by speakers, and so limit the number of solutions they consider. Overall, then, this type of extension, like metaphor, shows that the human mind cannot be regarded as a machine which gives a fixed set of responses. Active computation is required, in which the various factors involved have to be assessed, and a decision reached. And this seems to be true of the creation of new words also, as we shall see in the next chapter.

Summary

This chapter has considered how people extend the usage of existing words, looking primarily at metaphor, secondly at metonymy, and finally at a type of extension which overlaps with the creation of new words.

Metaphor utilizes normal processes of word interpretation, in that a metaphor is primarily the use of a word with a broken typicality condition, something which happens all the time in speech. There is therefore no clear difference between a word used in a non-prototypical way and a metaphor.

However, when humans consciously use metaphor, they subconsciously follow certain guidelines. They tend to compare items from different semantic fields, which share minor but obvious characteristics. This enables hearers to recognize that an unusual comparison is being made, and helps them to pinpoint the relevant similarities – although some poetic metaphors purposely lead hearers to multiple interpretations.

Comprehension of metaphor is also aided by the fact that, in any era, certain topics become the locus of metaphors. Some sources, especially the human body, are tied to folk beliefs which may have been in existence for centuries. They affect future metaphors, and perhaps even behaviour. Metonymy, the use of a part for a whole, is at first sight simpler than metaphor, but on closer examination, it turns out to be equally complex.

Finally, a third, 'Napoleonic' type of extension has no fixed constraints, but narrowing down the context guides the hearer towards the intended interpretation. As with metaphor, hearers must actively match their existing knowledge against the requirements of the situation in order to interpret the sentence. The process bridges the gap between the extension of old words and the creation of new ones, which will be discussed in the next chapter.

15

Globbering Mattresses
— Creating new words —

> The mattress globbered. This is the noise made by a live, swamp-dwelling mattress that is deeply moved . . .
> 'I sense a deep dejectedness . . .' it vollued . . . 'and it saddens me. You should be more mattresslike. We live quiet retired lives in the swamp, where we are content to flollop and vollue and regard the wetness in a fairly floopy manner.'
> Douglas Adams, *Life, the Universe and Everything*

Humans are enormously clever at making up new words, as the passage above shows. This is a literary example, so the novelties are perhaps more carefully thought out than those produced in everyday speech. But they exemplify a skill permanently available to humans, the ability to coin new words at any time, even in the course of a conversation.

These new usages occur continually, though most are quite temporary visitors to the language. They may be used only once, or by one person. 'Come and see my fishling,' said a friend who had just acquired a tiny fish. A travel journalist noted that a small airline had gone in for *jumbification* – the use of jumbo jets (Alex Hamilton).[1] And in an advertisement, *Autoguzzlosaurus Rex* is a large car-like animal with an excessive thirst for petrol (gas) and in danger of extinction. It's possible that these novelties will come into general use, though not particularly likely. Many, many more new words are invented than come into firm existence, in the sense of eventually being listed in a printed dictionary. Only if a new coinage is sufficiently useful, and used by someone influential, is it likely to catch on. The few which spread to a wider audience and get accepted into the language are like the raindrops which get caught in a bucket. They are only a minute proportion of those which fall from the sky. The majority soak into the ground without trace. How then do humans perform this creative task?

The Rarity of Googols

Word formation is the 'deepest, most secret part of language', according to the nineteenth-century philosopher-linguist Wilhelm von Humboldt.[2] This viewpoint is probably wrong, in that the mechanisms behind word formation are fairly easy to identify. Most new words are not new at all, they are simply additions to existing words or recombinations of their components. Words which are invented out of nothing are extremely rare: the writer of a book on word formation was able to find only six words in this category[3] – though a seventh is *googol*, meaning 'the figure I followed by 100 zeroes', supposedly coined by a mathematician who had asked his young nephew to think up a word for a very big number.[4] There are, a few more if one includes trade or product names, such as *Kodak* and *Teflon*, which are sometimes computer-generated. But even these are only partially new, since they always follow the existing sound patterns of the language, which, as we noted in chapter 12, form a limited number of combinations: one might invent a new bath-cleaner called *Woft* or *Drillo* or *Frud* – but certainly not one called **Sfog* or **Bdift* or **Wozrfeh*.

At any one time in a language there are numerous possible word formation devices, though only a few of these are likely to be in common use. These 'productive' processes – those in active use for the production of new words – are attached to the mental lexicon, perhaps as an auxiliary component.[5] The use of this 'lexical tool-kit' is always available and always optional.[6] The situation may be somewhat like name-labelling at conferences. The organizers usually have name-labels ready for delegates, but there are sometimes unexpected arrivals, for whom the organizers simply write out extra labels as required. The lexical tool-kit, then, contains back-up mechanisms which supplement the existing lexicon with instructions as to how to make up new words if they are needed.

Words are 'needed' for various reasons. Take the sentence: 'Alexander decided to *unmurder* Vanessa, the *murderee*,' which contains two words from recent novels.[7] The first was coined to fill a lexical gap in a science-fiction story, the second, *murderee*, is more economical than *murder victim* or *person who was murdered*. An attempt to be funny and eye-catching is a further reason. *Glosh* perhaps covers all three. This word was coined by a journalist to describe the enormous soupy stew prepared for a sumo wrestler – perhaps from *glop* and *slosh* with overtones of *goulash:* 'I might have to reach 160 kilos if I am to become a grand champion,' says Kitade between mouthfuls of this glosh.[8]

No two researchers agree exactly on the nature of instructions for forming new words,[9] but certain facts are fairly clear. The devices used differ from language to language, though some occur widely.[10] In this chapter we shall consider some that are common in English (figure 15.1). First, we shall look at compounding – the juxtaposition of existing words, as in *cow-tree*, perhaps 'tree where cows shelter'. Second, we shall discuss conversion – the changing of one part of speech into another, as in 'He jam-jarred the wasp.' Third, we shall consider affixation – the

Figure 15.1   Common ways of creating new words

addition of a morpheme to the end, beginning, or middle of an existing word, as in *Donald Duck-ish*. Finally, we shall discuss the human ability to split up existing words in order to create new ones, as in *flopnik* from 'sputnik'. The aim of this investigation is to see how humans do this and how others manage to comprehend them. In this way we shall find out more about the working of the 'lexical tool-kit' and how it is attached to the 'lexicon proper'.

Owl Bowls and Pumpkin Buses

Headache pills demolish headaches, *fertility pills* produce fertility, and *heart pills* aid the heart. Moreover, *slug powder* kills slugs, *talcum powder* is made of purified talc, and *face powder* goes on faces. As these examples show, words can be put together in so many superficially illogical ways that one wonders how on earth people manage to understand one another when this is done afresh, as in 'You can have the owl bowl,' meaning 'You can have the bowl with the picture of the owl on it.'

There are quite a lot of different ways in which words can be combined.[11] The largest group of existing compounds involves nouns alongside other nouns, and this is possibly the commonest category for novel ones. Children can produce compounds of this type from around the age of 2, as in *sky-car* 'aeroplane' (age 18 months), *car-smoke* 'car exhaust' (age 28 months).[12]

There are no absolute constraints on the way in which nouns can be combined, though speakers show certain preferences, in that a smallish number of relation-ships are favoured.[13] Objects tend to be involved in compounds which specify their use, as in *banana fork* 'fork used for bananas', *spaghetti saucepan* 'saucepan for cooking spaghetti'. Animals and plants are likely to occur in compounds which describe their appearance or habitat, as in the *Widmoor fox* or the *marsh tulip*, and humans are likely to have their occupation or sexual or ethnic identity specified, as in *police demonstrators* or *women sailors*.

The new compound must, it seems, convey further information: the sequence *egg bird* was judged unacceptable as a compound on the grounds that all birds come from eggs, and *head hat* was rejected because 'All hats are worn on the head – so all hats are head hats.'[14] Furthermore, the relationship between the two parts of the compound was normally expected to be a permanent or habitual one: 'The person who says *owl-house* does not expect his hearer to interpret this as "a house that owls fall on" or "the house my owl flew by". Houses are not characterized by a general tendency to be fallen upon by owls.'[15] Similarly, the interpretation of 'a bus that ran over a pumpkin' was considered unlikely for the compound *pumpkin-bus*.[16] People were happier to consider it a bus that habitually carried pumpkins, or that looked like a pumpkin.

These preferences, therefore, help to narrow down the likely possibilities. They subconsciously guide speakers and also aid hearers in their interpretation, so they must be regarded as part of the lexical tool-kit. However, exact interpretation depends above all on the context and on the intelligence and cooperation of hearers: *plate-length hair* is hair which drags in the food, and *the apple-juice seat* was the chair in front of which the apple-juice was placed.[17] Once again, human word comprehension requires active matching skills, in which pre-existing information must be combined with information extracted from the context.

There is, incidentally, some intriguing evidence that highly educated people find it easier to cope with compounds, at least in the absence of strong contextual clues. Seven Ph.D. candidates and seven clerical workers were each asked what they thought *house-bird glass* was. Six of the Ph.D. candidates thought that it was some kind of glass relating to house-birds, but only one of the clerical workers made this suggestion. The six others made fairly bizarre proposals, such as 'a glass bird-house', 'a house-bird made from glass', 'house-bird that's in a glass'.[18] This finding suggests that familiarity with the particular compounding processes used by one's own language is important for understanding less obvious combinations of words – a question which requires further research. Let us now turn to conversions.

Lightning Conversions

'Marigold chocolated the cake,' 'Peregrine abouted the car,' 'Let's do a wash-up.' The process of converting one part of speech into another is particularly common in English,[19] possibly because the basic form of verbs and nouns is often identical, as with *play* (noun or verb). This process is easily extended, not only by adults but also by children: 'He's keying the door,' commented a 3-year-old, watching someone unlock a door. 'Is it all needled?' queried another 3-year-old as a pair of pants were mended. 'I'm shirting my man,' said a 5-year-old dressing a doll. 'Will you nut these?' requested a 6-year-old, when she wanted some walnuts cracked.[20]

There are many more nouns than verbs in a language, so the conversion of a noun to a verb is considerably more common than the other way about. One simply has to add a verbal ending. The point of doing this, for an adult, seems to be to use fewer words: 'Marigold chocolated the cake' is shorter than 'Marigold covered the cake with chocolate.' As with compounding, there are relatively few constraints on this process, but a number of preferences can be detected.[21] It is particularly common when the noun involves some type of implement, and so the corresponding verb means to use the implement in a characteristic way: 'Henry Moulinexed the vegetables' (referring to a brand of food processor); 'John squeegeed the floor' (a type of floor-mop known as a squeegee). It is also employed to describe where something has been put: 'Henry kennelled the dog'; 'The dog treed a raccoon'; 'Mavis jam-jarred the wasp.'

Other relationships are possible, but are not so common in adult language. Adults do not normally say 'I'm caking' for 'I'm eating a cake' – though children sometimes use this kind of activity construction: 'I'm souping,' said a 2-year-old as he ate soup. 'I'm lawning,' said another, playing with a toy lawnmower.[22]

In general, then, adults use these conversions in certain conventional ways, which simplifies the problem of interpretation for the hearer. The hearer, however, as in the previous examples of extended and novel formations, has to take the current context into consideration, since the same word might mean something different on different days: *Sammy pizza-ed the floor* might mean 'Sammy dropped pizza all over the floor' on one day, but *Felicity pizza-ed the dough* could signify 'Felicity made the dough into pizzas' on the next. As elsewhere, active computation is essential, integrating existing knowledge with the current situation. Let us now move on to affixation.

The Undebeakability of Donald Duck

'Undebeakability is the test of true Donald Duckishness.' This sentence, though containing 'words' which have probably never been uttered before, would be quite comprehensible to a speaker of English, especially if it occurred in an article explaining that Donald Duck could be easily distinguished from fakes by the fact that his beak could not be twisted off. The new words make use of highly productive word formation processes – prefixation and suffixation – which allow them to be easily produced and readily understood.

Suffixation is the commonest method of forming new words in English, with certain suffixes being particularly favoured. The suffix *-ness*, for example, is enormously productive, so much so that an article in *Time* magazine entitled 'The Nesselrode to ruin' suggested that it may be a 'formidable enemy' of good English when it is extended indiscriminately to all kinds of words.[23] It is primarily added on to adjectives in order to create new nouns, as in *goodness, happiness, reasonable-ness*, but can also be attached to phrases, as in *broken-heartedness, matter-of-factness, up-to-dateness, hump-backed whaleishness, Donald Duckishness*, and occasionally other types of word as well, as in *whyness, thusness, whereness, oughtness*.

The suffix *-ness* illustrates several important characteristics of the suffixes found in the lexical tool-kit.[24] First, they are normally attached to whole words or phrases, not to bits of words: we find *politeness* not *poliness, *prettiness* not *prettness. Second, they are mostly added on to the major word classes – nouns, adjectives or verbs – in order to create another noun, adjective or verb: it is somewhat rare to find an ending added to a minor part of speech, as in *this-ness* or *about-ness*. Third, each word class has its own characteristic suffixes: nouns can be turned into adjectives by adding a suffix such as *-al* or *-ish*, as in *jumbificational, duckish*, but turning a verb into an adjective requires a different suffix, one such as *-able*, as in *debeakable*.

These three major characteristics are perhaps not surprising, in view of what we already know about the mental lexicon. We have noted that words are listed as wholes, so it seems reasonable that the most productive process is one which simply adds a piece on to a complete word. We know that 'full' words are treated separately from function words, which are closely related to the syntax, so it is not strange that only the former can normally employ the lexical tool-kit. Finally, we have seen that words are stored in word classes, so it makes sense that each class should have its own attachments.

Over time, words can accumulate several suffixes, as in *reason-able-ness*, or *department-al-iz-ation*. Like an onion, these words seem to have gathered increasing layers of outer skin. In general, this heaping-up of suffixes happened gradually. Each word became accepted as a lexical item before the next suffix was added, though it is not impossible to find two suffixes which appear to get added on at the same time, as in *Donald Duckishness*. A long word might change its word class several times in the course of being built, as with *Donald Duckishness*, which changes from a noun to an adjective and then back to a noun:

Donald Duck (NOUN) -ish
Donald Duckish (ADJ) -ness
Donald Duckishness (NOUN).

A useful way of showing this layering is by means of a tree diagram, where the topmost join or 'node' shows the overall result of adding various suffixes, which can be peeled off one by one (figure 15.2).

Prefixes, on the other hand, are not often combined, though this is not impossible, as shown by *undebeakability*. They are less numerous than suffixes, and only one or two of these change the word class, such as *de-* which can make nouns into verbs, as in *de-frost, de-bug, de-beak*. Infixes are even rarer. 'Ain't that fantastic! Oh, Jeez, isn't that fangoddamtastic! . . . Ain't that fanfuckingtastic?' This overexcited comment by a character in John Gordon Davis's novel *Leviathan* illustrates the use

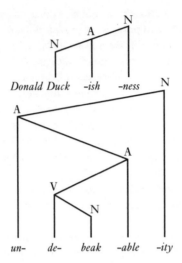

Figure 15.2   Layering of affixes

of infixes – a minor, occasional process in English, which never changes the word class. They are not random, however, but are controlled by a strict rhythmic principle, usually being inserted before the stressed syllable.[25]

Speakers, then, obviously have tools in their tool-kit which allow them to do this. Moreover, the tool-kit deals not only with sound segments, but also with adjustments to the rhythm of the original word, which may alter when a suffix is added. However, there is a further question which we need to discuss. Quite often there is more than one possible suffix in the tool-kit. How do speakers decide between them?

Scronkiness or Scronkity?

Suppose one came across a new word, *skronky*, meaning, perhaps, *scruffy* and *wonky*, and were asked to guess the noun which went with it, what would you say? *Scronkiness*? *Scronkity*? Most people judge that either is possible, but generally prefer *skronkiness*. Let us consider the guidelines which may lead to this decision.

There appear to be several 'rules of thumb' which speakers follow.[26] Frequent usage is the most obvious. There are more existing words ending in *-ness* than in *-ity*.[27] So *-ness* might just 'sound right' because it is so common. However, frequency of usage is not the only guideline.

The sound structure of the word is another factor that is taken into account. When people are asked to form a noun from a nonsense word such as *runcile*, the preference is for *runcility*: *runcileness* is judged possible, but not very likely. And this turns out to be the most usual suffix in the dictionary for adjectives ending in

-al, -ible or -ile, as in *nationality, possibility, fragility*.[28] So small portions of the lexicon have their own most probable ending.[29]

Phonetic factors are not always obvious to a casual observer. Why do we have the verbs *whiten* and *redden* but not **blonden* and **pinken?* You can say 'he reddened,' if someone blushes, though not **'he pinkened.'* The verbs *straighten* and *sharpen* exist, but not **rounden* or **blunten.* So you can say 'he straightened his tie,' but not **'she roundened the snowball.'* Why not? The answer is, look at the end of the adjectives from which these words are formed (*white, red, blond, pink; straight, sharp, round, blunt*). Only those which have a single final consonant allow the ending *-en* to be added. But for those in which *-n-* precedes the last consonant, the adding of *-en* is impossible.

A third consideration is the extent to which the existing word needs to be altered in order to produce the new one. In general, people try to retain the stress pattern of the base.[30] If you ask people to choose between *tulsivity* and *tulsiveness* as the noun for a nonsense adjective *tulsive*, they tend to choose *tulsiveness* not only because *-ness* is common, but also perhaps because it keeps the rhythm of the base word unchanged. This finding is supported by a moderately rare type of tongue-slip, in which new words are formed in the course of speech, probably because the existing one can't be accessed immediately, such as *deduce-ful* for 'deductive', *professor-al* for 'professorial' (chapter 11). The speaker tends to coin a word in which the base word is wholly reproduced. And in an experiment where people were asked to think of related words, the subjects sometimes replaced the base word even when it had been altered historically, initially saying *pompous-ity* instead of 'pomposity'.[31] Furthermore, if there is no way of keeping the original word whole, speakers prefer to keep the early part of the word intact and alter the sounds at the end, according to one researcher:[32] subjects who were asked if they preferred a verb *languidify* or *languify* as a derivative of the adjective *languid* came out in favour of *languify*. The experimenter attributed this to the fact that *languidify* would have altered the stress of the beginning of the word, and so made it hard to recognize – though another reason may be that the stress pattern of *languify* sounds more usual.

A further guideline which speakers use is the meaning. They are likely to prefer a suffix if it has a consistent meaning, so that there is a straightforward relationship between the old and the new word.[33] This is another reason for the general favouring of *-ness* over *-ity*. Words formed with *-ness* almost all denote abstract qualities, such as *kindness, cautiousness, mulishness.* Those in *-ity*, however, are less consistent. Some are abstract, as with *stability* and *equality*, but many of them also denote concrete people or institutions, as in *celebrity* and *university*. Furthermore, *-ty* endings can sometimes occur on adjectives, as in *crotchety* and *pernickety.*

The last two guidelines mentioned – a preference for keeping the base word intact and a preference for consistency in meaning – are both examples of a more general tendency found in language, a predilection for choosing formations which are 'transparent' or easily analysable and an avoidance of ones which are 'opaque' or hard to analyse.[34]

These guidelines – frequency of use, the sound structure of the base and a desire to avoid altering it, consistency of meaning in the suffix – are the main 'rules of thumb'. And there may be others which work intermittently. For example, there seems to be a resistance to having a suffix which repeats the previous sound: no one would be likely to agree to a formation *crotchety-ity* – *crotchetiness* would gain unanimous support.[35] Other sporadic preferences are less predictable: for example, a group of students thought *-ity* sounded better on nonsense words with a Latin flavour, such as *orbitality*, than on non-classical ones such as *plentifulity*.[36]

For infixes, rhythm has to be taken into account: *licketyfuckingsplit* is possible, but **lickfuckingetysplit* is not.[37] Speakers have to weigh up the guidelines. If they all reinforce one another, as sometimes happens, then the choice will be obvious. But where they clash, different speakers assess the situation in different ways. In brief, the lexical tool-kit does not work automatically. It quite often requires active decision-making, above all from the creator of the word, but also from the hearer.

Pickpocketees and Miniskirts

New words are perpetually filtering into English. But how does a new formation get itself established in the minds of speakers? This is a drip–drop process at first, which changes into a flood. People get progressively acclimatized to a new word-making device, as they hear it used more and more often.

Three things are necessary for the firm establishment of a new formation. First, the speakers must hear plentiful examples. Second, the formation must have a clear meaning. Third, it must be transparent, in the sense of being easily analysable. The acclimatization can be gradual, as in the case of the suffix *-ee*, or speedy, as in the case of *mini-*. These will be discussed below.

The ending *-ee*[38] has been around in England from the beginning of legal memory (officially dated to 1189). French was at that time used for legal matters, and 'legalese' is still spattered with terms such as *appellee*, *legatee*, *lessee*, all ending in the originally French suffix *-ee*.

Yet almost from the beginning, *-ee* was productive, that is, it produced new coinages, including non-legal ones. At first these new words were sparse. Between 1500 and 1800, 30 or fewer new *-ee* words are found in each century, though some of these became firmly embedded in the language. *Refugee*, for example, has been linked with the arrival of the Huguenots, French Protestants who fled to Britain to escape religious persecution in the seventeenth century.

Then the number of *-ee* words began to swell. About 100 were coined in the nineteenth century, though not all have remained. The words *biographee* 'someone whose biography is written' and *baptisee* 'someone baptized' now sound bizarre. So does *twistee*: 'one man did brutally twist the knee of another for a good ten minutes, and how the *twistee* groaned.' A further 200 or so have appeared in the twentieth century – though (as will be discussed below) they may not all be permanent residents in the language.

The *-ee* words were picked up by speakers fairly easily, because of their clear characteristics. They all refer to a person. An *abusee* 'someone abused' could not be a maltreated parrot or a broken window. Lack of control by the person in *-ee* is a further characteristic. The *-ee* person is often bracketed with someone in power, typically ending in *-er*, as *employer, employee*; *murderer, murderee*; *trainer, trainee*; *diner, dinee* 'someone forced to eat an unappetising meal'. Occasional exceptions to the control idea are found, as *fiancée*, though this word is usually pronounced differently, and spelled with an accent on the *-ee*. Mostly, the *-ee* person is powerless and passive, even when not part of an *-er/-ee* pair, as *amputee* 'someone whose limb has been amputated', *standee* 'someone forced to stand'.

In many cases, the *-ee* person is left in a powerless state for a long time, though a spate of recent words describes the passive recipient of a fairly brief, violent action, as *fuckee, muggee, pickpocketee* – though it's not yet clear whether these will remain in the language. The gradual accumulation of *-ee* words has therefore been going on for almost a thousand years. People have become used to hearing them, and are coining them in increasing numbers.

Other formations may take off much faster, as with words beginning with the prefix *mini-*,[39] as in *miniskirt, minicar*.

Mini- dates from 1845, according to the *Oxford English Dictionary* (*OED*). A *minibus*, a 'small bus', pronounced *MInibus* with stress on the first syllable, was offered for sale alongside an *omnibus*, a 'big bus', both of them horse-drawn, in an ad in the *Scotsman*:

> Important sale of horses, harness, and carriages . . . one excellent 12-inside omnibus, nearly as good as new . . . one handsome *minibus* in good order.

After this first occurrence, others eventually appeared, so people gradually got used to the formation. *Minicameras* are found in the 1930s. These were black box cameras, large by today's standards, but much smaller than the earlier cameras on tripods. *Mini-pianos* – small pianos which fitted into smallish homes – were found in the 1940s.

Once the *mini-* prefix was firmly established in a few words, their numbers soared. The take-off point occurred in the 1960s with transport words such as *minicabs, mini-cars* and *mini-vans*, and also clothing words: *miniskirts mini-coats, mini-dresses, mini-shorts*. Both the fashion magazine *Vogue* and the current affairs journal *The Economist* agree that 1965 was the year the *miniskirt* arrived.[40]

Then *mini-* crept on to other types of word. A writer noted that he must have been out of his *mini-mind* in 1966, and a *mini-boom* in economics happened in 1968. And new *mini-* formations continued to proliferate. The British newspapers *The Times* and *the Sunday Times* had a total of 125 stories containing a *mini*-prefix in the first three months of 1993, more than one a day, with words such as *mini-bar, mini-series, mini-enterprise, mini-conglomerate*. *Mini-* therefore came to be a dominant prefix in little over a century.

The cases of *-ee* and *mini-* show that new formations may be slow to get started, but typically they suddenly take off, especially if the word-formation process is clear both in form and meaning to new word-coiners.

Uncheesy Sandwiches

But as words pour into English, can researchers tell which word-formation processes are the most currently productive, in the sense that they are used most often by speakers to coin new words? If one simply counts words with, say, the suffix *-ness*, is it possible to distinguish the numerous existing words in *-ness* from the new coinages?

A clear-headed solution was proposed by some Dutch scholars.[41] They decided to compare the overall total of each of several endings with the number which were 'one-offs', technically *hapax legomena*, a Greek term meaning 'once said', in issues of the British newspaper *The Times*. They assumed that one-offs were thought-up on the spur of the moment, and so might diagnose which endings were in active production. They therefore listed all examples of the suffixes *-ness*, *-ity* and *-ly*, and the prefixes *un-* and *in-*, over a four-month period.

Overall, over 2,000 examples of *-ness* were found, approximately double the number of *-ity* forms. And *-ness* also had more one-offs, over 700, mostly nouns formed from adjectives, such as *crabbiness*. On the other hand, *-ity* had under 300, mostly preceded by *l*, as *anality*. The suffix *-ly* was also highly productive, with over 4,000 examples. The majority of these were adjectives formed from other adjectives, as in *breathcatchingly*. The prefix *un-*, as in the novel *uncheesy*, was more productive, than *in-* as in *inegalitarian*. The exact figures for these formations are shown in figure 15.3.

AFFIX	OVERALL	ONE-OFFS	EXAMPLE
-ness	2027	739	crabbiness
-ity	1020	280	anality
-ly	5196	1362	breathcatchingly
un-	1672	659	uncheesy
in-	243	48	inegalitarian

Figure 15.3 Productivity measured by one-offs (From Baayen and Renouf, 1996)

A number of other attempts have been made to assess productivity, and also word longevity.[42] These generally come to mainly similar conclusions, though with some clashing minor findings.

A Tronastery for Trunks

I wish I were a Tibetan monk
Living in a monastery.
I would unpack my trunk
And store it in a tronastery;
I would collect all my junk
And send it to a jonastery . . .

Ogden Nash, in his poem 'Away from it all', uses the fact that monks live in monasteries to reason that perhaps things that rhyme with *monk*, such as *trunk* and *junk*, are stored in places which rhyme with *monasteries* – *tronasteries* and *jonasteries*.

This is clearly a carefully thought-out play on words, but it parallels the type of analysis that goes on in everyday life:

Steven: This TV sure doesn't recept very well.
Mother: What do you mean, 'recept'?
Steven: You know, the reception's bad.

This conversation occurred between a woman and her 11-year-old son.[43] It shows that speakers sometimes form new words by analysing existing ones into segments – in this case the speaker had probably noted existing pairs of words in the lexicon such as *select*, *selection*, and *adopt*, *adoption*, and had figured that *recept*, *reception* was another pair in this category.

Analyses of this type form the basis of numerous new words. After the word *sputnik* was borrowed from Russian, following the launching of a Soviet satellite called a *sputnik*, *-nik* was detached, and *-nik* words were coined in profusion: a satellite launched with a dog inside it was referred to as a *dognik*, and a failed American satellite was referred to as a *flopnik*, a *goofnik*, an *oopsnik*, a *pfftnik*, a *sputternik* and a *stayputnik*.[44]

This particular type of construction – splitting words and forming new ones – relies above all on the assumption that the hearer can refer back to the original word which formed the pattern and analyse its make-up. In brief, 'words are formed from words.'[45]

Sweep-man and Smile-person

Children are enthusiastic coiners of new words. But they take a very long time to reach an adult-like ability, which probably isn't available until their teenage years. This is one piece of evidence that the lexical tool-kit can be regarded as a separate though linked component within the mental lexicon.

At first, children prefer compounds or conversion to affixation. In an experimental study, they mostly preferred compounds such as *baby wug* or *teeny wug* for a small 'wug' and *quirk-dog* for a dog covered in 'quirks',[46] in contrast to the adult *wuglet* and *quirky*. And spontaneous speech data show similar tendencies, with reports of words such as *smile-person* 'someone who smiles at people', *sweep-man* 'someone who sweeps things', *sharp* 'sharpen', as in 'How do you sharp this?'[47]

Youngsters produce a wide variety of innovations. However, many of these are illegitimate by adult standards. Children are slow to grasp adult constraints, apart from a few highly productive, very frequent suffixes. Affixes, when they develop, tend to be productive, transparent and regular, such as agentive *-er*, as in *hitter*.

Even at the age of 11, children are still a long way from an adult-type ability.[48] When asked about a 'small wug', those between the ages of 11 and 14 produced attempts such as *pug-wug*, *wuggist* and *wiggle*, with only a minority suggesting the adult preference of *wuglet*.[49] And the same was true for other processes, though the performance varied from task to task.

Researchers therefore agree that derivational endings become productive at different ages for different suffixes, and that there is 'a steady, positive development up through the adolescent period'[50] – and perhaps throughout life.

The Lexical tool-kit

Humans are able to split up words, even though (as we saw in chapter 11) this ability is not strictly necessary for existing words, since they are stored as wholes. The primary purpose of this ability, therefore, seems to be to enable speakers to make up new words of their own and to comprehend the novelties coined by others. Its secondary purpose may be as a memory aid to enable people to link up words containing similar morphemes. We noted in chapter 11 that many words had a set of back-up information attached to them. This showed how they are split up and specified links with other words containing the same morphemes. This back-up store also contains pointers to the lexical tool-kit, and it may be intermediate between that and the main lexicon. For example, *kindness* will be listed as *kindness* in the central lexicon, but in the back-up store it will be divided into *kind-ness*. There will be a link both to other words ending in *-ness*, such as *goodness* and *happiness*, and also to the tool-kit, to the rule which says that a new noun can be formed by adding *-ness* to an adjective (figure 15.4).

In this chapter, then, we have considered four types of word-formation process which are common in English: compounding, conversion, affixation and re-analysis. Although we have dealt with them separately, they can be combined. A possible word *spaghetti-sniffer*, presumably 'someone who sniffs spaghetti', involves putting a suffix on a verb, then attaching it to a noun, probably after analysing a word such as *glue-sniffer*. These mixed types behave in certain moderately predictable ways,[51] though they appear to be more complex, in that they take longer for children to learn.[52]

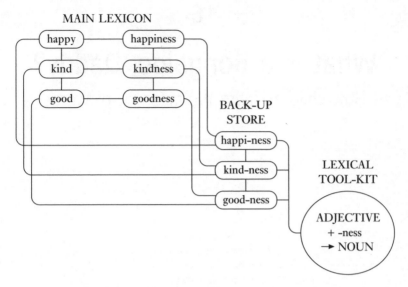

Figure 15.4 The lexical tool-kit and the back-up store

Summary

In this chapter, we examined the lexical tool-kit, the human facility for creating new words, an optional and always available ability, though one which develops slowly. We examined a number of common word-formation processes in English – compounding, conversion and affixation – and noted that these were flexible, in that there were relatively few overall constraints. However, there were a number of guidelines which narrowed down the range of new formations, and made inter-pretation easier for the hearers. Furthermore, the lexical tool-kit does not work in isolation. It has access to back-up information about each word, which helps it to deal with cases in which new words are formed by re-analysis.

Above all, the process of creating new words shows how enormously flexible the human mind is in coping with vocabulary. The creation of new words reinforces a viewpoint which we have already reached: that the mental lexicon is not a fixed dictionary with a set amount of information about each word, but an active system in which new links are perpetually being formed.

However, there is one important aspect of new words which has not yet been explored: that is, words which are new to the person learning them, though not new to the language. This will be the topic of the next two chapters, with a particular focus on the way children acquire words.

16

What is a Bongaloo, Daddy?

— How children learn the meaning of words —

'What is a Bongaloo, Daddy?'
'A Bongaloo, Son,' said I,
'Is a tall bag of cheese
Plus a Chinaman's knees
And the leg of a nanny goat's eye.'
Spike Milligan, 'The Bongaloo'

Children pick up words like a magnet picks up pins – possibly over ten a day.[1] Estimates vary as to vocabulary size at each age. On average, a 2-year-old actively uses around 500 words, a 3-year-old over 1,000, and a 5-year-old up to 3,000.[2] And this is far fewer than the number of words which can be understood. The passive vocabulary of a 6-year-old has been estimated at 14,000 by one researcher.[3]

Finding out how youngsters build up a store of words may provide additional clues to the mental lexicon. Of course, we cannot take it for granted that children store and retrieve words in the same way as adults. They may or they may not.

To return to the library analogy of chapter 3, one might as a first guess suggest that children are born owning a huge room lined with empty shelves. As they acquire each new word, they put it in its pre-ordained place, having been preprogrammed with the knowledge that certain words should be assigned to certain shelves or that particular types of words should be stored together. If this scenario is a realistic one, the difference between an adult's and a child's mental lexicon is primarily one of quantity. The words would be stored and retrieved in the same way, but the child would know fewer.

Alternatively, one might assume that the child initially organized its mental lexicon along the equivalent of a tiny shelf, in a fairly haphazard order. Only when she acquired too many words for the shelf or had problems finding a word she wanted, would she reorganize her system by setting up new shelves and arranging different types of words on different shelves. This process of enlarging the store and rearranging it might go on progressively as the child gets older. In this case, a child's mental lexicon might be somewhat different from an adult's, particularly in

Figure 16.1 Tasks involved in learning the meaning of words

the early stages. We shall be considering which of these scenarios is the most likely – or whether each of them encapsulates some portion of the truth.

How, then, do children acquire word meaning? According to the nineteenth-century psychologist James Sully, the task is a formidable one, so much so that the child can be likened to a 'little explorer' struggling over unknown terrain: 'Let us see what the little explorer has to do when trying to use verbal sounds with their right meanings . . . We shall find that huge difficulties beset his path, and that his arrival at the goal proves him to have been in his way as valiant and hard-working as an African explorer.'[4]

What are these 'huge difficulties'? Essentially, children are faced with three different but related tasks: a labelling task, a packaging task and a network-building task (figure 16.1). In the labelling task, youngsters must discover that sequences of sound can be used as names for things. In the packaging task, they must find out which things can be packaged together under one label. In the network-building task, they must work out how words relate to one another. Let us discuss these in turn.

The Labelling Task

Some people are surprised that one needs to ask how children learn to label things. They assume that the answer is obvious. Adults point to things, such as a toy duck or a glass of orange juice, and say, 'Duck', 'Juice'. Children in consequence learn to associate the names *duck* and *juice* with the things being pointed at.

The above view, however, is a considerable oversimplification. Symbolization – the realization that a particular combination of sounds 'means' or symbolizes a certain object – turns out to be quite a complex skill. It takes time to develop,[5] and need not emerge until well after a child's first birthday.[6]

Proud parents often find this comparatively late development hard to believe. Doting mothers and fathers frequently claim that babies under a year old can say *mama* and *papa*. But infants are unlikely to have attached the adult meaning to the words at this stage. In the early months of their life children experiment with making noises. Sounds formed at the front of the mouth are comparatively easy for a young child. So the sequences *mama*, *papa*, which are made with the lips, are likely to be babbled spontaneously from around six months, purely as random noises: 'Unprejudiced observers find that these babbling syllables have at first no meaning at all, are mere muscle exercises.'[7]

If the child says 'Mama' as its mother approaches it, it is understandable that the average mother will misinterpret this and impose her own meaning on the child, as was recognized by some early researchers such as the nineteenth-century German physiologist William Preyer: 'For the first articulate expression of concepts, some of those easily uttered syllables are employed which have been previously uttered by the child without consciousness or aim; the meaning is introduced into them wholly by the parents or nurse. Such syllables are *pa* and *ma*, with their reduplications, *papa*, *mama*, as appellations of the parents.'[8] Or, as a researcher noted some years later: 'It is natural that fond mothers, waiting for the traditional word joyfully interpret it as a reference to themselves; but dispassionate scholars should not follow them into this trap.'[9]

Even if proud parents accept this explanation for the early development of *papa* and *mama*, they are likely to point out equally young children who apparently know all the names in their alphabet book. But uttering particular sounds in response to different pictures does not guarantee that the child is genuinely 'naming' anything. This whole procedure may simply be a great game for the child. At the page where a large black fuzzy blob appears, a parent might point and say 'Cat'. The child's response shriek of 'Ga' may be a ritual response to a particular page of a particular book. The discovery that 'Ga' is the name for an object, a cat, could come some time later.[10]

The notion that many early 'words' are simply ritual accompaniments to a whole situation can be illustrated by the early utterances of young Adam.[11] 'Dut' ('duck') shrieked this 12-month-old child excitedly each evening at bathtime as he knocked a yellow toy duck off the edge of the bathtub. Adam said 'Dut' only when Adam himself knocked the duck off. And he never said 'Dut' when the duck was swimming in the bath. So *dut* seemed to be an unanalysed cry uttered as Adam swiped at the duck. It was a ritualized accompaniment to a whole scenario, and could perhaps be best translated as 'Whoopee' or 'Here goes'. At first, then, Adam had no realization that *dut* could label a particular part of the situation. And the same was true of his other early words. He said 'Chuff-chuff' only when he, Adam, was pushing his toy train across the floor. He did not say 'Chuff-chuff' when the train was still. And he said 'Dog' only when his father, and no one else, pointed to a picture of a dog on the bib he was wearing and said, 'What's that?'

A second stage occurred when Adam started to broaden the circumstances under which he produced these ritualized utterances. For example, he began to use the word *dog* not only when his father pointed to the dog on his bib and said, 'What's that?' but also when his mother or he himself did so. A third stage occurred when Adam finally dissociated each word from a whole event and started to use it as a label for a specific object or event. *Dut* was used to refer to his yellow toy ducks in any situation, and not just when they were being knocked off the bathtub. Later the word was used for real ducks, swans and geese. Similarly, *chuff-chuff* and *dog* were eventually widened out to include proper trains and dogs.

Adam's early 'words', then, became detached from whole situations in stages. There was considerable variability, in that they went through the stages at different times and at varying speeds. In addition, some words missed out a stage. But somewhere between the ages of one and two Adam reached a 'labelling stage'. Various researchers have remarked on a vocabulary spurt around this time. This may be due to the discovery that things have names, leading to a passion for attaching labels[12] – though other explanations are possible.[13]

The 'naming explosion' happens in most children, but not all. 'The word spurt is a myth,' according to one researcher.[14] The new names are often labels for objects, and tend to be words used frequently by parents.[15] Youngsters who show less of a spurt have a smaller vocabulary, but a wider range. Two researchers note: 'A "spurt" or "surge" may best describe children who concentrate their early linguistic efforts on a single strategy: learning names for things. This single-minded focus would allow children to accumulate words rapidly. Children who learn words at a more gradual pace may be manifesting an alternative strategy, one that attempts to encode a broad range of experience.'[16]

However, early vocabulary is hard to classify. It's not always easy to tell which words name things, as shown by 1-year-old Emma, who said *Hello* when greeting her father, when playing with a toy telephone and when pointing to a telephone in a book.[17] And is *drink* an object or not?[18]

Labelling, then, develops some time before the age of 2, but at different speeds in different children. It overlaps with the packaging task. Let us go on to consider this.

The Packaging Task

There is quite a lot of difference between applying a label such as *penguin* to one toy penguin and the ability to use that label correctly in all circumstances. How does a child come to apply the name *penguin* to a wider range of penguins? And how does she learn to restrict it to penguins alone, and not use it for puffins and pandas, which are also black and white? And what about blind children, who can't see black and white?

Superficially, at least, children seem to deal with words rather differently. By adult standards, both underextensions and overextensions occur: sometimes children assume that a word refers to a narrower range of things than it in fact does, whereas at other times they include far too much under a single name.

Underextensions seem quite understandable, as when 20-month-old Hildegard refused to accept that the word *white* could be used of blank pages, since she herself associated it only with snow.[19] She had acquired the word in a particular context, and it took time for her to realize that the word had a wider application. Similarly, a child quizzed on the words *deep* and *shallow* 'might respond correctly if he happens to be probed about ends of swimming pools . . . But if shown a picture of a deep puddle – a girl sinking into a mud puddle up to her knees – and asked "Is this a deep puddle?" the child might answer, "No, a big one." '[20] And in cases where words have abstract as well as concrete physical applications, it may be years before the child fully understands the range of meaning covered: in one experiment 3- and 4-year-olds readily called milk *cold*, water *deep*, boxes *hard* and trees *crooked*, but had no idea that these words could be extended to people, and some even denied that it was possible: 'I never heard of deep people anyway!' 'No people are cold!'[21] A period of underextension for a word, then, is quite normal, and the gradual enlarging of meaning to include an increasingly wide range does not seem particularly puzzling.

Overextensions are less common than underextensions, but are more noticeable, as the effects may be bizarre. 'One feature of the early tussle with our language is curious and often quaintly pretty,' commented the psychologist James Sully. 'Having at first but a few names, the little experimenter makes the most of these by extending them in new and surprising directions . . . The name "pin" was extended to a crumb . . . , a fly and a caterpillar . . . The same child used the sound "'at" (hat) for anything put on the head, including a hairbrush.'[22]

Three main types of explanation have been proposed for overextensions: gap-filling, 'mental fog' and wrong analysis. The first of these suggests that 'the dearth of words compels the child to use words for purposes to which they are not adapted from the adult point of view.'[23] He might recognize the difference between duck and a peacock but say *duck* for both because he doesn't yet know the word *peacock*. Or she might know the name *peacock*, but be unable to pronounce it, since some children consciously avoid sounds they find difficult to cope with.[24] Gap-filling explanations are possibly correct for some overextensions, but are unlikely to account for all of them, especially the more bizarre ones such as using the same word for a duck and a mug of milk.

'The child unquestionably perceives the world through a mental fog. But as the sun of experience rises higher and higher these boundaries are beaten back.'[25] This statement by an early twentieth-century psychologist typifies the 'mental fog' viewpoint. Its proponents argue that meanings are necessarily hazy and vague in the early stages, and that they gradually become more precise as children learn to discriminate more finely. At first, 'rough classifications suffice. With advancing maturity, finer subdivisions are needed, and new words are learned to satisfy the urge for expressing them.'[26]

Another version of this theory suggests that 'when the child first begins to use identifiable words, he does not know their full (adult) meaning: he has only partial entries for them in the lexicon . . . The acquisition of semantic knowledge, then, will consist of adding . . . to the lexical entry of the word until the child's . . . entry for that word corresponds to the adult's.'[27] The child might have learnt the word *dog* but only noticed certain outline characteristics: 'dogginess' might have been identified with 'being four-legged'. In that case, cows, sheep, zebras and llamas would wrongly be included in the category *dog*. But each of these lexical items would gradually be narrowed down. To the lexical entry for *dog* the child might attach the additional specifications 'makes barking sounds', 'is fairly small', while to *zebra* it might add 'striped' and 'fairly large', so distinguishing one from the other. Eventually, the child's lexical entries would have all the details filled in, and so be comparable to those of an adult.

This gradual narrowing down may apply to some words. But there are two facts which this type of theory does not explain. First, relatively few words are overextended – perhaps less than a third.[28] If the mental fog viewpoint was correct, one would expect many more words to start out by being too wide in their application. Second, many of the overextensions are bizarre and cannot easily be related to a lack of subdivisions in the adult word. This suggests that the child is not simply operating in a mental fog, in which he can only see broad outlines. Instead, he has made an analysis of the items concerned, but a wrong one by adult standards.

The Russian psychologist Vygotsky (1893–1934) discusses a child who used *qua* ('quack') for a duck swimming on a pond, a cup of milk, a coin with an eagle on it and a teddy bear's eye.[29] In his view, children are perfectly capable of analysis, but they tend to focus on only one aspect of a situation at a time and to generalize that alone. The child began with *qua* as a duck on a pond. Then the liquid element caught the youngster's attention, and the word was generalized to a cup of milk. But the duck had not been forgotten, and this surfaced in *qua* used to refer to a coin with an eagle on it. But then the child appeared to ignore the bird-like portion of the meaning and focus only on the roundness of the coin, so reapplied the word *qua* to a teddy bear's eye. Vygotsky calls this a 'chain-complex', because all the usages of *qua* are linked together in a chain. Each one is attached to the next, with no overall structure.

Another 'wrong analysis' theory suggests that children are working from proto-types. Perhaps they learn the meaning of words by picking on a typical example or 'prototype' which they analyse. They then match other possible examples of a category against the characteristics of the prototype, and if there is sufficient agreement, they assign the new object to the same category. According to this viewpoint, discrepancies between child and adult language occur because children analyse the prototype differently from adults. For example, between the ages of

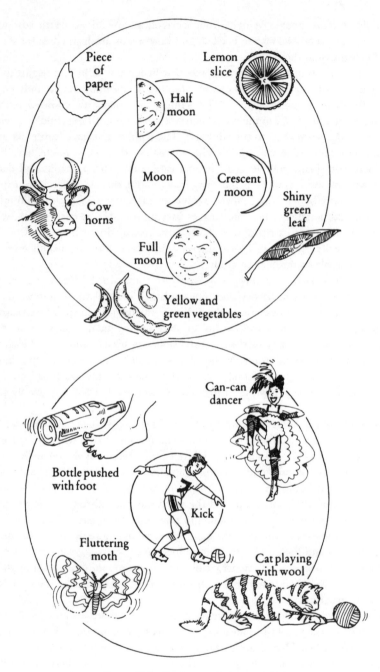

Figure 16.2　Eva's use of *moon* and *kick*

16 months and 2 years Eva used the word *moon* to refer not only to the moon but also to a slice of lemon, a shiny green leaf, curved cow horns, a crescent-shaped piece of paper and pictures of yellow and green vegetables on the wall of a store.[30] Most of these objects are crescent-shaped, which seemed to be an important property of moonhood for Eva. At first sight this observation supports mental fog theories: perhaps Eva simply thinks that *moon* means 'crescent'. But on examination there was more to it than this. First, Eva was able to recognize the moon in all its phases, when it was a full moon, a half moon or a quarter moon. So moons were not inevitably crescents, they were just typically crescents. Second, each of the objects labelled *moon* had something else apart from shape in common with the moon, though something different. The lemon slice shared its colour with the moon. The shiny green leaf shared the property of being shiny. The curved cow horns were seen from below. The green and yellow vegetables on the chart were seen against a broad expanse of background. So Eva had apparently identified several characteristics of the moon, the most crucial of which is its shape. Something was likely to be labelled *moon* if it shared both the shape and one other characteristic with the real moon (figure 16.2).

Similarly, at around the same age, Eva took someone kicking a ball as a prototype for the word *kick*.[31] She seems to have analysed this action as possessing three main characteristics: first, a waving limb, second, sudden sharp contact between part of the body and an object, third, propulsion forward of the object. This analysis could account for her labelling as *kick* a kitten with a ball of wool near its paw, dancers doing the can-can, a moth fluttering on a table, pushing a bottle with her feet and pushing a teddy bear's stomach against her sister's chest. All these things share characteristics with the prototypical *kick* but not the same ones (figure 16.2).[32]

Prototype theory therefore accounts for children's broad mental fog-type generalizations as well as the strange chain-complex ones. And it ties in with the way in which adults assign words to categories. Children, like adults, look for clusters of properties which belong to a prototype.[33]

Children differ from adults, however, in that they may not focus on the same features when they analyse words. In the early stages, they are over-influenced by appearance, especially shape.[34] When asked to name an object that was a crayon shaped like a car, younger children tended to call it a *car*, and older ones a *crayon*.[35]

Kindergarten-age children concentrate on superficial characteristics.[36] A child was asked if a friendly and cheerful woman who disconnected and removed a toilet bowl could be a robber. The reply was: 'No . . . 'cause robbers, they have to have guns and they do stickups, and this woman didn't do that, and she didn't have a gun, she didn't do a stickup.'[37] Another child argued that a hut containing dirty clothes which people paid to see couldn't be a museum, because 'a museum is something with dinosaur bones.' As children get older, they gradually alter their analyses to fit in with those of the people around them[38] – though this can go on into the teenage years.[39]

But what about blind children, who can't see all these superficial features? They lag behind sighted youngsters in the early stages of acquisition, but they soon catch up: 'By the third birthday, they are virtually indistinguishable from their sighted peers.'[40] And two to three years later, they can hold coherent conversations about visual matters, as shown by the responses of young Kelli:[41]

Researcher:	How do we see? What do we see with?
Kelli:	You guys see with your eyes.
Researcher:	And how about you?
Kelli:	No.
Researcher:	No?
Kelli:	I see with my hands.

When asked whether thunderstorms could be green, she said: 'Really not any colour – just out there roaring like a lion,' and when asked whether cars could be blue, she said: 'Our Toyota is blue . . . some cars are blue.'[42]

Kelli apparently started off by learning the names for various objects, like many sighted children. Then, she noticed which words could co-occur, again like other children.[43] She had heard people talk about blue cars, brown dogs and yellow flowers, so she knew what colours things could be – humans are particularly 'tuned in' to words which go together (chapter 8). Kelli reliably distinguished *look* and *see*, and used them correctly, because she payed attention to her mother's speech:

Look, here's how you wind the clock.
You look like a kangaroo.
Come and see the kitty.
See if you can put the slipper on.

But noticing which words co-occur is part of the network-building process. Let us go on to consider this.

Network-building

Somehow, words have to be fitted together into a semantic network. How does this happen?

The evidence is sometimes confusing. 'What's this?', asked $2\frac{1}{2}$-year-old Brian as he picked up a plastic horse. He was mimicking the behaviour of the experimenter who had just been testing him on word-names. The following conversation ensued:[44]

Experimenter:	It's an animal.
Brian:	No.
Experimenter:	Yes it is.
Brian:	No (laughs).
Experimenter:	Yes.
Brian:	No.

Experimenter:	This is an animal too.
Brian:	No.
Experimenter:	Yes.
Brian:	Horsie.
Experimenter:	It's also an animal.
Brian:	No.
Experimenter:	Just like you're Brian and you're a little boy.
Brian:	No.
Experimenter:	Yeah.
Brian:	No.
Experimenter:	You don't believe me.
Brian:	No.

Brian would not believe that a horse was an animal. This dialogue appears at first sight to confirm the view of the Swiss psychologist Jean Piaget that Brian was too young to understand the relationship of inclusion, the fact that horses are included in the category of animal.[45] But Piaget's claim seems rather strange, since children of 2 can respond to commands such as 'Pick up your toys.' Perhaps, alternatively, children may just be resistant to giving an object more than one name.[46] If a pig is a pig, then it can't be an animal. This seemed to be the reaction of around half of the 2-year-olds tested. They reserved the word *animal* for a bunch of assorted animals. And the 'one name only' preference has been confirmed by other researchers.[47]

The evidence, then, can be difficult to interpret. Apparent backward steps may be the best guide that network-building is taking place.[48] Two-year-old Christie used the words *put* and *give* appropriately, as in 'I *put* it somewhere,' '*Gimme* more gum.' Then, when she was 3, she started to use them interchangeably: 'You *put* ("give") me bread and butter,' 'Whenever Eva doesn't need her towel, she *gives* ("puts") it on my table.'[49] Perhaps, suggested Christie's mother, she had suddenly discovered that *put* and *give* had very similar meanings, but had not yet realized that one *puts* something on to a thing, but *gives* something to a person. Two more years elapsed before Christie used *put* and *give* correctly by adult standards.

Network-building takes place slowly. The 'lethargy of semantic development'[50] is a fairly general finding among researchers. Words which an adult would regard as related take time to get linked in the child's mind. This fits with the evidence from underextensions, the fact that children often learn a word in a particular context and only gradually extend it to a wider situation. Even fairly old children may find it hard to detach words from specific contexts. A group aged between 82½ and 102½ correctly guessed that the nonsense word *lidber* meant 'collect' from the sentence 'Jimmy lidbered stamps from all countries.' But when asked to interpret 'The police did not allow the people to lidber on the street,' a typical response was that the police did not allow people to collect stamps on the street.[51]

Slow network-building is seen in terms for family relations. 'A father is somebody who goes to work every day except Saturday and Sunday and earns money,' said a

5-year-old.[52] This response is partly due to a bias towards surface characteristics. But such replies are also caused by the way relatives get talked about: 'Uncle Buster gets blamed for everything' was a recurring statement in one family. It was far easier for the child to learn about Uncle Buster's 'badness' than about how uncles fit into the family setting.[53] Only at around the age of 7 does a child fit the various kinship terms together, as shown by comments such as: 'A niece is like a mother had a sister, and I'd be her niece.'[54]

The tortoise-like progress of network-building is confirmed by the literally dozens of studies which have explored how children cope with overlapping words, such as *tall*, *big*, *fat*, *high*, and opposites, such as *big–small*, *deep–shallow*, *tall–short*.[55] All the studies reported that these words acquire their adult meaning only gradually, sometimes with backward steps. One researcher found that children started out by using *big* to refer to gross overall size, but then mistakenly narrowed it down to meaning 'tall'.[56] Certain general trends emerge: the words *big* and *small* are used by younger children in preference to *tall–short*, *wide–narrow*, and children can cope with the larger of the two opposites better than the smaller: *fat* is learnt before *thin*, *high* before *low*, *long* before *short*. But the interpretation of these findings is disputed, since various other factors, such as children's preference for large rather than small objects and parental usage, complicate the situation.

Collocational links appear to have priority for children, while those between coordinates lag behind. This is shown by word association experiments: young children are likely to respond to 'table' with *eat*, to 'dark' with *night*, to 'send' with *letter* and to 'deep' with *hole*, whereas typical adult responses to these would be *chair*, *light*, *receive* and *shallow*.[57] As children get older, the more likely they are to give an adult-like response. A suggested explanation is that 'this change in word associations is a consequence of the child's gradual organization of his vocabulary into the syntactic classes called parts-of-speech.'[58] Another explanation is that children may take time to discover the criteria by which adults classify items as coordinates. A study conducted with a group of 3- to 5-year-olds showed that they were quite happy to agree that prototypical birds, such as sparrows or robins, were birds, but often argued that ducks or hens were not birds, they were ducks and hens.[59] It is unclear whether the children had come to this conclusion by themselves or whether they were simply reflecting the speech of their parents, since the same experimenter noted that parents tended to refer to typical birds as *birds* more often than atypical ones: 'Oh, look there's a bird, it's a robin'; 'That's a turkey, like the ones we saw at the turkey farm.'

Efficient retrieval may be another explanation for the importance of coordinates in adult speech. Fast word-finding is a skill that has to be acquired, and young children can be quite slow at naming objects such as *ice-cream*, *lion* and *bed*, whose names they know very well.[60] Perhaps the gradual shift-over comes in response to a need to organize and retrieve words quickly as the overall vocabulary gets larger.

Children, then, are continually acquiring new words. They begin by using each one in a restricted setting, then later fit it into an overall network as they detach it from the context in which it was learnt – and adults possibly learn words in a similar way. This continual integration of new words 'appears to be an extremely gradual process which may never be complete'.[61]

To return to the library analogy mentioned at the beginning of this chapter, both the 'large empty room' and the 'rearranging shelves' viewpoints are right to some extent. Children are constantly rearranging their 'mental shelves', yet both the original classification and any rearrangement are carried out in accordance with general principles which they seem to understand instinctively, and which are broadly the same as those followed by adults.[62]

Summary

In this chapter, we have looked at how children acquire the meanings of words. This involved three different tasks: labelling, packaging and network-building.

Labelling is not an automatic procedure. The ability to symbolize develops slowly, and probably emerges somewhere between the ages of one and two. It may be connected with a 'naming explosion' which often happens around this time.

Packaging, the classification of a number of objects under a particular label, leads to two common kinds of error: underextension and overextension. The gradual widening out of an over-narrow meaning is fairly straightforward. Overextension is often due to wrong analysis: children, like adults, seem to work from prototypes, even though they tend to analyse the characteristics of the prototype somewhat differently. They also pay attention to words which co-occur, as shown by the development of language in blind children.

Network-building happens gradually, and may continue throughout a person's life. Words are applied in a limited context only when they are first learned. Collocational links have a strong priority in early childhood. Gradually, words are integrated into the network, and links are built between coordinates, perhaps partly as a consequence of acquiring syntax and partly to allow for fast word-finding as the overall vocabulary increases.

Overall, children work from the same general principles as adults, but pay attention to different facets of these.

Let us now go on to consider how children handle the sound structure of these words.

17

Aggergog Miggers, Wips and Gucks

— How children cope with the sound structure of words —

Listen to me, angel tot,
Whom I love an awful lot . . .
When I praise your speech with glee
And claim you talk as well as me,
That's the spirit, not the letter.
I know more words, and say them better.
Ogden Nash, 'Thunder over the nursery'

Children mutilate words, by adult standards. Anyone who listens for only a few minutes to a young child is likely to hear forms such as *guck* for 'duck', *wip* for 'ship', *tat* for 'cat' or even *aggergog migger*, which appeared to mean 'helicopter' and 'cement mixer' interchangeably for one child.[1] In order to understand how children cope with the sound structure of words, we need to probe into these 'deformations'. Do they accurately represent the contents of the mental lexicon? Alternatively, perhaps the child's stored forms are more advanced but unpronounceable, so that only a mangled approximation remains: 'His articulatory organs cannot master the terrible words we put in his way, and he is driven to these short cuts and other makeshifts.'[2] These and other possible explanations need to be considered.

To an outsider, it may seem like a waste of time to try and unravel this gobbledegook. But the alterations are by no means haphazard, and in normal children there are consistent links between the child and adult forms. If a child says *dee* instead of 'tree', substituting [d] for [tr], then she is likely to say *dain* for 'train' and *duck* for 'truck' as well. Similarly, if she says *wip* for 'ship', then she will probably say *woo* for 'shoe' and *weep* for 'sheep'. Furthermore, the same types of alterations occur in languages all over the world. Certain substitutions seem to be typical of early child utterances. For example, sounds made near the back of the mouth are often replaced by sounds made near the front, as in *doose* for 'goose' or *tat* for 'cat'. Two consonants separated by a single vowel tend to 'harmonize', in the sense that they are likely to become similar, so 'cream' might become *meem* and

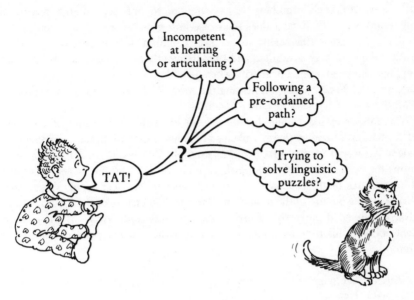

Figure 17.1   Theories about children's word 'deformations'

'lorry' might become *lolly*. Sounds at the ends of words tend to be devoiced –
produced without vibration of the vocal cords – as in *bet* for 'bed' and *ek* for 'egg'.
And there are numerous others.[3] What causes them?

Three main types of explanation have been put forward: physical incompetence,
pre-ordained paths and unsolved puzzles (figure 17.1). Incompetence explanations emphasize that children are just physically incapable, when compared with
adults. The poor little darlings can't hear properly, or they can't get their tongue
round the required sounds. Pre-ordained path theories suggest that children are
pre-programmed to cope with sounds in a certain way or certain order, and the
deformations are therefore predestined steps which the child must pass through
before acquiring the adult form. Puzzle-solving theories argue that the sound
structure of a language is a puzzle which each child has to solve slowly, and that
until it has done so, deformations will remain. Let us consider each of these in
turn.

The Cloth Ears Theory

'The child acquires the adult phonological system by way of his perception of
certain limited features of the adult form. These he reproduces . . . As his perception improves, the responses change. He discriminates more and attempts to
reproduce more.'[4] This represents the simplest hypothesis in relation to children's
'deformations', since it suggests that they are, to a large extent, reproducing what

they hear. At first children hear, or pay attention to, only certain gross features of the sound waves. Only later does their discrimination become 'fine-tuned'.

To some extent this seems to be true. Children do not perceive sounds in exactly the same way as adults,[5] and they frequently misperceive words.[6] Misperceptions can be identified primarily when a child gives an irrelevant response. For example, one French child, on hearing the word *Angleterre* ('England'), responded with the word for *pomme de terre* ('potato').[7]

But misperception cannot be the sole or even the main cause of children's 'deformations', because there is plenty of evidence that youngsters perceive considerably more than they produce. For example, 2-year-old Amahl had the same forms for *bus* and *brush, jug* and *duck, cart* and *card, mouse* and *mouth*. His father drew pictures of these objects and placed them in the next room. When asked 'Bring me the picture of the mouse' or 'Bring me the picture of the mouth,' Amahl always responded correctly.[8] Furthermore, he was quite aware of some of the deficiencies in his pronunciation, as when his father tried to persuade him to say 'Jump':

Father:	Say 'jump'.
Amahl:	Dup.
Father:	No, 'jump'.
Amahl:	Dup.
Father:	No, 'jummmp'.
Amahl:	Oli daddy gan day dup (= Only Daddy can say 'jump').

Further evidence of the discrepancy between what a child hears and what she says are provided by dialogues such as the following between an uncle and his niece Nicola, who called herself *Dicola*:

Uncle:	What's your name?
Nicola:	You know.
Uncle:	Is it Dicola?
Nicola:	No, Dicola.
Uncle:	Oh, Nicola.
Nicola:	Yes.

This is sometimes called the 'fis phenomenon' because of a child who called a plastic fish a *fis*. 'Is this your *fis*?' the researchers asked. 'No,' replied the child, 'My *fis*.'[9] As in this case, children are quite often puzzled if they are addressed in speech which resembles their own output. When a French mother addressed her child using his own deformations, the indignant youngster replied, 'Talk French to me, mummy.'[10] This would be unlikely to happen if he was reproducing what he heard.

'Backward steps' in pronunciation provide even stronger evidence of the gap between perception and production. At one point, Amahl said *dut* for both 'lunch' and 'shut'. Later he distinguished between them in pronunciation, saying *lut* for 'lunch' and *dut* for 'shut'.[11] But later still, he suddenly started pronouncing both of them as *lut*! Anyone maintaining that children say what they perceive would have to assume that this child at one time perceived the distinction between *lunch* and *shut*, but then suddenly failed to hear the difference any more. Furthermore, this is not an exceptional case. Forms which were once separate but later merge in the child's output are found quite often.[12] This phenomenon suggests that more is going on than simple misperception.

There is plenty of evidence, then, to suggest that children do not have 'cloth ears' – perhaps not surprisingly, considering the acuteness of the mammalian ear. Babies only a few weeks old can hear the difference between [b] and [p],[13] and so can rhesus monkeys and chinchillas.[14] The babies in the experiment sucked dummies which were hooked up to a sound system, so that each suck produced a pre-set sound, which at first was [p]. So they heard *pah-pah-pah-pah*. . . . As the babies got bored, their rate of sucking decreased. Then this [p] was changed to [b]. An acceleration in the sucking rate showed that the infants had noticed the change.

The difference between what children perceive and what they say, therefore, suggests that the words they utter might be somewhat different from those stored in their mental lexicons. So let us now go on to consider the theory that the problem is a purely mechanical one. According to this view, children have the words in their minds – they just can't get their tongue round certain sounds.

The Tongue-twister Theory

'I believe I can, on the foundation of my observations, state the following basic law: that the speech sounds are produced by children in an order which begins with the sounds articulated with the least physiological effort, gradually proceeds to the speech sounds produced with greater effort, and ends with the sounds that require the greatest effort for their production.'[15] This pronouncement in 1880 by Fritz Schultze, professor of philosophy and pedagogy at Dresden, became known as 'Schultze's Law', and was widely accepted at that time.

This 'tongue-twister' theory, like the 'cloth ears' theory, encapsulates a certain amount of truth. Particular sounds, such as English *th* [θ], as in *think*, are more difficult to cope with than others: they require extra precision and muscular tension. And some sound sequences, such as the cluster of consonants in *explain* [eksplein], may require more neuromuscular coordination than the child can manage. Nevertheless, children are physically capable of producing more sounds than they in fact do. Sounds which are not found in actual words may be present in babbling: a child may replace every [k] with [t] when it attempts to pronounce words, but may still babble long *kakakakaka* sequences.[16] Furthermore, a sound apparently unavailable in one word may be used in another word. Young Hildegarde used the sequence *moush* [mauʃ] for *mouth*, with a clear *sh* [ʃ] at the end, but she did not use *sh* in a word such as *shoe*.[17] In addition, she repeated the word *pretty* correctly when she first heard it, but later reverted to saying *pity*. This less accurate pronunciation fitted in with the way she dealt with other occurrences of [pr] which she pronounced as [p].

It is oversimple, therefore, to argue that children just can't pronounce things properly. Their muscles are not too floppy, nor their tongue too clumsy, as is sometimes supposed. The realization that children can both hear and pronounce more than they actually do has suggested to some researchers that there is some universal pre-ordained path which they are obliged to follow: some inbuilt constraint prevents them from articulating sounds that they are physically capable of producing, because they are genetically programmed to follow a particular route as they acquire sound patterns. Let us consider this viewpoint.

Pre-ordained Path Theories

The best-known pre-ordained path theory is that of Roman Jakobson, one of the pioneers in child language phonology, who claimed that speech contrasts are pre-programmed to emerge in a set order.[18] He proposed a set of 'implicational laws', according to which certain contrasts are unable to emerge until certain others have been acquired. For example, he stated that the first consonantal contrast a child makes will be between a nasal consonant (in which air is expelled through the nose) such as [m] and a non-nasal stop (sound produced with a complete stoppage of breath) made near the front of the mouth such as [p], as in *mama* and *papa*. After this, he suggested, the stop will be subdivided into labial – made with the lips such as [p] – and dental – made with the tongue against the teeth as in [t]. A contrast between these front stops must be acquired before one between a front stop and a back stop, such as [k], can be brought into the child's sound system. And so on (figure 17.2).

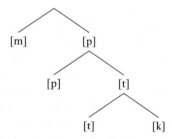

Figure 17.2   Jakobson's pre-ordained path theory

A number of researchers have examined these claims. There seems to be general agreement that Jakobson's 'laws' are statistical tendencies rather than obligatory universals.[19] Many children fit Jakobson's pattern to a reasonable extent, and some fit it perfectly.[20] But a number of others break it.[21] A statement of general tendencies can provide a useful guideline for charting normal development, but it does not explain why children 'deform' words.

A somewhat different pre-ordained path theory suggests that the human vocal organs are organized in such a way that certain sounds, or sound sequences, are more 'natural' than others.[22] For example, it is natural to have alternating consonants and vowels, so *abu* may be more 'natural' than *apple*. Similarly, it is natural to devoice sounds (produce them without vibrating the vocal cords) at the end of words, so *pik* may be more 'natural' than *pig*. According to this theory, words in which the natural tendencies are followed will be easier to learn, and those in which they are not – perhaps the majority – will be harder. In producing words, then, children must gradually suppress the universal tendencies they are born with, and learn the idiosyncratic rules of the particular language they are acquiring.

This theory, unlike Jakobson's, does not require all children to develop phonological structure in exactly the same order. Variation occurs partly because different processes may clash and children may choose to resolve the clashes in different ways, and partly because they may suppress different processes at different ages. For example, a word such as *duck* might be pronounced by one child as *dut* with the second consonant harmonizing with the first (both articulated at the front of the mouth) and by another as *guck* with the first consonant harmonizing with the second (both articulated at the back of the mouth). A mild tendency for the first consonant to harmonize with the second clashes with a tendency for sounds to be produced at the front of the mouth.

However, the fact that the theory allows so much variation is also its greatest weakness: whatever the child says can be attributed to a different natural process or a different order of suppression, with no overall guiding principle. One concludes that certain 'natural processes' – the ones which occur very widely, such as a tendency to devoice consonants at the end of words – are indeed built in to the way the articulatory organs work, but that the others – the weaker ones – do not 'explain' the deformations, since they need not happen.

But the main problem with the natural processes viewpoint is that it treats the child as a fairly passive individual, flattened by these universal tendencies and attempting to struggle out from under them. This does not tie in with the general impression that people have of children in the early stages of language development. They are mostly energetic little people who treat the world as a kind of puzzle which they are actively trying to solve. A third type of theory concerning children's deformations, then, regards the child as an active puzzle-solver, though one who often takes the 'easy way out' by using natural tendencies as intermediate solutions to problems provided by the sound structure.

Puzzle-solving Theories

Puzzle-solving theories argue that the sound structure of language presents youngsters with a series of different but interlinked problems which have to be solved

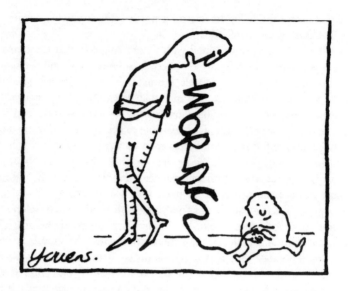

before they can have an adult-type grasp of the system. Children must identify words, work out which articulatory movements are paired with which sounds, and discover which sound sequences are permissible (figure 17.3). Let us therefore consider some of these problems in more detail.

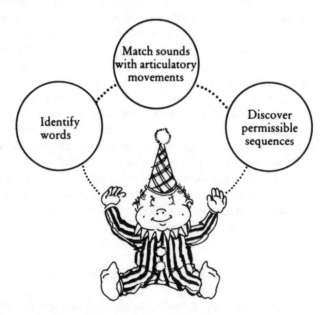

Figure 17.3   The sound puzzles facing children

Splitting up the stream of speech into word-sized chunks is a major task. Words are not spoken one by one but in a continual flow, in which the end of one word often sounds as if it begins the next, a fact exploited sometimes by humorous writers, as in the following extract from Eugene Field's poem 'A Play on Words':

> Assert ten barren love day made
> Dan wood her hart buy nigh tan day;
> Butt wen knee begged she'd marry hymn,
> The crewel bell may dancer neigh.

(A certain baron loved a maid / And wooed her heart by night and day; / But when he begged she'd marry him, / The cruel belle made answer 'Nay'.)

Learning how to split up the flow may cause the 'naming explosion' which often occurs between the ages of 1 and 2, according to one theory.[23] How do they do it?

At first, children may learn off whole chunks of sound, which are simply ritual accompaniments to particular actions (see chapter 16). Fourteen-month-old Minh said *Obedide* apparently in imitation of adult 'Open the door,' when he was pounding on a closed door and shouting to his older brother on the other side.[24] Another child used the phrase 'I carry you' as a request to be picked up, presumably imitating adult 'I'll carry you.'[25] Both these utterances seem to be unanalysed wholes, not yet divided into words.

Youngsters may be able to build up a small repertoire of words they have heard singly. But if they waited to hear every word in isolation, it would probably take years to learn to talk. They therefore have to analyse those which they do know and draw conclusions from these as to how to identify other words. For example, almost all English words have a strongly stressed syllable, and in the words which a child hears early and in isolation, this will often be the first: *daddy, mummy, kitty, dinner, broken*. So he might make a preliminary guess that words start with stressed syllables. It would then be fairly easy to identify words at the end of sentences, a hypothesis supported by the observation that children often make attempts to pronounce final words in an utterance, saying 'Teddy' in response to 'Let's look for teddy,' or 'Garden' when mother says, 'We're going into the garden.'[26]

Overall, the most important factors in splitting words up are probably stress and rhythm – though as the child becomes better acquainted with English, she can utilize certain additional clues. For example, [h] can never occur at the end of a word, and [ŋ] as in *sing* can never occur at the beginning.[27]

The matching task comes next. The child has to find out which sounds are paired with which lip and tongue movements. 'The situation is analogous to the problem which the older child faces in learning to draw geometric figures,' notes one writer. 'It is well-known that pre-schoolers can visually discriminate square, cross, triangle, etc., long before they can draw them. Learning to copy such figures involves progressive analysis of the forms in terms of the nature and position of the lines needed to make them.'[28] For example, one day Amahl rushed to his father and said, 'Daddy, I can say *quick*.'[29] He may well have had a good auditory image of the sound sequence *qu* [kw], but he had to discover the complicated set of articulatory movements needed to pronounce it by trial and error.

Matching the auditory image of a word to its actual pronunciation seems to be a fairly conscious process. Children often exploit their existing abilities, and avoid things which cause them trouble.[30] One child when asked 'Show me your thumb' could happily wiggle his thumb. Yet he himself referred to his thumb as *winger* (finger). He appeared to be purposely avoiding the sound *th* [θ] which he found hard to say.[31] Another child, Philip, substituted [m] or [n] as often as he could, often using consonant harmony, so he said *mim* for 'cream', *nanu* for 'sandwich', *nangu* for 'candle' and *mannow* for 'hammer'.[32] A further strategy is for children to seek out words they can say, and then to use the same output for words which they know are different but have certain similarities.[33] *Aggergog migger*, mentioned at the beginning of this chapter, for both 'cement-mixer' and 'helicopter' seems to be one of these, and another is *ebenin* used both for 'elephant' and 'ambulance'.[34]

The problem is not just one of matching individual segments, but also of stringing the sounds together fast and in the right order. If a child hits on a whole sequence it can reproduce quite easily, then it tends to overuse this. Learning to speak is partly learning to build up a library of these 'articulatory sub-routines'.[35] The sub-routines which the youngster learns to cope with early are likely to be those which fit in with the natural tendencies inherent in the human vocal apparatus – though some might be quite idiosyncratic. One boy, Christopher, had a strong preference for producing words ending in – *yat* or – *yan*. So he said *bayan* for 'banana', *payan* for 'panda', *kajat* for 'carrot', *pijat* for 'peanut' and *miyat* for 'steamer'.[36] Of course, some of this may have been a gap-filling strategy for words which he couldn't quite remember, as will be discussed in the next section.

So far, then, we have discovered that there is a considerable mismatch between the words in children's minds and what they say. Children's pronunciation can give us only very rough clues as to the form of words in their mental lexicons. Let us now go on to consider how words might be organized in their minds.

Mini-malapropisms

Please daddy, can I have an ice-cream *toilet* (cornet = cone).
At school we have a *concussion* (percussion) band.
We parked our car in a *naughty story* (multi-storey) car park.
Mummy, why have you got so many *burrows* (furrows) on your forehead?
Our new car's a *mistake* (estate) car.

The above are all cases in which children have, by adult standards, used the wrong word. The words which a child chooses to clump together with the same output, either intentionally or accidentally, can provide useful clues as to how they are stored, since presumably these words have been identified as 'similar' in some way.

An analysis of 170 'mini-malapropisms'[37] revealed that the rhythmic pattern was the feature most often retained, followed by the stressed vowel. The consonants, both those either side of the stressed vowel and those at the beginning and end, seemed to have lower priority, even after possible pronunciation problems had been taken into account. And this agrees with the findings of another researcher, who analysed a further 150 from several different languages.[38] This suggests that children, like adults, have some characteristics of the word stored more prominently than others, though these conspicuous characteristics do not seem to be the same as those attended to by adults, since children appear to give higher priority to rhythm and lower priority to consonants.

One study looked specifically at adult–child differences in malapropisms.[39] It found that in a majority of cases both adults and children preserved the same set of phonetic characteristics: number of syllables, rhythmic pattern, stressed vowel, consonants at the beginning and end of the word. However, when something went wrong, children preserved the number of syllables and rhythmic pattern, but tended to change the initial consonant. Adults, on the other hand, almost always preserved the initial consonant, preferring to change the number of syllables or the stressed vowel. Children gave the initial consonant the lowest priority of all, and preserved it less well than the consonant at the end of the word – a finding reported elsewhere.[40] The situation can be illustrated by the word *condiments* which occurred as a target among both the child and adult malapropisms:

Small girl: Pass the *monuments*, please.
Her brother: Don't be silly, you mean the *ornaments*.

In the adult example, a woman was boasting of old treasures she possessed: 'We have a lovely Victorian *condom* set in the attic.' The children could presumably have picked on a word beginning with *c* [k], and the adult could have chosen a three-syllable word. But they were naturally predisposed to make certain kinds of mistakes.

Children, then, seem to have mental representations of words which are in a number of ways similar to those of adults but which have different sections prominent: the 'bathtub effect' (chapter 12) is important for adults, but for children the rhythmic pattern and the stressed vowel are more important – and the younger the child, the more likely she is to preserve the rhythmic pattern.[41] Of course, sometimes children omit unstressed syllables, as in *efunt* for 'elephant' or *nana* for 'banana'. It's possible that they have become attuned to the most usual word pattern, which is 'dum-di' (strong + weak), as in *apple*, *lemon*, and haven't yet learned to handle the exceptions.[42]

In addition to certain sections of the word being more prominent for the child, certain types of words seem to be easier to remember than others. In one experiment, children between the ages of 4 and 9 were shown picture-books containing animals which they could mostly recognize easily, such as cows, dogs, elephants and rabbits.[43] But among these common creatures a few strange ones were inserted:

a bandicoot, a racoon (strange to British children), a lemming, a yak and so on. Whenever a strange one occurred, the child was taught its name, then was asked to continue naming the well-known animals. After a few minutes the strange animal would reappear and the child would try to recall its name, usually having partially forgotten it: 'Was it a *gandigoose* (bandicoot)?', 'It might have been *rack* (yak),' 'Something like *lemon* (lemming).' Certain words, or sections of words, turned out to be more memorable than others. It was easier for children to cope with words which began with the stressed syllable and in which nearby consonants agreed in voicing with one another. The beginnings of *lemming* and *bandicoot* were well remembered, but the first syllable of *racoon* and *kudu* turned out to be quite difficult.

When a word was difficult to recall, the children tended to implement 'natural' processes such as consonant harmony: 'racoon' was sometimes recalled as *cocoon*, and 'kudu' as *kuku* or *kutu*, a phenomenon also found by others.[44] And the youngsters tended to reproduce syllables composed of consonant + vowel, so 'armadillo' was remembered as *marmadillo*, and 'bandicoot' as *bandicoo*. These findings suggest that perhaps a few of the strange forms produced by children may be due to gap-filling strategies when they cannot remember the exact sounds, as in *riductor*, *ritack* and *rilastic* for 'conductor', 'attack' and 'elastic',[45] where the initial unstressed syllable might have proved difficult to recall. Possibly words which are relatively easy for the child to remember are in their mental lexicon in a fairly complete form, though with different sections prominent as compared to an adult's lexical entry. But difficult words may be somewhat different from the 'correct' form, since the details are liable to be forgotten.[46]

The Reorganization Process

If children have different sections of a word prominent in storage as compared with adults, this suggests that the overall organization of words by sounds is partially different, in that children tend to clump together different words in storage. Those with a similar rhythm will possibly be closely linked, whereas the beginnings of words will not be as important. They therefore gradually reorganize their lexicons as the years go by. In the animal learning experiment, 4-year-olds had more examples of consonant harmony than older children, but 9-year-olds still had some.[47] This suggests that the rearrangement may go on at least into adolescence, with minor reorderings perhaps continuing throughout a person's life as more words are built in to the lexicon.

However, perhaps we should ask why this reorganization is necessary. The portions of the word which children concentrate on seem to be the most naturally noticeable. So why switch over to the 'bathtub' system (chapter 12)?

Learning to read is an obvious factor. This focuses attention on the beginnings of words, especially when a person becomes familiar with dictionaries. But a more important reason may be the need for fast retrieval. An adult is likely to have a lexicon of around 50,000 actively used items (chapter 1), whereas up to the age of 5 a child's is probably less than a tenth of that number. As a person's vocabulary gets larger, fast retrieval may require an altered storage system, one which allows the speaker to home in on the required word quickly. A beginnings and endings strategy for clumping words together is fairly efficient, since it can narrow down the choice to a relatively small number of words. A rhythmic pattern and stressed vowel strategy, on the other hand, would produce much larger clusters, once the lexicon gets large: *ability, debility, facility, hostility, mobility, sterility, virility* and numerous others would all be together. So attention to the consonants is likely to be more useful for pinpointing a word.

Our general conclusion as to how children store words from the point of view of the sound pattern, then, is as follows. To a large extent children recall the same features as adults do. But their priorities are different. They pay attention above all to the rhythmic pattern and the stressed vowel, and they possibly organize their lexicon into clumps based on these features. The consonants, particularly those at the beginning of words, are ranked less highly. Then as children get older, learn to read and acquire a much larger vocabulary, they gradually switch to an adult-type system which is more efficient for finding words fast.

Summary

This chapter has looked at how children cope with the sound structure of words. We started by considering why children apparently 'deform' words, since we needed to know whether these deformations represent the contents of the mental lexicon.

We noted that children can perceive more than they can produce. Nor are the deformations simply due to articulatory problems. Children seem to be actively trying to solve the puzzles involved in acquiring sound structure – identifying words, linking up auditory images with articulatory routines and learning to cope with them fast. Word identification leads them to concentrate on the rhythmic structure, and many of the deformations are intermediate attempts to match up words and sounds, combined with fall-back strategies.

Children and adults possibly have somewhat similar lexical entries overall, though children have different characteristics prominent in storage, in particular the rhythmic pattern and the stressed vowel. They adopt an adult-like system gradually, as they learn to read and as their vocabulary increases.

We have now dealt with the main components of the mental lexicon. In the next chapter we will begin to consider how these all intermesh with one another.

Part IV
The Overall Picture

18

Seeking and Finding
— Selecting words —

Mrs Rooney: I remember once attending a lecture by one of these new mind doctors. I forget what you call them. He spoke . . .
Mr Rooney: A lunatic specialist?
Mrs Rooney: No, no, just the troubled mind. I was hoping he might shed a little light on my lifelong preoccupation with horses' buttocks.
Mr Rooney: A neurologist?
Mrs Rooney: No, no, just mental distress. The name will come back to me in the night.

Samuel Beckett, *All That Fall*

Humans behave like jugglers when they use the mental lexicon, in that they have to deal with semantic, syntactic and phonological information at the same time. We have not yet considered how all these ingredients are combined. Tracing the processes involved in putting them together, therefore, is likely to shed light on the organization of the various components in the human word-store.

In outline, production and recognition seem to be mirror images of one another. When producing a word, humans must pick the meaning before the sound. When recognizing a word, they must start with the sounds, then move on to the meaning. However, we cannot take it for granted that they utilize the same processes in a different order, just as we cannot automatically assume that going upstairs uses identical muscles to going down but in the reverse sequence. In this chapter, therefore, we shall consider word production, and in the next, word recognition.

Before we look at the intersecting processes involved in producing a word, the question of choice needs to be considered. Do people normally weigh up alternatives when they select words? Everyone knows that poets, in particular, are always seeking the apt word from among the various possibilities in their mental lexicons. T. S. Eliot in 'Little Gidding' vividly expresses the search for

The word neither diffident nor ostentatious,
An easy commerce of the old and the new,

The common word exact without vulgarity,
The formal word precise but not pedantic . . .

And Emily Dickinson describes a similar word-selection process:

Shall I take thee, the Poet said
To the propounded word?
Be stationed with the Candidates
Till I have finer tried –
The Poet searched Philology. . . .

There are also special occasions, such as wedding speeches, when words must be selected carefully, so much so that the phrase 'a few well-chosen words' has become a cliché. But in everyday conversation, when one is chatting to friends in a relaxed way, there is a general impression that decision-making is unnecessary: one just utters the first words that come to mind, as the poet Samuel Coleridge implied when he claimed that prose consisted of 'words in their best order', but poetry of 'the best words in the best order'. Is this assumption correct?

An Embarrassment of Riches

The notion that decision-making might be involved even in ordinary speech, though perhaps at a subconscious level, was suggested by the nineteenth-century psychologist William James: 'And has the reader never asked himself what kind of a mental fact is his intention of saying a thing before he has said it? It is an entirely definite intention . . . But as the words that replace it arrive, it welcomes them successively and calls them right if they agree with it, it rejects them and calls them wrong if they do not.'[1] There are several indications that James was quite right.

'Blends', when two words are melded into one, provide the clearest evidence that alternative words are often considered in the course of speech. 'Shun the frumious Bandersnatch,' said Lewis Carroll in the nonsense poem 'The Jabberwocky'. For those in doubt, he explains the word *frumious*: 'Take the two words "fuming" and "furious". Make up your mind that you will say both words, but leave it unsettled which you will say first. Now open your mouth and speak. If your thoughts incline ever so little towards "fuming", you will say "fuming-furious"; if they turn, by even a hair's breadth, towards "furious", you will say "furious-fuming"; but if you have that rarest of gifts, a perfectly balanced mind, you will say "frumious".'[2]

This example is a contrived, literary one, but it exemplifies a phenomenon which occurs quite unintentionally in real life, as in:

It's quite *ebvious* (evident + obvious) that you disagree.
Don't *frowl* (frown + scowl) like that!

Not in the *sleast* (slightest + least).
She *chuttled* (chuckle + chortle) at the news.
My *buggage* (baggage + luggage) is too heavy.
My *tummach* (tummy + stomach) hurts.

The large number of such examples suggests that we consider both options when there are two equally useful words to fill a slot, especially when these words have sounds in common. These are clear examples of cases in which speakers have failed to make up their mind between 'competing plans'.[3]

Blends can also be found in the speech of some aphasics. 'I forget seeing you before, sir. I remember the other documen and was plazed to see the other documen. My brother was with me. And he was queen that I was hoddle with our own little mm . . . bog, my thing of mogry, you know.'[4] This aphasic patient, a 72-year-old solicitor who had had a stroke, does a great many things wrong. But amidst this jumble, blends appear to predominate among the different types of errors.[5] *Documen* may be a blend of 'doctor' and 'gentleman', perhaps reinforced by 'document', a word which would have been very common in the patient's profession. *Plazed* might be a combination of 'pleased' and 'glad'. *I forget seeing you* may be a replacement of 'don't remember' with 'forget'. By themselves, these examples are not definitive evidence of blending, since it is easy to be fanciful in interpreting garbled utterances. But they are reinforced by other examples in this patient's speech. At least part of his problem, therefore, is that he is unable to choose the words he wants from the various alternatives which flash up, as it were, on his mental screen.

Both ordinary people and some aphasics, then, suggest that it is normal to consider more than one possibility, if there are several plausible candidates. There are, however, a number of indications that the selection process goes beyond this, and that humans automatically consider words that are inappropriate, provided they are in some way connected with the topic concerned.

Noshville, Greeceland and Freudian Slips

Blends are typically composed of two equally suitable words. But this is not inevitable. In some examples one word fits the sentence better than the other, as in *Noshville* (Nashville and Knoxville) where the speaker meant to name only one of these Tennessee towns, or *taquua* (tequila + kahlua) when only the first of these Mexican drinks was being ordered, or *Greeceland* (Greenland + Iceland) where Iceland alone was intended. Such errors suggest that it may be normal to activate a number of words in the area of the required word and then suppress those which are not wanted.

'Blocking' – when an interloper takes the place of a required word (chapter 12) supports this view.[6] 'I'm sure I know it, but this other one keeps popping up instead' is a common complaint, as if words were vying with one another for selection. Several weekend gardeners experienced this with plant names: *lobelia* blocked *buddleia*, *columbine* blocked *campanula*, and *gladioli* blocked *amaryllis*. And in a picture-naming experiment, *shark* was delayed if *whale* had been elicited earlier.[7]

Furthermore, overactivation might also be the explanation for errors such as *left* for 'right', *myrtle* for 'mimosa'. So far, we have assumed that the speaker accidentally picked up a neighbour and passed over the word which was required. But this is not the only possible explanation. Alternatively, the speaker may have activated both of them, and then erroneously suppressed the wrong one. Let us consider further evidence for this point of view.

The mind appears to inadvertently over-prepare itself quite often, as suggested by errors such as:

> The beach was flowing with *pebbles* (water).
> I bought eels and *snake* (skate).

In the first sentence, the speaker was describing a pebbly beach after a rainstorm, and there was no need for the word *pebbles* to have been uttered, but it had been subconsciously activated. In the second, the thought of eels triggered *snake* as well, which sounded sufficiently like *skate* to take its place. Sometimes, also, surrounding objects arouse words, even when they are not part of the topic of conversation: 'I'm waiting for the *snow* (butter) to melt.' Here, a woman was planning to make sandwiches, while watching the snow falling outside.[8]

Such examples are akin to genuine 'Freudian slips' – cases in which a person's secret thoughts and anxieties slip into a conversation. Although there are not as many of these as Freud assumed (as noted in chapter 2), they do sometimes occur. For example, Freud describes how, at a stormy meeting, the chairman announced: 'We shall now "quarrel" (*streiten*) to point four of the agenda,' instead of 'proceed' (*schreiten*).[9] Recently, after a fruitless discussion, a meeting was abandoned with the words 'And now, in *confusion* (conclusion) . . .' Such examples indicate that more words are prepared than normally surface. Usually the unwanted ones are suppressed, but occasionally they pop up inconveniently.[10]

This state of affairs has been reproduced experimentally. When a provocatively dressed female asked male subjects to read out pairs of words, many more subjects said *fast passion* for 'past fashion', *happy sex* for 'sappy hex' and *bare shoulders* for 'share boulders' than in a comparable control group.[11] In another experiment, bogus electrodes were wired on to subjects, and they were told that at some random moment they would be given a painful electric shock. Of course, as the 'electrodes' were not real ones, no shock was given. But the anxiety produced by this procedure was sufficient to make many more subjects say *damn shock* when they should have said 'sham dock', *carried volts* instead of 'varied colts' and *cursed wattage* instead of 'worst cottage' than in a comparable control group who had no anxiety about electricity. These experiments, therefore, give support to the notion that words are easily aroused in relation to topics one is thinking about, and so strengthen the idea that it is normal to activate many more words than one could ever use in a conversation.

The word salads – jumbles of apparently disconnected words and thoughts – of some schizophrenics may represent a similar phenomenon: 'I have distemper just like cats do, 'cause that's what we all are, felines. Siamese cat balls. They stand out. I had a cat, a manx, still around somewhere. You'll know him when you see him. His name is GI Joe: he's black and white. I had a little goldfish too, like a clown. Happy Hallowe'en down.'[12] Here the notion of cats leads on to different types of cat – Siamese, Manx – then cats lead on to goldfish. The goldfish presumably had big lips, like a clown, which triggers the idea of Hallowe'en, perhaps because in America this is a night when people sometimes dress up as clowns. And *clown* rhymes with *down*. When the same patient had a cigarette in her hand, she commented: 'This is holy smoke. It's a holy one. It goes in one hole and out the other and that makes it holy.'[13]

Part of this patient's problem is that her mind is overexcited. It is flashing up too many associations, and she cannot seem to distinguish between associations which should be secondary and in the background and those which are of vital importance to the topic under discussion. In this situation she jumps about among all of them, producing a seemingly incoherent jumble of images and ideas. Cases such as this indicate that when things go wrong, an inability to control and manipulate normal mechanisms may be the primary difficulty.[14] There is no need to assume that bizarre symptoms involve abnormal mechanisms. The opposite situation occurs with some aphasics, whose brain does not arouse sufficient information: only the occasional not particularly appropriate word is thrown up onto their mental screen.

There seems to be a good deal of evidence, then, that in speech production it is normal for the mind to activate many more words than are likely to be used in the course of a conversation. When we describe how humans find the words they want, we must show how people cope with this teeming mass of extra items. Let us now mention some other important factors which need to be taken into account when finding words.

What's-his-name and Thingummy

'Really,' cried Mrs. Skewton . . . 'one might almost be induced to cross one's arms upon one's frock, and say, like those wicked Turks, there is no What's-his-Name but Thingummy, and What-you-may-call-it is his prophet!'

Charles Dickens, *Dombey and Son*

The fictional Mrs Skewton produced this extraordinary quotation from the Koran because she was apparently unable to remember the words *God*, *Allah* and *Mohammed*. Like Mrs Rooney at the start of this chapter, she was experiencing a common phenomenon: that of knowing the word one wants, but being unable to think of the sounds: 'It is a universal fact of normal language experience that lexical form can be gallingly absent despite the lucid subjective presence of exquisite meaning detail' notes one researcher.[15] It happens most often with names, it also occurs with rarely used words, and gets worse with age.[16]

'Lexical selection and phonological encoding are wildly different processes'[17] it seems. Finding words involves at least two operations: selecting the abstract meaning and word class (the lemma), then finding the sounds to clothe this (the word form). Just about all researchers agree on this division,[18] which is clear from speech errors. Some involve only one of these, though others both (chapter 2):

MEANING: The *white* (black) sheep of the family.
                    They've *ended* (started) the third week of their strike.
SOUND: A *reciprocal* (rhetorical) question.
                    The *audience* (ordinance) survey map.
MEANING/SOUND: You're a *destructive* (disruptive) influence.
                    Look at this *badger* (beaver).

In all the above errors, outline specifications have been correctly selected: *white* and *black* are opposing colours (chapter 8), *reciprocal* and *rhetorical* have the same beginning, end and word rhythm (chapter 12), in *beaver* and *badger* the outline fits both the meaning and the sound.

In this chapter, therefore, we shall consider how humans carry out these two processes – lemma selection and finding the word form – and how they relate to one another.[19]

The Inadequacy of Stepping-stones

Let us now consider what might be going on in a person's mind as they select a word, taking into consideration the three important factors already mentioned in this chapter:

1 Lemmas may be separate from word forms, but this divide is not absolute, since errors frequently involve both meaning and form.
2 Outline specifications can be correct, but detailed specifications faulty.
3 Alternative words compete for selection.

We shall proceed by discussing in turn three possible scenarios: a stepping-stone model, a more complex waterfall model and finally an elaborate electricity model. Each of them envisages a somewhat different way of utilizing the basic components of words.

In the stepping-stone model, the speaker can be envisaged as someone crossing a stream, pausing at one stone before leaping to the next. Each stage is completed before the following one is started, and the various steps do not interact in any way.

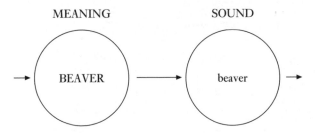

Figure 18.1   A basic stepping-stone model

According to this model, a person picks a lemma (meaning and word class) on the first stepping-stone – perhaps, for example, a smallish wild animal, which though not yet clothed in sounds, is known to be the noun BEAVER. On the second stepping-stone, the word form (sound) *beaver* is hooked on (figure 18.1).

Obviously this simple model needs to be elaborated. For a start, the first stepping-stone would have to be marked in some way to show speakers where to go next. So at the jumping-off point there would have to be a signpost saying where to go to in the next component. In the case of BEAVER there would be a sign pointing to a phonological 'area code': a two-syllable word beginning in *b-* and ending in *-er* (figure 18.2).

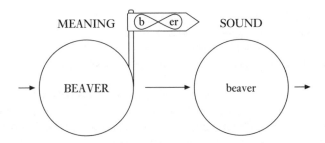

Figure 18.2   A stepping-stone model with signposting

But more refinements are needed. People activate a number of related words (as discussed earlier in this chapter), so the stepping-stones need to be broad at the entry end but progressively narrowed down as the target is approached. In the semantic component, OTTER, BEAVER, BADGER, RABBIT and other small wild animals might be activated at the early stage, then the choice narrowed down to BEAVER. Within the phonological component, numerous words with the same outline specification, *beaker, beaver, badger, bearer, beggar, burglar,* will at first be under consideration, then the target will be narrowed down to *beaver* (figure 18.3).

This model can explain errors such as *otter* for 'beaver' on the assumption that the speaker accidentally eliminated the correct word as the choice was narrowed

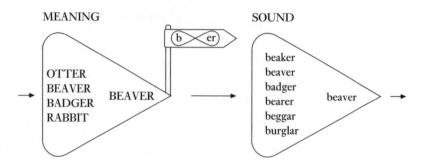

Figure 18.3   A stepping-stone model with narrowing down

down within the semantics. Similarly, *beaker* for 'beaver' would be an erroneous narrowing down within the phonology.

But there is one major flaw in the stepping-stone account: it cannot account for errors which are similar in both meaning *and* sound – perhaps the majority, according to some researchers.[20] *Badger* instead of 'beaver' is a typical one: both are smallish wild animals, neither is very common, and both have the same beginning and ending and the same rhythmic pattern. Other such errors were noted in chapter 2. Further examples are:

> Don't contact lenses make your *ears* (eyes) sore?
> I found it in the train *component* (compartment).
> There's a *sparrow* (swallow): summer's arrived.
> They picked up the language on trading *vehicles* (vessels).

The prevalence of this type of error is quite incomprehensible within a stepping-stone model, because each stage is over and done with before the next is started. But these errors suggest that memory of related words activated in the semantic component is still present while the phonology is picked. The stepping-stone model therefore has to be abandoned, and another one which can cope with this phenomenon needs to be proposed.

Waterfalls can't Flow Backwards

We need a model which incorporates some of the features of the elaborated stepping-stone model, notably signposting and gradual narrowing down of possibilities. But it must be one which allows a person still to be thinking about the meaning as they select the sound. These characteristics are found in a waterfall or 'cascade' model.[21] Here, all the information activated at the first stage is still available at the next stage: it is, as it were, cascading down to the next trough of water on the hillside. So, after a selection of word meanings has been activated, all

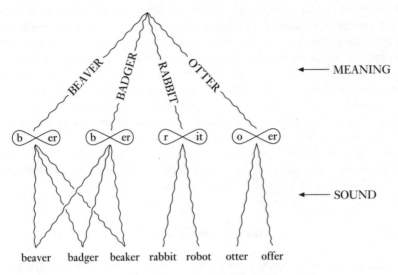

Figure 18.4   A waterfall model

of them remain available as a person deals with the sounds. They continue to be at hand until the required word has been pinpointed (figure 18.4).

In a waterfall model, therefore, the stages overlap. A speaker moves on to the sounds before the final choice is made between words such as OTTER, BEAVER, BADGER and RABBIT. Of course, this means that much more material is aroused than will eventually be required, since the outline phonology of several small animals will be triggered. But this overactivation fits with the evidence we discussed previously.

This model, then, encapsulates the fact that 'down-stream' processes still have access to earlier information. Furthermore, it suggests that word selection is not just a case of following one word through from beginning to end, like a dog chasing a particular rat, but is often a case of controlling and narrowing down a cascade of possible words which are pouring over one. The error *badger* for 'beaver' is explainable by assuming that the semantic information about small animals was cascading down as the outline phonology was picked. As there were two which shared the same outline, the wrong one happened to get picked in the final selection.

The waterfall model, therefore, is a great improvement, because it shows how the various stages overlap. Furthermore, it explains why humans activate so many extra words: this is inevitable, once one allows overlapping stages. But such a model has a serious drawback. Waterfalls can't flow backwards. Just as making the phonology precise requires semantic evidence, so phonology may be needed to narrow down the semantics.

A possible example of information flowing backwards and forwards is when people are prompted. If you say to someone, 'Think up the names of some woodland animals,' they might say, 'Rabbit, squirrel – I can't think of any more.' But if you prompt them 'Beginning with *b*', then *badger* or *beaver* might well spring to their lips. It's well known that this type of cueing helps both normal speakers and aphasics when they cannot think of words.[22] One way to account for this phenomenon is to assume that information can flow both ways: particular sounds can enable a speaker to activate meanings, just as meanings activate sounds. A waterfall or cascade model could account for this only if the animal name had already been subconsciously aroused and was among the cascade of information reaching the phonology. In this case, a prompt 'B . . b . . b . .' could help them to narrow down the field to *badger*. But it could not deal with an animal name which had not already been activated. Let us therefore go on to consider a model which allows information to flow both forwards and backwards.

Interactive Circuitry

We require a model which is in many ways like the waterfall model, but which allows information to flow backwards as well as forwards. An image of electricity might therefore be appropriate, with current flowing to and fro between various points in a complex electrical circuit.

In the production of speech the current is normally initiated in the semantic component, where a semantic field will be aroused, then narrowed down, perhaps to a clutch of woodland animals. Before a final choice has been made, the current flows to the phonological 'area code' of each, where a hoard of words will be triggered and those activated will feed back into the semantics, arousing more words there. All the links between the activated sections will metaphorically be lit up, with electric current rushing backwards and forwards. As it flows to and fro, it excites more and more related words. 'Spreading activation' or 'interactive activation' theories are the general name for models of this type, in which an initial impetus progressively fans out and activates more and more words as it spreads along the various connections[23] (figure 18.5).

As the activated links are inspected, those that are relevant get more and more excited, while those that are unwanted fade away: the rich get richer, and the poor get poorer, as it were. The initial list of animals gets gradually pared down, with those which are semantically inappropriate disappearing, suppressed by the attention paid to the more likely candidates. Since the current is flowing to and fro, anything which is particularly strongly activated in the semantics will cause extra activation in the phonology, and vice versa. If the outline phonology fits more than one animal, then both animals will become more excited in the semantics. So *beaver* and *badger* will both become highly activated. If the speaker is not paying sufficient attention, the wrong one might get picked.

This combination of progressive activation of likely candidates and the corresponding suppression of unwanted links goes on until one overall word wins out. The winner pops up, perhaps as in a toaster when the toast is ready. It is unclear

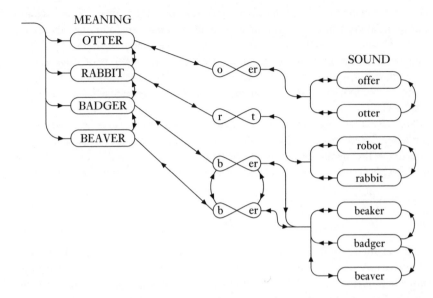

Figure 18.5   An interactive activation model

how to build this into the model – but we need to postulate some final point in selection at which one word emerges as the victor. Perhaps the current has to reach a certain level, or perhaps one word has to get much more excited than any of the others. Some researchers have envisaged a device which collects up relevant information about the various aspects of a word: as soon as sufficient has been gathered, a response is triggered and the device 'gives birth to' a word.[24] Different words require different levels of activation in order to be born: very frequently used words require relatively little to trigger them, while uncommon words are harder to arouse. Although the details are somewhat obscure, some such mechanism may be necessary.

A further requirement is possibly a 'monitoring device' – a double-check once the word has been chosen, to confirm that the right one has been selected: sometimes people are able to catch themselves as they utter the wrong word.[25]

Interactive activation models can account for all types of slip, including Freudian ones. Freudian slips occur because topics with which one is preoccupied get subconsciously activated – and once a topic is activated, then the whole range of related sound and meaning words get excited. Such slips are particularly likely to occur if there is some other link with the intended word, such as a sound link: 'I'll give her a *prescription* (subscription) for a magazine,' said someone who was trying to keep a doctor's visit a secret. Furthermore, it explains why we do not normally utter nonsense words: these do not exist, so cannot get excited.

A further advantage of interactive activation models is that they fit in with what we know about the brain. The human brain is known to contain billions of neurons, and many more billions of synapses connecting them. The excitation travelling along synapses in an area is likely to excite surrounding neurons, in much the same way as the spreading activation we have discussed. This model also suggests that the links between words are more important than their absolute location, and this also ties in with what we know about the human brain, where it is impossible to locate particular areas with as much accuracy as we can a heart or a kidney.

We have therefore outlined a plausible way in which words are selected for utterance,[26] and this has also given us some insight into how the various components in the mental lexicon might be linked. However, we now need to find out how people recognize words, and to see if a similar type of model is relevant.

Summary

In this chapter, we have looked at how people produce words from their mental lexicon when they are speaking. Three important facts need to be incorporated into any model of the process. First, humans activate many more words than they need as they plan speech, words which occasionally pop into an utterance inappropriately. Second, the lemma (meaning and word class) can be separated from its word form (sounds), though many errors are similar in both meaning and sound. Third, the word outline may be correctly selected, but the details filled in wrongly.

We then looked at a number of possible models of the retrieval process. First, we took a stepping-stone model, in which the meaning of a word was picked before the sound was considered. This did not work, because the various stages turned out to be interlinked and partly simultaneous. Second, we examined a waterfall or cascade model, in which information from the meaning was still available while the sounds were being selected. This could not account for the fact that meaning and sound seem to mutually influence each other. We therefore concluded that an interactive activation model was the most plausible. We likened the situation to complex electric circuitry, in which current flows backwards and forwards between particular points, and in so doing excites numerous other points around. The relevant points and links get more and more excited, and the irrelevant ones get suppressed, until finally one word wins out over the numerous others activated.

We now need to consider whether word recognition works similarly. This will be the topic of the next chapter.

19

Organized Guesswork

— Recognizing words —

> Some way ahead of them an awkward low shape was heaving itself wretchedly along the ground . . . It was moving so slowly that before too long they caught the creature up and could see that it was made of worn, scarred and twisted metal . . .
> 'What is it?' whispered Fenchurch in alarm . . .
> 'He's a sort of an old friend', said Arthur. 'I . . .'
> 'Friend!' croaked the robot pathetically. The words died away in a kind of crackle and flakes of dust fell out of his mouth. 'You'll have to excuse me while I try and remember what the word means. My memory banks are not what they were, you know, and any word which falls into disuse for a few zillion years has to get shifted down into auxiliary memory back-up. Ah, here it comes.'
> The robot's battered head snapped up a bit as if in thought.
> 'Hmmm', he said, 'what a curious concept.'
> Douglas Adams, *So Long and Thanks for All the Fish*

To casual onlookers, word recognition might seem straightforward. As a first guess, one might assume that hearers mentally record what they hear, then 'look up' the word in their mental lexicon, much as people find a word in a printed dictionary by matching it segment by segment. On investigation, however, this is a considerable oversimplification. Word recognition turns out to be a complex procedure which requires more skill than one might think.

There are a number of basic problems. First, in normal speech it is physically impossible to hear each segment: speech is just too fast. Twenty segments a second is not unlikely, but the brain cannot distinguish even half that number of separate sounds in that time.[1] Second, there is 'a discouraging lack of acoustic invariance in the speech signal.'[2] Sounds are altered by their neighbours, sometimes quite radically. The same sound produced artificially was interpreted by listeners as [p], [t] or [k], depending on the vowel following it.[3] Third, sound segments cannot be separated out, even in a laboratory. Each one merges into those on either side, like melting ice-cream. Although vowels can be sorted out, consonants cannot: 'If we take a piece of tape on which we have recorded the syllable [ba], and start cutting off pieces of tape from the consonant end, we eventually end up with . . . just the vowel [a]. But, if we cut the tape from the vowel end, we never get to a point where just the [b] sound is heard. As we cut pieces off, the syllable will get shorter and shorter until it suddenly turns into a sound like a chirp . . . a sound that doesn't even sound like speech, let alone a [b].'[4] Fourth, people's accents vary. Finally, we live in a noisy world, and whole chunks of words can get masked by cars honking or people coughing. How, in the circumstances, does anybody understand anyone else at all?

The Importance of Guesswork

One of the best-known facts about word recognition is that a lot of it is guesswork. People recognize words by choosing the 'best fit': they match the portion they have heard with the word in their mental lexicon that appears to be the most likely candidate, and they fill in gaps, often without noticing. One researcher played subjects sentences in which part of a key word such as *legislature* was hidden by a cough. Most people not only interpreted the word accurately, but also didn't notice that part of it was missing. They admitted hearing a cough, but thought it came somewhere else in the sentence.[5]

The routine use of guesswork has been demonstrated in a number of other experiments. In the following sentences the last word was played indistinctly:

> Paint the fence and the *?ate*.
> Check the calendar and the *?ate*.
> Here's the fishing gear and the *?ate*.

People reported hearing *gate* in the first, *date* in the second and *bait* in the third.[6] In another experiment, a sound half-way between [k] and [g] was artificially constructed. This was interpreted as [k] when followed by -*iss* [ɪs], making *kiss*, but as [g] when followed by -*ift* [ɪft] making *gift*.[7]

Furthermore, if the context is taken away, leaving hearers with nothing to guide them in their guesses, the result is often quite bizarre. Four people who were asked to listen to the somewhat unlikely utterance 'In mud eels are, in clay none are' came up with quite varied versions:[8]

> In muddies sar in clay nanar.
> In my deals are in clainanar.
> In my ders en clain.
> In model sar in claynanar.

So since guesswork is so important, how are these guesses made?

Sorting Out the Sound Waves

In word recognition, humans are faced with two different but interwoven problems: splitting up the stream of speech into words on the one hand, and identifying the words on the other. These two tasks proceed together, with people being perhaps slightly more efficient at the first than the second: 85 per cent of examples in a collection of 'slips of the ear' (cases in which people misheard what was said to them) involved a single word only, as in *Barcelona* for 'carcinoma', *simple* for 'sinful'.[9]

Obviously, listeners have to start out by analysing the sound waves, though there is relatively little agreement as to how they do this. A few researchers have argued that the acoustic signals are assembled piecemeal and matched directly against items in the mental lexicon.[10] The majority, however, have proposed an intermediate stage, in which the information culled from the sound waves is translated into a sequence of phonemes[11] or syllables[12] which are then fitted to words.

The reason behind the diverse viewpoints may be a simple one: perhaps there is no single way in which humans analyse sound waves. Some procedures may be more common than others, and the frequency with which they are used may vary from language to language.[13] Also, the techniques may vary depending on the type of speech: somewhat different strategies might be needed for coping with, say, a clear television newsreader and a foreigner at a noisy party.

In spite of all this uncertainty, certain outline facts have been ascertained. Rhythm may be the starting point for segmenting English words. 'BE ALERT! YOUR COUNTRY NEEDS LERTS! is an old joke, but it works. It turns up on bumper stickers, lapel badges, lavatory walls, even keyrings.'[14] It works because it ties in with speakers' expectations about where English word boundaries occur.[15] Listeners expect strong and weak syllables to alternate (chapter 12), and expect words to begin on a stressed syllable, as mishearings demonstrate:[16]

butter knife (heard instead of 'by tonight')
the skies (disguise)
The parade was an eagle. (The parade was illegal.)

Experiments confirm this. Subjects who listened to odd, faintly played sentences tended to segment them so that words started with stressed syllables:[17]

Some expect a blizzard (heard instead of 'Sons expect enlistment').
Angels pin their needles (Angels pinned beneath it).
A duck descends some pill (Conduct ascends uphill).

Rhythmic clues are supplemented by phonetic clues.[18] For example, [p], [t] and [k] are often strongly aspirated (pronounced with a puff of breath) at the beginning of words. And the start of a word may be obvious because the previous one has already been recognized.

Within words, vowels are perceived better than consonants.[19] Stressed vowels are particularly easy to hear, and they tend to be retained in slips of the ear, as in *coffee* for 'hockey', *horrible* for 'tolerable'.[20] Certain vowels vary less than others, notably [i], [u] and [a]. If one of these is present, it can form a peg round which the rest of a word can be built.[21] Consonants can usually be assigned to the 'natural class' to which they belong: [s] sounds rather different from [b], for example, even though it might get confused with [ʃ] as in *shin*.[22] All these factors can provide an outline framework.

Overall, then, the acoustic signal gives only a rough scaffold on which the hearer must work, and no portion of this can be relied upon, as a large sneeze might have masked any part of it. There are probably a number of different words in the mental lexicon which are compatible with the rough framework. It seems unlikely that humans just flail around, wildly testing possible words at random. There must be some principled way in which they narrow down the various possibilities. Let us therefore consider how they might do this.

'One after the Other' Theories

There are two main types of theory for word-matching: the one-by-one approach, and the horse-race approach. People test out probable words one after the other, according to some researchers, in a so-called 'serial' model of speech recognition. Others claim that all candidates are considered simultaneously, as if they were horses racing against one another, and so argue for 'parallel' processing. Some researchers have suggested combining the two. Let us consider the matter further.

One after the other theories depend on a single fact: that commonly used words are easier to find in the mental lexicon. Most people find the word *cat* faster than *panther* or *cheetah*, and the word *nose* faster than *pelvis* or *spleen*, simply because they use them more often. This fits in with our everyday experience, and has been confirmed time and again by psycholinguists: common words are recognized as words faster than uncommon ones, a fact first pointed out over a quarter of a century ago.[23] In some cases, common words are simply those which have been learnt earlier, so have become ingrained in one's memory. However, in terms of the mental lexicon, what does 'ingrained in one's memory' mean? Are common words kept, as it were, on top of the heap of words, so that they don't get buried or rubbed out? A number of psychologists have suggested just this. Perhaps words are organized within the sound system in heaps, or 'stacks', or 'bins', and within these bins perhaps the most frequently used words are kept on top.[24]

Those who envisage the mental lexicon as organized in this way suggest that, when fitting a word to sounds one has heard, a person first goes to the relevant bin and then conducts an orderly search, going from top to bottom of the heap, seeing if it matches. Bins, in the best-known model of this type,[25] are based on word beginnings, so one might go past common words such as *hammer* and *hanger* before getting to one that truly matched, say *hamper*. If the wrong word was accidentally

picked, it would have to be replaced in the bin as soon as the mistake was discovered, and the search would continue as before.

In another serial model, frequent words have a separate section of the lexicon to
themselves. According to this view, they are stored twice, once in an easily available
store and once in their proper place,[26] just as one might keep an abridged pocket
dictionary on one's desk for frequent fast consultation and a full-size lexicon the
other side of the room on a bookshelf. On hearing a word, therefore, a person
might check through the commonly used, readily available words first, and if it is
not there, move on to the full mental lexicon. This 'double storage' hypothesis was
put forward to account for the fact that frequent words are recognized faster in
lexical decision tasks when they occur among other frequent words than when they
occur among medium- and low-frequency words. The researchers suggested that
this difference in access time for the same words might be due to the fact that
hearers normally had only to zip through a relatively small store of frequent words.
The slower access time when they were among the middle- and low-frequency
words was because hearers had to seek them out from their proper place in the
overall lexicon.

The word frequency effect, then, is the main reason why some researchers have
argued for a serial model. They claim that faster processing of frequent words
must mean that these are checked first, and the remainder later. But the frequency
effect could have other explanations, and could be incorporated into a parallel
processing model. Perhaps a group of candidate lexical items are looked at simultaneously, but activation takes place faster for frequent words, just as, if one opened
the door of an aviary, some birds might rise from their perches faster than others.
Or the word frequency effect might be due to extra strength in the stored representation.[27] Perhaps frequent words are inked in more heavily, as it were, in one's
mental notebook. Furthermore, we recognize words so fast that perhaps parallel
access is inevitable. In addition, there is plenty of evidence to suggest that we think
about several words at once. Let us go on to consider this.

Multiple Meanings

'Look, no sooner had we got out there than the wind blew up . . .'
'And the house blew up. And your cruiser blew up. And Mrs Hutchmeyer blew
up and this Mr Piper . . .'
Hutchmeyer blew up.

The comic effect of this passage from Tom Sharpe's novel *The Great Pursuit* is
due to the different meanings of *blow up*. Studying how people cope with these
multiple meanings can lead to useful insights into word recognition. The crucial
question is this: do humans just latch on to the first plausible meaning that crosses
their mind? Or do they, as in speech production, consider many more options than
they actually use?

Psychologists have known for quite some time that, in cases where more than one meaning is plausible, subjects are likely to activate all of them, often without realizing it. In one experiment, subjects were asked to complete unfinished sentences, some of which contained ambiguous words, as quickly as they could.[28]

After taking the *right* (= 'correct' or 'right-hand') turn at the intersection I . . .
After taking the *left* turn at the intersection I . . .

Subjects took longer to begin completing the ambiguous sentences, and in dealing with them they stuttered more, sometimes repeated themselves and tended to produce ungrammatical sequences. This happened even when they claimed not to have noticed the ambiguity.

In another experiment, listeners were asked to wear earphones and were instructed to pay attention to a sentence being played into their right ear, which they would have to paraphrase.[29] This sentence was sometimes ambiguous, as in:

The spy *put out* (= 'extinguish' or 'display') the torch as our signal to attack.

Into the other, unattended ear the researchers played a sentence which could resolve the ambiguity:

The spy *extinguished* the torch in the window.
The spy *displayed* the torch in the window.

The subjects interpreted the attended sentence in accordance with the unattended to message, even though they were not consciously aware of having heard it: they had no idea why they chose the particular reading of *put out* that they did (figure 19.1). Once again, this suggests that people may subconsciously consider more meanings than they are aware of.

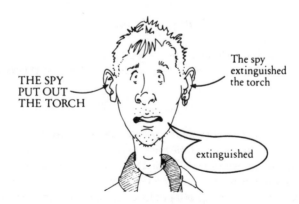

THE SPY PUT OUT THE TORCH

The spy extinguished the torch

extinguished

Figure 19.1   Subconscious processing

A similar conclusion was reached in a phoneme monitoring experiment: 'Press a button if you come to a word starting with B.'[30] Subjects monitored the required phoneme more slowly if the previous word was ambiguous, as in 'The seamen started to *drill* (drill holes or take part in a lifeboat drill?) before they were ordered to.' Once again, this happened even when those taking part claimed not to have noticed the ambiguity.

The overall conclusion to be drawn from these experiments is that when the same sequence of sounds has two meanings which fit equally well, people activate both and then select one, even if they are not aware of this process going on. But suppose a hearer is confronted with an ambiguous word in which one of the meanings is far less probable than the other. What happens then?

Take a sentence such as 'Aloysius was stuck in the jam for three hours.' Was Aloysius detained in congested and stationary traffic or in a preserve containing fruit? And how might one decide? Either one could briefly consider both meanings of the word, then choose the most appropriate one. Alternatively, the likelihood of being stuck in traffic rather than fruit preserve is so strong that one would initially think of the traffic meaning only. In this case, fruit preserve would be considered only when prompted, perhaps if the speaker continued: 'The soles of his shoes were glued to the sticky mess.' The hearer would then realize that he had been led 'up the garden path', and he would then retrace his steps, abandoning his original interpretation of congested traffic. Which of these scenarios is the most likely?

This question was investigated in an ingenious experiment.[31] People were asked to listen to sentences such as the following:

> For years the government building had been plagued with problems. The man was not surprised when he found several spiders, roaches and other bugs in the corner of his room.

While listening, the subjects were given a lexical decision task. Immediately after *bugs* – a word which is potentially ambiguous, though not in this context – three letters were flashed up onto a screen, and subjects were asked, 'Is this a word?' People responded to the task faster if the original sentence included a word related in meaning to the lexical decision item. Therefore, if they had just heard the word *bugs*, subjects responded faster to ANT than they did to SEW. But there was a further finding. After hearing the sentence above, where *bugs* clearly relates to insects, people responded as fast to SPY as they did to ANT (figure 19.2). This result suggests that subjects briefly activate both meanings of a homonym, even in cases where one of them is inappropriate. These extra meanings are available very briefly, probably for less than a second. If the lexical decision task was moved more than two or three syllables away from the ambiguous word, the 'priming' effect disappeared, suggesting that one's mind wipes away extra words quite fast, and does not leave them floating around indefinitely.

Of course, one might argue that anything to do with governments was bound to elicit the spy sense of *bug*. But this experiment cannot be explained away so easily,

WORD?

SPY

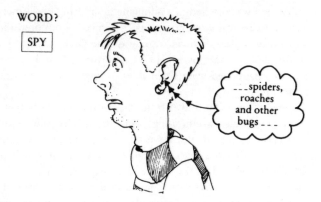

--_spiders,
roaches
and other
bugs _ _ _

Figure 19.2   Activation of irrelevant meanings

because a number of other researchers have confirmed that people activate irrelevant meanings.[32] In one experiment, the word *rose* activated both the flower and the meaning 'stood up'. Subjects were given a lexical decision task after hearing either 'They bought a *rose*' or 'They all *rose*.' They answered 'Yes' equally fast to FLOWER and STOOD in both *rose* sentences.[33] A further effect found in lexical decision tasks is that people respond faster to words with several meanings, an effect apparently unconnected with word frequency.[34]

The cumulative results of all these experiments suggest strongly that for a split second, hearers simultaneously activate more than one meaning for an ambiguous word, even when the context strongly biases them in one direction.

Humans, then, are capable of thinking in parallel, at least about ambiguous words. But this may be normal behaviour for *all* words, as outlined below.

Armies of Words

'By-the-bye, what became of the baby?' said the Cat. 'I'd nearly forgotten to ask.'
'It turned into a pig,' Alice answered. . . .
'Did you say "pig" or "fig"?' said the Cat.

When the Cheshire Cat failed to hear Alice's answer as to what had happened to the baby, it asked for clarification, meanwhile mentally considering both *pig* and *fig*. Recent findings indicate that this procedure is the norm. Humans routinely contemplate many more lexical items than the one that they actually select.

Speed of word recognition is an important strand of evidence. Humans can recognize words in a split second, sometimes before the word has been spoken (chapter 1).[35] This fast reaction time makes it likely that listeners have popped up several possible candidates, ready for selection.

The 'captain–captive' experiment confirms the arousal of more than one word.[36] Subjects were played either *captain* or *captive*, then asked to make a lexical decision about a written word which was linked in meaning to one of the *capt-* words: BOAT for *captain*, and GUARD for *captive*. When the written word was flashed up during the sequence *capt-*, subjects responded fast to both BOAT and GUARD, suggesting that both *captain* and *captive* had been activated. But when the written word occurred after the separation point, subjects said 'yes' faster to the linked-meaning word. And numerous other word-pairs supported this result.

Further evidence of multiple activation is provided by gating tasks, when a progressively longer portion of a word is let through before being chopped off by a 'gate' (chapter 2). When asked what word they were hearing, speakers easily made a wide variety of guesses in the early portions of a word.[37]

In speech recognition, then, speakers flash up on their mental screen, as it were, any word that is consistent with what they hear, then make use of all available evidence – syntactic and semantic – to narrow down the possibilities. The more information they are able to bring to bear on the situation, the faster they can come to a decision. They recognize words more quickly in normal, plausible contexts than in strange, unacceptable ones. People start doing this as soon as they hear any part of a word.

A whole army of words, it seems, marches up for consideration each time a word begins. Some researchers have suggested that this army is based largely on word beginnings.[38] A listener, on hearing the sequence *sta-*, immediately accesses the whole set of words beginning with *sta-* in the mental lexicon. This set is referred to as the 'word-initial cohort'. A cohort was originally a division of the Roman army, and one current dictionary definition is 'any band of warriors or associates'. So one must imagine metaphorically these serried ranks of words lined up ready for selection: *stab*, *stack*, *stag*, *stagger*, *stagnate*, *stalactite*, *stalagmite*, *stamina*, *stammer*, *stamp*, *stampede*, *stance*, *stand*, *standoffish*, *static* . . . and so on. (Although they are listed here for the sake of illustration in alphabetical order, there is no suggestion that this is their order in the cohort.)

The word-initial cohort then gets narrowed down. Suppose one heard:

John was trying to get some bottles down from the top shelf. To reach them he had to *sta* . . .

The words immediately preceding *sta* . . . would enable a hearer to cut down the range of possibilities by restricting the choice to verbs: *stab*, *stack*, *stagger*, *stagnate*, *stammer*, *stamp*, *stampede*, *stand* . . . and so on. The topic of the preceding sentence, John getting down bottles, would then narrow the choice down to *stack* or *stand*. So with these two possibilities in mind, a hearer can very quickly reject *stack* and select *stand* as soon as [n] is heard (figure 19.3).

This cohort model incorporates a number of important facts about word recognition: first, many more words are activated than are needed, second, speakers utilize all kinds of information in order to reach their decision, third, they reach this decision fast, often while the word is still being spoken.

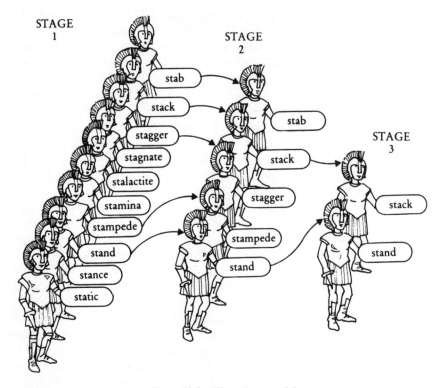

Figure 19.3 The cohort model

But there are disadvantages, at least with the earliest version of the cohort model, which required undistorted acoustic signals at the beginning of the word. It could not cope with the *?ate* (*gate*, *bait*, *date*) situation discussed earlier in the chapter, where the first sound was indistinct: if a wrong decision was made, the wrong cohort would be activated.

More recent versions of the cohort model have therefore moved towards a more fluid form of organization.[39] However, once the cohort model has been altered to become less rigid and more flexible, it begins to overlap with interactive activation models. Let us consider these.

Brain Circuitry Models

Electrical circuitry might be the best way to envisage an interactive activation model,[40] with current rushing backwards and forwards, as may happen in the human brain (chapter 18). Activation spreads from word to word, as each segment triggers new possibilities. Hearers start activating possible candidates as soon as a few segments have been heard. Any sound that is identified will immediately

PERCEIVED SEQUENCE

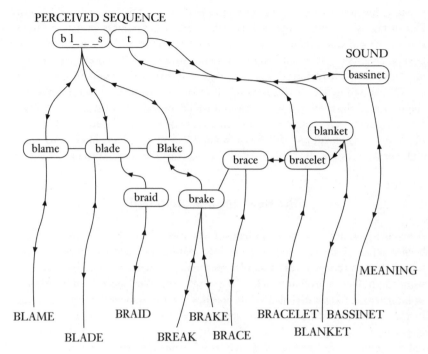

Figure 19.4 A spreading activation model

form links with all those words which contain a similar sound in approximately the same place.

Any candidate is then linked up with its possible meanings. Semantics influences the narrowing down of sounds, just as the sounds affect the meaning. As more information is added, some words will get an added boost, others will fade away. Take a word such as *bracelet*. Suppose this had initially been heard as *blace*. . . . At first, words such as *blame* and *blade* will be activated to a level higher than *bracelet*, but when these fail to match the overall word, *bracelet* eventually turns out to be a better fit, and the others are suppressed. Guesses about the word's identity are continually updated, partly due to hearing more, partly due to integrating what has been heard with the context (figure 19.4).

As in word production, the rich get richer and the poor get poorer. Words which are likely to fit get more and more excited, until one finally pops up. Those that are unwanted are gradually suppressed. The main difference between production and recognition is that the recognition process starts with sounds rather than meanings.

This interactive activation model can cope with indistinct acoustic information at any point in the word, even at the beginning. It allows new candidates to be considered at any time, and also allows listeners to alter their opinions.

Many researchers are coming round to the view that this represents a reasonable idea of how words are recognized. But there are still a number of details missing. Interactive activation models allow quite a lot of variation,[41] just as internal combustion engines can vary considerably from one to another. And the model described just now is in many ways somewhat vague. It has simply said that everything sets off everything else that is remotely connected with it. We need to know more about how all these excited words are controlled, especially as the interactive buzz-fuzz is so great that supporters of extreme versions have even queried whether one needs anything as cut and dried as a 'mental lexicon': perhaps interacting sounds and word-pieces are all that is needed. Let us consider some of the problems.

The Need for a Score-board

A major requirement is some mechanism which specifies when a firm decision has been reached. A device which collects information for each word was needed for word selection (chapter 18). A similar mechanism is needed for recognition. Each word might have a level at which it 'pops up', with allowances for different types of information to counterbalance one another: a lot of phonetic information might involve somewhat less semantic information, and vice versa.[42] Or a 'score-board' might be needed, which keeps track of the relative probability of different candidates. One might envisage a device which from moment to moment assigned to every item a relative probability rating for each of three factors: perceptual evidence, frequency weighting and contextual evidence[43] (figure 19.5).

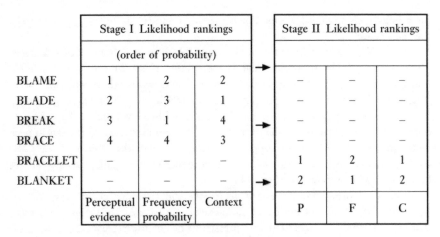

	Stage I Likelihood rankings				Stage II Likelihood rankings		
	(order of probability)						
BLAME	1	2	2	→	–	–	–
BLADE	2	3	1		–	–	–
BREAK	3	1	4	→	–	–	–
BRACE	4	4	3		–	–	–
BRACELET	–	–	–		1	2	1
BLANKET	–	–	–	→	2	1	2
	Perceptual evidence	Frequency probability	Context		P	F	C

Figure 19.5 Possible score-board system

But there are further aspects which need to be clarified. As in production, similar words not only activate one another, they may also 'block' one another. A highly activated word such as *bought* might inhibit a near neighbour such as *brought*. The relationships between activation and inhibition are still unclear, especially as both neigbourhood density and frequency of use have to be taken into consideration.[44]

Late recognition is another problem. The models discussed so far assume that all words will be recognized at least when they end. But this is unrealistic. Short words are often identified one or two words later. Their end may be signalled only by the arrival of the next word: a sequence *bun* could finish up as *bun, bundle, bunny, bunch* and so on. A provisional decision may have been made, but sure identification often takes place later.[45] In other cases, speakers may change their mind completely.

Finally, the models discussed mostly assume that there is a fixed number of recognizable words in a person's mental lexicon: it does not make allowance for novelties such as *fishling* (chapter 15) or compounds as in *verandah table sprays*.[46]

These shortcomings indicate that the interactive activation model is still incomplete. But the outline is clear.[47] Humans activate multiple words in the process of word recognition, and the human mind is capable of massive parallel processing. The major task for the future is not so much finding out how words are activated, as how the unwanted ones are suppressed, and how new ones are fitted into the picture.

Summary

This chapter has looked at word recognition. Owing to the impossibility of mentally recording the sound of a word in full, hearers have to rely on informed guesswork to fill in the gaps.

As in speech production, speakers consider many more words than they eventually select. A huge number are activated, then those that are not required are gradually suppressed. The same type of interactive activation model as that proposed for word production also applies to word recognition – even though many details are still obscure.

In the next chapter we will discuss how the various sections of the mental lexicon might be organized in relation to one another.

20

Odd Arrangements and Funny Solutions

— The organization of the mental lexicon —

> If God had designed a beautiful machine to reflect his wisdom and power, surely he would not have used a collection of parts generally fashioned for other purposes. Orchids were not made by an ideal engineer; they are jury-rigged from a limited set of available components . . . Odd arrangements and funny solutions are the proof of evolution – paths that a sensible God would never tread but that a natural process, constrained by history, follows perforce.
>
> Stephen Jay Gould, *The Panda's Thumb*

Is the mental lexicon a streamlined, well-designed device? Or is it a hotch-potch, which has been cobbled together in the course of evolution, like orchids in the quotation above? This is the question which we need to ask, as we piece together the conclusions reached in previous chapters.

Nature is an excellent tinkerer, not a divine artificer, according to one biologist.[1] Parts of living organisms get modified for new purposes, and compromises have to be made. The human mouth and throat are moderately useful for eating, speaking and breathing, but are not ideal for any of them. Jagged teeth might be better for eating, but would interfere with the production of sounds. Our streamlined throat is useful for speech, but makes it possible for us to choke, since the windpipe cannot be closed off. Language in general is an evolutionary mish-mash: 'Language has grown up like any big city: room by room . . . house by house, street by street . . . and all this is boxed together, tied together, smeared together.'[2] The mental lexicon is part of language. So do we find a similar collection of odd arrangements and funny solutions?

A Mix-up

Words, we have said, are like coins, with meaning and word class on the one side and sounds on the other. The fragility of the links between the two sides of the coin provides one piece of evidence that the mental lexicon is an evolutionary mish-mash. This link is easily broken (chapter 18), as when a professor said: 'Brain-half, but I can't think of its proper name,' Later she remembered *cerebral hemisphere*.

There is no intrinsic link between sound and meaning. The connection is arbitrary, apart from a small number of onomatopoeic words, such as *splash, bow-wow, quack-quack* – and even these differ from language to language: French ducks say *cancan*, and Danish ones go *rap-rap*. From time to time, individual languages may build up idiosyncratic associations between certain sound sequences and particular meanings.[3] For example, the sequence *-ump* in *bump, clump, dump, hump, lump, slump* and *thump* 'suggests a feeling of awkwardness or clumsy impact', according to a newspaper article,[4] and the writer George Orwell claimed that the words *plumb, plunge* and *plummet* indicate that 'the sound *plum-* or *plun-* has something to do with bottomless oceans.'[5] But such links are of minor importance, and variable.

There may be 'a thread of sound symbolism in language, a thread conceivably universal'[6] in the sense that certain sounds are reliably judged to be more appropriate for certain meanings than others. In a famous experiment German subjects were presented with two line drawings, one composed of curves, the other of spikes and angles.[7] *Takete* and *maluma*, they were told, were the names to be applied to them, and they were asked which name was appropriate for which drawing. Overwhelmingly the rounded drawing was labelled *maluma* and the spiky one *takete*, and this finding was replicated both in America[8] and in Tanganyika.[9] But in spite of this result, no natural language links up [t] and [k] with spikes, or [m] and [l] with curves. This slender thread of sound symbolism, therefore, appears to exist with respect to forced choices between nonsense words, but largely fades away in actual language use.[10]

So the sounds of words seem to be easily unhooked from their meaning and word class. Why should this be? Why in the course of time do meaning and sound not join up, since each word requires both ingredients? One possibility is that the two parts are inherently detachable because the component dealing with semantics and word class is arranged conveniently for production, whereas the phonology is organized primarily for speedy recognition. Let us explore this idea further.

Word lemmas (meaning and word class) seem to be organized in semantic fields, and within these fields there are strong bonds between coordinates which share the same word class, such as *lion, tiger*, or *knife, fork, spoon* (chapter 8). For producing speech, this is a useful arrangement. A speaker can then pick easily from a particular topic area, comparing several possible words which are linked closely together. 'Linked closely together' is more likely to mean 'having a direct and strong connection' than literally 'located near one another'. The meaning side of a word, therefore, seems to be organized primarily in a way which helps speech planning.

Word forms (sound structure), on the other hand, are organized with similar-sounding words closely linked, such as *referee* for 'refugee', *reciprocal* for 'rhetorical'. This is useful for word recognition. Hearers can compare candidates and find the best fit for what they have heard. This arrangement is quite inconvenient for producing speech, where it would be better if the sound of each word was far away from similar-sounding neighbours. Then nobody would ever have the embarrassing experience of accidentally saying *masturbate* instead of 'masticate' – a fairly common error. 'I always masturbate my food properly,' said someone explaining why he never got indigestion.

The lemma side of the coin, then, favours production in its organization, whereas the word-form side is better for recognition.[11] It follows from this observation that word forms are stored primarily as auditory images – what they sound like. And two further pieces of evidence support this.

First, in language learning, children – and adults – build up a passive vocabulary before they can actively use it. A child can take months to discover how to say a particular word she knows quite well (chapter 12).

Second, errors such as *moggy barsh* (boggy marsh), *reap of hubbish* (heap of rubbish), *leak wink* (weak link) suggest that words have to be converted into a form in which they can be pronounced. A 'scan-copying' mechanism perhaps comes into play. The speaker scans the mental representation, and copies it over into a form in which it can be articulated, checking off each segment as it is dealt with.[12] Occasionally, this mechanism goes wrong, and copies a sound onto the wrong word.

Sound structure-wise, then, the lexicon is stored primarily in auditory terms, and production requires a complicated conversion of an auditory representation into a sequence which can be pronounced. Recognition, in contrast, requires a 'matching and guessing' operation in which the signals in the sound waves are fitted to internal representations which are similar to what has been heard (figure 20.1).

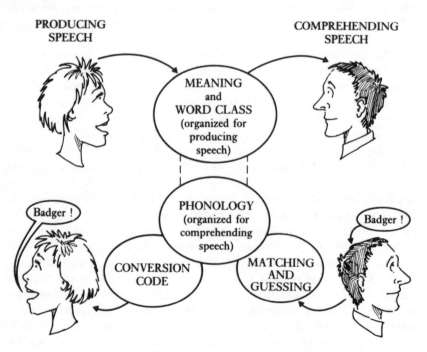

Figure 20.1   The fragility of the meaning–sound link

The mental lexicon, therefore, seems to be a mixed system which has found a workable compromise between the requirements of production and those of comprehension. The component that is required first in each case has imposed its demands on the organization. Production begins with the semantics and syntax, so these are arranged to suit production. Recognition begins with sounds, so these are organized to suit recognition. These differently organized components may be a hangover from a much earlier stage of evolution, when thoughts were not put into words and when listening for sounds was of major importance for survival. Now, meaning and sound are both required at the same time, but the links between them are relatively tenuous, and sometimes break down.

However, it may be an oversimplification to regard the mental lexicon as a simple tug-of-war between perception and production. There are signs that it has been further modified to take into account the needs of memory. Within each component, the set-up may have been modified not only to aid speedy retrieval but also to make words easier to remember. For example, the arrangement of words into word classes and into clumps of coordinates possibly occurs at least partly because the memory needs a more structured system in order to cope with the tens of thousands of words involved.

The mental lexicon, therefore, is a cobbled-together compromise in which the needs of production, perception and memory are all partially satisfied. But on closer inspection, it proves even messier, because of the way in which it overlaps with other aspects of cognition and language. Let us now consider this.

A Rough Map

In outline, the mental lexicon can be regarded as consisting of two major components: semantic–syntactic and phonological. Perhaps these components should be viewed as towns on a map: first, Semtown, which contains both meaning and word class specifications (the lemma), and second, Phontown, containing the sounds (the word form). Both these are linked to Novtown, which deals with the creation of new words (figure 20.2).

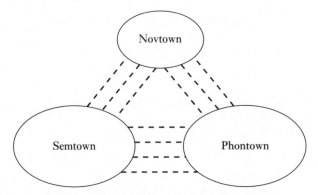

Figure 20.2 Components of the mental lexicon

To continue the map analogy, each town has only a small portion on the surface, and consists to a large extent of a vast underground network. On the surface, outline addresses are marked: the semantic fields in Semtown, the phonological 'area codes' in Phontown. These constitute the entrance points to the underground network. Then one can descend ever deeper, like Alice going down the rabbit-hole, until one finds the detailed information required. The further one travels in these subterranean tunnels, the more one can retrieve. Some of the tunnels are well worked and well lit, others have to be created afresh.

However, the underground tunnels stretch not only downwards but also sideways, linking up with tunnels from other 'towns'. The Semtown tunnels join up with tunnels from a person's general cognitive ability, allowing someone to link up an enormous amount of general knowledge and memory. Because the tunnels join, a tunnel starting in Semtown might be the same tunnel as one starting in a general memory section. It is therefore impossible to say where the 'meaning' of a word ends and general knowledge begins. Other tunnels from Semtown link up with the syntax of a language, with verbs in particular being intermingled with general syntactic rules. And all areas have links with the 'back-up' store, showing how words can be split up into morphemes, and via this, with the lexical tool-kit, which contains procedures for making new words (figures 20.3 and 20.4).

Finding a word in the mental lexicon can be envisaged as following a path through this complex network, with some network links being stronger than others. For well-known common words, the paths are well worn, and it is easy to travel fast. But for words used only occasionally, the paths are narrow and dimly

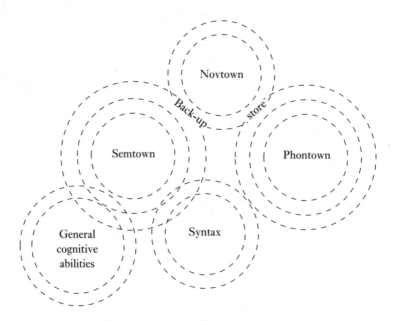

Figure 20.3 'Aerial' view of links with other components

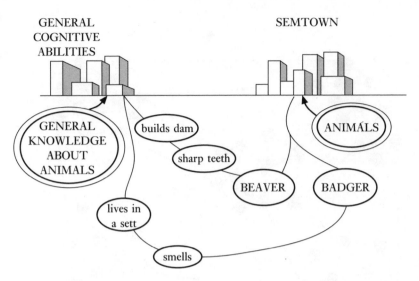

Figure 20.4 'Subterranean' view of some Semtown links

lit. Meanwhile, new tunnels are perpetually being dug. Furthermore, the word itself cannot ultimately be regarded as a finite package. Since each word has links with so many others, and with general memory information, all these connections are in a sense part of the sum total of what we mean by a 'word'.

The analogy of 'towns' and 'tunnels' is helpful, in that it emphasizes the multi-dimensional nature of the links. It also suggests that, as with real towns, it is hard to see exactly where one town ends and another begins: it is easier to identify them by their centres than their boundaries. But it is flawed, in that it suggests that the buildings and tunnels are fixed structures, with locations that can be pinpointed. This may be misleading, because the quality of the links in each case is probably more important than the exact location of the various pieces of information. The situation is somewhat like a life-support system in a hospital: what matters is the effectiveness of the pumps and tubes carrying blood and oxygen to the patient. The exact location of the equipment from which the tubes emerge is not of primary importance.

An alternative way of looking at the connections between these 'lexical towns', therefore, is one which focuses on the inhabitants rather than on fixed architecture. Any town in real life is likely to contain 'social networks', groups of people who know one another and interact fairly often.[13] Sometimes these networks are dense and multiplex, in that the same group of people live, work and play together. However, even in dense networks, some of these people are likely to have links outside their particular social group, though not such close ones. This analogy can be transferred to the mental lexicon. Each 'lexical town' will contain numerous clumps of words with strong ties to one another – though each clump will also have bonds, yet weaker ones, with other groups. In addition, there will be connections, weaker still,

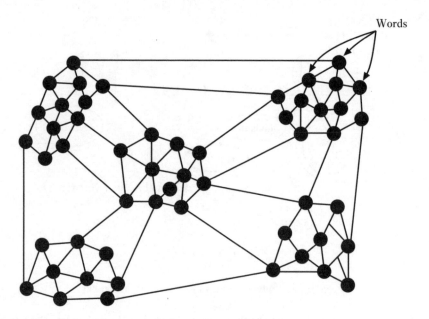

Words

Figure 20.5   Clumps of words

between individuals in different towns. Like social ties, these connections will fluctuate. Perhaps the most important difference between lexical networks and people networks is that the links between words are likely to be much more numerous than the social bonds which any one individual can contract (figure 20.5).

Basic specifications for Dumbella

Let us now return to Dumbella, the robot we talked about earlier (chapter 3). Our overall aim was to provide outline specifications for programming her, so that she would behave like a human being as far as her word-store is concerned. The overall layout for this was illustrated in figure 20.3. But, just to be clear that the robot-manufacturer has understood the main points made in this book, let us provide a summary list of the requirements, split into four sections: units, layout, processing, novelty.

Units

1   *Words*   The lexicon is to contain whole words.
2   *Meaning versus sound*   These whole words should be viewed as coins, in which one side is detachable from the other. On one side is the meaning and word class; on the other, the sound structure.

3   *Word analysis*   The sides of the word-coin are to be analysable, and the characteristics identified in the analysis are to form the basis of the ways in which each word is linked to the other words.

4   *Types of analysis*   Words are to be analysable in terms of meaning, word class, sounds and morphological structure.

Layout

5   *Modular organization*   The lexicon is to be composed of two main components or modules: semantic–syntactic, which contains the lemmas (meaning and word class), and phonetic phonological, which contains the word forms (sounds). These components are to be linked to a third subsidiary component, 'the lexical tool-kit', which contains procedures for creating new words. The link is to be via a back-up store showing how words can be divided into morphemes.

6   *Overlapping modules*   The modules should not have rigid boundaries, but should overlap each other and adjoining modules relating to syntax and general cognitive abilities.

7   *Network*   Each module is to be a complex network, with relatively tight links to other items within the module and somewhat looser links to items outside the module. Within each module there should be clusters of dense, multiplex mini-networks.

8   *Fluid structure*   The network must not be a fixed structure, although some links should be fairly durable. New links must be able to be added easily, and old ones must be alterable.

9   *Mixed organization*   The semantic–syntactic module is to be arranged conveniently for production, with words from the same semantic field linked closely. The phonetic–phonological module is to be organized for fast identification of sounds in speech comprehension, with words which sound similar tightly bonded together.

Processing

10   *Entry points*   There should be entry points into the network, which activate it: via a semantic field in word production, via acoustic signals in speech comprehension. These entry points can be envisaged as 'area codes' in a telephone directory, which provide access to more detailed information. Within each of the two main components, there should be 'signposts' to entry points in the other component.

11   *Parallel processing*   Numerous links must be activated simultaneously while the network is being used. This will involve links for many more words than will eventually be required.

12   *Interactive activation*   Any point or node in the network which has been activated must automatically activate those points with which it is most closely connected. Information must flow down the links in both directions.

13   *Excitation and inhibition*   Perpetual alteration and adjustment of the activated parts must be possible while the network is in use, with continuous arousal of extra

sections and damping down of previously aroused ones as processing proceeds. This excitation and inhibition must go on until a suitable word is found.

14   *Narrowing down*   A search for a word should involve first a broad sweep through a general area, in which numerous words which fulfil certain outline specifications are to be activated. The extra ones are to be gradually filtered out as the word required is selected. Narrowing down within each component should happen simultaneously, though the one which initiated the search should be in the lead.

Novelty

15   *Endless exploration*   The links which can be activated, both within the mental lexicon and in adjacent components, such as syntax and memory, must be potentially limitless. This is to allow full exploration to continue until enough have been activated to cope with the word being sought or until an alternative is found.

16   *Additional segmentation*   A word must optionally be able to be analysed into its component morphemes. This is primarily to aid comprehension of unfamiliar words or as a preliminary to creating new words.

17   *New word creation*   It must be possible to create a potentially infinite number of new words with the aid of the back-up information used in segmentation, and the 'lexical tool-kit'.

These outline specifications, at least, must be fulfilled if Dumbella is to behave at all like a human in her ability to cope with words.

The mental lexicon is therefore concerned above all with *links*, not locations. It pays attentions to *cores* of words, rather than peripheries, since it is impossible to say where knowledge about a word ends. And outline *frameworks* are more important than details, which are filled in creatively as speech proceeds.

Increasingly, the term 'mental lexicon' must be regarded as a metaphor:[14] the seething lexical connections in the mind are far from what we normally imagine a dictionary or lexicon to be.

Summary

This chapter has looked at the overall organization of the mental lexicon. It is an evolutionary mish-mash, in which the various parts have developed over the ages into a somewhat strange amalgam: the two main components are organized in different ways, one for easy production, the other for easy comprehension. And they both overlap and interact with other aspects of language and cognition.

Overall, the mental lexicon – a term which might need to be regarded as a metaphor – is concerned with links, not locations, with cores, not peripheries, and with frameworks, not fixed details.

The final chapter will deal with two topics. Can the contents of the mental lexicon be programmed into current computers? And what else do we need to know?

21

Last Word
— Final comments and future questions —

> Words, words, words, in songs and stories . . .
> If I only understood them . . .
> Would not this world be changed?
> Pete Seeger, 'Words, words, words'

'In the beginning was the word. But by the time the second word was added to it, there was trouble. For with it came syntax, the thing that tripped up so many people.'[1] This quotation represents the standard linguistic viewpoint over the past half-century – that syntactic structures are the most complex aspect of language, and consequently the area which merits the greatest attention. Words, in contrast, have been regarded as a collection of bric-à-brac, a jumble of miscellanea which speakers learn 'item by item, in a more or less rote fashion'.[2] They were treated as superficial trivia, 'brittle pieces of crystalline structure that may be picked up but not absorbed'.[3]

But there are signs that 'the time of the lexicon has set in':[4] 'The ability of children to conform to grammatical rules is only slightly more wonderful than their ability to learn new words. . . . What one tends to overlook is the sheer magnitude of the child's achievement. Simply learning the vocabulary is an enormous undertaking,' say two psychologists.[5] A neurologist notes: 'I must confess that I have always been more impressed with the capacity of the human brain to discriminate, characterize and store in memory the thirty thousand plus arbitrary words in active use than with the complexity claimed to be involved in learning a few dozen syntactic algorithmic rules.'[6] And a number of linguists have come round to the view that the lexicon is a central component of a person's internal grammar.[7]

In the previous chapter, we summarized the findings of this book. The most important were:

1   The mental lexicon contains whole words, which are viewed as coins with lemmas (meaning and word class) on one side and word forms (sounds) on the other.

2   Both sides of the coin have certain outline features engraved more strongly, the equivalent of area codes in a telephone directory. These provide entry points for retrieval, and are more durable in memory than the finer details.

3   Information about these two aspects of a word are in separate but linked 'modules'. These modules hook into a third, word-formation component.

4   Each module can be viewed as a dense, multiplex network, in which a few links are firm and durable, but many more temporary ones can be formed as the occasion requires.

5   The term 'the mental lexicon' may give a false impression of rigidity. The human mind is concerned with links not locations, with cores not peripheries, with outline frameworks not fixed structures.

In this chapter, we need to consider two main points. First, can we program this structure into Dumbella, the robot discussed at the beginning of the book (chapter 3), using a current-day computer? Second, what else do we need to know about the mental lexicon?

Can Dumbella be Programmed?

Hal (for Heuristically programmed Algorithmic computer, no less) was a master-work of the third computer breakthrough . . . Most of his communication with his shipmates was by means of the spoken word. Poole and Bowman could talk to Hal as if he were a human being, and he would reply in the perfect idiomatic English he had learned during the fleeting weeks of his electronic childhood.

This optimistic account of a talking computer occurs in Arthur Clarke's space fiction novel *2001: A Space Odyssey*. In real life, however, we are nowhere near being able to create robots like Hal. At the moment, it is simply impossible to program Dumbella with anything like the flexibility and power of the human mental lexicon. The most powerful device we have for producing models, the computer, is still inadequate: 'It is a striking fact that computers are virtually incapable of handling the routine mental feats of perception, language comprehension and memory retrieval that we humans take so much for granted.'[8] The most elaborate computer models of the lexicon so far are those which have attempted to simulate speech perception.[9] Yet not one of them has come near the overall requirements of human word recognition.

However, researchers may be on the right track with the new-style computers which take the human brain as their inspiration (chapter 3). The human brain is capable of massive parallel processing: an uncountable number of connections can be made simultaneously. It activates many more connections than are strictly needed for almost every brain process, then suppresses those which are not required. These properties are found in some 'connectionist' computer models with their intricate networks.[10]

But some fundamental problems need to be solved. Quantity-wise, the sheer number of interwoven links within the brain makes it almost inconceivable that a computer could handle them all. Quality-wise, the organization of this multiplex web is the key factor, yet is still a mystery. As one writer notes: 'If the cells and fibres in one human brain were all stretched out end to end, they would certainly reach to the moon and back. Yet the fact that they are not arranged end to end enabled man to go there himself. The astonishing tangle within our heads makes us what we are.'[11]

The mental lexicon accounts for a largish portion of this astonishing tangle – but how much of a tangle is it? Above all, is the mind an interlocking whole, or is it split up into components or modules? Can the mind 'be carved at its joints'?[12] This is known as the 'modularity question'.

If the mental network isn't divided up, then how does the human mind cope with the labyrinth? If it is split up, then how did the modules get there? Were they created as a side-effect of the way the mind-web works? Or were they pre-programmed to develop? And further questions arise. If modules exist, how self-contained are they? Is there a module overseer, to check that they link up properly? These are all unanswered questions.[13]

This book has argued strongly for interconnected modules. Relatively recently, computer scientists have started to pay serious attention to the mental lexicon, and interconnected modules form the solution proposed by some of them, as will be outlined below.

Interconnected Modules

The mental lexicon is an elaborate structure, with an enormous amount of information involved. Mostly, researchers have worked on individual sections. But a few people have (finally!) started to try to put all the pieces together. James Pustejovsky, a computer scientist, stresses the various levels of lexical information, the extensive amount of polysemy (multiple meanings, chapter 10), and the routine underspecification (lack of detail, the fact that the word *door* in to 'knock on the door' involves a hard object, but to 'walk through the door' implies an empty space, for example, chapter 10). Pustejovksy outlines the bare bones of a lexical model.[14] His work is significant partly because of its intrinsic interest, but also because he is one of the first computer scientists who has tried to specify the components, and 'put it all together'. His outline specifications partly overlap with proposals made by others, and partly add new insights of his own.

First, a word's role in the syntax of the sentence is important, he notes. This is uncontroversial. A verb's 'argument structure' must be specified, that is, the essential syntactic accompaniments (chapter 11). Its 'event structure' also needs to be listed, the kind of event which the verb describes. This is also uncontroversial, though less attention has been paid to this facet (chapter 11). A further requirement is its 'inheritance structure', for example, the word *suffocate* 'inherits' the more general meaning *die*, since it is a special instance of dying. This is again uncontroversial (chapter 9).

Any word has in addition what Pustejovksy calls its 'qualia structure', which specifies certain essential aspects of its meaning. *Qualia* have been described as 'raw feelings', 'the basic subjective feelings associated with consciousness'.[15] Classic examples include 'experience of the redness of red, the itchiness of an itch, and the painfulness of pain'.[16] According to Pustejovsky, the qualia structure of a word such as *novel* includes a 'constitutive aspect', the relation between the word and its component parts: a *narrative* is likely to be a linking thread. A 'telic aspect' provides information that a book's purpose is for reading, and an 'agentive aspect' specifies that the novel came into being because it was written. In short, the qualia structure includes everything that might be included in a good dictionary, and more. Pustejovsky not only outlines these basic requirements, but also makes some attempt at a preliminary formal specification (though the formal aspects of qualia structure are fairly specialised).[17]

At the very least, Pustejovksy's contribution has been to draw attention to the centrality of the lexicon, to explore some of its essential components, and to show how these might be handled by a computer, a radical turn-around from the way in which the lexicon was envisaged even some 20 years ago.

But however the lexicon is organized, there is increasing evidence that children are pre-programmed to arrange it in the way they do, as will be outlined below.

The Original Word Game

'The only way to begin to account for the child's wizardry as a word learner, given the sheer weight of how much there is to be learned, is to grant that the child brings a great deal to the "original word game".'[18] This comment by a psychologist is echoed by others working in language, notably the linguist Noam Chomsky: 'Similar problems [concerning the speed and efficiency of language learning] arise in the area of vocabulary acquisition, and the solution to them must lie along the same lines: in the biological endowment that constitutes the human language faculty.'[19]

What then could possibly be innate? Bees provide a partial answer. They unerringly fly to flowers, yet roses are very different from marigolds or delphiniums. So bees cannot have been born with an encyclopaedia of all flowers in their minds. Instead, they have to learn. And they learn fast because they are predisposed to pay attention to certain flower features: a combination of shape, colour and scent. Similarly, humans are predisposed to pay selective attention to certain aspects of their environment, and to label these with words. This phenomenon is known as 'innately guided learning'. In short, strong biases are inbuilt in perhaps all animal species.[20]

The basic features which humans attend to are unclear, and many writers are somewhat vague about them. Many also may overestimate the 'ready-made' nature of the concepts. 'The child approaches language with an intuitive understanding of such concepts as physical object, human intention, volition, causation, goal, and so on,'[21] says Chomsky, arguing that 'The speed and precision of vocabulary acquisition leaves no real alternative to the conclusion that the child somehow has the concepts available before experience with language and is basically learning labels for concepts that are already part of his or her conceptual apparatus.'[22]

More recently, however, researchers have attempted to be more specific about these basics, suggesting, for example, that humans are tuned into things, events and states, and that these correlate with aspects of language.[23] Children notice particularly the shape of objects (chapter 16), and are able to describe objects in considerable detail – though they are much less good at locating these objects in space.[24] Stress and rhythm are highly salient aspects of sound structure, especially for children (chapter 17). In brief, we are beginning to understand what humans are pre-set to notice – but there is still a long way to go. This whole area is an important question for the future.

The characteristics into which meaning and sound are analysed are similar the world over. This suggests that the modules containing the lemmas on the one hand, and the sound structure on the other, are possibly pre-programmed in outline, and available from a very young age. But they have a fluid structure, which develops gradually into its mature state.

Judging from recent work, only broad outlines are pre-ordained. For much of the detail, youngsters are highly influenced by their own language, from a fairly young age.[25] An analysis of the spontaneous speech of English and Korean children between the ages of 1 and 3 showed that they talked about similar events, such as putting on and taking off clothing, opening and closing containers. But from the age of 18 months, they diverged in the way they dealt with spatial terms.[26] The English children used particles and prepositions such as *up*, *down*, *in*, *out*, *on*, *off*, whereas the Korean children used only verbs. English makes a firm distinction between *put on*, as putting a cup *on* a flat surface such as a table, and *put in*, as putting an apple into a container such as a bowl. Korean, on the other hand, systematically distinguishes via the verbs used between putting things into a tight container, such as fitting a piece into a jigsaw puzzle, and putting things into a loose container, such as putting a book into a bag. The children reliably followed these distinctions, and even their errors tended to be language-specific, as when a child used the 'tight-fitting' word *kkita* for sticking a fork into an apple, which for adults would be outside the *kkita* category. The researchers concluded that spatial semantic development is highly responsive to the properties of the input language.

A similar picture emerged from the exploration of children's acquisition of the Mayan language Tzeltal.[27] Tzeltal speakers talk as if the whole world tilted down northwards, so one can speak of the 'uphill' end of a table. Children do not start out with any pre-linguistic concepts such as vertical, the writer argues. Youngsters observe instances of vertical and also land slope in actual use. Consequently, learning the word in context provides the concepts.

In short: 'Many linguistic categories are simply not natural in any straightforward sense at all: they have to be learnt from usage,' argues one influential researcher: 'Languages *construct* concepts that otherwise might not have been.'[28]

Other Languages

This book has concentrated on the lexicon underlying the spoken language of native English speakers. Other languages have been mentioned only intermittently. But English is just one of the 50,000 or so languages spoken in the world. There is no reason to believe that it is superior or inferior to the others. It happens to have been studied in more depth than most other languages. But is it representative?

So far, the answer for the mental lexicon appears to be both 'yes' and 'no'. Certain areas of other languages have been studied, and these suggest that there are both similarities and differences in the ways in which the mental lexicon is organized. To take some random examples, a study of child language acquisition in Telegu, a Dravidian language spoken in south India, showed that the semantic errors of children acquiring Telegu are very like those found among English-speaking children.[29] And, in a miscellaneous collection of Indian languages, many of the word-formation processes have strong similarities to English ones.[30] Work on Italian has confirmed a difference between inflectional and derivational morphology.[31] Analysis of a French aphasic showed that she formed new words from the fragments of words which she could remember, by a back-up procedure which was similar to that used by English speakers.[32]

On the other hand, studies of Welsh slips of the tongue indicate that phonological storage might be somewhat different from that for English words, especially as the initial consonant of Welsh words 'mutates' systematically, depending on the preceding word.[33] Spanish slips of the tongue show some differences from English ones, perhaps due to the different rhythmic pattern of the language.[34] French speakers perhaps pay more attention to syllables than English speakers when they recognize words.[35] Polish speakers are reported to respond somewhat differently from English speakers in word association experiments.[36] Turkish is an 'agglutinative' language, one which 'glues together' strings of morphemes in a clear-cut way (as in English *know-ing-ly*): its speakers probably assemble words in the course of speech to a greater extent than speakers of English.[37] Serbo-Croatian speakers probably deal with morphologically related words in an un-English way: one inflected form seems to be at the hub of an array of related forms, an arrangement sometimes spoken of as a 'satellite organization'. The central form is linked more closely to each of the satellites than any of them are to each other.[38] The treatment of morphology may also be partially different from English in Italian,[39] German,[40] and Dutch[41] – though there is some controversy over this, with some work on Dutch indicating a closer relationship to English results.[42]

These various papers suggest that it is important to compare and contrast findings obtained from English with those from other languages. Only in this way will we be able to confidently distinguish universal features of the mental lexicon from those which are due to the structure of an individual language.[43]

Furthermore, native speakers of English may be unrepresentative of the inhabitants of the world in two ways. First, a large proportion of them are literate. This may have affected lexical storage. Many English adults report that they are unable to remember a word unless they see it written down. And spelling can play a role in lexical decision tasks involving spoken words.[44] This suggests that the spoken form of a word can be affected by its written representation. And the reverse is true: whether or not someone can read a word may depend on features of its spoken form, such as the rhythm.[45] There is now a large, informative body of work on reading and spelling.[46] But the interrelationship between the spoken and written forms still requires exploration.[47]

A second biasing factor is that many English speakers are monolingual, a situation somewhat unusual in the world at large, where it is common for humans to use more than one language. There is no general agreement as to how the various lexicons are organized in the minds of bilingual and multilingual speakers[48] – though there is increasing evidence for a single integrated network.[49] If a person knows two languages reasonably well, words are possibly subconsciously activated in both languages, then the language which is not wanted is suppressed.[50] The fact that words from both languages are activated is shown by the occurrence of blends, such as *Springling* (a blend of the English word *spring* and the equivalent German word *Frühling*). When one language is better known than the other, words in both languages may still be activated – but the more weakly activated will be suppressed, and the highly activated will 'block' access to it (chapter 18). This may be why it is sometimes so difficult to remember a word in a foreign language. However, considerably more work is needed in order to understand fully how the various languages known by a single speaker are interwoven.

Much Desire to Learn . . .

'Where there is much desire to learn, there of necessity will be much arguing, much writing, many opinions; for opinion in good men is but knowledge in the making.' These words of the seventeenth-century poet John Milton[51] are entirely applicable to the research going on around the mental lexicon today. This book has attempted to summarize a number of important findings, and tried to provide an overall picture of how people store and find words. Hopefully, it is on the right track – though undoubtedly some sections of it will be controversial, and others might be proved wrong by future research.

However, as a wise elderly monk William said in Umberto Eco's novel *The Name of the Rose*: 'Books are not made to be believed, but to be subjected to enquiry.'[52] My overall hope is that this book will act as a jumping-off point – that many people will, like me, be captivated by the importance and mystery of words, and will work to fill in the gaps in our knowledge. Perhaps in the foreseeable future we shall solve the secrets of the human word-store, much as our ancestors solved the mystery of the circulation of the blood:

On a huge hill,
Cragged and steep, Truth stands, and he that will
Reach her, about must, and about must goe;
And what the hills suddennes resists, win so.

John Donne 'Satyre III'

Notes

Where two dates appear together, e.g., Freud, S. (1901/1975), the first is the date of the original publication of the work, the second the date of the edition listed in the references.

Chapter 1 Welcome to Dictionopolis!

1 Chand, n.d.: 3–4.
2 Quoted by Vygotsky, 1934, in Saporta, 1961: 509.
3 Butterworth, 1979.
4 Milton, *Paradise Lost*, v. 622–4.
5 For useful summaries of work on memory, see Gregg, 1986; Baddeley, 1990; Gathcrcole and Baddeley, 1993.
6 Seashore and Eckerson, 1940: 14.
7 Farrar, 1865: 59.
8 Bresler, 1983.
9 Seashore and Eckerson, 1940.
10 For further discussion, see Diack, 1975; R. C. Anderson and Freebody, 1981; McKeown and Curtis, 1987.
11 For further refinements, see Aitchison and Koppel, 1990; Nation, 1993.
12 Nagy and Anderson, 1984; Nagy and Herman, 1987.
13 G. A. Miller, 1991; G. A. Miller and Gildea, 1987: 86.
14 Wallman, 1992; Aitchison, 1998.
15 Lenneberg, 1967.
16 Marslen-Wilson and Tyler, 1980, 1981.
17 Ibid.
18 Shakespeare, *Henry V*, III. iv.
19 Butterworth, 1980a.
20 H. H. Clark and Gerrig, 1983.
21 Ibid.
22 Hudson, 1984a: 74. The information included by dictionaries has varied from century to century. On the history of dictionaries, see Green (1996); Béjoint (2000), ch. 3; Landau (2001), ch. 2.

23 Fodor, 1981: 287.
24 Ibid.: 288.
25 Ayto, 1980: 45.
26 Kilgarriff, 1997.
27 For early attempts to list its contents, see Fillmore, 1971; Butterworth, 1983b.
28 For other recent attempts to examine its content, see Lipka, 1992; Carter, 1998; Singleton, 2000.

Chapter 2   Links in the Chain

1 Ohala, 1981.
2 James, 1890/1981: 615.
3 Ibid.: 243.
4 Freud, 1901/1975: 96–7.
5 Goodglass et al., 1984.
6 Meringer and Mayer, 1895/1978: vii.
7 Fromkin, 1971.
8 There is a useful appendix of speech errors in Fromkin, 1973, from which some of the examples in this book have been taken.
9 Ellis, 1980.
10 Freud, 1901/1975: 146–7.
11 Fromkin, 1973: 248.
12 Zwicky, 1982.
13 Cutler, 1982a. Further problems with slips of the tongue are discussed in Ferber, 1991, 1995; Meyer, 1992.
14 Quoted by Critchley, 1970/1973: 60.
15 Gardner, 1974.
16 Ibid.: 70.
17 Benson, 1979: 313.
18 Ellis, 1985a: 108.
19 Freud, 1891/1953: 13.
20 Ellis, 1985a.
21 Benson, 1979.
22 Ibid.: 302.
23 Ibid.: 303.
24 Bateman, 1892, quoted in Ellis, 1985a: 116.
25 Butterworth, 1993.
26 Galton, 1883: 145.
27 Postman and Keppel, 1970.
28 R. Brown and McNeill, 1966.
29 R. Brown, 1970: 234.
30 Balota and Chumbley, 1984.
31 Gordon, 1983.
32 Swinney, 1979.
33 Marslen-Wilson, 1989a.
34 For discussions of priming, see, e.g., Monsell, 1985; Schriefers et al., 1992; Wheeldon and Monsell, 1992, 1994.

35 Cutler and Norris, 1979.
36 Grosjean, 1980.
37 Marslen-Wilson, 1989a.
38 Carey, 1978; Aitchison and Chiat, 1981.
39 Aitchison and Chiat, 1981.
40 Whaley, 1978.
41 Labov, 1973: 340.
42 Householder, 1966: 100.
43 E. K. Brown, 1984: 10.
44 Kempson, 1977: 102.
45 Bloomfield, 1933: 274.
46 Chomsky and Halle, 1968: 12.
47 E. K. Brown, 1984.
48 Blumstein, 1995; Posner and Raichle, 1994.
49 Hillyard, 1993; Kutas and van Petten, 1994.
50 Johnson, 1755.
51 Aston and Burnard, 1997.
52 Biber et al., 1998: 6. On the use of corpora, see also Aijmer and Altenberg, 1991; Barnbrook, 1996; Biber, Conrad and Reppen, 1998; Kennedy, 1998; Ooi, 1998; Renouf, 1998; Thomas and Short, 1996.

Chapter 3   Programming Dumbella

1   Milton, *Paradise Lost*, viii. 76–80.
2   Weizenbaum, 1976/1984: xvii.
3   Ibid.: 24.
4   E. K. Brown, 1984.
5   Chomsky, 1978: 202.
6   Baddeley, 1983: 12.
7   Matthei and Roeper, 1983.
8   J. Miller, 1978: 9.
9   Marshall, 1977; Draaisma, 2000.
10 Plato, *Theaetetus* 197d–e.
11 Cicero, *De Oratore* I. 5. 18.
12 Conan Doyle, 1930/1981: 21.
13 Quoted in Marshall, 1977: 479.
14 Thomson, 1907, quoted in Marshall, 1977: 479.
15 Marshall, 1977.
16 Hodges, 1983/1985.
17 Rumelhart et al., 1986: 75.
18 Kintsch, 1984.
19 See, e.g., Lyons, 1968; Palmer, 1984; E. K. Brown, 1984; Aitchison, 1992c.
20 Parlett, 1981: 198.
21 Kilgarriff, 1997: 142.

Chapter 4   Slippery Customers

1 Waugh, quoted in J. Green, 1982: 254.
2 Herbert, 1935.
3 Lakoff, 1972: 183.
4 Labov, 1973: 341.
5 Collingwood, 1938.
6 Johnson-Laird, 1983.
7 Quine, 1961/1985: 49.
8 For a useful summary of the differing standpoints of philosophers and psychologists, see Johnson-Laird, 1983; Murphy, 1991.
9 Quine, 1971: 142.
10 G. A. Miller and Johnson-Laird, 1976: 212.
11 Aitchison, 1985.
12 Tulving, 1972; Baddeley, 1976.
13 R. Brown, 1958: 85.
14 Titchener, 1909, quoted in ibid.: 90.
15 E. Smith and Medlin, 1981.
16 Fillmore, 1975.
17 Quoted in a letter to *The Times*.
18 Gowers, 1986: 39.
19 Katz and Fodor, 1963.
20 *COD* (1982).
21 *LCED* (1982).
22 Armstrong et al., 1983.
23 Putnam, 1975.
24 Johnson-Laird, 1983: 195.
25 Dupré, 1981.
26 Fodor, 1987.
27 Labov, 1973.
28 Ibid.: 340.
29 Ibid.: 341.
30 Wittgenstein, 1958: 66.
31 Ibid.
32 Ibid.: 67.
33 Weinreich, 1966: 190, 186.
34 See Pulman, 1983; D. Sperber and Wilson, 1986; Murphy, 1991, for further discussion on this.

Chapter 5   Bad Birds and Better Birds

1 e.g., Lenneberg, 1967; Berlin and Kay, 1969.
2 Rosch, 1975: 198.
3 Armstrong et al., 1983.
4 Rosch, 1975.
5 Pulman, 1983.

6 Shakespeare, *As You Like It*, V. iv.
7 L. Coleman and Kay, 1981.
8 Ibid.: 31.
9 Jackendoff, 1983.
10 Aitchison, 1985.
11 Fillmore, 1982; Jackendoff, 1990; J. R. Taylor, 1995.
12 Aitchison, 1981.
13 Shakespeare, *Hamlet*, II. ii.
14 *LDEL*.
15 Summarized and discussed by Geeraerts 1992, 1993. See also J. R. Taylor, 1992; Kilgarriff, 1992.
16 Zwicky and Sadock, 1975.
17 e.g., Lakoff, 1987; J. R. Taylor, 1989; Geeraerts, 1992.
18 On *old*, see also J. R. Taylor, 1992, whose treatment differs somewhat from the account below.

Chapter 6   Whispering Chambers of the Imagination

1 Armstrong et al., 1983.
2 Osherson and Smith, 1981.
3 *Guardian*, November 1984.
4 G. A. Miller and Johnson-Laird, 1976: 41.
5 Bulmer, 1967.
6 Jackendoff, 1983; Geeraerts, 1989.
7 Geeraerts, 1989: 606.
8 Geeraerts, 1989.
9 Aitchison, 1992b.
10 Cruse, 1990.
11 Rosch et al., 1976.
12 Most notably, Wierzbicka, 1985, 1990, 1992a.
13 Geeraerts, 1989, 1992; Bolinger, 1992; Lakoff, 1987; Minda and Smith, 2001. See also book reviews, Aitchison, 1990, 1993.
14 Posner, 1986: 59.
15 Lakoff, 1987.
16 See Markman, 1989, for a useful discussion.
17 English week, Fillmore, 1982; Inca week, Aveni, 1990.
18 Dahrendorf, 1982.
19 Lakoff, 1987.
20 Lakoff and Johnson, 1980; Lakoff, 1987.
21 Mental models: Johnson-Laird, 1983; frames: Fillmore, 1982; scripts: Schank and Abelson, 1977; ICMs: Lakoff, 1987; cognitive domains: Langacker, 1987, 1988.
22 Minsky, 1975.
23 For various views on frames and domains, see G. Brown and Yule, 1983; Lehrer and Kittay, 1992; Ungerer and Schmidt, 1996; Clausner and Croft, 1999.
24 Barsalou, 1992: 29.
25 Barsalou, 1985.
26 Barsalou, 1983.

27   Hampton, 1991.
28   Barsalou, 1992: 64.
29   Shank and Abelson, 1977; Ungerer and Schmidt, 1996.

Chapter 7   The Primordial Atomic Globule Hunt

1   G. A. Miller and Johnson-Laird, 1976: 237.
2   Armstrong et al., 1983.
3   Lucretius, *De rerum natura*, v. 422–6.
4   Bierwisch, 1970: 182.
5   Leibniz, quoted in Wierzbicka, 1992c: 9.
6   Chomsky, 1965: 160.
7   Schank, 1972.
8   G. A. Miller and Johnson-Laird, 1976.
9   Schank, 1972.
10   G. A. Miller and Johnson-Laird, 1976.
11   Ibid.: 38.
12   Ibid.: 688.
13   Ibid.
14   Wierzbicka, 1996. The quotes from her book are on pp. 11, 22, 180.
15   Johnson, 1987.
16   Fodor et al., 1975.
17   Cutler, 1983.
18   e.g., Wason, 1965.
19   Kintsch, 1974; Fodor et al., 1980.
20   Pulman, 1983: 31.
21   e.g., Katz, 1975.
22   e.g., Chomsky, 1965: 160.
23   Fodor et al., 1980: 266.
24   Ayto, 1984: 50.
25   *COD*, 7th edn, 1982. This definition was updated in the 9th edn, 1990.
26   1978.

Chapter 8   Word-webs

1   Fodor, 1983: 80.
2   Jenkins, 1970.
3   e.g., Deese, 1965; Postman and Keppel, 1970.
4   E. B. Coleman, 1964.
5   Jenkins, 1970.
6   Ibid.
7   Garrett, 1992.
8   Freud, 1901/1975: 96–7.
9   R. Brown and McNeill, 1966.
10   Butterworth et al., 1984.
11   Ibid.: see Funnell, 1995a, 1995b, for further confusions of this type.

12 Goodglass and Baker, 1976.
13 Howard et al., 1981.
14 Hotopf, 1980.
15 Garrett, 1992.
16 Ibid.: 383.
17 Warrington, 1981.
18 Goodglass et al., 1966.
19 Warrington, 1981.
20 Hart et al., 1985.
21 Ibid.: 439.
22 Garrett, 1993; Damasio, 1990; Warrington and Shallice, 1984; Shallice, 1988; Cohen et al., 1997; Lucchelli et al., 1997.
23 Goodglass and Baker, 1976.
24 Howard et al., 1981.
25 *NSOD*, 1993.
26 *Wimp* examples from *Sunday Times*, July and August 1993; *Cosmopolitan*, July 1984; Aitchison and Lewis, 1995.
27 On freezes, see Fenk-Oczlon, 1989.
28 *Longman Dictionary of English Idioms*, 1979. See also Wray, 2002.
29 Nunberg et al., 1994: 492.
30 Nunberg et al., 1994.
31 Jackendoff, 1997a.
32 Pitt and Katz, 2000.
33 According to Igor Mel'cuk, quoted in Pawley, 2001.
34 Cowie, 1998.
35 Kay and Fillmore, 1999.
36 Jackendoff, 1997b.
37 Ibid.
38 Kay and Fillmore, 1999: 30; Jackendoff, 1997a.
39 Aitchison and Lewis, 1996. The data are from the BNC. As explained in ch. 2, this is a database of real examples from both spoken and written language.
40 Aitchison and Lewis, 1996.
41 Hotopf, 1980.
42 Johnson-Laird, 1983: 214.
43 From *A Selection from Symbolic Logic* (1895), in Carroll, 1988: 1119.
44 Lyons, 1981; Hurford and Heasley, 1983; Cruse, 1986.
45 Lyons, 1981: Lyons distinguishes binary antonymy (here labelled the either–or type), gradable antonymy (hidden scale type), converseness (differing viewpoint type).
46 Cruse, 1992; Murphy and Andrew, 1993.
47 Charles and Miller, 1989; Fellbaum, 1992.
48 The reasoning can be carried through to hyperonyms. For example, a *carrot* is not a *metal* because it is a *plant*, and plants and metals are incompatible.
49 Cruse, 1986; Tversky, 1990; Chaffin, 1992.
50 For further details of lexical links, see Cruse, 1986; Lipka, 1992.

Chapter 9 Lexical All-sorts

1 Wittgenstein, 1958: 11.
2 e.g., Fromkin, 1971.
3 Hopper and Thompson, 1984.
4 Levelt, 1989.
5 Hotopf, 1980.
6 Deese, 1965.
7 Allport and Funnell, 1981; Hand et al., 1979.
8 Bird et al., 2000; Black and Chiat, 2001; Chiat, 2002.
9 Hotopf, 1980.
10 G. A. Miller, 1990b; Fellbaum, 1998.
11 G. A. Miller, 1990a.
12 Ibid.
13 R. Brown, 1958; Rosch et al., 1976.
14 Tversky, 1990.
15 Ibid.: 339.
16 Cruse, 1986.
17 Chaffin, 1992.
18 Cruse, 1986.
19 G. A. Miller, 1990a; G. A. Miller and Fellbaum, 1992.
20 Gross and Miller, 1990.
21 For further complexities involving adjectives, see Gross et al., 1989.
22 For experimental evidence, see Murphy and Andrew, 1993.
23 Fellbaum, 1990.
24 McCawley, 1983: 263.
25 McCawley, 1983.
26 Theoretical linguists regard nouns, verbs, adjectives and prepositions as the four major word classes. For an outline account of this viewpoint, see Napoli, 1993.
27 Grodzinsky, 1990.
28 Wittgenstein, 1958: 12.
29 Friederici, 1982, 1985.
30 Gardner, 1974: 61.
31 Jakobson, 1956.
32 Kean, 1977: 10.
33 Goodglass and Menn, 1985; Caplan, 1987, 1992.
34 Cutler and Isard, 1980; Butterworth, 1989.
35 Bradley, 1983; Bradley et al., 1980.
36 Gordon and Caramazza, 1982, 1985.
37 Friederici, 1985.
38 Shillcock and Bard, 1993, provide further experimental evidence.

Chapter 10 Verb Power

1 Carroll, 1872, in Carroll, 1988: 197.
2 G. A. Miller and Fellbaum, 1991: 214.

3 *CED*, according to a count made by G. A. Miller and Fellbaum, 1992. They point out that the ratio is partially counteracted by the polysemy count: 2.11 for verbs, 1.74 for nouns.
4 Anon., *First Grammar Book for Children* (London: Walker, n.d.).
5 Hopper and Thompson, 1984.
6 Advertisement for medical equipment in *British Journal of Hospital Medicine*, January 1980.
7 Hand et al., 1979.
8 Aitchison and Koppel, in prep.
9 Levin, 1991: 208.
10 Levin, 1991.
11 Levin, 1991; Levin and Rappaport Hovav, 1996.
12 Levin, 1993.
13 Ibid.
14 Levin and Rappaport Hovav, 1992.
15 Ibid.: 138.
16 Fillmore and Atkins, 1992.
17 Ibid.
18 Ibid. and Fillmore and Atkins, 1994.
19 See, e.g., *LLA*, 1993.
20 Carlson and Tanenhaus, 1988; Tanenhaus and Carlson, 1989; Tanenhaus et al., 1990, 1993.
21 See esp. Fillmore, 1968; and Jackendoff, 1972, for early work on the topic; Talmy, 1985; Rappaport and Levin, 1988; Dixon, 1989; and Jackendoff, 1990, for more recent work.
22 Jackendoff, 1990.
23 Gruber, 1965/1976, whose work became well known through its development in Jackendoff, 1972.
24 The main proponents of a single role are the group of researchers surrounding the American Noam Chomsky, who controversially regard thematic roles as syntactic, not semantic. In this approach, the term *thematic roles* has been shortened to *theta-roles*, or θ-roles, and a verb is regarded as having a *thematic grid*, which summarizes the set of thematic roles associated with it. For a summary, see Haegeman, 1994, for further discussion, Grimshaw, 1990.
25 An important proponent of more than one is Jackendoff, 1987, 1990.
26 See Pullum, 1991, for the history of the controversy.
27 e.g., Dowty, 1991; Levin and Rappaport Hovav, 1992.
28 Levin and Rappaport Hovav, 1992.
29 Levin and Rappaport Hovav, 1994, 1995.
30 Levin and Rappaport Hovav, 1994, 1995; Rappaport Hovav and Levin, 1998.
31 McKoon and MacFarland, 2000.
32 Vendler, 1967.
33 Pustejovsky, 1997; Pustejovsky and Boguraev, 1996; Pustejovsky, 2001.

Chapter 11 Bits of Words

1 See Aitchison, 1999; Spencer, 2001, for outline discussions.
2 Jarvella and Meijers, 1983.

3　e.g., Mackay, 1979.
4　Chomsky and Halle, 1968: 12.
5　Butterworth, 1983b.
6　For other differences between inflection and derivation, see S. R. Anderson, 1988a, 1992: 75; Aronoff, 1994; Marslen-Wilson and Tyler, 1998. On morphology in general, see esp. Spencer, 2001, 1991; also S. R. Anderson, 1992; Matthews, 1991; Carstairs-McCarthy, 1992; Jensen, 1990.
7　This conclusion is further supported by the speech errors analysed by Stemberger and MacWhinney, 1986.
8　Garrett, 1976, 1980.
9　Butterworth, 1983b.
10　See also Chialant and Caramazza, 1995; Tyler and Cobb, 1987. The latter found a patient with a deficit only for inflectional morphology.
11　Examples from Ayto, 1990.
12　Cheshire, 1982.
13　e.g., Cutler, 1983.
14　Murrell and Morton, 1974; Stanners et al., 1979.
15　Fowler et al., 1985. See Schriefers et al., 1992, for possible causes of the discrepancy.
16　e.g., Napps and Fowler, 1987; J. P. Stemberger and MacWhinney, 1988; Napps, 1989.
17　Stemberger, 1985; Stemberger and MacWhinney, 1986.
18　Taft and Forster, 1975.
19　Taft, 1981; Taft et al., 1986, though more recently Taft has shown signs of doubt, Taft, 1988, 1994.
20　Taft, 1981: 296.
21　Fay, 1977.
22　See Butterworth, 1983b; Cutler, 1983; Henderson, 1985, for a summary of the early years of the dispute.
23　Rubin et al., 1979.
24　Aronoff, 1976.
25　Aitchison, 1983–4.
26　Ibid.
27　Tyler et al., 1988.
28　Aitchison, 1983–4.
29　Cutler et al., 1985; Hawkins and Cutler, 1988.
30　e.g., Aronoff, 1976.
31　e.g., Mackay, 1979.
32　See Spencer, 1991; Jensen, 1990, for details of these 'levels' of derivation.
33　As pointed out, e.g., by Chomsky, 1970; Aronoff, 1976; Giegerich, 1999.
34　Aitchison and Straf, 1982; Aitchison, 1987.
35　Aitchison, 1987.
36　Anshen and Aronoff, 1988: 647.
37　Anshen and Aronoff, 1988, suggest that -ness suffixes are added on in the course of speech.
38　Summaries in Cutler, 1983; Henderson, 1989; see also Tyler et al., 1993.
39　Manelis and Tharp, 1977.
40　Bergman et al., 1988.
41　Manelis and Tharp, 1977.

42 S. R. Anderson, 1988b; Bergman et al., 1988; Aitchison, in press.
43 A similar proposal is made in Anshen and Aronoff, 1988.
44 Tyler et al., 1993; Sandra, 1994. See also Marslen-Wilson and Zhou, 1999.

Chapter 12 Taking Care of the Sounds

1   For an introduction to phonology, see Giegerich, 1992. For a psycholinguistic viewpoint, see Bybee, 2002. For views on the segment, see Ohala, 1992; Cutler, 1992.
2   Greenberg and Jenkins, 1964.
3   R. Brown and McNeill, 1966.
4   e.g., Koriat and Lieblich, 1974; Rubin, 1975; Browman, 1978. For a survey of the TOT experience, see A. S. Brown, 1991.
5   Tweney et al., 1975.
6   Fay and Cutler, 1977; Hurford, 1981; Aitchison and Straf, 1982.
7   Aitchison and Straf, 1982.
8   Room, 1979.
9   Browman, 1978.
10 Ibid.: 48.
11 Aitchison and Straf, 1982.
12 Fay and Cutler, 1977: 514n. They claim that the first vowel matched the target in 83% of malapropisms.
13 R. Brown and McNeill, 1966.
14 Fay and Cutler, 1977: 87%; but Aitchison and Straf, 1982: 67%.
15 R. Brown and McNeill, 1966; Aitchison and Straf, 1982.
16 Hayes, 1983, 1984.
17 Liberman and Prince, 1977; Selkirk, 1980, 1984; Halle and Vergnaud, 1987. For an introduction, see Giegerich, 1992; Ewen and van der Hulst, 2001; Kager, 1995.
18 Browman, 1978; Aitchison and Straf, 1982.
19 Browman, 1978.
20 Stemberger, 1990.
21 Barton, 1971.
22 Goodglass et al., 1976.
23 Treiman, 1989. The breaks were first noted by Mackay, 1972, though mainly in German examples. Laubstein, 1988; and S. Davis, 1989, disagree with this view.
24 Treiman, 1989: 36.
25 Blevins, 1995.
26 Treiman, 1989.
27 See, e.g., Vincent, 1986; Wells, 1990; Giegerich, 1992.
28 For a useful summary, see Halle and Clements, 1983.
29 Fay and Cutler, 1977.
30 For overlapping, but divergent views, see Jakobson et al., 1952; Chomsky and Halle, 1968; van den Broecke and Goldstein, 1980; Ladefoged, 1993; Maddieson, 1984.
31 Fay and Cutler, 1977.
32 Shattuck-Hufnagel and Klatt, 1979.
33 Berg, 1991b, notes that all words seem to be fully listed, so there is considerable redundancy: knowledge of syllable structure does not lead to words being constructed by rule.

Chapter 13   Drifting Words

1   The quote at the top of the chapter is from Trench (1855). The Byron lines are from 'Hints from Horace', 89.
2   Trench, 1856: 192.
3   Lewis Carroll *Through the Looking-Glass* (1872). In *The Complete Works of Lewis Carroll*. London: Penguin, 1982, p. 196.
4   Georg von der Gabelentz, 1891, in Hopper and Traugott, 1993.
5   Hughes, 1988: 14.
6   Bréal, 1883, quoted in Ullmann, 1962: 6.
7   Hughes, 1988: 2–3.
8   This list is from Burchfield, 1985.
9   The example of *buff* is from Ayto, 1990.
10   Ullmann, 1962: 197.
11   Meillet, 1905–6.
12   *Soup*, from Ayto, 1990.
13   Paul Bryers, *The Prayer of the Bone*. London: Bloomsbury, 1998, p. 45. On euphemisms, see Ayto, 1993.
14   Bloomfield, 1933: 347.
15   Aitchison, 2001, summarizes Labov's findings.
16   Paul, 1880/1920.
17   Hopper and Traugott, 1993: 100. For more on polysemy, see Geeraerts, 1992, 1993; Nerlich and Clarke, 1997.
18   *Chambers 21st Century Dictionary*, 1996.
19   Hopper and Traugott, 1993: 100.
20   Pustejovsky and Boguraev, 1996: 2, whose terminology is used in the rest of this section.
21   The examples in this and the next section are taken from Aitchison and Lewis, in press, and ultimately come from the BNC.
22   *New Oxford Dictionary of English*, 1998.
23   Aitchison and Lewis, in press.
24   Otto Jespersen in 1925, quoted in Warren, 199: 125.
25   Aitchison, 1996.

Chapter 14   Interpreting Ice-cream Cones

1   G. A. Miller and Johnson-Laird, 1976: 292.
2   M. K. Smith and Montgomery, 1989.
3   H. H. Clark and Gerrig, 1983.
4   Aristotle, *De Arte Poetica*, 1457b.
5   The subject of the metaphor is often called the *tenor* (e.g., nipples), and the new name the *vehicle* (e.g., ice-cream cones).
6   Pollio et al., 1990.
7   Lakoff and Johnson, 1980: 3.
8   D. Sperber and Wilson, 1985/6.
9   On the pervasiveness of metaphor and its overlap with 'ordinary' language, see also Lakoff, 1987; Pollio et al., 1990.

10 Lehrer, 1983.
11 Derek Cooper, quoted in Lehrer, 1983: 1.
12 H. R. Pollio et al., 1977.
13 A large number of books on metaphor have been published in recent years. For varied views, see Gibbs, 1994; Goatly, 1997; Kittay, 1987; Ortony, 1993; Steen, 1994.
14 Grice, 1975.
15 Brownell et al., 1984.
16 Quoted in Cohen and Cohen, 1980: 240.
17 Quoted in ibid.: 260.
18 Quoted in Lehrer, 1983: 14.
19 Chaucer, *Canterbury Tales*, Prologue, 152.
20 Blackburn, 1984: 175. The metaphor was coined by T. S. Eliot.
21 Shakespeare, *Macbeth*, II. ii.
22 Quoted in Cohen and Cohen, 1980: 183.
23 La Mettrie's watch metaphor (1748) is quoted in MacCormack, 1985: 11. See also H. Sperber, 1930.
24 Quoted in H. R. Pollio et al., 1977: 4.
25 M. K. Smith et al., 1981; Draaisma, 2000 explores changing metaphors for memory.
26 Lakoff, 1987; Johnson, 1987, 1992; Lakoff and Turner, 1989; Sweetser, 1990; Aitchison, 1997.
27 Lakoff, 1987; Lakoff and Kövecses, 1987; Kövecses, 1988.
28 Gibbs and O'Brien, 1990.
29 Osella and Osella, 1991.
30 Lakoff, 1987. See also Deignan, 1997.
31 Aitchison, 1992a.
32 Sweetser, 1990; Wierzbicka, 1992c.
33 Lakoff and Johnson, 1980; Lakoff, 1987; Johnson, 1987, 1992; Heine, 1997.
34 H. R. Pollio et al., 1977; M. R. Pollio and Pickens, 1980.
35 Lyric by Jimmy Kennedy, 1935.
36 On metonymy, see Lakoff and Johnson, 1980; Lakoff and Turner, 1989; Panther and Radden, 1999; Ungerer and Schmid, 1996.
37 H. H. Clark and Gerrig, 1983.
38 Ibid.

Chapter 15   Globbering Mattresses

1 *Guardian*, November 1984.
2 Humboldt, quoted in Bauer, 1983: 292.
3 Bauer, 1983.
4 The definition of *googol* quoted is from *Merriam-Webster's Collegiate Dictionary*, 10th edn (1993). Technically, a googol is 10 to the power of 100 (Chambers 21st century dictionary). Ayto (1999) relates the incident of the young nephew's coinage.
5 On measuring productivity, see this chapter, pp. 184–5.
6 Aronoff, 1976.
7 Noted by Kastovsky, 1986, who points out the need to distinguish between reasons for word formation.
8 Robert Philip, *Daily Telegraph*, 20 August 1993.

9 For differing but overlapping views, see Aronoff, 1976; Selkirk, 1982b; Dressler, 1985; Matthews, 1991; S. R. Anderson, 1992.
10 Cutler et al., 1985.
11 Adams, 1973; Bauer, 1983.
12 E. V. Clark, 1981.
13 Downing, 1977.
14 Ibid.: 832.
15 Gleitman and Gleitman, 1970: 92.
16 Downing, 1977.
17 Ibid.
18 Gleitman and Gleitman, 1979.
19 Adams, 1973; Bauer, 1983.
20 E. V. Clark, 1982.
21 E. V. Clark and H. Clark, 1979.
22 E. V. Clark, 1982.
23 *Time*, May 1962.
24 Aronoff, 1976.
25 McCarthy, 1982.
26 Aronoff, 1976; Romaine, 1983.
27 Lehnert, 1971.
28 Ibid.
29 Romaine, 1983.
30 Cutler, 1980, 1981.
31 Romaine, 1983.
32 Cutler, 1980.
33 Aronoff, 1976; Romaine, 1983.
34 Aitchison, 1991.
35 Menn and MacWhinney, 1984.
36 Randall, 1980.
37 Bauer, 1983: 90; McCarthy, 1982.
38 This ending was discussed in Marchand, 1969; Bauer, 1994; Barker, 1998.
39 Aitchison, 1994. Dictionaries are inconsistent in the spelling of *mini-* words. Sometimes they are hyphenated, as *mini-skirt*, at other times they are written as a single unhyphenated word, as *miniskirt*. The hyphen seem to be omitted as the words become more familiar.
40 According to the *OED*.
41 Baayen and Renouf, 1996.
42 Algeo, 1993, 1998; Anshen and Aronoff, 1988; Ayto, 1996; Kastovsky, 1986; Matthews, 1991.
43 S. H. Taylor, 1978: 352.
44 Bauer, 1983: 255.
45 Aronoff, 1986: 46.
46 Berko, 1958.
47 E. V. Clark and Hecht, 1982; Clark, 1993.
48 Sterling, 1983.
49 Aitchison, 2000.
50 Derwing and Baker, 1986: 331.
51 Marchand, 1969.
52 E. V. Clark et al., 1986; Clark, 1993.

Chapter 16   What is a Bongaloo, Daddy?

1   Chomsky (1988: 27) suggests that the rate is 12 a day; G. A. Miller and Gildea (1987: 86) suggest 13. A few moments of arithmetic can confirm the approximate average figure, assuming that an educated adult knows at least 50,000 words (ch. 1).

2   These guesstimates were produced by averaging out figures from various sources: M. E. Smith, 1926, whose estimates are assumed to be on the low side; N. V. S. Smith, 1973; Macnamara, 1982.

3   Carey, 1978.

4   Sully, 1897, in Bar-Adon and Leopold, 1971: 31.

5   Bates et al., 1979.

6   There is considerable variation between children (Harris et al., 1988): a few seem to be aware that words are symbols from a very young age.

7   Leopold, 1948, in Bar-Adon and Leopold, 1971: 2.

8   Preyer, 1882, in ibid.: 31.

9   Leopold, 1948, in ibid.: 2.

10 McShane, 1979, 1980; Kamhi, 1986.

11 Barrett, 1983, 1986, 1995.

12 McShane, 1979, 1980; Kamhi, 1986.

13 See ch. 16 for a phonological explanation, Plunkett, 1993; also Gopnik and Meltzoff, 1987, who argue that the spurt is connected with the development of the ability to categorize.

14 Goldfield and Reznick, 1990; Bloom, 2000: 35.

15 Goldfield and Reznick, 1990; Harris et al., 1988; Goldfield, 1993; Nelson et al., 1993.

16 Goldfield and Reznick, 1990: 180.

17 Lieven et al., 1992; Nelson, 1973, made the now famous distinction between 'referential' and 'expressive' vocabulary. Problems are pointed out by Lieven et al., 1992; Nelson has developed her ideas since then; see Nelson et al., 1993.

18 Nelson et al., 1993.

19 Leopold, 1948, in Bar-Adon and Leopold, 1971: 98.

20 Carey, 1978: 288.

21 Asch and Nerlove, 1960.

22 Sully, 1897, in Bar-Adon and Leopold, 1971: 37.

23 Leopold, 1948, in Bar-Adon and Leopold, 1971: 98. Gap-filling is also discussed in Hoek et al., 1986.

24 Ferguson and Farwell, 1975.

25 Chambers, 1904, quoted by Leopold, 1948, in Bar-Adon and Leopold, 1971: 99.

26 Leopold, 1948, in ibid.: 101.

27 E. V. Clark, 1973: 72.

28 Nelson et al., 1978.

29 Vygotsky, 1934/1962: 70.

30 Bowerman, 1980.

31 Bowerman, 1978.

32 For further examples of extensions explainable by prototypes, see Griffiths, 1986.

33 Markman, 1989.

34 Landau et al., 1988, 1992; Baldwin, 1992.

35 Merriman et al., 1993.

36 Keil and Batterman, 1984.

37 Ibid.: 229.
38 Anglin, 1970; Keil and Batterman, 1984; Keil, 1989.
39 Aitchison, 1992b.
40 Landau and Gleitman, 1985: 22.
41 Ibid.: 91.
42 Ibid.: 165.
43 Gropen et al., 1992.
44 Macnamara, 1982.
45 Inhelder and Piaget, 1964.
46 Macnamara, 1982.
47 The 'one name only' preference comes under different names: e.g., 'principle of contrast', E. V. Clark, 1987, 1993; 'mutual exclusivity', Merriman and Bowman, 1989 – though there is some discussion as to whether it is relevant at all ages (Merriman, 1991).
48 Bowerman, 1978, 1982.
49 Bowerman, 1978.
50 Anglin, 1970: 99.
51 Werner and Kaplan, 1950.
52 Haviland and Clark, 1974.
53 Goldfield and Snow, 1992.
54 Haviland and Clark, 1974.
55 For a useful survey, see Richards, 1979.
56 Maratsos, 1973.
57 Entwisle, 1966; R. Brown and Berko, 1960.
58 R. Brown and Berko, 1960: 14.
59 White, 1982.
60 Wiegel-Crump and Dennis, 1986.
61 Anglin, 1970: 99.
62 For other overviews of the development of word meaning, see Pease et al., 1993; Griffiths, 1986. For a more detailed discussion, see Markman, 1989.

Chapter 17 Aggergog Miggers, Wips and Gucks

1   N. V. S. Smith, 1973.
2   Sully, 1897, quoted in Bar-Adon and Leopold, 1971: 36.
3   For fuller lists, see Chiat, 1979; Ingram, 1986, 1989; Menn and Stoel-Gammon, 1993.
4   Waterson, 1970: 23.
5   Fourcin, 1978.
6   Vihmann, 1981.
7   Bloch, 1921, quoted in Vihmann, 1981: 248.
8   N. V. S. Smith, 1973.
9   Berko and Brown, 1960.
10 Jakobson, 1941/1968: 23.
11 N. V. S. Smith, 1973.
12 Vihmann, 1981.
13 Eimas et al., 1971; Eimas, 1985.
14 Morse, 1976; Kuhl and Miller, 1974, 1975.

15 Schultze, 1880, in Bar-Adon and Leopold, 1971: 28.
16 Jakobson, 1941/1968.
17 Leopold, 1947.
18 Jakobson, 1941/1968.
19 e.g., Macken, 1980.
20 e.g., Leopold, 1947.
21 e.g., Velten, 1943.
22 Stampe, 1969, 1979.
23 For an excellent and thorough overview of child phonology, see Vihmann, 1996. For a briefer but useful recent overview, see Menn and Stoel-Gammon, 1995. For children with language problems, see Chiat, 2000. The idea that the 'naming explosion' is due to word identification is in Plunkett, 1993.
24 Peters, 1983.
25 R. Clark, 1974.
26 Dupreez, 1974; Blasdell and Jensen, 1970.
27 For a fuller account of how children identify words, see Chiat, 1979, 1983. On the importance of stress and rhythm, see Gleitman et al., 1988; Echols and Newport, 1992; Echols, 1993; see also Jusczyk, 1993.
28 Braine, 1974: 283.
29 N. V. S. Smith, 1973.
30 Ferguson and Farwell, 1975; Menyuk and Menn, 1979.
31 Drachman, 1973.
32 Ingram, 1986.
33 Vihmann, 1981.
34 N. V. S. Smith, 1973.
35 Menn, 1978.
36 Priestley, 1977.
37 Aitchison, 1972.
38 Vihmann, 1981.
39 Aitchison and Straf, 1982.
40 e.g., Slobin, 1973; Vihmann, 1981.
41 Vihmann, 1981; Echols, 1993.
42 Wijnen et al., 1994.
43 Aitchison and Chiat, 1981.
44 Vihmann, 1978.
45 N. V. S. Smith, 1973.
46 Gathercole and Baddeley, 1989; Papagno and Vallar, 1992, have found that long-term storage of words depends critically on phonological short-term memory.
47 Aitchison and Chiat, 1981.

Chapter 18   Seeking and Finding

1 James, 1890/1981: 245.
2 Carroll, 1876/1967: 42.
3 Baars, 1980.
4 Butterworth, 1979.
5 Bickerton, 1981.

6   On blocking, see A. S. Brown, 1991; Burke et al., 1991; Jones and Langford, 1987; Jones, 1989.
7   Wheeldon and Monsell, 1994.
8   My own examples, but see Harley, 1990, for more on 'environmental contamination'.
9   Freud, 1901/1975: 112.
10   See Motley, 1985a, who brings *double entendres* into this category.
11   Motley, 1985b.
12   Chaika, 1974: 261.
13   Ibid.: 260.
14   D. Green, 1986.
15   Garrett, 1993: 146.
16   A. S. Brown, 1991; Burke et al., 1991.
17   Levelt, 1993a: 17.
18   e.g., Levelt, 1989, 1993a; Garrett, 1993; Schriefers et al., 1990; Roelofs, 1993a; Dell and O'Seaghdha, 1993; Caramazza, 1997.
19   There is no good evidence for an earlier phase: 'Piece together your thoughts into a lemma' (ch. 7), though some researchers disagree (e.g., Levelt, 1989). Others propose a 'higher' level of whole concepts (e.g., Roelofs, 1992, 1993a, b).
20   Browman, 1978.
21   McClelland, 1979.
22   Ellis, 1985a.
23   e.g., Dell and Reich, 1980; Dell, 1986, 1988; Stemberger, 1985; Ellis, 1985b; Roelofs, 1992, 1993a, b; Knott et al., 1997.
24   Morton, 1979.
25   Laver, 1980.
26   For other accounts of the lexicon in speech production, see Levelt, 1989, 1992; Garman, 1990. For a set of papers, see Levelt, 1993b.

Chapter 19   Organized Guesswork

1   Liberman et al., 1957.
2   Matthei and Roeper, 1983: 43.
3   Liberman et al., 1957.
4   Matthei and Roeper, 1983: 37.
5   R. M. Warren, 1970.
6   Bond and Garnes, 1980; Garnes and Bond, 1980.
7   Ganong, 1980.
8   Reddy, 1976, quoted in Cole, 1980: 137.
9   Browman, 1980.
10   e.g., Klatt, 1981, 1989.
11   e.g., Cole and Jakimik, 1980.
12   e.g., Segui, 1984; Mehler, 1981.
13   Norris and Cutler, 1985; Frauenfelder, 1985; Dupoux, 1993.
14   Cutler and Butterfield, 1992: 218.
15   Cutler, 1989, 1990; Cutler and Butterfield, 1992; Grosjean and Gee, 1987.
16   From Cutler, 1990.
17   Cutler and Butterfield, 1992.

18 Lehiste, 1960, 1972; Frauenfelder, 1985; Church, 1987.
19 Browman, 1980.
20 Bond and Garnes, 1980; Garnes and Bond, 1980. See Bond, 1999, for a full account of 'ear-slips'.
21 Matthei and Roeper, 1983.
22 For a list of sounds which easily get confused, see G. Miller and Nicely, 1955; Wang and Bilger, 1973; Goldstein, 1980.
23 Solomon and Howes, 1951. See also Balota and Chumbley, 1984; Allen et al., 1992.
24 Forster, 1976.
25 Forster, 1976 – though Forster has revised his ideas to some extent; see Forster, 1989.
26 Glanzer and Ehrenreich, 1979.
27 Morton, 1979.
28 Mackay, 1966.
29 Lackner and Garrett, 1972.
30 Foss, 1970.
31 Swinney, 1979.
32 e.g., Seidenberg et al., 1982; Kinoshita, 1986.
33 Tanenhaus et al., 1979.
34 Jastrzembski, 1981.
35 Marslen-Wilson and Tyler, 1980; Marslen-Wilson, 1987, 1990; Tyler, 1989.
36 Marslen-Wilson, 1987, 1990.
37 Tyler, 1984, 1989.
38 Marslen-Wilson and Tyler, 1980, 1981; Marslen-Wilson, 1987, 1989, 1990; Tyler, 1984, 1989.
39 Marslen-Wilson, 1987, 1989b, 1990, 1993.
40 McClelland and Elman, 1986.
41 Elman and McClelland, 1984; McClelland and Elman, 1986; Elman, 1990, and various other papers in Altmann, 1990.
42 Morton, 1979.
43 Norris, 1986; also Norris, 1990.
44 Luce et al., 1990; Shillcock, 1990; Bard and Shillcock, 1993.
45 Grosjean, 1985; Bard et al., 1989.
46 Sparck-Jones, 1984.
47 For further brief accounts of word recognition, see Tyler and Frauenfelder, 1987; Forster, 1989; Garman, 1990. For more extended discussions, see the papers in Frauenfelder and Tyler, 1987; Marslen-Wilson, 1989b; Altmann, 1990.

Chapter 20   Odd Arrangements and Funny Solutions

1 Jacob, 1977.
2 Fritz Mauthner, quoted in Blackburn, 1984: 8.
3 Chapman, 1984.
4 John Ayto, *Observer*, November 1985.
5 Quoted in Bolton, 1984: 34.
6 R. Brown et al., 1955: 389.
7 Köhler, 1947.
8 Holland and Wertheimer, 1964.

9   R. Davis, 1961.
10 Ultan, 1984; Woodworth, 1991; Hinton et al., 1994.
11 Fay and Cutler, 1977.
12 Shattuck-Hufnagel, 1979.
13 Milroy, 1987.
14 Günther, 1989.

Chapter 21   Last Word

1   Simon, 1981: 111.
2   Katz and Fodor, 1963: 183.
3   Bolinger, 1965: 571.
4   A. Hakulinen, quoted in Bauer, 1983: 1.
5   G. A. Miller and Gildea, 1987: 86.
6   Marin, 1982: 64.
7   e.g., Hudson, 1984b.
8   Elman and McClelland, 1984: 337.
9   e.g., Elman and McClelland, 1984; McClelland and Elman, 1986; Marcus, 1984; Klatt, 1980.
10 McClelland and Rumelhart, 1986; Rumelhart and McClelland, 1986; Elman, 1990. For an introduction, see Bechtel and Abrahamsen, 1991.
11 Blakemore, 1977: 85.
12 Garfield, 1978: 1.
13 On modularity in general, see Garfield, 1987, on modularity and the lexicon, see esp. Tanenhaus et al., 1987.
14 Pustejovsky, 1995; Pustejovksy and Boguraev, 1996; Pustejovsky, 1998, 2001.
15 Cotterill, 1998: 481.
16 Ibid.
17 Pustejovsky, 1998.
18 Carey, 1987: 265.
19 Chomsky, 1988: 27.
20 Gould and Marler, 1987; Aitchison, 1989; Markman, 1992.
21 Chomsky, 1988: 32.
22 Ibid.: 28.
23 Jackendoff, 1983, 1990.
24 Landau and Jackendoff, 1993.
25 Bowerman and Levinson, 2001.
26 Bowerman and Choi, 2001.
27 Brown, 2001.
28 Levinson, 2001: 584.
29 Nirmala, 1981.
30 Krishnamurti and Mukherjee, 1984.
31 Laudanna et al., 1992.
32 Pillon et al., 1991.
33 Meara and Ellis, 1982.
34 Berg, 1991a.
35 Mehler, 1981.

36 Grover Stripp and Bellin, 1985.
37 Hankamer, 1989.
38 Lukatela et al., 1980; Feldman and Fowler, 1987.
39 Burani and Laudanna, 1992.
40 Mackay, 1979; Clahsen et al., 2001.
41 Jarvella and Meijers, 1983; Jarvella et al., 1987.
42 Schriefers et al., 1991.
43 See Frauenfelder and Cutler, 1985, for a useful set of papers on cross-linguistic language processing.
44 Jakimik et al., 1985.
45 Black and Byng, 1986.
46 For a useful summary, see Ellis, 1984.
47 For a useful set of papers, see Allport et al., 1987; for a model of the lexicon based on evidence from dyslexia 'reading difficulties', see Fromkin, 1987; for an approach to psycholinguistics which gives equal weighting to spoken and written evidence, see Garman, 1990.
48 For a useful bibliography on vocabulary in a second language, see Meara, 1983; on some differences between bilinguals and monolinguals in their treatment of vocabulary items, see Merriman and Kutlesic, 1993.
49 D. Green, 1986; Kirsner et al., 1984.
50 D. Green, 1986.
51 Milton, *Areopagitica*.
52 Umberto Eco, *The Name of the Rose*, trans. William Weaver. London: Pan, 1984, p. 316.

References

Adams, V. (1973). *An Introduction to Modern English Word-formation*. London: Longman.

Aijmer, K. and Altenberg, B. (eds) (1991). *English Corpus Linguistics*. London: Longman.

Aitchison, J. (1972). Mini-malapropisms. *British Journal of Disorders of Communication*, 7, 38–43.

—— (1981). Mad, bad and dangerous to know. *Literary Review*, July, 81–2.

—— (1983–4). The mental representation of prefixes. *Osmania Papers in Linguistics*, 9–10 (Nirmala Memorial Volume), 61–72.

—— (1985). Cognitive clouds and semantic shadows. *Language and Communication*, 5, 69–93.

—— (1987). Reproductive furniture and extinguished professors. In R. Steele and T. Threadgold (eds), *Language Topics*, vol. 2. Amsterdam: John Benjamins.

—— (1989). *The Articulate Mammal: An Introduction to Psycholinguistics*, 3rd edn. London: Routledge.

—— (1990). Review of Lakoff (1987), in *International Journal of Lexicography*, 3, 147–9.

—— (1992a). Chains, nets or boxes? The linguistic capture of love, anger and fear. In W. G. Busse (ed.), *Anglistentag 1991 Düsseldorf, Proceedings*. Berlin: Mouton de Gruyter.

—— (1992b). Good birds, better birds and amazing birds: the development of proto-types. In H. Béjoint and P. Arnaud (eds), *Vocabulary and Applied Linguistics*. London: Macmillan.

—— (1993). Review of Tsohatzidis (1990), in *International Journal of Lexicography* 6, 215–21.

—— (1994). *Language Joyriding*. Oxford: Clarendon Press.

—— (1996). *The Seeds of Speech: Language Origin and Evolution*. Cambridge: Cambridge University Press.

—— (1997). *The Language Web: The Power and Problem of Words*. Cambridge: Cambridge University Press.

—— (1998). *The Articulate Mammal: An Introduction to Psycholinguistics*, 4th edn. London: Routledge.

—— (1999). *Linguistics*, 5th edn. London: Hodder and Stoughton TY Books. Also published as *Linguistics: An Introduction*, 2nd edn. Hodder and Stoughton.

—— (2000). Shuddering halt or sudden spurt? The linguistic development of (pre-)adoles-cents. In H. W. Kam and A. Pakir (eds), *Recent Developments and Issues in Applied Linguistics: A Collection of SAAL (Singapore Association for Applied Linguistics) Lectures*. Singapore: EPB.

—— (2001). *Language change: Progress or decay?* 3rd edn. Cambridge: Cambridge University Press.

—— (in press). Speech perception and production. In. *Morphology: A Handbook for Inflection and Word Formation*, vol. 2. Berlin: Walter de Gruyter.

Aitchison, J. and Chiat, S. (1981). Natural phonology or natural memory? The interaction between phonological processes and recall mechanisms. *Language and Speech*, 24, 311–26.

Aitchison, J. and Koppel, A. (1990). *The lexicon in 11–14 year olds*. Mimeo.

Aitchison, J. and Lewis, D. M. (1995). How to handle wimps: incorporating new lexical items as an adult. *Folia Linguistica*, 29, 7–20.

—— (1996). The mental word web: forging the links. In Svartvik (1996).

—— (in press). Polysemy and bleaching. In B. Nerlich et al. (eds), *Patterns of Meaning in Mind and Language*. Berlin: Mouton de Gruyter.

Aitchison, J. and Straf, M. (1982). Lexical storage and retrieval: a developing skill. In Cutler (1982a). Originally published in *Linguistics*, 19 (1981), 751–95.

Algeo, J. (1993). Desuetude among new English words. *International Journal of Lexicography*, 6, 282–93.

—— (1998). Vocabulary. In S. Romaine (ed.), *The Cambridge History of the English Language*, vol. 4, 1776–1997. Cambridge: Cambridge University Press.

Allen, P. A., McNeal, M. and Kvak, D. (1992). Perhaps the lexicon is coded as a function of word frequency. *Journal of Memory and Language*, 31, 826–44.

Allport, A. and Funnell, E. (1981). Components of the mental lexicon. *Philosophical Transactions of the Royal Society of London* B, 295, 397–410. (= *Psychological Mechanisms of Language*. London: The Royal Society and the British Academy).

Allport, A., Mackay, D. G., Prinz, W. and Scheerer, E. (eds) (1987). *Language Perception and Production: Relationships between Listening, Speaking, Reading and Writing*. London: Academic Press.

Altmann, G. T. M. (ed.) (1990). *Cognitive Models of Speech Processing: Psycholinguistic and Computational Perspectives*. Cambridge, MA: MIT Press.

Altmann, G. T. M. and Shillcock, R. (eds) (1993). *Cognitive Models of Speech Processing*. Hove: Lawrence Erlbaum.

Anderson, R. C. and Freebody, P. (1981). Reading comprehension and the assessment and acquisition of word knowledge. In J. T. Guthrie (ed.), *Comprehension and Teaching*. Newark, DE: International Reading Association.

Anderson, S. R. (1988a). Inflection. In Hammond and Noonan (1988).

—— (1988b). Morphology as a parsing problem. *Linguistics*, 26, 521–49.

—— (1992). *A-morphous Morphology*. Cambridge: Cambridge University Press.

Anglin, J. M. (1970). *The Growth of Word Meaning*. Cambridge, MA: MIT Press.

Anshen, F. and Aronoff, M. (1988). Producing morphologically complex words. *Linguistics*, 26, 641–56.

Arbib, M. A., Caplan, D. and Marshall, J. C. (eds) (1982). *Neural Models of Language Processes*. New York: Academic Press.

Armstrong, S. L., Gleitman, L. R. and Gleitman, H. (1983). What some concepts might not be. *Cognition*, 13, 263–308.

Aronoff, M. (1976). *Word Formation in Generative Grammar*. Linguistic Inquiry Monograph 1. Cambridge, MA: MIT Press.

—— (1994). *Morphology by Itself*. Cambridge, MA: MIT Press.

Asch, S. E. and Nerlove, H. (1960). The development of double-function terms in children: An exploratory investigation. In B. Kaplan and S. Wapner (eds), *Perspectives in*

Psychological Theory. New York: International Universities Press. Also in De Cecco (1967).

Aston, G. and Burnard, L. (1997). *The BNC Handbook: Exploring the British National Corpus with SARA*. Edinburgh: Edinburgh University Press.

Aveni, A. (1990). *Empires of Time: Calendars, Clocks and Cultures*. London: I.B. Tauris.

Ayto, J. (1980). When is a meaning not a meaning?. *Times Educational Supplement*, 25 April, 45.

—— (1984). The vocabulary of definition. In D. Goetz and T. Herbst (eds), *Theoretische und praktische Probleme der Lexicographie*. Munich: Max Hueber Verlag.

—— (1990a). *Bloomsbury Dictionary of Word Origins*. London: Bloomsbury.

—— (1990b). *The Longman Register of New Words*, vol. 2. London: Longman.

—— (1993). *Euphemisms: Over 3,000 Ways to avoid Being Rude or Giving Offence*. London: Bloomsbury.

—— (1996). Lexical life expectancy – a prognostic guide. In Svartvik (1996).

—— (1999). *20th Century Words*. Oxford: Oxford University Press.

Baars, B.J. (1980). The competing plans hypothesis: an heuristic viewpoint on the causes of errors in speech. In H. W. Dechert and M. Raupach (eds), *Temporal Variables in Speech*. The Hague: Mouton.

Baayen, H. and Lieber, R. (1991). Productivity and English derivation: a corpus-based study. *Linguistics*, 29, 801–45.

Baayen, R. H. and Renouf, A. (1996). Chronicling *The Times*: productive lexical innovations in an English newspaper. *Language*, 72, 69–96.

Baddeley, A. (1983). *Your Memory: A User's Guide*. Harmondsworth: Penguin.

—— (1986). *Working Memory*. Oxford: Oxford University Press.

—— (1990). *Human Memory: Theory and Practice*. Hove: Lawrence Erlbaum.

Baldwin, D. A. (1992). Clarifying the role of the shape assumption. *Journal of Experimental Child Psychology*, 54, 392–416.

Balota, D. A. and Chumbley, J. I. (1984). Are lexical decisions a good measure of lexical access? The role of word-frequency in the neglected decision stage. *Journal of Experimental Psychology: Human Perception and Performance*, 10, 340–57.

Bar-Adon, A. and Leopold, W. F. (eds) (1971). *Child Language: A Book of Readings*. Englewood Cliffs, NJ: Prentice-Hall.

Bard, E. G. and Shillcock, R. (1993). Competitor effects during lexical access: Chasing Zipf's tail. In Altmann and Shillcock (1993).

Bard, E. G., Shillcock, R. C. and Altmann, G. T. M. (1989). The recognition of words after their acoustic affect: effect of subsequent context. *Perception and Psychophysics*, 44, 395–408.

Barker, C. (1988). Episodic -*ee* in English: a thematic constraint on new word formation. *Language*, 74, 695–727.

Barnbrook, G. (1996). *Language and Computers: A Practical Introduction to the Computer Analysis of Language*. Edinburgh: Edinburgh University Press.

Barrett, M. (1983). Scripts, prototypes and the early acquisition of word meaning. *Working Papers of the London Psycholinguistics Research Group*, 5, 17–26.

—— (1986). Early semantic representations and early word usage. In S. A. Kuczaj and M. D. Barrett (eds), *The Development of Word Meaning*. New York: Springer.

—— (1995). Early lexical development. In Fletcher and MacWhinney (1995).

Barsalou, L. W. (1983). Ad hoc categories. *Memory and Cognition*, 11, 211–27.

—— (1985). Ideals, central tendency, and frequency of instantiation as determinants of graded structure in categories. *Journal of Experimental Psychology: Learning, Memory and Cognition*, 11, 629–54.

—— (1992). Frames, concepts and conceptual fields. In Lehrer and Kittay (1992).

Barton, M. (1971). Recall of generic properties of words in aphasic patients. *Cortex*, 7, 73–82.

Bates, E., Benigni, R., Bretherton, L., Camioni, R. and Volterra, V. (1979). *The Emergence of Symbols: Communication and Cognition in Infancy*. New York: Academic Press.

Bauer, L. (1983). *English Word-formation*. Cambridge: Cambridge University Press.

—— (1994). *Watching English Change*. London: Longman.

Bechtel, W. and Abrahamsen, A. (1991). *Connectionism and the Mind: An Introduction to Parallel Processing in Networks*. Oxford: Basil Blackwell.

Béjoint, H. (2000). *Modern Lexicography: An Introduction*. Oxford: Oxford University Press.

Benson, D. F. (1979). Neurologic correlates of anomia. In H. Whitaker and H. A. Whitaker (eds), *Studies in Neurolinguistics*, 4. New York: Academic Press.

Berg, T. (1991a). Phonological processing in a syllable-timed language with pre-final stress: Evidence from Spanish speech error data. *Language and Cognitive Processes*, 6, 265–301.

—— (1991b). Redundant feature coding in the mental lexicon. *Linguistics*, 29, 903–25.

Bergman, M. W., Hudson, P. T. W. and Eling, P. A. T. M. (1988). How simple complex words can be: morphological processing and word representations. *Quarterly Journal of Experimental Psychology*, 40A, 41–72.

Berko, J. (1958). The child's learning of English morphology. *Word*, 14, 150–77.

Berko, J. and Brown, R. (1960). Psycholinguistic research methods. In P. H. Mussen (ed.), *Handboook of Research Methods in Child Development*. New York: John Wiley.

Berko Gleason, J. (ed.) (1993). *The Development of Language*, 3rd edn. New York: Macmillan.

Berlin, B. and Kay, P. (1969). *Basic Color Terms: Their Universality and Evolution*. Berkeley and Los Angeles: University of California Press.

Bever, T. G., Carroll, J. M. and Miller, L. A. (eds) (1984). *Talking Minds*. Cambridge, MA: MIT Press.

Biber, D., Conrad, S. and Reppen, R. (1998). *Corpus Linguistics: Investigating Language Structure and use*. Cambridge: Cambridge University Press.

Bickerton, K. (1981). Jargon aphasia: a headache in aphasiology. *Working Papers of the London Psycholinguistics Research Group*, 3, 13–24.

Bierwisch, M. (1967). Some semantic universals of German adjectivals. *Foundations of Language*, 3, 1–36.

—— (1970). Semantics. In J. Lyons (ed.), *New Horizons in Linguistics*. Harmondsworth: Penguin Books.

Bird, H., Howard, D. and Franklin, S. (2000). Why is a verb like an inanimate object? Grammatical category and semantic deficits. *Brain and Language*, 72, 246–309.

Black, M. and Byng, S. (1986). Prosodic constraints on access in reading. *Cognitive Neuropsychology*, 3, 369–409.

Black, M. and Chiat, S. (in press). Noun–verb dissociations: a multi-faceted phenomenon. *Journal of Neurolinguistics*.

Blackburn, S. (1984). *Spreading the Word: Groundings in the Philosophy of Language*. Oxford: Clarendon Press.

Blakemore, C. (1977). *Mechanics of the Mind*. Cambridge: Cambridge University Press.

Blasdell, R. and Jensen, P. (1970). Stress and word position as determinants of imitation in first language learners. *Journal of Speech and Hearing Research*, 12, 193–202.

Blevins, J. (1995). The syllable in phonological theory. In Goldsmith (1995).

Bloom, P. (2000). *How Children Learn the Meanings of Words*. Cambridge, MA: MIT Press.

Bloomfield, L. (1933). *Language*. New York: Holt, Rinehart, Winston.

Blumstein, S. E. (1995). The neurobiology of language. In J. L. Miller and P. D. Eimas (eds), *Speech, Language and Communication*. San Diego: Academic Press.

Bolinger, D. (1965). The atomization of meaning. *Language*, 41, 555–73.

—— (1992). About furniture and birds. *Cognitive Linguistics*, 3, 111–17.

Bolton, W. F. (1984). *The Language of 1984*. Oxford: Basil Blackwell.

Bond, Z. S. (1999). *Slips of the Ear: Errors in the Perception of Casual Conversation*. London: Academic Press.

Bond, Z. S. and Garnes, S. (1980). Misperceptions of fluent speech. In Cole (1980).

Boomer, D. S. and Laver, J. D. M. (1968). Slips of the tongue. *British Journal of Disorders of Communication*, 3, 1–12. Also in Fromkin (1973).

Bouma, H. and Bouwhuis, D. G. (eds) (1984). *Attention and Performance X: Control of Language Processes*. Hillsdale, NJ: Lawrence Erlbaum.

Bowerman, M. (1978). Systematizing semantic knowledge: changes over time in the child's organization of meaning. *Child Development*, 49, 977–87.

Bowerman, M. (1980). The structure and origin of semantic categories in the language learning child. In D. Foster and S. Brandes (eds), *Symbol as Sense: New Approaches to the Analysis of Meaning*. New York: Academic Press.

—— (1982). Reorganizational processes in lexical and syntactic development. In Wanner and Gleitman (1982).

Bowerman, M. and Choi, S. (2001). Shaping meanings for language: universal and language-specific in the acquisition of spatial semantic categories. In Bowerman and Levinson (2001).

Bowerman, M. and Levinson, S. C. (eds) (2001). *Language Acquisition and Conceptual Development*. Cambridge: Cambridge University Press.

Bradley, D. C. (1983). *Computational Distinctions of Vocabulary Type*. Bloomington, IN: Indiana University Linguistics Club.

Bradley, D. C., Garrett, M. F. and Zurif, E. B. (1980). Syntactic deficits in Broca's aphasia. In Caplan (1980).

Braine, M. D. S. (1974). On what might constitute learnable phonology. *Language*, 50, 270–99.

—— (1990). Can children use a verb without exposure to its argument structure? *Journal of Child Language*, 17, 313–42.

Bresler, F. (1983). *The Mystery of Georges Simenon*. London: Heinemann.

Browman, C. P. (1978). *Tip of the Tongue and Slip of the Ear: Implications for Language Processing*. UCLA Working Papers in Phonetics 42.

—— (1980). Perceptual processing: Evidence from slips of the ear. In Fromkin (1980).

Brown, A. S. (1991). A review of the tip-of-the-tongue experience. *Psychological Bulletin*, 109, 204–23.

Brown, G. and Yule, G. (1983). *Discourse Analysis*. Cambridge: Cambridge University Press.

Brown, P. (2001). Learning to talk about motion UP and DOWN in Tzeltal: is there a language specific bias for verb learning? In Bowerman and Levinson (2001).

Brown, R. (1958). *Words and Things*. New York: Free Press.

Brown, R. (ed.) (1970). *Psycholinguistics: Selected Papers*. New York: Free Press.

Brown, R. and Berko, J. (1960). Word association and the acquisition of grammar. *Child Development*, 31, 1–14. Also in De Cecco (1967).

Brown, R. and McNeill, D. (1966). The 'tip of the tongue' phenomenon. *Journal of Verbal Learning and Verbal Behaviour*, 5, 325–37. Also in Brown (1970).

Brown, R., Black, A. H. and Horowitz, A. E. (1955). Phonetic symbolism in natural languages. *Journal of Abnormal social Psychology*, 50, 388–93. Also in Brown (1970).

Brownell, H. H., Potter, H. H. and Michelow, D. (1984). Sensitivity to lexical denotation and connotation: a double dissociation? *Brain and Language*, 22, 253–65.

Bulmer, R. (1967). Why is the cassowary not a bird? *Man*, NS 2, 5–25. Also in M. Douglas (ed.), *Rules and Meanings*. Harmondsworth: Penguin, 1973.

Burani, C. and Laudanna, A. (1992). Units of representation for derived words in the lexicon. In R. Frost and L. Katz (eds), *Orthography, Phonology, Morphology and Meaning*. Elsevier Science.

Burchfield, R. (1985). *The English Language*. Oxford: Oxford University Press.

Burke, D. M., Mackay, D. G., Worthley, J. S. and Wade, E. (1991). On the tip of the tongue: What causes word finding failures in young and older adults? *Journal of Memory and Learning*, 30, 542–79.

Butterworth, B. (1979). Hesitation and the production of neologisms in jargon aphasia. *Brain and Language*, 8, 133–61.

—— (1980a). Evidence from pauses in speech. In Butterworth (1980b).

—— (ed.) (1980b). *Language Production*, vol. 1. New York: Academic Press.

—— (ed.) (1983a). *Language Production*, vol. 2. New York: Academic Press.

—— (1983b). 'Lexical representation'. In Butterworth (1983a).

—— (1989). Lexical access in speech production. In Marslen-Wilson (1989).

—— (1993). Disorders of phonological encoding. In Levelt (1993). Originally published in *Cognition*, 42 (1992), 261–86.

Butterworth, B., Howard, D. and Mcloughlin, P. (1984). The semantic deficit in aphasia: the relationship between semantic errors in auditory comprehension and picture naming. *Neuropsychologia*, 22, 409–26.

Bybee, J. L. (2002). *Phonology and Language Use*. Cambridge: Cambridge University Press.

Caplan, D. (1980). *Biological Studies of Mental Processes*. Cambridge, MA: MIT Press.

—— (1987). *Neurolinguistics and Linguistic Aphasiology*. Cambridge: Cambridge University Press.

—— (1992). *Language: Structure, Processing and Disorders*. Cambridge, MA: MIT Press.

Caramazza, A. (1997). How many levels of processing are there in lexical access? *Cognitive Neuropsychology*, 14, 177–208.

Carey, S. (1978). The child as word learner. In M. Halle, J. Bresnan, and G. A. Miller (eds), *Linguistic Theory and Psychological Reality*. Cambridge, MA: MIT Press.

Carlson, G. and Tanenhaus, M. (1988). Thematic roles and language comprehension. In Wilkins (1988).

Carroll, L. (1967). *The Annotated Snark*, ed. M. Gardner. Harmondsworth: Penguin.

—— (1988). *The Complete Works of Lewis Carroll*. Harmondsworth: Penguin.

Carstairs-McCarthy (1992). *Current Morphology*. London: Routledge.

Carter, R. (1998). *Vocabulary: Applied Linguistic Perspectives*, 2nd edn. London: Routledge.

Chaffin, R. (1992). The concept of a lexical relation. In Lehrer and Kittay (1992).

Chaika, E. O. (1974). A linguist looks at 'schizophrenic' language. *Brain and Language*, 1, 257–76.

Chand, N. (n.d.). *Improve your Vocabulary*. New Delhi: New Light Publications.

Chapman, R. (1984). *The Treatment of Sounds in Language and Literature*. Oxford: Basil Blackwell.

Charles, W. G. and Miller, G. A. (1989). Contexts of antonymous adjectives. *Applied Psycholinguistics*, 10, 357–75.

Cheshire, J. (1982). *Variation in an English Dialect: A Sociolinguistic Study*. Cambridge: Cambridge University Press.

Chialant, D. and Caramazza, A. (1995). Where is morphology and how is it processed? The case of written word recognition. In L. B. Feldman (ed.), *Morphological Aspects of Language Processing*. Hove: Lawrence Erlbaum.

Chiat, S. (1979). The role of the word in phonological development. *Linguistics*, 17, 591–610.

—— (1983). Why Mikey's right and my key's wrong: the significance of stress and word boundaries in learning to output language. *Cognition*, 14, 275–300.

—— (2000). *Understanding Children with Language Problems*. Cambridge: Cambridge University Press.

Chomsky, N. (1965). *Aspects of the Theory of Syntax*. Cambridge, MA: MIT Press.

—— (1970). Remarks on nominalization. In R. A. Jacobs and P. Rosenbaum (eds), *Readings in English Transformational Grammar*. Waltham, MA: Ginn.

—— (1978). On the biological basis of language capacities. In G. A. Miller and E. Lenneberg (eds), *Psychology and Biology of Language and Thought*. New York: Academic Press. Also in Chomsky (1980).

—— (1980). *Rules and Representations*. Oxford: Basil Blackwell.

—— (1988). *Language and Problems of Knowledge: The Managua Lectures*. Cambridge, MA: MIT Press.

Chomsky, N. and Halle, M. (1968). *The Sound Pattern of English*. New York: Harper and Row.

Church, K. W. (1987). Phonological parsing and lexical retrieval. In Frauenfelder and Tyler (1987).

Clahsen, H., Eisenbeiss, S., Hadler, M. and Sonnenstuhl, I. (2001). The mental representation of inflected words: an experimental study of adjectives and verbs in German. *Language*, 77, 510–43.

Clark, E. V. (1973). What's in a word? On the child's acquisition of semantics in his first language. In T. E. Moore (ed.) *Cognitive Development and the Acquisition of Language*. New York: Academic Press.

—— (1981). Lexical innovation: how young children learn to create new words. In W. Deutsch (ed.), *The Child's Construction of Language*. London: Academic Press.

—— (1982). The young word maker: A case study of innovation in the child's lexicon. In Wanner and Gleitman (1982).

—— (1987). The principle of contrast: a constraint on language acquisition. In B. MacWhinney (ed.), *Mechanisms of Language Acquisition*. Hillsdale, NJ: Lawrence Erlbaum.

—— (1993). *The Lexicon in Acquisition*. Cambridge: Cambridge University Press.

Clark, E. V. and Berman, R. A. (1984). Structure and use in the acquisition of word formation. *Language*, 60, 542–94.

Clark, E. V. and Clark, H. (1979). When nouns surface as verbs. *Language*, 55, 767–811.

Clark, E. V. and Hecht, B. F. (1982). Learning to coin agent and instrument nouns. *Cognition*, 12, 1–24.

Clark, E. V., Hecht, B. F. and Mulford, R. C. (1986). Coining complex compounds in English: affixes and word order acquisition. *Linguistics*, 24, 7–30.

Clark, H. H. and Gerrig, R. J. (1983). Understanding old words with new meanings. *Journal of Verbal Learning and Verbal Behavior*, 22, 591–608.

Clark, R. (1974). Performing without competence. *Journal of Child Language*, 1, 1–10.

Clausner, T. C. and Croft, W. (1999). Domains and image schemas. *Cognitive Linguistics*, 10, 1–31.

Cohen, J. M. and Cohen, M. J. (1980). *Dictionary of Modern Quotations*, 2nd edn. Harmondsworth: Penguin.

Cohen, L., Verstichel, P. and Dehaene, S. (1997). Neologistic jargon sparing numbers: a category-specific phonological impairment. *Cognitive Neuropsychology*, 14, 1029–61.

Cole, R. A. (ed.) (1980). *Perception and Production of Fluent Speech*. Hillsdale, NJ: Lawrence Erlbaum.

Cole, R. A. and Jakimik, J. (1980). A model of speech perception. In Cole (1980).

Coleman, E. B. (1964). Supplementary report: on the combination of associative probabilities in linguistic contexts. *Journal of Psychology*, 57, 95–9.

Coleman, L. and Kay, P. (1981). Prototype semantics: the English word *lie*. *Language*, 57, 26–44.

Collingwood, R. G. (1938). *The Principles of Art*. Oxford: Oxford University Press.

Collins, A. M. and Quillian, M. R. (1969). Retrieval time from semantic memory. *Journal of Verbal Learning and Verbal Behavior*, 8, 240–47.

Conan Doyle, A. (1981). *The Complete Sherlock Holmes*. Harmondsworth: Penguin.

Cooper, W. and Walker, E. C. T. (eds) (1979). *Sentence Processsing*. Hillsdale, NJ: Lawrence Erlbaum.

Cotterill, R. (1998). *Enchanted Looms: Conscious Networks in Brains and Computers*. Cambridge: Cambridge University Press.

Cowie, A. P. (1998). *Phraseology: Theory, Analysis and Applications*. Oxford: Clarendon Press.

Crick, F. H. C. (1979). Thinking about the brain. *Scientific American*, 241, 219–30.

Critchley, M. (1973). Articulatory defects in aphasia: the problem of Broca's aphasia. In Goodglass and Blumstein (1973).

Cruse, D. A. (1986). *Lexical Semantics*. Cambridge: Cambridge: University Press.

—— (1990). Prototype theory and lexical semantics. In Tsohatzidis (1990).

—— (1992). Antonymy revisited: Some thoughts on the relationship between words and concepts. In Lehrer and Kittay (1992).

Curtis, M. E. (1987). Vocabulary testing and vocabulary instruction. In McKeown and Curtis (1987).

Cutler, A. (1980). Productivity in word formation. *Papers from the Sixteenth Regional Meeting, Chicago Linguistic Society*, 45–51.

—— (1981). Degrees of transparency in word formation. *Canadian Journal of Linguistics*, 26, 73–7.

—— (1982a). *Slips of the Tongue and Language Production*. Berlin: Mouton. Originally published as *Linguistics*, 19 (1981).

—— (1982b). The reliability of speech error data. In Cutler (1982a). Originally published in *Linguistics*, 19 (1981).

—— (1983). Lexical complexity and sentence processing. In Flores d'Arcais and Jarvella (1983).

—— (1989). Auditory lexical access: where do we start? In Marslen-Wilson (1989).

—— (1990). Exploiting prosodic probabilities in speech segmentation. In Altmann (1990).

—— (1992). Psychology and the segment. In Docherty and Ladd (1992).

—— (1993). Language-specific processing: does the evidence converge? In Altmann and Shillcock (1993).

Cutler, A. and Butterfield, S. (1992). Rhythmic cues to speech segmentation: Evidence from juncture misperception. *Journal of Memory and Language*, 31, 218–36.

Cutler, A. and Isard, S. (1980). The production of prosody. In Butterworth (1980b).

Cutler, A. and Norris, D. (1979). Monitoring sentence comprehension. In Cooper and Walker (1979).

Cutler, A., Hawkins, J. A. and Gilligan, G. (1985). The suffixing preference: a processing explanation. *Linguistics*, 23, 723–58.

Dahrendorf, R. (1982). *On Britain*. London: BBC.

Damasio, A. R. (1990). Category related recognition deficits as a clue to the neural substrates of knowledge. *Trends in Neuroscience*, 13, 95–8.

Davis, R. (1961). The fitness of names to drawings. a cross-cultural study in Tanganyika. *British Journal of Psychology*, 52, 259–68.

Davis, S. (1989). On a non-argument for the Rhyme. *Journal of Linguistics*, 25, 211–17.

De Cecco, J. P. (ed.) (1967). *The Psychology of Thought, Language and Instruction*. New York: Holt, Rinehart and Winston.

Deese, J. (1965). *The Structure of Associations in Language and Thought*. Baltimore, MD: John Hopkins Press.

Deignan, A. (1997). Metaphors of desire. In K. Harvey and C. Shalom (eds), *Language and Desire*. London: Routledge.

Dell, G. S. (1986). A spreading-activation theory of retrieval in sentence production. *Psychological Review*, 93, 283–321.

—— (1988). The retrieval of phonological forms in production: Tests of predictions from a connectionsit model. *Journal of Memory and Language*, 27, 124–42.

Dell, G. S. and O'Seaghdha, P. G. (1993). Stages of lexical access in language production. In Levelt (1993). Originally published in *Cognition*, 42, 287–314.

Dell, G. S. and Reich, P. A. (1980). Toward a unified model of slips of the tongue. In Fromkin (1980).

Derwing, B. L. and Baker, W. J. (1986). Assessing morphological development. In Fletcher and Garman (1986).

Diack, H. (1975). *Standard Literacy Tests*. St Albans: Hart-Davis.

Dixon, R. M. W. (1989). Subject and object in universal grammar. In D. Arnold et al., *Essays on Grammatical Theory and Universal Grammar*. Oxford: Clarendon Press.

Docherty, G. J. and Ladd, D. R. (eds) (1992). *Papers in Laboratory Phonology: Gesture, Segment, Prosody*. Cambridge: Cambridge University Press.

Downing, P. (1977). On the creation and use of English compound nouns. *Language*, 53, 810–42.

Dowty, D. (1991). Thematic proto-roles and argument selection. *Language*, 67, 547–619.

Draaisma, D. (2000). *Metaphors of Memory: A History of Ideas about the Mind*, trans. P. Vincent. Cambridge: Cambridge University Press.

Drachman, G. (1973). Some strategies in the acquisition of phonology. In M. J. Kenstowicz and C. W. Kisseberth (eds), *Issues in Phonological Theory*. The Hague: Mouton.

Dressler, W. (1985). *Morphophonology: The Dynamics of Derivation*. Ann Arbor, MI: Karoma.

Dupoux, E. (1993). The time course of prelexical processing: the syllabic hypothesis. In Altmann and Shillcock (1993).

Dupré, J. (1981). Natural kinds and biological taxa. *Philological Review*, 40, 66–90.

Dupreez, P. (1974). Units of information in the acquisition of language. *Language and Speech*, 17, 369–76.

Echols, C. H. (1993). A perceptually-based model of children's earliest productions. *Cognition*, 46, 245–96.

Echols, C. H. and Newport, E. L. (1992). The role of stress and position in determining first words. *Language Acquisition*, 2, 189–220.

Eimas, P. (1985). The perception of speech in early infancy. *Scientific American*, 252, 34–40.

Eimas, P., Siqueland, E., Jusczyk, P. and Vigorito, J. (1971). Speech perception in infants. *Science*, 171, 303–6.

Ellis, A. W. (1980). On the Freudian theory of speech errors. In Fromkin (1980).

—— (ed.) (1985a) *Progress in the Psychology of Language*, 2 vols. London: Lawrence Erlbaum.

—— (1985b). The production of spoken words: a cognitive neuropsychological perspective. In Ellis (1985a), vol. 2.

—— (1993). *Reading, Writing and Dyslexia: A Cognitive Analysis*, 2nd edn. Hove: Lawrence Erlbaum.

Elman, J. L. (1990). Representation and structure in connectionist models. In Altmann (1990).

Elman, J. and McClelland, J. L. (1984). Speech perception as a cognitive process: the interactive activation model. In N. Lass (ed.), *Speech and Language: Advances in Basic Research and Practice*, vol. 10. New York: Academic Press.

Entwisle, D. R. (1966). *Word-associations of Young Children*. Baltimore, MD: John Hopkins Press.

Ewen, C. J. and van der Hulst, H. (2001). *The Phonological Structure of Words: An Introduction*. Cambridge: Cambridge University Press.

Farrar, F. W. (1865). *Chapters on Language*. London: Longmans Green.

Fay, D. (1977). Prefix errors. Paper presented at the 4th Salzburg International Linguistics Meeting, Aug. 1977.

Fay, D. and Cutler, A. (1977). Malapropisms and the structure of the mental lexicon. *Linguistic Inquiry*, 8, 505–20.

Feldman, L. B. (ed.) (1995). *Morphological Aspects of Language Processing*. Hove: Lawrence Erlbaum.

Feldman, L. B. and Fowler, C. A. (1987). The inflected noun system in Serbo-Croatian: lexical representation of morphological structure. *Memory and Cognition*, 15, 1–12.

Fellbaum, C. (1990). English verbs as a semantic net. *International Journal of Lexicography*, 3, 278–301.

—— (1992). Co-occurrence and antonymy. *CSL Report*, 52. Cognitive Science Laboratory, Princeton University.

Fellbaum, C. (ed.) (1998). *WordNet: An Electronic Lexical Database*. Cambridge, MA: Bradford Books (MIT Press).

Fenk-Oczlon, G. (1989). Word frequency and word order in freezes. *Linguistics*, 27, 517–56.

Ferber, R. (1991). Slip of the tongue or slip of the ear? On the perception and transcription of naturalistic slips of the tongue. *Journal of Psycholinguistic Research*, 20, 105–22.

—— (1995). Reliability and validity of slip-of-the-tongue corpora: a methodological note. *Linguistics*, 33, 1169–90.

Ferguson, C. A. and Farwell, C. B. (1975). Words and sounds in early language acquisition. *Language*, 51, 439–91.

Fillmore, C. J. (1968). The case for case. In E. Bach and R. Harms (eds), *Universals in Linguistic Theory*. New York: Holt, Rinehart and Winston.

—— (1971). Types of lexical information. In Steinberg and Jakobovits (1971).

—— (1975). An alternative to check-list views of meaning. *Proceedings of the 1st Annual Meeting, Berkeley Linguistics Society*, 123–31.

—— (1982). Frame semantics. In Linguistic Society of Korea, *Linguistics in the Morning Calm*. Seoul: Hanshin.

Fillmore, C. J. and Atkins, B. T. (1992). Towards a frame-based lexicon: The semantics of RISK and its neighbours. In Lehrer and Kittay (1992).

—— (1994). Starting where dictionaries stop: The challenge of corpus lexicography. In B. T. Atkins and A. Zampolli (eds), *Computational Approaches to the Lexicon*. Oxford: Oxford University Press.

Fillmore, C. J., Kay, P. and O'Connor, M. C. (1988). Regularity and idiomaticity in grammatical constructions: the case of *let alone*. *Language*, 64, 501–38.

Fletcher, P. and Garman, M. (eds) (1986). *Language acquisition*, 2nd edn. Cambridge: Cambridge University Press.

Fletcher, P. and MacWhinney, B. (eds) (1995). *The Handbook of Child Language*. Oxford: Blackwell.

Flores d'Arcais, G. B. and Jarvella, R. J. (eds) (1983). *The Process of Language Understanding*. New York: Wiley.

Fodor, J. A. (1981). *Representations: Philosophical Essays on the Foundations of Cognitive Science*. Cambridge, MA: MIT Press.

—— (1983). *The Modularity of Mind*. Cambridge, MA: MIT Press.

—— (1987). *Psychosemantics: The Problem of Meaning in the Philosophy of Mind*. Cambridge, MA: MIT Press.

Fodor, J. D., Fodor, J. A. and Garrett, M. F. (1975). The psychological unreality of semantic representations. *Linguistic Inquiry*, 6, 515–31.

Fodor, J. A., Garrett, M. F., Walker, E. C. T. and Parkes, C. H. (1980). Against definitions. *Cognition*, 8, 263–367.

Forster, K. (1976). Accessing the mental lexicon. In Wales and Walker (1976).

Forster, K. I. (1989). Basic issues in lexical processing. In Marslen-Wilson (1989b).

Foss, D. (1970). Some effects of ambiguity upon sentence comprehension. *Journal of Verbal Learning and Verbal Behavior*, 9, 699–706.

Fourcin, A. J. (1978). Acoustic patterns and speech acquisition. In N. Waterson and C. Snow (eds), *The Development of Communication*. Chichester: Wiley.

Fowler, C. A., Napps, S. E. and Feldman, L. (1985). Relations among regular and irregular morphologically related words in the lexicon as revealed by repetition priming. *Memory and Cognition*, 13, 241–55.

Frauenfelder, U. H. (1983). Cross-linguistic approaches to lexical segmentation. *Linguistics*, 23, 669–88.

Frauenfelder, U. H. and Cutler, A. (1985). *Cross-language Psycholinguistics: Sublexical and Lexical Processing. Linguistics*, 23 (special issue).

Frauenfelder, U. H. and Tyler, L. K. (eds) (1987). *Spoken Word Recognition*. Cambridge, MA: MIT Press. Originally *Cognition*, 25 (1987).

Freud, S. (1891/1953). *On Aphasia*, trans. E. Stengel. New York: International University Press.

—— (1975). *The psychopathology of everyday life*, trans. A. Tyson. Harmondsworth: Penguin.

Friederici, A. (1982). Syntactic and semantic processes in aphasic deficits: the availability of prepositions. *Brain and Language*, 15, 249–58.

—— (1985). Levels of processing and vocabulary types: evidence from on-line comprehension in normals and agrammatics. *Cognition*, 19, 133–66.

Fromkin, V. (1987). The lexicon: evidence from acquired dyslexia. *Language*, 63, 1–22.

Fromkin, V. A. (1971). The non-anomalous nature of anomalous utterances. *Language*, 47, 27–52. Also in Fromkin (1973).

—— (ed.) (1973). *Speech Errors as Linguistic Evidence*. The Hague: Mouton.

—— (1980). *Errors in Linguistic Performance: Slips of the Tongue, Ear, Pen, and Hand*. New York: Academic Press.

Funnell, E. (1995a). A case of forgotten knowledge. In. *Broken memories*. Oxford: Blackwell.
—— (1995b). Objects and properties: a study of the breakdown of semantic memory. *Memory and Cognition*, 3, 497–518.

Galton, F. (1883). *Inquiries into Human Faculty and its Development*. London: Dent.

Ganong, W. F. (1980). Phonetic categorization in auditory word perception. *Journal of Experimental Psychology: Human Perception and Performance*, 6, 110–25.

Gardner, H. (1974). *The Shattered Mind*. New York: Random House.

Garfield, J. L. (ed.) (1987). *Modularity in knowledge representation and natural-language understanding*. Cambridge, MA: MIT Press.

Garman, M. (1990). *Psycholinguistics*. Cambridge: Cambridge University Press.

Garnes, S. and Bond, Z. (1980). A slip of the ear: a snip of the ear? A slip of the year? In Fromkin (1980).

Garrett, M. F. (1976). Syntactic processes in sentence production. In Wales and Walker (1976).
—— (1980). Levels of processing in sentence production. In Butterworth (1980).
—— (1992a). Lexical retrieval processes: semantic field effects. In Leherer and Kittay (1992).
—— (1992b). Disorders of lexical selection. *Cognition* 42, 143–80. Also in Levelt (1993).

Gathercole, S. E. and Baddeley, A. D. (1989). Development of vocabulary in children and short-term phonological memory. *Journal of Memory and Language*, 28, 200–13.
—— (1993). *Working Memory and Language*. Hove: Lawrence Erlbaum.

Geeraerts, D. (1989). Prospects and problems of prototype theory. *Linguistics*, 27, 587–612.
—— (1992). Polysemy and prototypicality. *Cognitive Linguistics*, 3, 219–31.
—— (1993). Vaguenesses puzzles, polysemy's vagaries. *Cognitive Linguistics*, 4, 223–72.

Gibbs, R. W. (1994). *The Poetics of Mind: Figurative Thought, Language and Understanding*. Cambridge: Cambridge University Press.

Gibbs, R. W. and Gonzales, G. P. (1985). Syntactic frozenness in processing and remembering idioms. *Cognition*, 20, 243–59.

Gibbs, R. W. and O'Brien, J. E. (1990). Idiom and mental imagery: the metaphorical motivation for idiomatic meaning. *Cognition*, 36, 35–68.

Gibbs, R. W., Nayak, N. P. and Cutting, C. (1989). How to kick the bucket and not decompose: analyzability and idiom processing. *Journal of Memory and Language*, 28, 576–93.

Giegerich, H. J. (1992). *English Phonology: An Introduction*. Cambridge: Cambridge University Press.
—— (1999). *Lexical Strata in English: Morphological Causes, Phonological Effects*. Cambridge: Cambridge University Press.

Glanzer, M. and Ehrenreich, S. L. (1979). Structure and search of the internal lexicon. *Journal of Verbal Learning and Verbal Behavior*, 18, 381–98.

Gleitman, H. and Gleitman, L. (1979). Language use and language judgement. In C. J. Fillmore, D. Kempler and W. S.-Y. Wang (eds), *Individual Differences in Language Ability and Language Behavior*. New York: Academic Press.

Gleitman, L. R. and Gleitman, H. (1970). *Phrase and Paraphrase: Some Innovative Uses of Language*. New York: Norton.

Gleitman, L. R., Gleitman, H., Landau, B. and Wanner, E. (1988). Where learning begins: initial representations for language learning. In F. Newmeyer (ed.), *Linguistics: The Cambridge Survey*, vol. 3. Cambridge: Cambridge University Press.

Goatly, A. (1997). *The Language of Metaphors*. London: Routledge.

Goldfield, B. A. (1993). Noun bias in maternal speech to one-year-olds. *Journal of Child Language*, 20, 85–99.

Goldfield, B. A. and Reznick, J. S. (1990). Early lexical acquisition: rate, content and the vocabulary spurt. *Journal of Child Language*, 17, 171–83.

Goldfield, B. A. and Snow, C. E. (1992). 'What's your cousin Arthur's mommy's name?' Features of family talk about kin and kin terms. *First Language*, 12, 187–205.

Goldsmith, J. A. (ed.) (1995). *The Handbook of Phonological Theory*. Oxford: Blackwell.

Goldstein, L. (1980). Bias and asymmetry in speech perception. In Fromkin (1980).

Goodglass, H. (ed.) (1978). *Selected Papers in Neurolinguistics*. Munich: Wilhelm Fink Verlag.

Goodglass, H. and Baker, E. (1976). Semantic field, naming and auditory comprehension in aphasia. *Brain and Language*, 3, 359–74. Also in Goodglass (1978).

Goodglass, H. and Blumstein, S. (1973). *Psycholinguistics and Aphasia*. Baltimore, MD: Johns Hopkins University Press.

Goodglass, H. and Menn, L. (1985). Is agrammatism a unitary phenomenon?. In M.-L. Kean (ed.), *Agrammatism*. Orlando, FL: Academic Press.

Goodglass, H., Barton, M. I. and Kaplan, E. F. (1968). Sensory modality and object naming in aphasia. *Journal of Speech and Hearing Research*, 11, 488–96. Also in Goodglass (1978).

Goodglass, H., Kaplan, E., Weintraub, S. and Ackerman, N. (1976). The 'tip-of-the-tongue' phenomenon in aphasia. *Cortex*, 12, 145–53.

Goodglass, H., Klein, B., Carey, P. and James, K. J. (1966). Specific semantic word categories in aphasia. *Cortex*, 2, 74–89.

Goodglass, H., Theurkauf, J. C. and Wingfield, A. (1984). Naming latencies as evidence for two modes of lexical retrieval. *Applied Psycholinguistics*, 5, 135–46.

Gopnik, A. and Meltzoff, A. (1987). The development of categorization in the second year and its relation to other cognitive and linguistic developments. *Child Development*, 58, 1523–31.

Gordon, B. (1983). Lexical access and lexical decision: mechanisms of frequency sensitivity. *Journal of Verbal Learning and Verbal Behaviour*, 22, 22–44.

Gordon, B. and Caramazza, A. (1982). Lexical decision for open and closed class items: Failure to replicate differential frequency sensitivity. *Brain and Language*, 15, 143–80.

—— (1985). Lexical access and frequency sensitivity: frequency saturation and open/closed class equivalence. *Cognition*, 21, 95–115.

Gould, S. J. (1983). *The Panda's Thumb*. Harmondsworth: Penguin.

—— (1984). *Hen's Teeth and Horse's Toes*. Harmondsworth: Penguin.

Gould, S. J. and Marler, P. (1987). Learning by instinct. *Scientific American*, 256, 62–73.

Gowers, E. (1973). *The Complete Plain Words*. London: Her Majesty's Stationary Office.

Green, D. (1986). Control, activation and resource: a framework and a model for the control of speech in bilinguals. *Brain and Language*, 27, 210–23.

Green, J. (1982). *A Dictionary of Contemporary Quotations*. London: Pan Books.

—— (1996). *Chasing the Sun: Dictionary Makers and the Dictionaries they Made*. London: Jonathan Cape.

Greenberg, J. H. and Jenkins, J. J. (1964). Studies in the psychological correlates of the sound system of American English. *Word*, 20, 157–77.

Gregg, V. H. (1986). *Introduction to Human Memory*. London: Routledge and Kegan Paul.

Grice, H. P. (1975). Logic and conversation. In P. Cole and J. Morgan (eds), *Syntax and Semantics 3: Speech Acts*. New York: Academic Press.

Griffiths, P. (1986). Early vocabulary. In Fletcher and Garman (1986).

Grimshaw, J. (1990). *Argument Structure*. Cambridge, MA: MIT Press.

Grodzinsky, Y. (1990). *Theoretical Perspectives on Language Deficits*. Cambridge, MA: MIT Press.

Gropen, J., Pinker, S., Hollander, M. and Goldberg, R. (1991). Affectedness and direct objects. *Cognition*, 41, 153–96. Also in Levin and Pinker (1992).

Grosjean, F. (1980). Spoken word recognition processes and the gating paradigm. *Perception and Psychophysics*, 28, 267–83.

—— (1985). The recognition of words after their acoustic offset: evidence and implications. *Perception and Psychophysics*, 38, 299–310.

Grosjean, F. and Gee, J. P. (1987). Prosodic structure and spoken word recognition. *Cognition*, 25, 135–56. Also in Frauenfelder and Tyler (1987).

Gross, D. and Miller, K. J. (1990). Adjectives in WordNet. *International Journal of Lexicography*, 3, 265–77.

Gross, D., Fischer, U. and Miller, G. A. (1989). The organization of adjectival meanings. *Journal of Memory and Language*, 28, 92–106.

Grover Stripp, M. and Bellin, W. (1985). Bilingual linguistic systems revisited. *Linguistics*, 23, 123–36.

Gruber, J. S. (1965/1976). *Lexical Structures in Syntax and Semantics*. Amsterdam: North Holland.

Günther, H. (1989). Wörter im Kopf? Gedanken zu einen Buch von Jean Aitchison. In G. Kegel, T. Arnhold, K. Dahlmeier, G. Schmid and B. Tischer (eds), *Sprachwissenschaft und Psycholinguistik 3*. Westdeutchser Verlag.

Haegeman, L. (1994). *An Introduction to Government and Binding Theory*, 2nd edn. Oxford: Basil Blackwell.

Halle, M. and Clements, G. N. (1983). *Problem Book in Phonology*. Cambridge, MA: MIT Press.

Halle, M. and Vergnaud, J. R. (1980). Three-dimensional phonology. *Journal of Linguistic Research*, 1, 83–105.

—— (1987). *An Essay on Stress*. Cambridge, MA: MIT Press.

Hammond, M. and Noonan, M. (eds) (1988). *Theoretical Morphology: Approaches in Modern Linguistics*. New York: Academic Press.

Hampton, J. (1991). The combination of prototype concepts. In Schwanenflugel (1991).

Hand, C. R., Tonkovich, J. D. and Aitchison, J. (1979). Some idiosyncratic strategies utilized by a chronic Broca's aphasic. *Linguistics*, 17, 729–59.

Hankamer, Jorge. (1989). Morphological parsing and the lexicon. In Marlsen-Wilson (1989b).

Harley, T. A. (1990). Environmental contamination of normal speech. *Applied psycholinguistics*, 11, 45–72.

Harris, M. Barrett, M., Jones, D. and Brookes, S. (1988). Linguistic input and early word meaning. *Journal of Child Language*, 15, 77–94.

Hart, J., Berndt, R. S. and Caramazza, A. (1985). Category-specific naming deficit following cerebral infarction. *Nature*, 316, 439–40.

Haviland, S. E. and Clark, E. V. (1974). This man's father is my father's son: a study of the acquisition of English kin terms. *Journal of Child Language*, 1, 23–47.

Hawkins, J. A. and Cutler, A. (1988). Psycholinguistic factors in morphological assymetry. In J. A. Hawkins (ed.), *Explaining Language Universals*. Oxford: Basil Blackwell.

Hayes, B. (1983). A grid-based theory of English meter. *Linguistic Inquiry*, 14, 357–93.

—— (1984). The phonology of rhythm in English. *Linguistic Inquiry*, 15, 33–74.

Heine, B. (1997). *Cognitive Foundations of Grammar*. Oxford: Oxford University Press.

Henderson, L. (1985). Towards a psychology of morphemes. In Ellis (1985a), vol. 1.

—— (1989). On mental representation of morphology and its diagnosis by measures of visual access speed. In Marslen-Wilson (1989b).

Herbert, A. P. (1935). *What a Word!* London: Methuen.

Hermann, P. (1880/1920). *Prinzipien der Sprachgeschichte*. Halle an der Scale.: Max Niemeyer.

Hillyard, S. A. (1993). Electrical and magnetic brain recordings: contributions to cognitive neuroscience. *Current Opinion in Neurobiology*, 3, 711–17.

Hinton, L., Nichols, J. and Ohala, J. J. (eds) (1994). *Sound Symbolism*. Cambridge: Cambridge University Press.

Hodges, A. (1983/1985). *Alan Turing: The Enigma of Intelligence*. London: Hutchinson, Unwin Paperbacks.

Hoek, D., Ingram, D. and Gibson, D. (1986). Some possible causes of children's early word overextensions. *Journal of Child Language*, 13, 477–94.

Holland, M. K. and Wertheimer, M. (1964). Some physiognomic aspects of naming, or *maluma* and *takete* revisited. *Perception and Motor Skills*, 19, 111–17.

Hopper, P. J. and Thompson, S. A. (1984). The discourse basis for lexical categories in universal grammar. *Language*, 60, 703–52.

Hopper, P. J. and Traugott, E. C. (1993). *Grammaticalization*. Cambridge: Cambridge University Press.

Hotopf, W. H. N. (1980). Semantic similarity as a factor in whole-word slips of the tongue. In Fromkin (1980).

Householder, F. W. (1966). Phonological theory: a brief comment. *Journal of Linguistics*, 2, 99–100.

Howard, D. V., McAndrews, M. P. and Lasaga, M. I. (1981). Semantic priming of lexical decisions in young and old adults. *Journal of Gerontoloy*, 36, 707–14.

Hudson, R. (1984a). *Invitation to Linguistics*. London: Martin Robinson.

—— (1984b). *Word Grammar*. Oxford: Basil Blackwell.

Hughes, G. (1988). *Words in Time: A Social History of English Vocabulary*. Oxford: Blackwell.

Hurford, J. (1981). Malapropisms, left-to-right listing, and lexicalism. *Linguistic Inquiry*, 12, 419–23.

Hurford, J. and Heasley, B. (1983). *Semantics: A Coursebook*. Cambridge: Cambridge University Press.

Ingram, D. (1979). Phonological patterns in the speech of young children. In Fletcher and Garman (1979).

—— (1989). *First Language Acquisition: Method, Description and Explanation*. Cambridge: Cambridge University Press.

Inhelder, B. and Piaget, J. (1964). *The Early Growth of Logic in the Child*. London: Routledge and Kegan Paul.

Jackendoff, R. (1972). *Semantic Intepretation in Generative Grammar*. Cambridge, MA: MIT Press.

—— (1983). *Semantics and Cognition*. Cambridge, MA: MIT Press.

—— (1987). The status of thematic relations in linguistic theory. *Linguistic Inquiry*, 18, 369–412.

—— (1990). *Semantic Structures*. Cambridge, MA: MIT Press.

—— (1997a). *The Architecture of the Language Faculty*. Cambridge, MA: MIT Press.

—— (1997b). Twistin' the night away. *Language*, 73, 534–59.

Jacob, F. (1977). Evolution and tinkering. *Science*, 196, 1161–6.

Jakimik, J., Cole, R. A. and Rudnicky, A. I. (1985). Sound and spelling in spoken word recognition. *Journal of Memory and Language*, 24, 165–78.

Jakobson, R. (1956). Two aspects of language and two types of aphasic disturbance. In R. Jakobson and M. Halle, *Fundamentals of Language*. The Hague: Mouton.

—— (1968). *Child Language, Aphasia and Phonological Universals*. The Hague: Mouton.

Jakobson, R., Fant, G. and Halle, M. (1952). *Preliminaries to Speech Analysis: The Distinctive Features and their Correlates*. Cambridge, MA: MIT Press.

James, W. (1890/1981). *The Principles of Psychology*, 2 vols. Cambridge, MA: Harvard University Press.

Jarvella, R. J., Job, R., Sandström, G. and Schreuder, R. (1987). Morphological constraints on word recognition. In Allport et al. (1987).

Jarvella, R. J. and Meijers, G. (1983). Recognizing morphemes in spoken words: some evidence for a stem-organized mental lexicon. In Flores d'Arcais and Jarvella (1983).

Jastrzembski, J. E. (1981). Multiple meanings, number of related meanings, frequency of occurrence, and the lexicon. *Cognitive psychology*, 13, 278–305.

Jenkins, J. J. (1970). The 1952 Minnesota word association norms. In Postman and Keppel (1970).

Jensen, J. T. (1990). *Morphology: Word Structure in Generative Grammar*. Amsterdam: John Benjamins

Johnson-Laird, P. N. (1983). *Mental Models*. Cambridge: Cambridge University Press.

Johnson, M. (1987). *The Body in the Mind: The Bodily Basis of Meaning, Imagination and Reason*. Chicago: University of Chicago Press.

—— (1992). Philosophical implications of cognitive semantics. *Cognitive Linguistics*, 3, 345–66.

Johnson, S. (1755). *A Dictionary of the English Language*. London: Knapton, Longman et al. Facsimile published 1990 by Longman Group UK Ltd. CD-ROM published 1996 by Cambridge University Press.

Jones, G. V. (1989). The role of interlopers in the tip of the tongue phenomenon. *Memory and Cognition*, 17, 69–76.

Jones, G. V. and Langford, S. (1987). Phonological blocking in the tip of the tongue state. *Cognition*, 26, 115–22.

Jusczyk, P. W. (1992). Developing phonological categories for the speech signal. In C. A. Ferguson, L. Menn and C. Stoell-Gammon (eds), *Phonological Development: Models, Research, Implications*. Parkton, MD: York Press.

Kager, R. (1995). The metrical theory of word stress. In Goldsmith (1995).

Kamhi, A. G. (1986). The elusive first word: the importance of the naming insight for the development of referential speech. *Journal of Child Language*, 13, 155–61.

Kastovsky, D. (1986). The problem of productivity in word formation. *Linguistics*, 24, 585–600.

Katz, J. J. (1975). Logic and language: an examination of recent criticisms of intensionalism. In K. Gunderson and G. Maxwell (eds), *Minnesota Studies in Philosophy of Science*, vol. 6. Minneapolis: University of Minnesota Press.

Katz, J. J. (ed.) (1985). *The Philosophy of Linguistics*. Oxford: Oxford University Press.

Katz, J. J. and Fodor, J. A. (1963). The structure of a semantic theory. *Language*, 39, 170–210. Also in J. A. Fodor and J. J. Katz (eds), *The Structure of Language*. Englewood-Cliffs, NJ: Prentice-Hall, 1964.

Kay, P. and Fillmore, C. J. (1999). Grammatical constructions and linguistic generalizations: the What's X doing Y? construction. *Language*, 75, 1–33.

Kean, M.-L. (1977). The linguistic interpretation of aphasic syndromes: agrammatism in Broca's aphasia, an example. *Cognition*, 5, 9–46.

Keil, F. C. (1989). *Concepts, Kinds and Cognitive Development*. Cambridge, MA: MIT Press.

Keil, F. C. and Batterman, N. (1984). A characteristic-to-defining shift in the development of word meaning. *Journal of Verbal Learning and Verbal Behavior*, 23, 221–36.

Kempson, R. (1977). *Semantic Theory*. Cambridge: Cambridge University Press.

Kennedy, G. (1998). *An Introduction to Corpus Linguistics*. London: Longman.

Kilgarrif, A. (1992). *Polysemy*. Cognitive Science Research Paper 261. Falmer: University of Sussex, School of Cognitive and Computing Sciences.

—— (1997). Putting frequencies in the dictionary. *International Journal of Lexicography*, 10, 135–55.

Kinoshita, S. (1980). Sentence context effect on lexically ambiguous words: evidence for a postaccess inhibition process. *Memory and Cognition*, 13, 579–95.

Kintsch, W. (1974). *The Representation of Meaning in Memory*. Hillsdale, NJ: Lawrence Erlbaum.

Kintsch, W. (1984). Approaches to the study of the psychology of language. In Bever, Carroll and Miller (1984).

Kirsner, K., Smith, M. C., Lockhart, R. S., King, M. L. and Jain, M. (1984). The bilingual lexicon: language-specific units in an integrated network. *Journal of Verbal Learning and Verbal Behavior*, 23, 519–39.

Kittay, E. F. (1987). *Metaphor: Its Cognitive Force and Linguistic Structure*. Oxford: Clarendon Press.

Klatt, D. H. (1980). Speech perception: a model of acoustic-phonetic analysis and lexical access. In Cole (1980).

—— (1981). Lexical representations for speech production and perception. In Myers, Laver and Anderson (1981).

—— (1989). Review of selected models of speech perception. In Marslen-Wilson (1989).

Knott, R., Patterson, K. and Hodges, J. R. (1997). Lexical and semantic binding effects in short-term memory: evidence from semantic dementia. *Cognitive Neuropsychology*, 14, 1165–1216.

Köhler, W. (1947). *Gestalt Psychology*. New York: Liveright.

Koriat, A. and Lieblich, I. (1974). What does a person in a 'TOT' state know that a person in a 'don't know' state doesn't know. *Memory and Cognition*, 2, 647–55.

Kövecses, Z. (1988). *The Language of Love*. London and Toronto: Associated University Presses.

Krishnamurti, Bh. and Mukherjee, A. (1984). *Modernization of Indian Languages in News Media*. Osmania Publications in Linguistics 2. Hyderabad: Osmania University.

Kuhl, P. and Miller, J. D. (1974). Discrimination of speech sounds by the chinchilla: /t/ vs /d/ in CV syllables. *Journal of the Acoustical Society of America*, 56, series 42 (abstract).

—— (1975). Speech perception by the chinchilla: phonetic boundaries for synthetic VOT stimuli. *Journal of the Acoustical Society of America*, 57, series 49 (abstract).

Kutas, M. and van Petten, C. (1994). Psycholinguistics electrified: event-related brain potential investigations. In M. A. Gernsbacher (ed.), *Handbook of Psycholinguistics*. New York: Academic Press.

Labov, W. (1973). The boundaries of words and their meanings. In C.-J. N. Bailey and R. W. Shuy (eds) *New Ways of Analyzing Variation in English*. Washington, DC: Georgetown University Press.

Lackner, J. R. and Garrett, M. F. (1972). Resolving ambiguity: Effects of biasing context in the unattended ear. *Cognition*, 1, 359–72.

Ladefoged, P. (1975). *A Course in Phonetics*. New York: Harcourt Brace Jovanovich.

Lakoff, G. (1972). Hedges: a study in meaning criteria and the logic of fuzzy concepts. *Papers of the Eighth Regional Meeting, Chicago Linguistic Society*, 183–228.

——— (1987). *Women, Fire and Dangerous Things*. Chicago: University of Chicago Press.

Lakoff, G. and Johnson, M. (1980). *Metaphors We Live By*. Chicago: University of Chicago Press.

Lakoff, G. and Kövecses, Z. (1987). The cognitive model of anger inherent in American English. In D. Holland and N. Quinn (eds), *Cultural Models in Language and Thought*. Cambridge: Cambridge University Press.

Lakoff, G. and Turner, M. (1989). *More than Cool Reason: A Field Guide to Poetic Metaphor*. Chicago: University of Chicago Press.

Landau, B. and Gleitman, L. R. (1985). *Language and Experience: Evidence from the Blind Child*. Cambridge, MA: Harvard University Press.

Landau, B. and Jackendoff, R. (1933). 'What' and 'where' in spatial language and spatial cognition. *Behavioral and Brain Sciences*, 16, 217–65.

Landau, B., Smith, L. B. and Jones, S. (1988). The importance of shape in early lexical learning. *Cognitive Development*, 3, 299–321.

——— (1992). Syntactic context and the shape bias in children's and adults' lexical learning. *Journal of Memory and Language*, 31, 807–25.

Landau, S. I. (2001). *The Art and Craft of Lexicography*, 2nd edn. Cambridge: Cambridge University Press.

Langacker, R. W. (1987). *Foundations of Cognitive Grammar, I: Theoretical Prerequisites*. Stanford, CA: Stanford University Press.

——— (1988). Review of Lakoff (1987), in *Language*, 64, 384–95.

——— (1991). *Concept, Image and Symbol*. Berlin: Mouton de Gruyter.

Laubstein, A. S. (1988). *The Nature of the 'Production Grammar' Syllable*. Bloomington, IN: Indiana University Linguistics Club.

Laudanna, A., Badecker, W. and Caramazza, A. (1992). Processing inflectional and derived morphology. *Journal of Memory and Language*, 31, 333–48.

Laver, J. (1980). Monitoring systems in the neurolinguistic control of speech production. In Fromkin (1980).

Lehiste, I. (1960). *An Acoustic-phonetic Study of Internal Open Juncture*. *Phonetica*, Supplement 5.

——— (1972). The timing and utterances of linguistic boundaries. *Journal of the Acoustical Society of America*, 51, 2018–24.

Lehnert, M. (1971). *Rückläufiges Worterbuch der englischen Gegenwartssprache*. Leipzig: VEB.

Lehrer, A. (1983). *Wine and Conversation*. Bloomington: Indiana University Press.

Lehrer, A. and Kittay, E. F. (eds) (1992). *Frames, Fields and Contrasts*. Hillsdale, NJ: Lawrence Erlbaum.

Lenneberg, E. (1967). *Biological Foundations of Language*. New York: Wiley.

Leopold, W. F. (1947). *Speech Development of a Bilingual Child*, vol. 2: *Sound-learning in the First Two Years*. Evanston, IL: Northwestern University Press.

Levelt, W. J. M. (1989). *Speaking: From Intention to Articulation*. Cambridge, MA: MIT Press.

——— (1992). Accesssing words in speech production. *Cognition*, 42, 1–22. Also in Levelt (1993).

Levelt, W. J. M. (ed.) (1993). *Lexical Access in Speech Production*. Oxford: Blackwell. Originally published as *Cognition*, 42 (1992).

Levin, B. (1991). Building a lexicon: the contribution of linguistics. *International Journal of Lexicography*, 4, 205–226.

——— (1993). *English Verb Classes and Alternations: A Preliminary Investigation*. Chicago: University of Chicago Press.

Levin, B. and Pinker, S. (eds) (1992). *Lexical and Conceptual Semantics*. Oxford: Blackwell. Originally published as *Cognition*, 41 (1991).

Levin, B. and Rappaport Hovav, M. (1991). Wiping the slate clean: a lexical semantic exploration. *Cognition*, 41, 123–52. Also in Levin and Pinker (1992).

—— (1994). A preliminary analysis of causative verbs in English. *Lingua*, 92, 38–77.

—— (1995). *Unaccusativity: At the Syntax-lexical Semantics Interface*. Cambridge, MA: MIT Press.

—— (1996). Lexical semantics and syntactic structure. In S. Lappin (ed.), *The Handbook of Contemporary Semantic Theory*. Oxford: Blackwell.

Levinson, S. C. (2001). Covariation between spatial language and cognition, and its implications for language learning. In Bowerman and Levinson (2001).

Liberman, A. M., Harris, K. S., Hoffman, H. S. and Griffith, B. C. (1957). The discrimination of speech sounds within and across phoneme boundaries. *Journal of Experimental Psychology*, 54, 358–68.

Liberman, M. and Prince, A. (1977). On stress and linguistic rhythm. *Linguistic Inquiry*, 8, 249–336.

Lieber, R. (1981). *The Organization of the Lexicon*. Bloomington: Indiana University Linguistics Club.

Lieven, E. V. M., Pine, J. L. and Barnes, H. D. (1992). Individual vocabulary differences in early vocabulary development: redefining the referential-expressive distinction. *Journal of Child Language*, 19, 287–310.

Lipka, L. (1992). *An Outline of English Lexicology*, 2nd edn. Tübingen: Niemeyer.

Lucchelli, F., Muggia, S. and Spinnler, H. (1997). Selective proper name anomia: a case involving only contemporary celebrities. *Cognitive Neuropsychology*, 14, 881–900.

Luce, P. A., Pisoni, D. B. and Goldinger, S. D. (1990). Similarity neighbourhoods of spoken words. In Altmann (1990).

Lukatela, G., Gligorijevic, B., Kostic, A. and Turvey, M. T. (1980). Representation of inflected nouns in the internal lexicon. *Memory and Cognition*, 8, 415–23.

Lyons, J. (1968). *Introduction to Theoretical Linguistics*. Cambridge: Cambridge University Press.

—— (1981). *Language, Meaning and Context*. London: Fontana.

McCarthy, J. J. (1982). Prosodic structure and expletive infixation. *Language*, 58, 574–90.

McCawley, J. D. (1983). The syntax of some English adverbs. *Papers of the Nineteenth Regional Meeting, Chicago Linguistic Society*, 263–82.

McClelland, J. L. (1979). On the time relations of mental processes: an examination of systems of processes in cascade. *Psychological Review*, 86, 287–330.

McClelland, J. L. and Elman, J. E. (1986). The TRACE model of speech perception. *Cognitive Psychology*, 18, 1–86.

McClelland, J. L. and Rumelhart, D. E. (1986). *Parallel Distributed Processing: Explorations in the Microstructure of Cognition, vol.2: Psychological and Biological Models*. Cambridge, MA: MIT Press.

MacCormac, E. R. (1985). *A Cognitive Theory of Metaphor*. Cambridge, MA: MIT Press.

Mackay, D. G. (1966). To end ambiguous sentences. *Perception and Psychophysics*, 1, 426–36.

—— (1972). The structure of words and syllables: evidence from errors in speech. *Cognitive Psychology*, 3, 210–27.

—— (1979). Lexical insertion, inflection, and derivation: creative processes in word production. *Journal of Psycholinguistic Research*, 8, 477–98.

Macken, M. A. (1980). The acquisition of stop systems: a cross-linguistic perspective. In G. Yeni-Komshian, J. Kavanagh and C. A. Ferguson (eds), *Child Phonology*, vol. I: *Perception and Production*. New York: Academic Press.

McKeown, M. G. and Curtis, M. E. (eds) (1987). *The Nature of Vocabulary Acquisition*. Hillsdale, NJ: Lawrence Erlbaum.

McKoon, G. and Macfarland, T. (2000). Externally and internally caused change of state verbs. *Language*, 76, 833–58.

Macnamara, J. (1982). *Names for Things*. Cambridge, MA: MIT Press.

McShane, J. (1979). The development of naming. *Linguistics*, 17, 879–905.

—— (1980). *Learning to Talk*. Cambridge: Cambridge University Press.

Maddieson, I. (1984). *Patterns of Sounds*. Cambridge: Cambridge University Press.

Makkai, A. (1972). *Idiom Structure in English*. The Hague: Mouton.

Manelis, L. and Tharp, D. A. (1977). The processing of affixed words. *Memory and Cognition*, 5, 690–5.

Maratsos, M. P. (1973). Decrease in the understanding of the word 'big' in preschool children. *Child Development*, 44, 747–52.

Marchand, H. (1969). *The Categories and Types of Present-day English Word-formation*, 2nd edn. Munich: Bech.

Marcus, S. M. (1984). Recognizing speech: on the mapping from sound to word. In Bouma and Bouwhuis (1984).

Marin, O. S. M. (1982). Brain and language: the rules of the game. In Arbib, Caplan and Marshall (1982).

Markman, E. M. (1989). *Categorization and Naming in Children*. Cambridge, MA: MIT Press.

—— (1992). Constraints on word learning: speculations about their nature, origins, and domain specificity. In M. R. Gunnar and M. Maratsos (eds), *Modularity and Constraints in Language and Cognition*. The Minnesota Symposium on Child Psychology, vol. 25. Hillsdale, NJ: Lawrence Erlbaum.

Marshall, J. C. (1977). Minds, machines and metaphors. *Social Studies of Science*, 7, 475–88.

Marslen-Wilson, W. D. (1987). Functional parallelism in spoken word recognition. *Cognition*, 25, 71–102. Also in Frauenfelder and Tyler (1987).

—— (1989a). Access and integration: projecting sound onto meaning. In Marslen-Wilson (1989b).

—— (ed.) (1989b). *Lexical Representation and Process*. Cambridge, MA: MIT Press.

—— (1990). Activation, competition, and frequency in lexical access. In Altmann (1990).

Marslen-Wilson, W. D. and Tyler, L. K. (1980). The temporal structure of spoken language understanding. *Cognition*, 8, 1–71.

—— (1981). Central processes in speech understanding. *Philosophical Transactions of the Royal Society of London* B, 295, 317–32. Also published as *Psychological Mechanisms of Language*. London: Royal Society and British Academy).

—— (1998). Rules, representations, and the English past tense. *Trends in Cognitive Sciences*, 2, 428–535.

Marslen-Wilson, W. D. and Zhou, X. (1991). Abstractness, allomorphy and lexical architecture. *Language and Cognitive Processes*, 14, 321–52.

Matthei, E. and Roeper, T. (1983). *Understanding and Producing Speech*. London: Fontana.

Matthews, P. (1991). *Morphology*, 2nd edn. Cambridge: Cambridge University Press.

Meara, P. (1983). *Vocabulary in Second Language*. Specialised Bibliography 3. London: Centre for Information on Language Teaching and Research.

Meara, P. and Ellis, A. W. (1982). The psychological reality of deep and surface phonological representations: evidence from speech errors in Welsh. In Cutler (1982a). First published in *Linguistics*, 19 (1981).

Mehler, J. (1981). The role of syllables in speech processing: infant and adult data. *Philosophical Transactions of the Royal Society of London* B, 295, 333–52. Also published as *Psychological Mechanisms of Language*. London: Royal Society and British Academy.

Meillet, A. (1905–6). Comment les mots changent de sens. *Année Sociologique*, 1–38. Reprinted in A. Meillet, *Linguistique historique et linguistique générale*, vol. 1. Paris, Champion, 1948, 230–71.

Menn, L. (1978). Phonological units in beginning speech. In A. Bell and J. B. Hooper (eds), *Syllables and Segments*. Amsterdam: and North-Holland.

Menn, L. and MacWhinney, B. (1984). The repeated morph constraint. *Language*, 60, 519–41.

Menn, L. and Stoel-Gammon, C. (1993). Phonological development: learning sounds and sound patterns. In Berko Gleason (1993).

—— (1995). Phonological development. In Fletcher and MacWhinney (1995).

Menyuk, P. and Menn, L. (1979). Early strategies for the perception and production of words and sounds. In Fletcher and Garman (1979).

Meringer, R. and Mayer, K. (1978). *Versprechen und Verlesen: Eine Psychologisch-Linguistische Studien*. Amsterdam: John Benjamins.

Merriman, W. E. (1991). The mutual exclusivity bias in children's word learning: a reply to Woodward and Markman. *Developmental Review*, 11, 164–91.

Merriman, W. E. and Bowman, L. L. (1989). *The Mutual Exclusivity Bias in Children's Word Learning. Monographs of the Society for Research in Child Development*, 54.

Merriman, W. E. and Kutlesic, V. (1993). Bilingual and monolingual children's use of two lexical acquisition heuristics. *Applied Psycholinguistics*, 14, 229–49.

Merriman, W. E., Scott, P. D. and Marazita, J. (1993a). An appearance-function shift in children's object naming. *Journal of Child Language*, 20, 101–18.

Mervis, C. B. (1987). Child basic object categories and early lexical development. In U. Neisser (ed.), *Concepts and Conceptual Development: Ecological and Intellectual Factors in Categorization*. Cambridge: Cambridge University Press.

Meyer, A. S. (1992). Investigation of phonological encoding through speech error analyses: Achievements, limitations, and alternatives. *Cognition*, 42, 181–211. Also in Levelt (1993).

Miller, G. and Nicely, P. (1955). An analysis of perceptual confusions among English consonants. *Journal of the Acoustical Society of America*, 27, 338–52.

Miller, G. A. (1990a). Nouns in WordNet: A lexical inheritance system. *International Journal of Lexicography*, 3, 245–64.

—— (1990b). *Wordnet: An On-line Lexical Database*. Special issue of the *International Journal of Lexicography*, 34.

—— (1991). *The Science of Words*. New York: Scientific American Library.

Miller, G. A. and Fellbaum, C. (1991). Semantic networks of English. *Cognition*, 41, 197–229. Also in Levin and Pinker (1992).

Miller, G. A. and Gildea, P. M. (1987). How children learn words. *Scientific American*, 257, 86–91. Also in Wang (1991).

Miller, G. A. and Johnson-Laird, P. N. (1976). *Language and Perception*. Cambridge: Cambridge University Press.

Miller, J. (1978). *The Body in Question*. New York: Random House.

Minda, J. P. and Smith, J. D. (2001). Prototypes in category learning: the effects of category size, category structure, and stimulus complexity. *Journal of Experimental Psychology: Learning, Memory and Cognition*, 27, 775–99.

Minsky, M. (1975). A framework for representing knowledge. In P. H. Winston (ed.), *The Psychology of Computer Vision*. New York: McGraw Hill.

Monsell, S. (1985). Repetition and the lexicon. In Ellis (1985a), vol. 2.

Morse, P. A. (1976). Speech perception in the human infant and rhesus monkey. In S. Harnad, H. Steklis and J. Lancaster (eds), *Origins and Evolution of Language and Speech. Annals of the New York Academy of Sciences*, 280.

Morton, J. (1979). Word recognition. In Morton and Marshall (1979).

Morton, J. and Marshall, J. C. (eds) (1979). *Psycholinguistics 2: Structure and Processes*. London: Elek.

Motley, M. T. (1985a). Slips of the tongue. *Scientific American*, 253, 114–19.

—— (1985b). The production of verbal slips and double entrendres as clues to the efficiency of normal speech production. *Journal of Language and Social Psychology*, 4, 275–93.

Murphy, G. L. (1991). Meaning and concepts. In Schwanenflugel (1991).

Murphy, G. L. and Andrew, J. M. (1993). The conceptual basis of antonymy and synonymy in adjectives. *Journal of Memory and Language*, 32, 301–19.

Murrell, G. A. and Morton, J. (1974). Word recognition and morphemic structure. *Journal of Experimental Psychology*, 102, 963–8.

Myers, T. Laver, J. and Anderson, J. (eds) (1981). *The Cognitive Representation of Speech*. Amsterdam: North Holland.

Nagy, W. E. and Anderson, R. (1984). The number of words in printed school English. *Reading Research Quarterly*, 19, 304–30.

Nagy, W. E. and Herman, P. A. (1987). Breadth and depth of vocabulary knowledge: implications for acquisition and instruction. In McKeown and Curtis (1987).

Napoli, D. J. (1993). *Syntax: Theory and Problems*. Oxford: Oxford University Press.

Napps, S. E. (1989). Morphemic relationships in the lexicon: are they distinct from semantic and formal relationships? *Memory and Cognition*, 17, 729–39.

Napps, S. E. and Fowler, C. A. (1987). Formal relationships among words and the organization of the mental lexicon. *Journal of Psycholinguistic Research*, 16, 257–72.

Nation, I. S. P. (1993). Using dictionaries to estimate vocabulary size: essential, but rarely followed procedures. *Language Testing*, 10.

Nelson, K. (1973). *Structure and Strategy in Learning to Talk. Monographs of the Society for Research in Child Development*, 38.

Nelson, K., Hampson, J. and Kessler Shaw, L. (1991). Nouns in early lexicons: evidence, explanations and implications. *Journal of Child Language*, 20, 61–84.

Nelson, K., Rescorla, L., Gruendel, J. and Benedict, H. (1978). Early lexicons: what do they mean? *Child Development*, 49, 960–8.

Nerlich, B. and Clarke, D. D. (1997). Polysemy: patterns in meaning and patterns in history. *Historiographia Linguistica*, 24, 359–85.

Nirmala, C. (1981). *First Language (Telegu) Development in Children: A Short Descriptive Study*. Unpublished doctoral dissertation, Osmania University, Hyderabad.

NODE (1998). *The New Oxford Dictionary of English*. Oxford: Oxford University Press.

Norris, D. (1986). Word recognition: context effects without priming. *Cognition*, 22, 93–136.

—— (1990). A dynamic-net model of human speech recognition. In Altmann (1990).

Norris, D. and Cutler, A. (1985). Juncture detection. *Linguistics*, 23, 689–706.

Nunberg, G., Sag, I. A. and Wasow, T. (1994). Idioms. *Language*, 70, 491–538.

Ohala, J. H. (1992). The segment: primitive or derived? In Docherty and Ladd (1992).

—— (1981). Articulatory constraints on the cognitive representation of speech. In Myers, Laver and Anderson (1981).

Ooi, V. B. Y. (1998). *Computer Corpus Lexicography*. London: Longman.

Ortony, A. (ed.) (1993). *Metaphor and Thought*, 2nd edn. Cambridge: Cambridge University Press.

Osella, C. and Osella, F. (1991). Sneham: emotion or bodily fluid? Paper presented at London University Language and Communication Seminar, June 1991.

Osherson, D. N. and Smith, E. E. (1981). On the inadequacy of prototype theory as a theory of concepts. *Cognition*, 9, 35–58.

Palmer, F. (1984). *Grammar*. Harmondsworth: Penguin.

Panther, Klaus-U. and Radden, G. (eds) (1999). *Metonymy in Language and Thought*. Amsterdam: John Benjamins.

Papagno, C. and Vallar, G. (1992). Phonological short-term memory and the learning of novel words: The effect of phonological similarity and item length. *Quarterly Journal of Experimental Psychology*, 44A, 47–67.

Parlett, D. (1981). *Botticelli and Beyond: 100 of the World's Best Word Games*. New York: Pantheon Books.

Pawley, A. (2001). Phraseology, linguistics and the dictionary. *International Journal of Lexicography*, 14, 122–34.

Pease, D. M., Berko Gleason, J. and Pan, B. A. (1993). Learning the meaning of words: semantic development and beyond. In Berko Gleason (1993).

Peters, A. (1983). *The Units of Language Acquisition*. Cambridge: Cambridge University Press.

Pillon, A., de Partz, M.-P., Raison, A.-M., Seron, X. (1991). 'L'orange, c'est le fruitier de l'orangine': a case of morphological impairment? *Language and Cognitive Processes*, 6, 137–67.

Pitt, D. and Katz, J. J. (2000). Compositional idioms. *Language*, 76, 409–32.

Plunkett, K. (1993). Lexical segmentation and vocabulary growth in early language acquisition. *Journal of Child Language*, 20, 43–60.

Pollio, H. R., Barlow, J. M., Fine, H. J. and Pollio, M. (1977). *Psychology and the Poetics of Growth: Figurative Language in Psychology, Psychotherapy and Education*. Hillsdale, NJ: Lawrence Erlbaum.

Pollio, H. R., Smith, M. K. and Pollio, M. R. (1990). Figurative language and cognitive psychology. *Language and Cognitive Processes*, 5, 141–67.

Pollio, M. R. and Pickens, J. D. (1980). The developmental structure of figurative competence. In R. P. Honeck and R. R. Hoffman (eds), *Cognition and Figurative Language*. Hillsdale, NJ: Lawrence Erlbaum.

Posner, M. (1986). Empirical studies of prototypes. In C. Craig (ed.), *Noun Classes and Categorization*. Amsterdam: John Benjamins.

Posner, M. I. and Raichle, M. E. (1994). *Images of Mind*. New York: W. H. Freeman (Scientific American Library).

Postman, L. and Keppel, G. (eds) (1970). *Norms of Word Associations*. New York: Academic Press.

Priestley, T. M. S. (1977). One idiosyncratic strategy in the acquisition of phonology. *Journal of Child Language*, 4, 45–66.

Pullum, G. (1991). *The Great Eskimo Vocabulary Hoax*. Chicago: Chicago University Press.

Pulman, S. G. (1983). *Word Meaning and Belief*. London: Croom Helm.

Pustejovsky, J. (1995). *The Generative Lexicon*. Cambridge, MA: MIT Press.
—— (1998). Generativity and explanation in semantics. *Linguistic Inquiry*, 29, 289–311.
—— (2001). Type construction and the logic of concepts. In P. Bouillon and F. Busa (eds), *The Language of Word Meaning*. Cambridge: Cambridge University Press.
Pustejovsky, J. and Boguraev, B. (eds) (1996). *Lexical Semantics: The Problem of Polysemy*. Oxford: Clarendon Press.
Putnam, H. (1975). The meaning of 'meaning'. In K. Gunderson (ed.), *Language, Mind and Knowledge. Minnesota Studies in the Philosophy of Science*, vol. 7. Minneapolis: University of Minnesota Press.
Quine, W. V. (1971). The inscrutability of reference. In Steinberg and Jakobovits (1971).
—— (1985). The problem of meaning in linguistics. In Katz (1985).
Randall, J. H. (1980). *-ity*: a study in word formation restrictions. *Journal of Psycholinguistic Research*, 9, 523–33.
Rappaport, M. and Levin, B. (1988). What to do with theta-roles. In Wilkins (1988).
Rappaport Hovav, M. and Levin, B. (1992). Classifying single argument verbs. Mimeo.
—— (1998). Building word meanings. In M. Butt and W. Geuder (eds), *The Projection of Arguments: Lexical and Compositional Factors*. Stanford, CA: CSLI Publications.
Renouf, A. (ed.) (1998). *English Corpus Linguistics: The State of the Art – Papers from the Eighteenth International Conference on English Language Research on Computerised Corpora (ICAME 18)*. Amsterdam: Rodopi.
Richards, M. M. (1979). Sorting out what's in a word from what's not: evaluating Clark's semantic features acquisition theory. *Journal of Experimental Child Psychology*, 27, 1–47.
Roelofs, A. (1992). *Lemma Retrieval in Speaking: A Theory, Computer Simulations, and Empirical Data*. Nijemegen: Nijmegen Insitute for Cognition and Information.
—— (1993a). A spreading-activation theory of lemma retrieval in speaking. In Levelt (1993). Originally published in *Cognition*, 42 (1992), 107–42.
—— (1993b). Testing a non-decompositional theory of lemma retrieval in speaking: Retrieval of verbs. *Cognition*, 47, 59–87.
Romaine, S. (1983). On the productivity of word formation: Rules and limits of variability in the lexicon. *Australian Journal of Linguistics*, 3, 177–200.
Room, A. (1979). *Room's Dictionary of Confusibles*. London: Routledge and Kegan Paul.
Rosch, E. (1975). Cognitive representations of semantic categories. *Journal of Experimental Psychology: General*, 104, 192–233.
Rosch, E., Mervis, C. B., Gray, W. D., Johnson, D. M. and Boyes-Braem, P. (1976). Basic objects in natural categories. *Cognitive Psychology*, 8, 382–439.
Rubin, D. C. (1975). Within word structure in the tip-of-the-tongue phenomenon. *Journal of Verbal Learning and Verbal Behavior*, 14, 392–397.
Rubin, G. S., Becker, C. A. and Freeman, R. H. (1979). Morphological structure and its effect on visual word recognition. *Journal of Verbal Learning and Verbal Behavior*, 18, 757–67.
Rumelhart, D. E. and McClelland, J. L. (eds) (1986). *Parallel Distributed Processing: Explorations in the Microstructure of Cognition, vol.1: Foundations*. Cambridge, MA: MIT Press
Rumelhart, D. E., Hinton, G. E. and McClelland, J. L. (1986). A general framework for parallel distributed processing. In Rumelhart and McClelland (1986).
Sandra, D. (1994). The morphology of the mental lexicon: internal word structure viewed from a psycholinguistic perspective. *Language and Cognitive Processes*, 9, 227–69.
Saporta, S. (1961). *Psycholinguistics: A Book of Readings*. New York: Holt, Rinehart and Winston.

Scalise, S. (1988). Inflection and derivation. *Linguistics*, 26, 561–81.

Schank, R. C. (1972). Conceptual dependency: a theory of natural language understanding. *Cognitive Psychology*, 3, 552–631.

Schank, R. C. and Abelson, R. P. (1977). *Scripts, Plans, Goals and Understanding: An Enquiry into Human Knowledge Structures*. Hillsdale, NJ: Erlbaum.

Schriefers, H., Friederici, A. and Graetz, P. (1992). Inflectional and derivational morphology in the mental lexicon: Symmetries and asymmetries in repetition priming. *Quarterly Journal of Experimental Psychology*, 44A, 373–90.

Schriefers, H., Meyer, A. S. and Levelt, W. J. M. (1990). Exploring the time course of lexical access in language production: picture-word interference studies. *Journal of Memory and Language*, 29, 86–102.

Schriefers, H., Zwitserlood, P. and Roelofs, A. (1991). The identification of morphologically complex spoken words: continuous processing or decomposition. *Journal of Memory and Language*, 30, 26–47.

Schwanenflugel, P. J. (ed.) (1991). *The Psychology of Word Meanings*. Hillsdale, NJ: Lawrence Erlbaum.

Seashore, R. H. and Eckerson, L. D. (1940). The measurement of individual differences in general English vocabularies. *Journal of Educational Psychology*, 31, 14–38.

Segui, J. (1984). The syllable: a basic perceptual unit in speech processing? In Bouma and Bouwhuis (1984).

Seidenberg, M. S., Tanenhaus, M. K., Leiman, J. M. and Bienkowski, M. (1982). Automatic access of meanings of ambiguous words in context: some limitations of knowledge based processing. *Cognitive Psychology*, 14, 489–537.

Selkirk, E. O. (1980). The role of prosodic categories in English word stress. *Linguistic Inquiry*, 11, 563–605.

—— (1982). *The Syntax of Words*. Linguistic Inquiry Monograph 7. Cambridge, MA: MIT Press.

—— (1984). *Phonology and Syntax: The Relation between Sound and Structure*. Cambridge, MA: MIT Press.

Shallice, T. (1988). *From Neuropsychology to Mental Structure*. Cambridge: Cambridge University Press

Shattuck-Hufnagel, S. (1979). Speech errors as evidence for a serial-ordering mechanism in sentence production. In Cooper and Walker (1979).

Shattuck-Hufnagel, S. and Klatt, D. H. (1979). The limited use of distinctive features and markedness in speech production: evidence from speech error data. *Journal of Verbal Learning and Verbal Behavior*, 18, 41–55.

Shillcock, R. (1990). Lexical hypotheses in continuous speech. In Altmann (1990).

Simon, J. (1981). *Paradigms Lost*. London: Chatto and Windus.

Singleton, D. (2000). *Language and the Lexicon: An Introduction*. London: Arnold.

Slobin, D. I. (1973). Cognitive prerequisites for the development of grammar. In C. A. Ferguson and D. I. Slobin (eds), *Studies of Child Language Development*. New York: Holt.

Smith, E. and Medlin, D. (1981). *Categories and Concepts*. Cambridge, MA: Harvard University Press.

Smith, M. E. (1926). An investigation of the development of the sentence and the extent of vocabulary in young children. *University of Iowa Studies in Child Welfare*, 35.

Smith, M. K. and Montgomery, M. B. (1989). The semantics of winning and losing. *Language in Society*, 18, 31–57.

Smith, M. K., Pollio, H. R. and Pitts, M. K. (1981). Metaphor as intellectual history: Conceptual categories underlying figurative usage in American English from 1675–1975. *Linguistics*, 19, 911–35.

Smith, N. V. S. (1973). *The Acquisition of Phonology*. Cambridge: Cambridge University Press.

Solomon, R. L. and Howes, D. H. (1951). Word frequency, personal values and visual duration threshholds. *Psychological Review*, 58, 256–70.

Sparck-Jones, K. (1984). Compound noun interpretation problems. In F. Fallside and W. A. Woods, *Computer Speech Processing*. Englewood Cliffs, NJ: Prentice-Hall.

Spencer, A. (1991). *Morphological Theory*. Oxford: Basil Blackwell.

Spencer, A. (2001). Morphology. In M. Aronoff and J. Rees-Miller (eds), *The Handbook of Linguistics*. Oxford: Blackwell.

Sperber, D. and Wilson, D. (1986). *Relevance: Communication and Cognition*. Oxford: Blackwell.

Sperber, D. and Wilson, D. (1985/6). 'Loose talk'. *Proceedings of the Aristotelian Society*, NS 86, 153–71.

Sperber, H. (1930). *Einführung in die Bedeutungslehre*, 2nd edn. Leipzig: K. Schroeder Verlag.

Stampe, D. (1969). The acquisition of phonemic representation. *Proceedings of the Fifth Regional Meeting, Chicago Linguistic Society*, 433–44.

Stampe, D. (1979). *A Dissertation on Natural Phonology*. New York: Garland Press.

Stanners, R. F., Neiser, J. J., Hernon, W. P. and Hall, R. (1979). Memory representation for morphologically related words. *Journal of Verbal Learning and Verbal Behavior*, 18, 399–412.

Steen, G. (1994). *Understanding Metaphor in Literature*. London: Longman.

Steinberg, D. D. and Jakobovits, L. A. (eds) (1971). *Semantics: An Interdisciplinary Reader in Philosophy, Linguistics and Psychology*. Cambridge: Cambridge University Press.

Stemberger, J. P. (1990). Wordshape errors in language production. *Linguistics*, 35, 123–57.

Stemberger, J. P. and MacWhinney, B. (1986). Frequency and the lexical storage of regularly inflected words. *Memory and Cognition*, 14, 17–26.

—— (1988). Are inflected forms stored in the lexicon? In Hammond and Noonan (1988).

Stemberger, N. (1985). *The Lexicon in a Model of Speech Production*. New York: Garland.

Sterling, C. M. (1983). The psychological productivity of inflectional and derivational morphemes. In D. Rogers and A. J. A. Sloboda, *The Acquisition of Symbolic Skills*. NY: Plenum Press.

Svartvik, J. (ed.) (1996). *Words*. Stockholm: Swedish Academy (KVHAA Konferenser 36).

Sweetser, E. E. (1990). *From Etymology to Pragmatics: Metaphorical and Cultural Aspects of Semantic Structure*. Cambridge: Cambridge University Press.

Swinney, D. A. (1979). Lexical access during sentence comprehension: (Re)consideration of context effects. *Journal of Verbal Learning and Verbal Behavior*, 18, 645–59.

Swinney, D. A. and Cutler, A. (1979). The access and processing of idiomatic expressions. *Journal of Verbal Learning and Verbal Behavior*, 18, 523–34.

Taft, M. (1981). Prefix stripping revisited. *Journal of Verbal Learning and Verbal Behavior*, 20, 289–97.

—— (1988). A morphological-decomposition model of lexical representation. *Linguistics*, 26, 657–68.

—— (1994). Interactive-activation as a framework for understanding morphological processing. In D. Sandra and M. Taft (eds). *Morphological Structure, Lexical Representation and Lexical Access*. Hove: Lawrence Erlbaum.

Taft, M. and Forster, K. I. (1975). Lexical storage and retrieval of prefixed words. *Journal of Verbal Learning and Verbal Behavior*, 15, 607–20.

Taft, M., Hambly, G. and Kinoshita, S. (1986). Visual and auditory recognition of prefixed words. *Quarterly Journal of Experimental Psychology*, 38A, 351–66.

Talmy, T. (1985). Lexicalization patterns. In T. Shopen (ed.), *Language Typology and Syntactic Description. III: Grammatical Categories and the Lexicon*. Cambridge: Cambridge University Press.

Tanenhaus, M. K. and Carlson, G. N. (1989). Lexical structure and language comprehension. In Marslen-Wilson (1989b).

Tanenhaus, M. K., Dell, G. S. and Carlson, G. (1987). Context effects and lexical processing: a connectionist approach to modularity. In Garfield (1987).

Tanenhaus, M. K., Garnsey, S. M. and Boland, J. (1990). Combinatory lexical information and language comprehension. In Altmann (1990).

Taylor, J. R. (1992a). How many meanings does a word have? *Stellenbosch Papers in Linguistics*, 25, 133–68.

—— (1992b). Old problems: adjectives in cognitive grammar. *Cognitive Linguistics*, 3, 1–35.

—— (1995). *Linguistic Categorization: Prototypes in Linguistic Theory*, 2nd edn. Oxford: Clarendon Press.

Taylor, S. H. (1978). On the acquisition and completion of lexical items. In D. Farkas, W. M. Jacobsen and K. W. Todrys (eds), *Papers from the Parasession on the Lexicon*. Chicago, IL: Chicago Linguistic Society.

Thomas, J. and Short, M. (eds) (1996). *Using Corpora for Language Research*. London: Longman.

Tourangeau, R. and Sternberg, R. J. (1982). Understanding and appreciating metaphors. *Cognition*, 11, 203–44.

Treiman, R. (1989). The internal structure of the syllable. In G. N. Carlson. and M. K. Tanenhaus (eds), *Linguistic Structure in Language Processing*. Dordrecht: Kluwer.

Trench, R. C. (1855). *On the Study of Words*, 6th edn. London: J. W. Parker.

—— (1856). *English Past and Present*, 3rd rev. edn. London: J. W. Parker.

Tsohatzidis, S. (ed.) (1990). *Meanings and Prototypes: Studies in Linguistic Categorization*. London: Routledge.

Tulving, E. (1972). Episodic and semantic memory. In E. Tulving and W. Donaldson (eds), *Organization of Memory*. New York: Academic Press.

Tversky, B. (1990). Where partonomies and taxonomies meet. In Tsohatzidis (1990).

Tweney, R., Tkacz, S. and Zaruba, S. (1975). Slips of the tongue and lexical storage. *Language and Speech*, 18, 388–96.

Tyler, L. K. (1984). The structure of the initial cohort. *Perception and Psychophysics*, 36, 417–27.

—— (1989). The role of lexical representations in language comprehension. In Marslen-Wilson (1989).

Tyler, L. K. and Cobb, H. (1987). Processing bound morphemes in context: the case of an aphasic patient. *Language and Cognitive Processes*, 2, 245–62.

Tyler, L. K. and Frauenfelder, U. H. (1987). The process of spoken word recognition: an introduction. *Cognition*, 25, 1–20. Also in Frauenfelder and Tyler (1987).

Tyler, L. K., Marslen-Wilson, W. D., Rentoul, J. and Hanney, P. (1988). Continuous and discontinuous access in spoken word-recognition: the role of derivational prefixes. *Journal of Memory and Language*, 27, 368–81.

Tyler, L. K., Waksler, R. and Marslen-Wilson, W. D. (1993). Representation and access of derived words in English. In Altmann and Shillcock (1993).

Ullmann, S. (1962). *Semantics: An Introduction to the Science of Meaning*. Oxford: Blackwell.

Ultan, R. (1984). Size-sound symbolism. In J. Greenberg (ed.), *Universals of Human Language*, vol. 4. Stanford, CA: Stanford University Press.

Ungerer, F. and Schmid, H. J. (1996). *An Introduction to Cognitive Linguistics*. London: Longman.

Van den Broecke, M. P. R. and Goldstein, L. (1980). Consonant features in speech errors. In Fromkin (1980).

Van Velin, R. D. (1990). Semantic parameters of split intransitivity. *Language*, 66, 221–60.

Velten, H. V. (1943). The growth of phonemic and lexical patterns in infant language. *Language*, 19, 281–92. Also in Bar-Adon and Leopold (1971).

Vendler, Z. (1967). *Linguistics in Philosophy*. Ithaca, NY: Cornell University Press.

Vihmann, M. M. (1978). Consonant harmony: its scope and function in child language. In J. H. Greenberg (ed.), *Universals of Human Language*. Stanford, CA: Stanford University Press.

Vihmann, M. M. (1981). Phonology and the development of the lexicon: evidence from children's errors. *Journal of Child Language*, 8, 239–64.

—— (1996). *Phonological Development: The Origins of Language in the Child*. Oxford: Blackwell.

Vygotsky, L. S. (1962). *Thought and language*, trans. E. Hanfmann and G. Vakar. Cambridge, MA: MIT Press.

Wales, R. J. and Walker, E. (eds) (1976). *New Approaches to Language Mechanisms*. Amsterdam: North-Holland.

Wallman, J. (1992). *Aping Language*. Cambridge: Cambridge University Press.

Wang, M. D. and Bilger, R. C. (1973). Consonant confusions in noise: a study of perceptual features. *Journal of the Acoustical Society of America*, 54, 1248–66.

Wang, W. S.-Y. (ed.) (1991). *The Emergence of Language: Development and Evolution*. New York: W. H. Freeman.

Wanner, E. and Gleitman, L. R. (eds) (1982). *Language Acquisition: The State of the Art*. Cambridge: Cambridge University Press.

Warren, B. (1992). *Sense Developments: A Contrastive Study of the Development of Slang Senses and Novel Standard Senses in English*. Stockholm: Almqvist and Wiksell.

Warren, R. M. (1970). Perceptual restoration of missing speech sounds. *Science*, 167, 393–5.

Warrington, E. K. (1981). Neuropsychological studies of verbal semantic systems. *Philosophical Transactions of the Royal Society of London* B, 295, 411–23. Also published as *Psychological Mechanisms of Language*. London: The Royal Society and the British Academy.

Warrington, E. K. and Shallice, T. (1984). Category specific semantic impairments. *Brain*, 107, 829–54.

Wason, P. (1965). The contexts of plausible denial. *Journal of Verbal Learning and Verbal Behavior*, 4, 7–11.

Waterson, N. (1970). Some speech forms of an English child: a phonological study. *Transactions of the Philological Society*, 1–24.

Weinreich, U. (1966). On the semantic structure of language. In J. H. Greenberg (ed.), *Universals of Language*, 2nd edn. Cambridge MA: MIT Press.

Weizenbaum, J. (1984). *Computer Power and Human Reason: From Judgement to Calculation*. Harmondsworth: Penguin.

Wells, J. (1990). Syllabification and allophony. In S. Ramsaran (ed.), *Studies in the Pronunciation of English*. London: Routledge.

Werner, H. and Kaplan, E. (1950). Development of word meaning through verbal context: an experimental study. *Journal of Psychology*, 29, 251–7. Also in De Cecco (1967).

Whaley, C. P. (1978). Word-nonword classification time. *Journal of Verbal Learning and Verbal Behavior*, 17, 143–54.

Wheeldon, L. R. and Monsell, S. (1992). The locus of repetition priming of spoken word production. *Quarterly Journal of Experimental Psychology*, 44A, 723–61.

—— (1994). Inhibition of spoken word production by priming a semantic competitor. *Journal of Memory and Language*, 33, 332–56.

White, T. G. (1982). Naming practices, typicality, and underextension in child language. *Journal of Experimental Child Psychology*, 33, 324–46.

Wiegel-Crump, C. A. and Dennis, M. (1986). Development of word finding. *Brain and Language*, 27, 1–23.

Wierzbicka, A. (1985). *Lexicography and Conceptual Analysis*. Ann Arbor, MI: Karoma.

—— (1990). 'Prototypes save': on the uses and abuses of the notion of 'prototype' in linguistics and related fields. In Tsohatzidis (1990).

—— (1992a). Furniture and birds: a reply to Dwight Bolinger. *Cognitive Linguistics*, 3, 119–23.

—— (1992b). Semantic fields and semantic primitives. In Lehrer and Kittay (1992).

—— (1992c). *Semantics, Culture, and Cognition*. Oxford: Oxford University Press.

—— (1996). *Semantics: Primes and Universals*. Oxford: Oxford University Press.

Wijnen, F., Krikhaar, E. and den Os, E. (1994). The (non)realisation of unstressed elements in children's utterances: Evidence for a rhythmic constraint. *Journal of Child Language*, 21.

Wilkins, W. (ed.) (1988). *Syntax and Semantics 21: Thematic Relations*. New York: Academic Press.

Wittgenstein, L. (1958). *Philosophical investigations*, trans. G. E. M. Anscombe, 2nd edn. Oxford: Basil Blackwell.

Woodworth, N. L. (1991). Sound symbolism in proximal and distal forms. *Linguistics*, 29, 273–300.

Wray, A. (2002). *Formulaic Language and the Lexicon*. Cambridge: Cambridge University Press.

Zwicky, A. (1982). Classical malapropisms and the creation of a mental lexicon. In L. K. Obler and L. Menn (eds), *Exceptional Language and Linguistics*. New York: Academic Press.

Zwicky, A. and Sadock, J. (1975). Ambiguity tests and how to fail them. In J. Kimball, *Syntax and Semantics*, 4. New York: Academic Press.

Index

This is primarily a topic index. It contains only the names of people noted in the text; it does not include those mentioned only in the notes or the list of references.